The Tour Book
How to Get Your Music on the Road

Andy Reynolds

Course Technology PTR
A part of Cengage Learning

COURSE TECHNOLOGY
CENGAGE Learning·

Australia • Brazil • Japan • Korea • Mexico • Singapore • Spain • United Kingdom • United States

COURSE TECHNOLOGY
CENGAGE Learning™

The Tour Book
How to Get Your Music on the Road
Andy Reynolds

Publisher and General Manager, Course Technology PTR: Stacy L. Hiquet

Associate Director of Marketing: Sarah O'Donnell

Manager of Editorial Services: Heather Talbot

Marketing Manager: Mark Hughes

Acquisitions Editor: Orren Merton

Marketing Assistant: Adena Flitt

Project Editor/Copy Editor/ Development Editor: Cathleen D. Small

PTR Editorial Services Coordinator: Erin Johnson

Interior Layout Tech: ICC Macmillan Inc.

Cover Designer: Mike Tanamachi

Indexer: Sharon Shock

Proofreader: Kate Welsh

For product information and technology assistance, contact us at
Cengage Learning Customer & Sales Support, 1-800-354-9706

For permission to use material from this text or product, submit all requests online at **cengage.com/permissions**
Further permissions questions can be emailed to
permissionrequest@cengage.com

Library of Congress Catalog Card Number: 2006909687

ISBN-13: 978-1-59863-371-9

ISBN-10: 1-59863-371-6

Course Technology
25 Thomson Place
Boston, MA 02210
USA

Cengage Learning is a leading provider of customized learning solutions with office locations around the globe, including Singapore, the United Kingdom, Australia, Mexico, Brazil, and Japan. Locate your local office at: **international.cengage.com/region**

Cengage Learning products are represented in Canada by Nelson Education, Ltd.

For your lifelong learning solutions, visit **courseptr.com**

Visit our corporate website at **cengage.com**

Printed in the United States of America
08 09 10 11 12 TW 10 9 8 7 6 5 4 3 2

For Eileen and Lily

Acknowledgments

My thanks and love go out to:

Mum and Dad, Jeremy, Sara, and Katie. You always believed in me.

Tracey, Ruby, and Megan Nelson.

Noel Kilbride (this is your fault!), Nick Jevons (always!), Joey Jevons and Carmel Kilbride, Pete and Jenny Darnborough, and Glen Neath and Lizzie.

All the crew I have had the honour to serve with over the years, especially Andy Dimmack, Ricky Ricketts, Tim Hardstaff, Paul Myers, Rich Bell, Jock Bain, Sean Gerrard, Chris Taplin, Mark Parsons, Timm Cleasby, Nigel Reeks and The DCL "Top Gun." See you in catering.

Everyone who consented to be interviewed. I hope I have used your words of wisdom in the best way.

The many bands and artists, booking agents, promoters, and artist managers who have put up with my eccentric style of tour management. "There has been a terrible mistake."

Cop Shoot Cop—the finest band ever to walk this planet. Your conviction and integrity made me question my own.

Ryoko Mutasono, for the camera and my daughter's hairstyles.

Orren Merton, Stacy Hiquet, Cathleen Small, all the good people at Cengage Course Technology PTR, and Guy Rose. You made this happen—thank you!

Eileen. Just for being you.

About the Author

Andy Reynolds has worked as an international concert tour manager and audio engineer for 17 years. He has toured continuously during this time, working on an average of 200 shows per year. Andy has worked for such bands as All-American Rejects, House of Pain, Machine Head, Nightmares On Wax, Pavement, Roots Manuva, Super Furry Animals, Skunk Anansie, Squarepusher, and The White Stripes. He has worked with bands on tours by such acts as U2, Whitney Houston, Manic Street Preachers, and Foo Fighters. His touring experience encompasses stadiums, arenas, theatres, pubs, bars, clubs, outdoor festivals, rooftops, subway stations, cruise ships, mountainsides, and very, very muddy fields.

Andy has taught sound engineering and modern tour management at Red Tape Studios in Sheffield, and he appeared as guest lecturer at Liverpool University and City College Manchester.

Learn more about Andy at www.tourconcepts.com.

Contents

Chapter 5
Preparation for the Show   95

Chapter 6
Equipment   125

Chapter 7
At the Show   181

Chapter 10
Marketing
329

Chapter 11
Getting Onstage: Advanced Information
341

Epilogue: That Story!   403

Appendix   417

Index   421

Introduction

"The top 10 percent of artists make money selling records. The rest go on tour."

—Scott Welch, manager for Alanis Morissette and LeAnn Rimes

Live music is a huge industry. In 2005, concert ticket sales totaled $3.1 billion in North America alone! Playing live is an integral part of the success of any musician, band, or artist. There is a huge difference between writing and recording your songs in your home studio or rehearsal space and going out and putting on a show. If you can't cut it live, then you really are not going to impress any audience, let alone gain a record deal and sell your music.

But how do you make sure your show has the maximum impact? How do you appear professional and knowledgeable in an industry that has its own conventions, language, and baffling technical terms? How do you get booked into a venue and get paid? How do you then get bigger and better shows?

These are all questions to which you should find the answers.

The music industry is extraordinarily fickle, and often people only get one chance. By being unprepared and unprofessional, you run the risk of making mistakes that could lead to the end of your career before you even get started!

If you are serious about working or performing in the live industry, you need some help to avoid those mistakes.

That's where I come in. I can help. Let me tell you why. . . .

The Book

The Tour Book is not a "how to get rich playing music in public" book. It is not a "careers in the music industry" book. Nor is it a "behind the scenes" fact book.

The Tour Book is all those things and more. It is obvious that we have already entered into a new era of music distribution, and the live show is becoming not only a place to show off your performing talent, but also an immediate marketplace to sell and distribute your songs.

I have been a concert tour manager and audio engineer for nearly 20 years now. I have toured all around the world and I have learned a considerable amount about how a rock show works. The aim of my book is to share my knowledge and experience (and that of the musicians, road crew, artist managers, promoters, booking agents, and record label people I know) to give you a valuable insight into the live-music performing culture. Some of this knowledge may help you make money. Some of this information will definitely help you save money! Most of this information is just really useful. Whether you are a part of an alternative rock band, a DJ, a fledgling concert promoter, a music course leader, or a concerned parent of a teenage musician, this book should be useful to you.

The Tour Book will help you to put on your show in a more professional manner, enabling you to produce your own contracts, work schedules, and marketing materials. *The Tour Book* will give you advice on insurance, foreign taxation, merchandise, and commissions. This book contains everything—and I mean *everything*—you need to know to get your show on the road.

Please do not feel you have to read the whole book straight through to get your show on the road. The subject is far too expansive for that. Instead, use *The Tour Book* as a reference and dive in and out to the parts you need. Think of *The Tour Book* as a manual. Write in it, doodle on it, make notes, fold down pages, and leave it in the bottom of your guitar case.

To help you get the most from *The Tour Book,* I have divided the information into four parts:

Part I: The Live Music Business. This Part covers how it all works and who does what.

Part II: How to Get Your Music on the Road. This Part describes everything you need to know about a live show—equipment, rehearsing, sound checks, marketing, getting paid, getting more shows, and more advanced information for when you have made it big!

Part III: Working in the Live Music Industry. This Part provides a more detailed examination of how to gain and keep a successful career in live music.

Part IV: The Future. This Part discusses your future and the future of live music.

And who am I to tell you all this? Well, read on....

Me

By the time I was 14, I was besotted with music and the idea of being in a successful band. At 16 I was in bands with friends, knocking out Beatles covers and trying to write prog-rock epics. I am not saying I am a brilliant musician—I really only wanted to emulate my heroes.

My devotion to and obsession with music was noticed by the head of my year, who advised me to go to art college. That way I could meet other rock-star wannabes in the same way that John and Paul and Mick and Keef did. (My parents were less than impressed with this career advice.) I did go to Art College and the advice paid off, as I did indeed meet other like-minded people—people who also happened to be musicians.

I left the college after a year to pursue a career as a rock star.

Rock stardom initially passed me by, and while writing and rehearsing my own music, I learned how to record and mix on four-track Portastudios. (These were revolutionary cassette tape–based devices that enabled anyone to do multitrack recording at home. They must have been good, because Sting had one.) My first recordings were awful. The whole process seemed so complicated! Busses, auxiliaries, signal path, drop ins—there were all these new terms and technologies to master! At the same time, though, the process was fascinating. My friends and I could not help but marvel at the fact that our own bedrooms were now more powerful than Abbey Road studios at the time of recording the first Beatles albums!

Wanting to understand, I went away and read magazines and books and persevered until I really understood audio engineering. I gained part-time engineering jobs in local professional recording studios. Other local musicians, sensing I had good ears and some engineering skills, would ask me to come to their shows and mix the live audio.

I soon learned there is a *huge* difference in mixing recorded and live audio. I also learned to love the one-shot take of mixing live show audio and the instant reaction of the band and audience when I did a good job.

I did not really tout myself as an engineer because I was still plugging away, trying to be the next John Lennon/Kurt Cobain/Madonna, but I would take live sound engineering jobs for the money. I also did some work for local sound rental companies, setting up, running, and tearing down the PA (public address system) at shows. During this time I built up some experience regarding how shows work and, more importantly, the importance of a positive personality in this job.

At some point I finally accepted that the world was not ready for my music (you fools!), but somehow I had a new career, and one that I really enjoyed. Around this time, I met a tour manager who needed an engineer for an upcoming tour.

That was the start of it, really. I loved it. I was getting paid to make really loud bands even louder, travel the world, and have a bloody good time. I toured as an engineer for about five years, learning all the time. Although I had played as a musician and I thought I knew about equipment, while touring I also involved myself in setting up the bands' equipment in order to learn backline skills. I watched other touring engineers and asked lots of relevant questions. I read more books about audio engineering and even learned rudimentary lighting skills.

After a couple of years of touring I began to get slightly bored. (I know, it sounds stupid now, but you know how that goes.) I was mixing audio for a lot of punk/rock bands, touring around the same old venues, meeting the same "don't give a f**k" local crews, and generally feeling a bit understimulated. Long travel days (especially in the US) also meant I was not busy for 8 to 10 hours of the working day; I hate not being busy.

I began looking at alternatives and realized I loved the life; I just needed a better job on the road. I looked at the tour managers because they seemed to be permanently busy during the show day and able to change situations that were not right, whereas I was just the "noise boy" who had to put up with it (whatever "it" might be in any particular case).

Tour managers also got paid more than me! So, while on tour, I began asking questions, volunteering for tasks, and generally making myself useful. My break came when a band I had worked with for years as an FOH engineer announced a tour but had no TM. I really wanted to get into tour management, so I came up with a proposal: I would be TM for the tour. I knew the band really well, I knew their personal style and we were all great friends. Great, right?

Wrong! The band flew in from the States, and that first day was a disaster. Everything that could go wrong did go wrong. I had not anticipated the sheer amount of advance preparation that needs to go into any kind of performance tour, let alone a full-on alternative rock band tour!

I was grossly unprepared. It seemed to me that I knew nothing, and there was *so* much to do on a day-to-day basis.

After that first show I was ready to go home. The band, sensing my disillusionment, took me to one side and helped me to see the positive side of what I had achieved. They also told me that I should carry on as tour manager. I took that encouragement and advice, and the band and I continued to tour together for many years after that. Thanks to that one completely challenging situation, I gained both experience and confidence. I was now a band tour manager!

I have been touring successfully now for nearly 20 years. I work on an average of 200 shows every year as a tour manager, audio engineer, or a combination of both. I know a vast number of amazing musicians, road crew, artist managers, promoters, booking agents, and record label people. I have interviewed and asked them for their hints, tips, and advice because, like me, they want to teach you about working and performing live shows and, in so doing, share the vast amounts of information and experience we have all gained.

I have seen hundreds of bands, musicians, and artists perform live. I know what it takes to perform a good show, to connect with an audience, and to win them over. And I have seen musicians (and crew) really mess it up for themselves by being unprepared, unprofessional, or ignorant. It always strikes me as a shame when artists and crew act that way. Surely this is the dream you have been working toward, so why throw away the chance of a lifetime by being unprepared?

You

The motto for *The Tour Book* is "Get your show on the road." I do not necessarily mean taking a band and going on tour. I mean kick-start your career in the live industry. You could be a musician looking to perform a better show, get more shows, or get more money for your performance. You could also be fantasizing about working for a rock band on tour, experiencing the travel, the "glamour," and the free deli trays. (Some people do fantasize about free deli trays, you know.)

You might be looking at setting up as a concert promoter or a live booking agent or building a rehearsal studio. Whatever your fantasy path—performer or behind the scenes—I can help you get your show on the road.

One final thought: If you cast your ear beyond the iTunes/MTV/FM radio sphere of music, you will hear impassioned music from around the world that has nothing to do with four white kids in a garage dreaming of sex, drugs, and rock 'n roll. With my experience, it is easy for me to get into the "Western rock" mindset. Obviously that is where most of the music industry does its business, and certainly that is where most of my experience lies. The examples, hints, and tips contained in this book are mostly based on modern rock or electronic music tours and events. Live music is live music, though, and you will be able to apply the examples to any live performance situation in which you may find yourself.

Andy Reynolds, June 2007

The Live Music Business

 # Industry Overview

Gigs! Concerts! Touring! Imagine the performers, conveyed to a concert hall in sleek tour buses, surrounded by an entourage of beautiful people, security personnel, and managers. They take the stage and are amplified and lit by state-of-the-art show production equipment. Imagine the audience, basking in the god-like radiance of their heroes and abandoning their inhibitions in an orgy of singing, shouting, and dancing....

After this vision of communal ecstasy, it may be difficult to regard live music as an industry. After all, industry is business, and many of us think of business as being somewhat dull and unrewarding.

However, let us not forget that live music *is* a business and a huge industry in its own right. With an increasing emphasis on a do-it-yourself path for younger and established musicians alike, live music is seen as where it's at in terms of an artist's career. This is reflected in the increasing number of tours and shows per year, which translates to an increased amount of work for behind-the-scenes people and performers.

You too could be a part of this burgeoning industry! You are obviously serious about your career (because you have bought this book), so to get you all fired up, have a look at these figures:

- In *Numbers 2006*, the IFPI Global Recording Industry reported that live performance of music generated a total of $14.4 *billion* in 2005. That is an increase of 11 percent over the 2004 figures!

- According to Michael Rapino, CEO of Live Nation (a concert promoter), Live Nation produces 29,500 shows per year around the world.

- *Counting the Notes,* a 2003 report by the National Music Council, reported that the live music sector in the UK was valued at £656 million ($1.2 billion) a year in 2003. Live music provides the second greatest income in the £3.6 billion music industry after recording, which generates more than £1 billion in revenue. Music industry professionals in the UK (managers, agents, and promoters) made £132 million ($246 million) in 2003.

- "The Value of Music in London," a 2000 article by Dave Laing and Norton York, stated that in 2000 there were 600 significant music venues in London alone, along with 1,000 licensed by local authorities for public entertainment!

- *Counting the Notes* also reported that a survey conducted by researchers covering a week in November 2000 identified 720 music events in the London area alone.

- According to research company TNS, the average price that 16- to 24-year-olds were prepared to pay for a music festival in 2006 was £81 ($151).

- Pollstar.com reported that the top 10 tours in North America grossed $809.2 million in 2005. The leader was the Rolling Stones, with gross ticket sales of $162.4 million on an average ticket price of $133. This beat the Stones' old record of $121.20 per ticket for the 1994 Voodoo Lounge tour.

- The average international touring band employs 10 crewmembers on tour. Wages start at £80 ($140) a day and can go up to £350 ($610) a *day*!

- According to the *Guardian* newspaper, tickets for two Kylie Minogue concerts in London sold out in two hours, despite the fact that Kylie has not released a non-compilation album since 2003. And according to *Audience* magazine, 35,000 tickets for the UK's 2007 T In The Park festival were sold in one day—only two days after the 2006 festival had finished!

Touring History

So how did this all start? Ladies and gentlemen, please welcome Mr. Mick Jagger, courtesy of *Fortune* magazine:

> In the beginning when we started, there wasn't any money to be made from touring. There wasn't a touring industry. As far as rock music was concerned, there wasn't really any money in it. The touring shows in the old days were lots of lots of acts. There might be eight to ten acts; you'd go out and do your two numbers, your hit record or your next one or your last one, and that was your lot. And that's how we started. And that's how tours were. Obviously there was somebody maybe who made money, but it certainly wasn't the act. And if you were lucky, you got to do your own show, but I don't think you ever made money out of that, not really. And then if you were really good in America, for instance, you got to play in Vegas, and that was the only time you made money. Elvis never toured, so there was no role model, for whatever reasons, who cares, but he never did and the only thing he ever did was Vegas. Why was that? Well, it was perceived that the only time you could make money was in Vegas. So Elvis did Vegas, [but] he never did a tour. It was a stupid idea, because he could have done all right. There was no touring industry until approximately 1969, when we were one of the first bands to create or be part of the burgeoning touring industry. Of course by then records were selling a lot. Recorded music and the business of it is a totally separate subject from the road and it has a completely different business model, and of course one's linked to the other. But for years they were never really linked at all. In fact, you could never get the two groups to talk to each other. It was a nightmare.

Musicians from every musical style have always performed live, giving impromptu shows or planned concerts. Musicians have also always traveled to give shows in other cities or countries as demand dictated. Despite what Mick Jagger says, contemporary musicians from the 1930s onward were sufficiently motivated and successful enough to participate in regular tours in Europe and the USA. A definitive history of concert tours before the 1960s is outside the scope of this book, but it should be noted that established agents and promoters were very successful at organizing and selling concert tours. However, these tours often simply went where the work was and were far removed from the complex productions we have come to expect today.

However, Jagger is right to claim responsibility for inventing or defining the modern touring industry as we know it (even if the Stones should share that title with Led Zeppelin). Before 1969, acts would simply travel by whatever mode of transportation was available to them, use whatever in-house sound and lighting equipment was available to them, and rely on an untrained and inexperienced "crew" to help them try to get a show together. Remember, at their peak the Beatles were playing to 5,000 people two times a night, but were still provided with only two microphones amplified through cinema speakers and were still using the film projector as a lighting source! The Beatles, the Rolling Stones, Elvis, Buddy Holly and the Crickets, Little Richard, and any other bands of that era were forced to endure the same conditions. It is hard to imagine today how terrible those shows must have sounded and looked, both for the band and for the audience.

By 1966 the Beatles had had enough of touring; the production limitations clashed with their sonic experimentation. Elvis never ventured beyond the States and ended up playing yearlong residences in Las Vegas. Many artists were discovering that television was helping them reach a larger, younger audience. Other bands, however, were continuing to sell lots of records and do concert tours. The Stones continued to succeed and were in a position to fundamentally change things for the better. Following the success of 1969's *Let it Bleed*, they found they were capable of selling two shows a day in a mix of arenas and stadiums throughout the US. However, growing weary of accepting below-standard local sound and lights, the Stones invested time and money in procuring their own talented and experienced crew, sound, lights, and staging. The 1969 US tour is considered a watershed in the touring industry in terms of its success both in sales and production values.

Other areas were changing as well. Traditionally bands were booked by agents or bookers who would take care of all the financial details.

This included picking up the money and disbursing it to the artists. Less scrupulous agents and promoters were prone to deceiving their artists and withholding or not declaring income. This was especially true in the late 1950s and early 1960s in the States and the UK, where a thriving "package tour" scene had emerged. (A package tour was simply a package of four or five acts on tour together, as Mick Jagger explained in the quote at the start of this chapter.) Artists often found it difficult to understand contracts and payment details and were clearly in the dark as to how and when they should be paid. Ray Phillips of the Nashville Teens recounts:

> We were working every night. The only money we really made was from gigging.... I think the money then was about £350 to £400 [$560 to $620]. That was good money. We got that on a lot of gigs, but with publicity there was never anything instigated from the office.... It was hit-and-miss all the time.... We had to go up and barter for the money. If we were owed a grand [Don Arden would] say, "Would you settle for £600 ($1,200)?" We'd be sitting in the office waiting for some money to get to a gig. He'd keep us waiting 'til the banks closed. "Oh, I've got no money now. I've got some here—would you settle for that?" Little did you know, that's it— you were paid off.

Many artists were aware of the financial situation, though, and had retained good management to take care of these matters. The emphasis moved away from agents and promoters taking care of all the money and trickling down fees to the bands; now acts were employing road or tour managers who not only administrated the increasingly complex touring production, but also collected and accounted for all monies. Only when the band had been paid in full could the agents and promoters expect their commissions—not before. Both the Stones and the up-and-coming Led Zeppelin operated in this way—they created the concert systems we know today.

By the mid 1970s, bands such as the Stones, Led Zeppelin, and Pink Floyd were playing to crowds of 50,000 to 60,000 people a night in the US. Concert revenue was an average of £120,000 ($223,000), which would translate to approximately £470,500 ($886,000) today. They were also spending £21,250 ($59,500)—which would translate to £115,000 ($214,500) today—a night on staging the show. Bands now toured with their own sound systems, lighting and projection systems, staging, catering, merchandise, wardrobe, and administration. They employed 10 to 20 people full time on tour and up to 50 people per night as loaders, riggers, runners, concessionaires, and other roles that I will explain in Chapter 2, "How the Concert Industry Works: Who Does What." Bands had their own trucks, buses, and jet planes. Specialized companies sprang up to meet the demands of this new industry, drawing on skills learned in theatre, sports, and even at theme parks.

The 1980s saw the touring music industry refining its art. Artists, their management, and promoters realized they could stage more ambitious stage shows and still tour them around the world, thus drawing in more ticket-buying fans. The evolving sound, staging, and light technology meant that equipment could be smaller, lighter, and easier to set up and break down. (It did not get cheaper, though! Pink Floyd lost $800,000 (£416,600)—which translates to approximately $1,877,000 (£977,600) today—despite performing *The Wall* to 750,000 people in the US and Europe in 1980.) Technological advancements also meant shows could be louder and brighter and therefore seen by more people at once, resulting in greater ticket sales and increased return per show.

It was not all stadiums and arenas, though. The success of so many touring bands also meant revitalizing the smaller club and theatre circuit. As the "big boys" got to experiment with million-dollar budgets for sound and lights, the equipment manufacturers suddenly had a lot of cash to inject into research and development of smaller and cheaper sound and light equipment. Concertgoers, used to seeing huge flashy stadium shows, demanded the same audio quality at the smaller shows.

Also, punk had arrived. This highly energetic music suited live performance, and people clamored to see live the bands that had been banned. New studio technology, such as synthesizers and drum machines, had led to a wave of new electronic and experimental bands. These bands could also now perform "live" thanks to multichannel sound mixing desks and computerized lighting effects. All this led to a prolific time for touring acts and for the touring industry as a whole. Many of the top promoters, agents, equipment manufacturers, and suppliers of today came to prominence during the late 1970s and early 1980s.

This is where we are at today. Technology is constantly evolving, but the fundamentals of putting on a show have not changed much since the late 1960s. You still need a band, some sound and lighting equipment, someone to put it all up, someone to promote the show, someone to collect the money, and someone to take down all the equipment and transport it and the artist to the next city. In the next chapters, I will explain in detail every aspect of modern touring: the reasons for touring; production and legal/financial requirements; logistics; contracts and riders; the roles of agents, promoters, and managers; and everything else in between.

"Play as many venues as possible in the early days, but later it's more important to select what you do. The band should have fun and do it for themselves, and people will come to you."

—Olly Parker, A&R, Rough Trade Records.

2 How the Concert Industry Works: Who Does What

Whether you are just starting out or you consider yourself to be highly experienced, it is always useful to know the components of your business. I have met many successful musicians who still do not know the difference between promoters and booking agents, for example. I remember working on my first professional tours and the assumptions and mistakes I made about the tour organizers, promoters, and various crew I met. Although the relative roles in the professional setting may seem irrelevant to you now, it is vitally important that you understand how a show is put together and who does what and why. In this section I will outline briefly each person's role in the planning, booking, or running of a show. More detailed analysis of job roles and responsibilities can be found in Part III, "Working in the Live Music Industry."

Remember you only have one chance when pitching for a prestigious opening slot or applying for a crew job. A little research now will prevent embarrassing mistakes later. Make sure you know who you are talking to and you understand their responsibilities!

> "Every act I've ever worked with has played live. People want to see their artists in the flesh. It's pretty fundamental."
>
> —Andy Ross, A&R Director, Food Records

The Management

Although managers are not 100-percent involved in the day-to-day mechanics of a show or event, I have included information about them here because, as a performer or behind-the-scenes person, you will invariably run into managers as your first point of contact. Trying

11

to get an opening slot on a show, applying for a touring job, trying to arrange an artist interview or book a show—in all these cases, you will need the permission of the management!

The artist manager (otherwise known as the personal manager in the U.S.) is the spoke around which the wheel of the artist's career should revolve. The manager's job is to represent the artist in all business areas and to guide him or her toward the best logistical and financial decisions. Obviously this role extends to recordings, publishing, and non-performance promotional activities, but it is the role of the artist manager in shows and touring that is relevant here.

Note: No Manager? Read This Anyway! If you are an artist without management or you represent yourself, then please read this section anyway. YOU will be taking on the roles and responsibilities I am talking about here.

I'm not going to waffle on about artist managers too much—for more detailed information about how to find and work with a manager, you should read the very excellent *All You Need About the Music Business* (Simon & Schuster, 2000) by Donald S. Passman. At this point you do need to know that an artist will approach or be approached by a manager who agrees to handle his or her affairs for a percentage of the artist's gross earnings (usually between 10 and 20 percent, with most managers taking 15 percent). The manager and artist should sign a contract to stipulate this arrangement or at very least sign an agreement stating the intentions of each party over a given time period, say six months or a year. (Generally, "Make me rich and famous by next week" is not a suitable artist/manager agreement!)

Although not strictly involved in the booking of a show or tour, the managers to whom I spoke were unanimous in their support for playing live. "It's fundamental that a band plays live, especially in the current climate," says Ben Kirby, manager of the Subways. "There's such a fast turnover of acts these days, and it's vital to gig your arse off and build a solid fan base that will still be there in five years and will see you through any downturns."

Andy Farrow, manager for Paradise Lost, Million Dead, and Skindred, agrees: "For a rock act to get signed, they have to cut it live, so it's of the utmost importance." A good manager should therefore be looking to make sure the act he or she represents is capable and ready to play live, both to perhaps score a record deal and, more importantly, to gain a strong audience fan base.

Because touring can be expensive, you will need a manager who can raise finances and keep good track of expenses. As well as handling finances and publicity and organizing and overseeing rehearsals, the manager can either find work for the artist himself or find and use a booking agent. In the early days, most managers will have to book shows for their artists themselves; after a degree of success (or a label signing), the artist management will likely work with a booking agent.

Remember, the manager's job is to secure the most lucrative and wide-reaching activities for his or her act; simply advising the team to "go out and get loads of shows" is not good business sense. The artist manager has to present logistical and financial information to the booking agent in order for the agent to work effectively. Performing shows or touring should complement any other activities in which the artist is involved, and good lines of communication should exist between the artist manager, the booking agent, the record company, the publicity departments, and the tour crew.

Once the manager is presented with a list of potential concert dates by the booking agent, it is his or her job to make sure the tour or show is viable for the artist. The manager will work out a budget or employ a tour manager (hey, that's me!) to work out a budget for her. The booking agent will have given the manager a list of the fees (income from ticket sales) the band will receive on the tour. The person responsible for the budget should then subtract cost figures for the following likely expenses:

- Wages
- Per diems
- Accommodations
- Transportation

- Sound

- Lighting

- Video

- Production—other items necessary to create the show

- Visas and work papers

- Rehearsals

- Agent's commission

- Management commission

- Foreign Artist tax

The show/tour income minus the expenses listed will give either the profit or loss figure for the tour. A loss is called a *shortfall*. We will be looking more closely at budgets and costs in Chapter 11, "Getting Onstage: Advanced Information."

Once a budget has been worked out to the manager's approval, a couple of things may happen. If the budget shows a profit or if the band is not beholden to any record label or other financial concern (in other words, if they are U2 or the Rolling Stones), then the manager will approve the tour and tell the agent to go ahead and confirm the shows. The tour is then on!

If the budget shows a loss/shortfall, then the band can either cancel the proposed tour or try to find extra income from somewhere. The most common route (if applicable) is to go to the record label and ask for tour support. Tour support is money advanced to the act by the label to enable the act to go off and tour. The thinking is that the touring will help to promote the act and sell more records, so record companies see a benefit and will grant tour support. Obtaining a decent amount of tour support is difficult these days because the fortunes of the record companies have suffered setbacks recently. (One enterprising manager once described record company advances in general and particularly tour support as a "big, fat interest-free loan." While the analogy makes the process easy to explain, I would certainly seek proper legal advice if entering into a recording contract!)

If you're applying for tour support, the record company accountants will want to see a copy of the proposed budget. The budget will be scrutinized and objections will be made regarding any unauthorized or unnecessary expenses. Even though the tour support is recoupable from the artist and is basically a loan, record companies have very clear guidelines about what they will and will not fund when supplying tour support. You will see more about record company tour support and budgets in Chapter 11.

The manager's responsibility to his or her artist is to ensure the budget/ list of expenses for the tour is reasonable and bona fide. Once the label's accountant is satisfied, he will approve the budget and arrange for the amount of the shortfall to be paid to the band. The manager then makes a final decision and if he or she feels the tour is viable, the manager will inform the agent to confirm the gigs. The tour is on (again)!

Note: How Tour Support Is Paid The record company will usually stagger the payment of the tour support. They do not just hand over £50,000 (roughly $96,000 USD) and let you climb into the back of a Transit van with your band mates and head off on tour! A typical scenario for payment of tour support is a 25/75 ratio, where 25 percent of the shortfall is paid before the start of the tour and the remaining 75 percent is payable on receipt of the tour accounts at the end of the tour. This is important because many tour suppliers (crew, trucking companies, PA and lighting suppliers, and so on) ask for or demand large down payments for their services before the tour starts. (As I mentioned, rock and roll is a fickle business, and there have been a "few" cases of people not being paid for their tour-related work.) Because there is only 25 percent of the tour support available before the tour starts, the manager and any tour suppliers need to be realistic about how much can be paid out in pre-tour deposits or payments.

The manager is also responsible for overseeing the expenses incurred on the road—even if he or she has employed a tour manager. The tour manager should have responsibility for expenditures in line with the agreed budget, but if there is an emergency or if an unpredicted expense arises, then the tour manager should definitely seek the manager's approval before spending any more money. At the end of the day the manager has to justify the expenses and any budget overrun to the label accountant. If the label feels the expenses are over and above what was agreed upon, they can withhold the remaining shortfall or deduct unwarranted expenses from the due amount. The effect of this could bankrupt a band. A manager therefore has to have a firm grip on touring expenses.

There is a (probably) apocryphal story that illustrates this point. The story goes that a UK band touring the US became so miserable on the road that they demanded the tour manager arrange hotel rooms for them each night, in addition to the very expensive sleeper bus they were already using. This was obviously not an approved expense and it caused the shortfall to expand considerably. In desperation the artist manager applied to the label for more tour support. The label agreed, but used money allocated for recording the next album to fund this extra tour support. All tour expenses were paid in full, but the following album had to be recorded on a much tighter budget.

Whether or not it is true, the story illustrates just how careful a manager has to be in keeping touring costs in check.

Okay, so that's how the established/signed acts do it. Suppose you are just starting your career as a performer or a behind-the-scenes person—how does the role of the manager affect you?

As a beginner to the world of live performance, you are going to have to do everything just described yourself. You will have to book your shows, work out the costs and the budgets, keep a grip on expenses, produce and maintain publicity, as well as get up there onstage and perform! This may all seem a little daunting but don't worry—everything you need to know about putting on a show is contained in this book. I am even going to give you performance hints and tips! You will still work with artist managers, though—there will come a time when you may need to approach someone about officially representing you or just to try to secure that all-important opening slot!

> "This is a brilliant time for young bands, and it's increasingly easy to produce fantastic demos. But the live show *has* to back it up. If the performance is lackluster, then the wrong message is being put across. You only get one chance to make a first impression."
>
> —Flash Taylor, A&R, Sony Music Publishing

The Agent

The booking agent (or talent agent) books the concerts/shows/gigs for the act. The booking agent does not actually put on shows. An agent presents the artist to promoters who may want to put on a show featuring that artist.

There are two main types of agents:

- **Concert agents.** Concert agents are usually part of larger agencies composed of a number of agents. The agents are responsible for their own revenues and use the agency's infrastructure (including telephone, ISP, legal and accountancy services) to help run their own "micro-business" within the overall framework of the agency. The agency then takes a cut of the agent's revenue to pay for these services and to (hopefully) generate a profit. This type of agent usually represents professional acts that have a recording contract. This agent works closely with the manager and also the record labels to coordinate a promotional schedule based on concert touring. Major agencies include Creative Artists Agency, William Morris, Little Big Man Booking, the Agency Group, and Helter Skelter.

- **Talent agents.** Talent agents usually run a stable of similar acts, such as DJs, tribute bands, presenters, or blues acts. They provide a service to these acts by supplying them to venues and markets demanding that type of act. In general, they represent semi-professional or niche artists.

In this book, I will mostly be referring to concert agents.

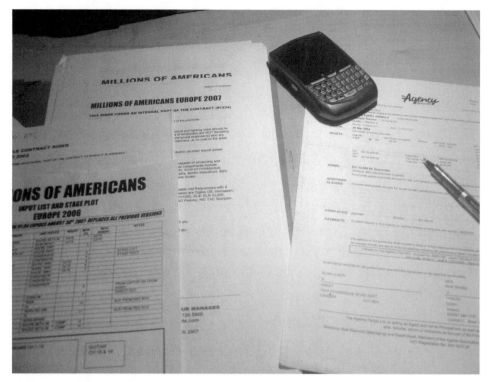

Figure 2.1 Paperwork, paperwork, and more paperwork—the life of a booking agent!

In either case the agent works along similar principles. Having worked with the act or manager, the agent has a rough idea of the logistical and financial expectations his or her artists will have for performing live. This information can then be summarized in the contract and contract rider information (see Chapter 3, "Contracts and Riders") that will legally bind any booking made by the agent. Contracts mean paperwork, and being a booking agent means a lot of paperwork, as you can see from Figure 2.1!

An agent makes money by charging a percentage of the artist's gross income for the performance. (Figures vary, but 10 percent of the gross seems to be the norm.) If an agent makes a deal with a promoter that sees the promoter providing non-cash additions, such as hotels or executive transportation, then the agent will often calculate the cash equivalent of these "special terms and conditions" and charge a percentage of the perceived value of these items when calculating the commission due. After all, the agent did negotiate very strenuously on behalf of the artist to secure these non-cash perks; it is therefore only fair that the agent should be compensated further. It is thus very important that the artist manager has access to a highly experienced accountant who can verify the true cash worth of these intangibles. What percentage of the Sony PlayStation included backstage should your booking agent charge for?

Having agreed upon a period of touring or concert activity with the artist's manager, the agent will approach promoters and offer the artists services. The conversation may go like this:

AGENT: Hey, Mr. Promoter. Millions of Americans has a new album out in October and they are looking to tour to support it. Do you have any dates to fill at your venue from the second week in October?'

PROMOTER: Millions of Americans? Oh yeah, the hotly tipped young rock band from Sheffield. I heard their single quite a bit on the radio. I reckon they might sell quite a few tickets! What's the deal?

A: Depending on your capacity, we could do $500 plus PA, lights, and catering. [PA stands for "public address," an outdated term that refers to the sound system. You will learn more about this in Chapter 6, "Equipment."]

P: $500? I can get [*insert name of even more successful alternative rock band here*] for that!

A: But they have massive record-company backing, and the manager tells me they have the cover of *Spin* next week.

P: That's what you said about [*insert name of "used to be successful but last time they played here they stiffed" rock band here*]. You are having a laugh!

And on and on. It is the agent's job to negotiate the deals with the promoter based on what he or she knows of the act's status, the city or venue he or she is pitching to, and the relationship with the promoter. It is no good trying to get $1,000 for a newly signed act in a pub on a Sunday night in Huddersfield, regardless of how much record-company backing and how many rock magazine covers you are getting. All good agents will have developed working relationships with the promoters to the extent that most of the negotiating is unsaid; each knows the other's business well.

This relationship also means that managers can rely on superstar agents to help break their acts. Agents such as Marty Diamond (the US agent for Coldplay, Snow Patrol, KT Tunstall, and Artic Monkeys) would obviously be more able to persuade a promoter to take on a small, unknown act. The understanding would be that if the promoter works with this act now, then the agent will offer the promoter the chance to book a bigger act in the future. Having said that, you will see later on that it is extremely difficult to be taken on by an agent at the start of your career.

When booking shows, the agent has to take into account geographical and seasonal matters, as well as keep an eye on the competition. An agent will try to plan the routing of the tour when pitching to promoters. In the aforementioned example, the agent simply asked for any dates in October. In practice, promoters will be offered their pick of dates depending on the location of the venue they are booking. For instance, in North America the agent will approach all promoters based in the Northwest (Portland, Seattle, Vancouver) with available dates in the first four days of the tour. Then he or she will approach promoters in California (San Francisco, Los Angeles, San Diego, and so on) with possible openings for the following four or five days. In the UK it would be openings in Scotland for the first couple of days, and then maybe promoters in Liverpool, Manchester, and Carlisle would be approached for the next week of the tour. Hopefully, the agent can then present a fairly logical routing for the tour, such as north to south or clockwise around the country. This will ensure less traveling and cheaper transportation costs.

This type of planning has to be done well in advance (typically three to four months) to ensure availability in the regions wanted. Sometimes it is just not possible, and you end up with the much-dreaded "Star of David" tour in which every show seems to be at the geographical opposite from the previous performance!

Seasonal matters also come into play. It is pointless to try to book a club tour of Europe between June and August if you represent an indie/alternative act. The vast majority of music fans will be headed for one of the many festivals, such as Carling: Reading & Leeds, Pukkelpop, and Roskilde, and these music fans will include your smaller club pro-moters! Likewise, a coast-to-coast tour of Canada in January/February would be pretty pointless. Even if you could make it through the snow, would the audience turn up?

Finally, both agents and promoters should have a keen eye on interna-tional sports fixtures. These events are direct competition to music events and, unfortunately, music always loses!

When the agent has provisionally booked the act into various cities, he or she will inform the artist manager of the dates on offer and the fees expected. If the manager and label (as discussed earlier) approve the tour, the agent will issue contracts to the promoters. The agent will then be available to answer any further questions or concerns the man-ager or promoters may have before the tour and will act as a go-between should any disagreements arise during the tour itself.

So how does an agent help you? Certainly, as a performer, having a good and successful agent will enable you to get more shows and, more importantly, bigger shows opening up for larger acts. However, getting a good agent will be just as hard as getting a record deal! Geoff Meall (the UK agent for Nickelback, Muse, My Chemical Romance, and Super Furry Animals) says that any band he considers for repre-sentation should be "either signed or close to being signed because [he is] not going to waste [his] time on touring something that has nothing outside of just being a live band." Most of Geoff's acts come to him through direct recommendation or request from artist managers and labels he has had successful relationships with in the past. Ed Stringfellow, also of the Agency Group, agrees: "There are not enough agents out there to deal the number of good emerging bands," he says.

It may therefore be a distraction to spend time and money trying to secure an agent at the start of your career. Although an agent can get you shows, and a good agent can get you *really* good shows, you have to remember that superstar agents such as Geoff Meall have a reputation, and his involvement with an act really only starts when the act has some success. "We are approached daily by bands that have no record deal, basically have a MySpace page, have done some recording, and want to release some demos. Obviously I could go and take this band and book it

20 shows around the country, but, in reality, what would be the point of that? They wouldn't enjoy it because there wouldn't be any marketing behind them. Very few booking agents will get involved with a band from day one," Geoff says. Bob Gold, managing director of booking agent GAA, admits, "We rarely deal with unsigned bands unless something comes up that's really exciting." Bob looks after such acts as REM, Annie Lennox, and Maroon 5. He adds, "If [the band] has got good management, we may take them forward." It does seem like a catch-22 situation: You need gigs to build your potential career, and you need a successful career to get the shows! Please do not despair, though—you've made the right choice in buying this book. In Chapter 8, "How to Get the Shows," I will show you how those really prestigious shows are booked and the types of acts that get those shows.

After reading this book, you may be in a position to approach an agent when you are trying to get your band onto a bill with one of his or her existing acts. I mentioned you would have to speak to the manager of the act about this. The agent will also be trying to get more of his or her acts on this bill as well, for two reasons: 1) It keeps her other artist managers happy, and 2) she will earn more commission from the same bill!

In this section I am merely introducing you to all the components of the live show process. It is obvious to me that in the early days you will have to act as your own booking agent, so in Chapter 9, "Getting Paid," I am also going to teach you the skills to negotiate fees and produce contracts.

> "If you can't hack it live, then you are not really going anywhere. People connect to live music in a different way [than] to records, so you need to be able to do both well."
>
> —Kevin Doran, A&R Manager, EMI Records

The Promoter

In the UK and Europe, these people are known as *promoters;* in the US they are known as *talent buyers.* Whatever the terminology may be, these are the brave souls who decide they can make money out of putting on a show or event. (The term *promoter* is because they promote an event to make money; *talent buyer* is because they er, buy the, er ... talent that will, er ... sell tickets. You get the idea!)

Figure 2.2 The promoters job is simple—put bums in seats!

The promoter's goal is simple: Put bums/asses on seats (see Figure 2.2). This means the promoter takes an event, puts it into a suitable venue, and sells tickets to the public. Some venues manage their promotions (in-house), but usually venues are hired by the promotions team to stage the show. There is an enormous risk involved with promotion, but a good promoter will look at turning a profit over the long term by developing good relationships with the booking agents. A good relationship with the agents means direct access to the agent's roster and his or her more successful acts.

Most promoting today is done by companies that (like booking agencies) consist of a number of individual promoters. As we have seen, there is a lot of money to be made from concerts. The last 20 years have seen the creation of several huge concert-promoting companies. The major players in the US are Live Nation and AEG LIVE, with a host of smaller companies such as Outback Concerts and Paragon doing well. In the UK, Live Nation is again very strong, along with MFMG (Mean Fiddler Music Group), SJM, and Metropolis Music Group.

So how does it all work? Promoters are approached by an agent, manager, or artist to stage a show, or (very importantly) they scout around for good moneymaking opportunities. The recent success of re-formed bands from the 1970s and 1980s is due in no small part to promoters seeing the financial potential. Mags Revell, a promoter at Metropolis Music Group, worked hard to persuade the original members of Motley Crüe to re-form for a concert tour. After a gap of nearly seven years and with no record to promote, the band hit the road in 2005, playing in 60 cities and grossing $40 million in North America alone!

Whether the attraction is a superstar act, such as Motley Crüe, or an unknown and unproven act, such as Millions of Americans, the principle is the same: The promoter will examine the costs involved in staging the event and the profit potential to himself and to the act. He will then propose a financial offer to the act that will incorporate what he knows about the act's technical production requirements. At this point the promoter will probably not have a full contract and rider from the agent (you will learn about contracts and contract riders in Chapter 3), but he can make an educated guess about what he is going to offer based on similar acts and his experience.

The promoter is then responsible for advertising the show and selling the tickets. If he doesn't advertise and sell tickets, he isn't going to make any money! He will work with the act's record company, PR, and plugging firms to ensure maximum publicity for the event. Additionally, and depending on the act's contract terms, the promoter may also be responsible for arranging sound and lighting equipment, transportation, accommodations, and catering for the band and its crew.

As I mentioned, promoting can be an enormously risky venture and possibly the most risky role out of the management/agent/promoter relationship. The fickleness of the concert-going public should never be under-estimated. This uncertainty is the reason why specialized promotion companies, employing many individual promoters, handle most of the concert touring promotion these days. As production demands from the artists and tickets prices both increase, the potentially huge financial losses are too great for a one-man band or a small company. Recent years have therefore seen consolidation, buyouts, and mergers of talent buyers creating larger, more powerful promotions companies.

Note: Live Nation—the Future of Music Promotion? The biggest of the modern promotion companies is Live Nation, a US-based behemoth that promoted or produced more than 28,500 events in 2005. The original Live Nation was called SFX Entertainment. SFX itself was pretty big after founder Robert F. X. Sillerman began purchasing US radio and television stations in 1992. Based on this success, he formed a company named SFX Broadcasting. In 1997, SFX created a division called SFX Concerts and entered the live entertainment industry by aggressively purchasing other smaller concert promoters and venues in the UK, Europe, and the US.

In 2000, Clear Channel (a radio and billboard advertising company) acquired SFX and re-branded it Clear Channel Entertainment (CCE). CCE continued to acquire promoters and venues worldwide, snapping up some of Europe's largest promoters in the process. Late in 2005, Live Nation was spun-out from Clear Channel as a stand-alone publicly owned company.

At this point I can hear you all saying, "Thanks for the business lesson, Andy, but what does that have to do with me?" I know you are impatient to get your show on the road. However, I did say you need to learn all the components to avoid making mistakes. A common mistake is to assume that the person who promotes the show is the same person you deal with over the phone and on the day. Let me explain.

All promoting companies, whether large or small, rely on new talent to create continual cash. Live Nation, SJM, DEAG, and so on all need input from agents and the acts themselves as to what's hot and what's not. Promotion companies will employ two or three people who are the *actual* people constantly on the lookout for new talent, fielding calls from booking agents and working on the deals. These are the big guys (and girls) who make the calls, do the math, and sign the deal. Wham, deal is done, and then onto the next one. They do not have time to sort out sound and lights, print up dressing room signs, or arrange parking for 16 tour buses. Other people in the organization are employed for those roles, and it is very important that *you*, as a performer or crew person, do the research to find the right person to deal with.

For example, the majority of the bands that I tour with will do some UK shows that are promoted by SJM Concerts. (There are other promoters, such as Live Nation and Metropolis Music, to whom this example applies just as well.) Based in Manchester, SJM promotes shows throughout England, ranging in size from 350-capacity club shows to stadium shows. Chris Yorke, as one of the heads of SJM, is responsible for doing the deals; therefore, every contract I receive for an SJM show bears his name. As tour manager, I am very unlikely to be in a position to question or change the deal the promoter has offered, and therefore I have very rarely spoken to Chris. What I need to sort out is load in, sound check and show times, bus parking, dressing room riders, PA and light specifications, curfew times, merchandising fees, and myriad other details. For this I speak to a very nice guy named Wayne Larner.

Wayne deals with the "production" of the show—the nuts and bolts. He has a huge database of every venue that SJM uses, so he can send me over information including stage sizes, power for buses, and whether the venue has stairs to the stage (very important!). Wayne also receives information from Chris about the other acts playing on the show and how much is in the budget for catering. Wayne can therefore tell me what the show times will be and how many cans of cheap lager and supermarket sandwiches/ deli trays he will give me for the "rider." (You'll find an explanation of riders in Chapter 3.) I get all this information from Wayne for each SJM-promoted show on the tour and I make sure it fits in with what I am expecting and with what our contract stipulates. If challenges and issues arise, we try to come to a sensible arrangement, always bearing in mind that the financial deal for the show has already been done. If I start demanding extravagant sound equipment and tons of booze for backstage, based on the show deal already signed, the promoter will lose money. And because the promoter does not want to lose money, it is very unlikely that he or she will agree to my demands.

When I have all my information from Wayne (and the equivalent Waynes from the other promoters), I then set off on tour. On arriving at the first SJM show, I will see neither Chris nor Wayne. Chris is in the office doing deals, and Wayne is in the office supplying advance information for future SJM shows. Besides, a large promoter such as SJM has an average of 10 to

20 shows per night happening. The promoters are not leaving me to fend for myself, though; they send down a representative.

The Promoter's Representative

The promoter's representative (or *rep*) is your point of contact for the promoter. Regardless of whether you are a performer, a tour manager, backline crew, or someone handing out flyers, if you want to speak to the promoter at a show, you will actually need to speak with the rep. The actual promoter will not be around until much later, if at all.

So the promoter is not at the show, and you have to deal with this rep. What can the rep do for you? Well, the rep's job is to be a liaison between the venue and the artist and to look out for the interests of the promoter. The rep will arrive at the same time as the main load in starts and is basically in charge of the show until the end of the night. The rep is there to ensure that the show goes smoothly, the band is paid correctly, the law is observed, and everything else in between goes well. Please do not assume I am talking about huge shows in theaters or arenas here. Remember, a successful promotions company may have 10 to 20 shows going on each night. Whether you are opening up in a 250-capacity bar or as a support DJ at a festival, you are going to be dealing with reps, not necessarily the person who has booked you for your show.

Note: I'm on the Guest List .... If you ever have difficulty trying to get into a show as a guest (in other words, you are on the guest list), always ask to speak with the promoter and/or the rep. Arguing with the door security people is a waste of time. Door staff and security people have a job to do; this does not involve trying to second-guess your intentions in arguing about guest list places. The door staff has the list and has no power or special privileges to grant you entry if your name happens not to be on that list. Instead, you should ask to speak with the rep, who will usually have submitted the guest list to the box office and will be able to help you if a genuine mistake has been made.

You will see more about the day-to-day responsibilities of a promoter's rep in Chapter 7, "At the Show." The fact that you know a show is booked by a promoter but the day is handled by someone different should make your life a bit easier!

The Venue

Table 2.1 shows the basic types of venues in which you will work and/or perform. Some of the venue types are unique to the US and other warmer climates. For instance, "sheds" are mixed-type venues with large, covered seated areas and grass-covered outdoor amphitheatres. Up to 75 percent of the audience is outdoors, and obviously this arrangement can only work in warmer, less wet climates!

I mentioned that some venues run their own promotions and that most promoters hire venues for their shows. When dealing with an in-house promotion, you will probably experience the same split in job roles as discussed earlier. There will be a promoter making the deals, and all the technical details and marketing will be handled by other people. This applies to even the smallest bar operations in my experience, so always make sure you are asking for the right people when you are trying to book a show, confirm running times, and so on.

In smaller venues you may not have a promoter's rep; instead, look out for the bar manager, night manager, or house manager. This person will be in charge of the venue from when it is open to the public (or from a specified time if the venue is open to the public all day). I have often found that the bar/night/house manager starts to work from a later time (such as 7:00 P.M.) and will not be there during the day when you arrive for setup and sound check. Technical details will be dealt with by the house sound and/or light people, but usually questions about payment, guest lists, and hospitality riders are the responsibility of the bar/night/house manager. Find out in advance if this is the case.

The bar/night/house manager is not there just to deal with your show. He or she is paid to run the operation of the venue, and that includes dealing with the public and the in-house staff. Venues exist to make money. An obvious point, maybe, but the fact a venue has booked you and your show does not necessarily mean everyone who works in the venue shares your

Table 2.1 Venues in Which You Will Work

Type	Description	Audience Capacity	In-House Promotion	Outside Promotion	In-House Sound and Lights	Music Shows per Week	Show Types	Example
Bar, pub		20–80	Yes. Owner or manager, hobby-type interest	Very occasionally	Maybe basic PA. Maybe no stage!	2 or 3	DJs, local bands, talent nights, tribute bands	Anywhere!
Music bar or pub		81–300	More dedicated promotions team	Occasionally	Basic PA and lights. Stage.	5 to 7 A more dedicated business	Local bands, smaller touring acts, talent night, and tribute bands	Bull & Gate, London. Euclid Tavern, Cleveland, Ohio.
Music venue		301–1,000	Yes, but lots of outside hire	Yes, national promoters	Good PA and lights, backstage rooms, and so on. Options to bring in production.	4 to 7	Touring acts, showcases, discos, and theme nights on weekends	Leadmill, Sheffield. Troubador, Hollwood.
Theater/ large club		1,000–2,000	Occasionally unless privately owned	Yes, national promoters	PA for disco events but probably have to hire in all sound and lights	4 to 6	National touring acts, showcases	Rock City, Nottingham. Irving Plaza, New York City.
Large theater		2,001–5,000	Occasionally	Yes, national promoters	No existing PA or lights	3 to 4	National touring acts, one-offs, and multiple runs	Brixton Academy, London. Warfield Theater, San Francisco.

(Continued)

Table 2.1 Continued

Type	Description	Audience Capacity	In-House Promotion	Outside Promotion	In-House Sound and Lights	Music Shows per Week	Show Types	Example
Sheds	Amphitheatre with seated and open areas	5,000–15,000	Occasionally	Yes	Very basic	3 to 4 seasonal	National touring acts	Smirnoff Music Centre, Dallas, Texas.
Large halls	Part of purpose-built venue (university or arena complex)	5,001–10,000	Promoter may own venue (such as Live Nation)	Yes	No existing PA or lights	1 to 3	International touring acts and multiple runs, sporting events	A.J. Palumbo Center, Pittsburgh, Pennsylvania.
Arenas		10,001–30,000	Mixed. Some festivals run by national promoters.	Mixed. Some festivals run by national promoters.	No existing PA or lights	1 or 2	International touring acts and multiple runs, sporting events, ice events	Wembley Arena, London. United Center, Chicago, Illinois.
Outdoor	Festival and green field sites plus larger sheds	25,000–50,000 per day	No	Yes	No	1 seasonal	International touring acts	Roskilde. Carling: Reading & Leeds. Vans Warped Tour.
Stadiums		25,000–100,000	No unless venue owned/operated by promotion company	Yes	No	1 seasonal	Superstar touring acts	Wembley Stadium, London. Feyenoord, Rotterdam.

view regarding the importance of your act and tonight's show. And although the venue may be making some money off the show, the majority of the cash received will be from the bars, food, coat check, and parking facilities that the venue provides. On a larger scale, an arena venue such as the SECC in Glasgow makes £7.25 million ($13.5 million) per year from these "concessions" at its music shows. The fewer problems you present to the manager on the night of the show, the better! Many smaller venues (especially in the US) have their technical team deal with payment, guest lists, and so on as a way of saving costs. I am not a fan of this approach; it puts too much responsibility on one (often underpaid) person.

The Production Office

The incoming musical act with the trucks, sound and lighting equipment, set, costume, video, radios, trailers, and crew is known as the "production." As you will see, it takes an immense amount of advance planning to get all these people and this equipment on the road, and that planning continues when the act is actually on tour. As in any organization, the planning and administration takes place in offices, and on tour those offices are set up in each venue on the tour for the duration of the production's stay. It is here that the computers, printers, broadband routers, fax machines, photocopiers, filing cabinets, walkie-talkies, and shredders that the tour may carry are set up each day. Most modern venues will have some kind of dedicated production office (see Figure 2.3), even it takes the form of a space in the cloakroom with a desk and a telephone!

The production office (once set up) acts as the nerve center for the tour day. The tour manager, production manager, assistants, and (unless he or she has a separate office) promoter's rep will have a desk or desk space in the production office and will pretty much spend all the tour day in here. All information flows into and out of this office. When walking into a venue to find a promoter, tour manager, or other touring staff, you should always ask for and locate the production office first.

Marketing

So you play music, as a band or solo performer, and you have been offered a show at a local music venue. You obviously make sure you

Figure 2.3 A typical venue production office.

put the date on your website and your MySpace site, print flyers and posters, and start to spread the word of mouth. All that activity is to be expected if you are taking your music career seriously, but is there something else you can be doing? Absolutely!

The venue and/or promoter wants the show to sell as many tickets as you do, so make sure you work with them when it comes to publicizing the show. Keep in mind the fact that promoters and venues put on shows for a living, literally. They probably have more access to more media outlets than you do, and they regularly produce advertisements in the local and national press, as well as radio spots and features on their websites and in magazines. It is vital that you work with them to get the maximum publicity and ticket sales. At the very least, you should make sure the promoter's publicity department has a good-quality graphic file of your logo (in JPEG or GIF format), a concise and up-to-date press release/bio, and a list of the other acts with whom you may have played. You should also make sure the dates are entered into any national and regional show listings, either print- or web-based. The promoter will probably contact you for this information, so do not be surprised when they do. If the venue/promoter does not ask you for this material, then make sure you get it to them anyway! At the very least, it shows you care about making the show a success for the both of you. You will learn more about this subject in Chapter 10, "Marketing."

The Crew

So far you have met the artist manager, the booking agent, the promoter (and his or her representatives), the venue manager, and the publicity people. All these people are directly involved in putting on a modern music performance. You will meet them all in various incarnations as soon as you step inside any venue to work.

The final set of people you will meet and have to work with at a show are the technical staff, or the *crew*. A full examination of various crew jobs and functions is included in Part III of this book; for now I will concentrate on their roles in relation to planning and executing a show.

When you step in the venue as a performer or crew person, you will meet two types of crew people (depending on the size of venue)—house/local crew and touring/visiting crew.

House/Local Crew

The main person working on a show from the house/venue crew will be the audio technician. This person is employed to set up, run, and maintain the venue's sound system for visiting acts. If you are playing in a tiny pub or bar, if you carry your own PA, or if you create unamplified music, then you will probably not meet the venue's audio technician (a.k.a. the "house sound guy"). If, on the other hand, you create music that needs to be amplified—in other words, pretty much any contemporary music—then the house engineer will help you when you arrive to perform your show.

Do not assume I am only talking about small-capacity (150 to 700 people) venues with in-house sound equipment here. If you perform or work on a stage at an outdoor festival, then you will be working with the house guys. Their house is a tent, but they are still there to supply sound services to the incoming acts, regardless of whether you have/are your own engineer.

Note: The House Sound Guy Everyone I have ever worked with has an opinion about the venue audio technician, usually along the lines of, "Jeez, that house sound guy was such a jerk," blaming that person for a bad show. Experience shows me that the house audio tech is a very easy target. But don't blame them—read this book and learn how to make your show better from the start! It is true that there are inexperienced house engineers out there, but everyone has to start somewhere, which again is why you are reading this book.

In the many years I have been working, I still see bands and DJs turn up at small venues with substandard, broken equipment and expect the sound onstage and in the house to be perfect. There is a popular saying: "You cannot polish a turd." There is no magic with live sound. If your instruments sound thin, crackly, buzzy, and out of tune onstage, then that is how they will sound to the audience, only amplified and therefore louder! Think about that concept, accept the limitations of the environment, and be prepared!

The house audio tech is there to place microphones and monitor wedges that will amplify your instruments and enable you to hear yourself onstage. He or she then will mix your sound for you unless you have (or are) your own engineer. Bear in mind the house guy also has to do the same for all the other bands on the bill that night, which hopefully will only total two acts, but usually means four or five bands on "local band" or talent nights! I will go into sound check etiquette in Chapter 7, but the lesson here is that it is a sound check, not a rehearsal. Never, *ever* think you will have time to rehearse that new song during sound check. Get your instruments set up and plugged in, and listen to what the house audio tech asks you to do. Do not play or sing until you are asked to do so, and keep looking at the house guy all the time so you will catch his "stop playing" signals. Sound checks have been known to cause a great deal of frustration to musicians, technicians, house staff, promoters, artist managers, and booking agents. I will therefore be devoting a good deal of time to the etiquette of sound checks in Chapter 7.

The other people you will find yourself working with in the venue are the local crew, or *humpers*. These people are employed by the venue and/or the promoter specifically to assist the touring or visiting crew with load in and load out the PA, lights (if applicable), and the musicians' equipment—speaker cabinets, amplifiers, drums, keyboards, and stands—known as the *backline*. (On larger shows the local crew will be employed to load in all the set, staging, lights, PA, wardrobe, catering, and production equipment. A typical large theater/arena-type show will involve about 20 to 40 local crew for each the load in and load out.)

If you are working as an opening act on a large show, you might not see the locals because their work will have been done by the time you arrive for sound check. It is common practice, however, to retain two to four local crewmembers to help load in the opening band's equipment and then to assist with changing over the support band's equipment during the show. This will probably be your first contact with the local crew if you are an opening act. The local crew will appear side-stage as you (or the band you work for) finish the performance, and then they will help take your equipment offstage in preparation for the next band coming onstage.

Many venues in the US are union regulated, and you are therefore not allowed to load/unload your own equipment. The unloading, loading, and carrying of all the visiting production equipment has to be done by a workforce designated by the local union.

Note: Accept Available Help! When you arrive at a larger show, you should not automatically load in your equipment. A good tip is to send someone inside and inquire as to whether there are any local crew people to assist you. Why carry your gear when someone is being paid to help you?

Other vital members of the local crew are the runners. The equivalent of "gofers" (as in "go for this, go for that") from the film world, runners are local people with access to transportation who can therefore go on errands for the band's production personnel.

The runner will make himself or herself known to the arriving production during load in. Bear in mind that the job of the runner is to go on errands/shopping trips for the act; the runner will put up a blank shopping list in the production office or dressing room, along with his or her mobile number. If you need something during the day, such as musical equipment spares, photocopying, batteries, or laundry, you either phone the runner or write your request on the list, along with your name. The runner will then go and purchase whatever is necessary, having been given a cash float by the tour/production manager or tour accountant.

After you have played, the local crew will help you get your gear offstage to make way for the next band. They will also help you load out the gear and pack your van/car/bus. Remember, they have nothing to do with the other acts and are paid as part of running the show. These guys were probably there at 8:00 in the morning and will work at the venue until 2:00 the next morning; they still have to have to tear down PA and lights and pack big smelly trucks. My advice for dealing with local crews is to be bloody nice to them! Always make sure you ply local crews with band T-shirts, water, and whatever else they might like.

Security

Any gathering of people has to be organized to include emergency medical and evacuation procedures. This includes modern concerts, whether classical orchestral or alternative rock. The role of the security and stewarding personnel is primarily to oversee and assist with the safety of the audience. When attending any modern concert, you will see these security people at the public entrances and exits and also in the "pit" (the area in front of the stage between the stage and the crush barrier). The promoter and/or venue pay for these security personnel. Most countries that stage entertainment events have very strict laws regarding the amount and type of security personnel and stewards that have to be supplied for each event. Although the majority of security people at a large show or festival are employed on a casual basis, the companies that supply security and stewarding teams provide full-time and highly trained experts to oversee the casual labor at each event.

Security personnel are also used to guard certain areas of the venue, such as the dressing rooms and areas containing expensive sound, light, and video equipment, as well truck and bus parking areas. Access to these areas is based on a pass system, with the passes being issued by the tour/production manager and the promoter. The touring band and crew will usually have laminated passes ("laminates") that will specify the wearer has "Access to All Areas" or AAA. AAA personnel may have "escort" privileges, meaning they can escort non-AAA guests or workers into areas that are off limits to non-AAA personnel.

Opening acts, guests, photographers, promoter's reps, and other working personnel are given sticky passes that indicate their role on the day and the access privileges they hold.

To avoid confusion, the security personnel on the day will be given a *pass sheet*. A pass sheet is a copy of the passes issued on the day, arranged on one or two sheets of paper with detailed explanations of the access levels for each pass. This pass sheet is then issued to all relevant security personnel and also posted at every "sensitive" access point.

Audiences, crew, and band members alike all have opinions and stories about security people, most of them negative. Although the scope of this book does not allow me to really address views and complaints from the concert-going public regarding security/stewarding personnel, it is a perfect place to lay down a few truths for all the bands and crews out there that have a less-than-favorable view toward security and stewarding at shows.

- Truth 1: Venue security people are employed to protect *you*.
- Truth 2: Venue security people are employed to make sure *your* expensive sound/light/video/recording/catering/production equipment does not get stolen or damaged.

There really is no attempt to create any kind of inner sanctum or exclusive world when issuing passes and employing venue security staff. Pass-based controls are put in place to limit the number of people who have access to certain areas at a show or event for both health and safety reasons. Having a pass to a backstage area of the show does not mean you are any more important than anybody else viewing or participating in the running of the show. Having this kind of accreditation merely means you are necessary or accountable to the band's organization or you are amicable or trustworthy. This is great!

Note: AAA Passes: Who Should Get Them? The touring artists and crew will get AAA passes issued to them by the tour manager. These passes will be recognized (with a few notable exceptions) by the security and stewarding personnel in the shows in which you are working. Heads of record companies, artist managers, guitarists' girlfriends/boyfriends, and booking agents will also insist on AAA laminates to enable them to walk into any show on a tour they are involved with.

Politically, it is a good idea to give out the same AAA passes as for the rest of the touring personnel—these agents, managers, label people, and girlfriends/boyfriends are important to the continued success of your band; these people are all working hard on behalf of the band and should therefore be afforded the same status as the rest of the touring organization. However, it is not a good idea to give all these people the same access privileges as the full-time touring party; you really do not want guests (however important they may be) escorting a load of their drunken friends to the backstage areas. The backstage area of a modern concert is a working environment. There are offices filled with laptops and printers, clothes, and personal effects, as well as the sound and light equipment. There are amplifier racks, lighting dimmer racks, mains distributions boards, hundreds of cables, and other trip hazards. There may also be pyrotechnics. It's not a safe place to be, especially if you have had a few beers.

So you need to give "higher" access to these VIPs, and at the same time you need to control just how much access they have without pissing them off. You will definitely run the risk of offending these special guests if you give them sticky passes. Also, you cannot tell security people, "This person with an AAA can escort, but this person with an AAA cannot." So how do you get around this problem? A common solution is to have dots on the laminates—small sticky stars or circles (or whatever) that signify different or special privileges. These dots are indicated on the pass sheet issued to the security people. The guests can still go anywhere they want, but they are unable to bring non-AAA guests with them. No one is offended, and a sensible amount of access is granted to everyone.

Wherever possible, I restrict escort privileges for the band members on a tour. In my experience the musicians get far too much pressure from friends and family to get them backstage. I am not trying to create some bizarre personal kingdom. However, the backstage area of a modern concert is a working environment, and safety is of the utmost importance. Therefore, I always feel it necessary to restrict the number of people traipsing through these areas to the necessary working personnel only. There is always the hotel bar for socializing!

It may be necessary for acts to travel with their own security/close protection personnel. You have read stories or seen videos of divas and hip-hop luminaries being escorted by these "man mountains." It is an unfortunate sign of the times that celebrities from all entertainment fields may be threatened; the music world is no different. In my experience, close protection security employed by bands act more as travel/movement coordinators; this helps to take the pressure off the tour manager. Touring security are also good at explaining the rules of the road to opening bands and local crew and can read the riot act if necessary. I once had an interesting "lecture" from the head of security of the headline act after one of my band's guitarists lobbed a glass across a crowded nightclub. It was explained to me in no uncertain terms that this kind of behavior goes straight into the papers and that journalists really do not care whether the "bad boy" from the headline act threw the glass—stories like that sell papers and ruin reputations. My charge was given the opportunity to apologize....

Touring/Visiting Crew

This section assumes you are working on a show with other acts that are perhaps touring or playing a one-off. In any case, the band will employ its own crew that works directly for the act and/or for the suppliers (PA, lights, and so on) and is touring with the band. There is a massive list of people who accompany a band on tour, but for the purposes of this brief "who does what" section, I will introduce you to a few of the staff. They are no more or less important than anyone who works for a touring act, but you are likely to interface with these people at a show and likely to cause offense if you do not observe the proper etiquette!

Tour Manager

The tour manager is the primary contact for a band and its crew. If you are opening up either as a one-off or as part of a tour, you should take the time to introduce yourself to the TM of the headline act (preferably before the first day of the tour) and supply him or her with all relevant information. This should consist of the following:

- The number of people in your touring/show entourage. (Do *not* forget your drivers!)

- The role of each person in your touring entourage.

- A contact number for you/your tour manager.

- The type of vehicle(s) for you and your gear.

- An input list, stage plan, and any special production equipment you may be bringing for the show, such as backdrops, banners, lasers, and so on.

On arrival at the first show, make time to briefly introduce yourself and then get the hell out of the way! If you are part of a tour, there will be plenty of time for socializing later.

Audio Crew

You may be working in a venue with in-house sound and lights (100 to 1,000 capacity). You may be working on a show where the promoter or headline act has bought in its own (rented) PA system. (Venues greater than 2,000 capacity rarely have an in-house sound system.) Either way, the band may have its own crew, or there will certainly be the house crew or the system crew. (The supplier will send along technicians when supplying a PA system for the tour or event. Because they work for the supplier, they are the "system crew.")

You probably won't have much to do with the artist's own audio crew but, as mentioned, you will work with the house/system crew. Local crew will help you get your gear onstage, and the house/system crew will place microphones and monitor wedges. Hopefully you will have provided them with an input list well in advance. (An input list is a list of all the instruments you use, what microphones or DI boxes you need, plus other specific audio information. More details on this in Chapter 3.) The house/system crew will also mix your monitor/stage sound and your FOH sound for you unless you are the engineer or your band has an engineer.

Note: The Evil Practice of Charging for System Techs! There is a practice that exists when dealing with touring systems crew that I want to bring to your attention. Standard practice is to pay the system techs to mix your sound for you if you do not have your own FOH or monitor engineer. This is often called "opening/support band money." The argument is that the system techs are employed to run sound for the headline act, work a very long day anyway, and therefore should be paid overtime to mix the sound for other acts. However, I do not see why the opening acts, often with no money (if they had money, they would employ their own engineers), have to then stump up cash to the audio crew.

Don't get me wrong; I have often worked as a system audio tech and, yes, I worked really hard all day, and the opening/support band money was a good incentive. However, I totally disagree with this convention because your show contract should stipulate that the promoter agrees to provide PA and lights "at no cost to the artist/producer." If your contract does say this, then the promoter should be paying the support band money to the system crew, not you. After all, you do not have to pay for festival sound systems techs or in-house techs. As I say, I have allegiances on both sides, but having been a TM for struggling young acts, it strikes me that the whole system is extremely exploitative. Make sure you check your contract and tackle the issue well in advance of the show; you could be paying out an extra £30 (approximately $58) a night!

Backline Crew

These are the boys and girls who tend to the personal instruments, amplifiers, and effects of the band musicians themselves. When you arrive, they will often have filled the stage with the band's gear, plus toolboxes, guitar worlds (areas at the side of the stage that the backline crew uses to set up, tune, and maintain guitars and basses), and production cases. You will have to negotiate what space you can have to set up your gear with them. Again, if you have spoken to the TM and/or backline crews of all the bands on the bill in advance, you may be able to negotiate sharing equipment and stage space. Always be prepared to change your setup to fit in with their existing production. For example, if the headline act's keyboard rig is stage left, then all the DI boxes, monitor wedges, and so on will be there at stage left. Providing outputs, power, and monitors for you is going to be time consuming if your keyboard stage setup is stage right. And time is one thing you are really short of if you want to get all your gear onstage and obtain a decent sound check. To save this time and technical hassle for the house/system crew, you should consider changing your setup to stage left. Then you can simply set up your rig in front of the existing keyboard setup; the house/system crew will only have to extend a few cables and move a monitor speaker. Voilà! Everyone is happy, and you are set up and able to sound check in minutes. Make sense, doesn't it?

Lighting Crew

The lighting crew is split into two types, as is the audio crew—there are people who work directly for the band, and then there are house/system crew who work in the venue or tour with the rented lighting rig. A large tour (700-person capacities and upward) will often carry its own lighting equipment. This will supplement or replace the existing house lighting system. The headline act will be renting this system, and the promoter will be contributing to this cost as per his contracted agreement to "supply PA and lights to the artist's specifications." (We will see more about this in Chapter 3.) The headline act and crew has arranged, designed, trucked, and set up this system. Because the show will contain special effects and set pieces, you will probably not be given access to the full range of lights in the system. Common practice for support bands is to light them using the generic PAR-type lights, which will be controlled by one of the touring system crew. On a large tour with a touring rig, you will probably be asked to pay for one of the system crew to operate the lights for you during your show. Because the system crew will not know your material and will only have some general lamps to work with, you are not going to get much of a show! I would therefore argue against this charge and simply and politely ask for a static wash for the whole of your set. (A "wash" is a mix of colors from the lights that will illuminate you and nothing else—in other words, the lights will wash over you.)

Caterers

Okay, you can lose your patience with the backline people, insult the tour manager, and even refuse to pay the systems crew. There is one set of people, however, whom you should approach on your knees and hail as gods—the caterers!

On a large-scale show (700-capacity and upward), it is common practice to bring in people to cook hot, highly nutritious meals for the bands, the touring crew, and (occasionally) the local crew. This catering crew either tours with the act or is locally sourced for each venue. In both cases, the catering crew starts work extremely early and finishes late. Caterers have to bring in ovens, gas bottles, fridges, flatware, ice machines—everything! They cook three main meals a day, as well as provide running buffets for up to 250 people a day, depending on the size of the production. And the food is always amazing, considering the environment it is prepared in. Many of the world's venues are not very good for producing music shows, let alone cooking!

I mention all this because, as with all modern show production, there is etiquette. Actually, it is just plain manners. Three things to remember when filing into catering:

- These people are *not* your Mum, and it is not a commercial restaurant. These people got up at 7:00 A.M. and will not finish until 1:00 A.M. It really is tough if you do not like what they have prepared. If you have a major dietary concern, then you have to inform someone well in advance—such as your tour manager.

- Catering is the heart and soul of any touring show or one-off event. People come here to meet up, to eat, to talk, and to relax. Be really careful what you say here, especially if you are thinking of bitching about someone! Save that for your own transportation, your hotel room, or for when you have finished the tour.

- Clear your plates, cutlery, and waste when you have finished. Again, the caterers are *not* your Mum, and it is not a commercial restaurant.

You may think I am overdoing it with the advice here. Unfortunately I have worked with people who had no respect or manners for anyone on the show. As I keep saying, you only get one shot at making an impression. If someone is going to put that much hard work into something so integral to life, health, and happiness as your food, then you had better show them some respect!

> "[Playing live] is probably the most important thing a band can do. It's where a band builds a following, improves musically, gets tighter, and it's the best way of spreading awareness."
>
> —Joe Etchells, A&R, BMG Publishing.

3 | Contracts and Riders

According to Fortune.com, "[b]y the mid-'60s the Stones had reportedly sold ten million singles, including 'Satisfaction,' and five million albums, but the band was still living hand to mouth. 'I'll never forget the deals I did in the '60s, which were just terrible,' says Jagger. 'You say, "Oh, I'm a creative person, I won't worry about this." But that just doesn't work. Because everyone would just steal every penny you've got.'"

Although artists today are generally more aware of the business dealings that surround them, this does not mean that the potential for misunderstanding or illegality does not exist. It is vital to get some kind of written agreement, preferably a contract, before undertaking any paid work in the music industry. Continuing with our introduction to the live music business, we will see in this chapter that contracts are a mundane but useful tool.

The Contract

There is a lot of money, prestige, and ego involved when performing a show or tour. Things can and do go wrong; organizers can misunderstand their responsibilities, arrangements can be misinterpreted, and people can get greedy. If this happens and things get sticky between the various parties (artist, promoter, agent, venue, and so on), then it will always help you to have a legally binding bit of paper to wave around to prove your point.

> **Note: Always Seek Advice from a Legally Qualified Person!** This section is meant as an overview of the process of issuing contracts for live performance. You are encouraged to *always* seek qualified legal counsel when writing or administering any legal documents, including live performance contracts.

With the majority of contemporary music shows, everything runs smoothly, and the issuing of a contract is a formality, but a formality that is strictly adhered to.

You have seen how a show is booked, with the artist/agent hassling the promoter (or vice versa) to book a show or tour at a certain time. When the agent and promoter have agreed to the show and the terms in principle, the agent will then produce a contract for each show (or set of shows) and send the contract to the promoter. This contract sets out the terms under which the artist agrees to perform and lists any special technical or production stipulations specific to that engagement.

An example of a contract is reproduced on the next page. Take time to study it; explanations of the various clauses follow.

This is obviously an example; concert contracts take many different forms and are specific to one show. A decent contract should, at the very least, contain the points and clauses discussed in the following sections.

Date of Agreement

"An agreement between *x* and *y*"—who is the agreement between? The parties could be artist and promoter, or artist manager and promoter, or agent and promoter. All parties involved need to be named and contract terms must be applied. The promoter will usually be referred to as "the promoter," "the purchaser," or "the buyer" for the rest of the contract. The artist or artist manager will be referred to as "the producer," "the artist," or "the management." In this case, P. Romoter is the promoter/purchaser, and Mr. Ron Decline is the manager who is signing this contract on behalf of his client, the band called Millions of Americans. It is very rare for the agent to be named as a contracting party. After all, the agent acts to bring the two contractors together and is not involved in the financial transaction.

Contract No.: **1234**

An Agreement made the 01st day of January 2007

Between **P. Romoter pp TKN Concerts, 123 Gig Street, London** hereinafter referred to as the 'Promoter' of the one part
AND **Ron Decline pp Millions of Americans** hereinafter referred to as the 'Artiste' of the other part.

WITNESSETH that the Promoter hereby engages the Artiste and the Artiste agrees to the engagement to appear/perform as **Millions of Americans** at the venues(s), on the dates and for the periods and at the salary stated hereto.

SCHEDULE

The Artiste agrees to appear at ONE (1) performance as follows:

At the:	**Fleapit**
	1 Deedah Street
	Sheffield
	S1
On the:	**Saturday, 25th April 2006**
Capacity:	**350**
Ticket price:	**$6.00 in advance**
For a salary of:	**$300.00 plus PA/lights + catering or 80% of door receipts (after $1116.43 costs) whichever is the greater**

SPECIAL STIPULATIONS

1)   The exact running times for this engagement are to be advised.

Signed _____ Date _____

This agency is not responsible for any non-fulfillment of contracts by Proprietors, Managers or Artists but every reasonable safeguard is assured.

Contract No.: 1234 continued

2) Payment

The guaranteed fee for this engagement is $300.00 + 80% of door receipts, after costs, which is payable to the Artiste as follows:

a) A deposit of 50% of the fee, i.e. $150.00, is payable to by certified check to TKN CONCERTS CLIENTS ACCOUNT and should be posted to TKN Concerts, 123 Gig Street London. **Deposit due immediately on receipt of contract.** In the event of cancellation by the Promoter, this will be retained by the Artiste.

For the purposes of this clause time is of the essence.

b) The balance of the fee, i.e. $150.00, plus any percentage payments due, is payable to the Artiste in cash pounds Sterling on the night of the performance.

c) The fee should be net and free of all local taxation.

3) Sound and Lights

Promoter are to provide and pay for a first class P.A. and Monitor system and Lighting systems to the Artiste's specification and approval (see attached technical specifications). All the necessary crew is to be in attendance throughout sound check and for the duration of Artiste's entire performance.

4) Sponsorship and Endorsement

The name or logo of Millions of Americans or any of its members shall not be used by any sponsor or be tied to any commercial product or company, nor there be any sign, banner or advertising at or within 30 meters of the stage throughout the entire engagement. Promoter is specifically prohibited from associating Artiste's name with any product or sponsorship or promotion whatsoever without Artiste's prior approval and written consent.

5) Merchandising

The Artiste shall have the exclusive right but not obligation to sell souvenirs, posters, programs, shirts and all other merchandise directly pertaining to and/or bearing the likeness of the Artistes at the engagement and to retain ALL monies received from the sale thereof.

Promoter shall ensure that there is sufficient space for suitable stands to be erected for this purpose at no cost to Artiste.

6) Unauthorized Recording

a) The Promoter agrees that no part of the performance may be taped, filmed, or otherwise recorded in any way whatsoever. Promoter shall place a sign at the entrance(s) to the engagement which clearly states this limitation.

b) Promoter shall ensure that no recordings take place and shall confiscate or otherwise detain any sound or visual recording materials by visually screening all persons attending the engagement for any recording equipment. Promoter agrees to cooperate fully with Artistes to prevent such recordings and agree to act promptly and diligently to all Artiste's requests in fulfilment of this clause.

c) It is agreed and understood that in no instance whatsoever will the Artistes allow filming, recording, or broadcasts of any type at the aforementioned venue (by persons known or unknown) including but not limited to TV, film, radio, video tape and digital media unless the Artiste gives prior written consent.

7) Decline to Perform

The Artiste reserves the right to decline to perform without prejudice to the full agreed fee in the event of any reason beyond the control of the Artiste including but not limited to strike, lock out, war, fire, or serious or dangerous weather conditions.

Signed _____ Date _____

Description of Services Supplied

Who is performing and under what name? It may be obvious that Millions of Americans is the band performing, but many solo performers play under different names. DJs have pseudonyms and also perform under their real names. For instance, Soulwax (a Belgian rock band) also perform as 2 Many DJs (a hip DJ team). Soulwax/2 Many DJs regularly perform in both incarnations at festivals and will probably issue separate contracts.

Where and When Will the Concert Take Place?

This is the venue, street address, and show date. This should be obvious, I know, but I have seen more than one contract issued with the wrong show date!

Capacity

This information will give you and the tour manager (if applicable) insight into the physical size of the venue. You will also be able to work out whether the promoter's costs are reasonable after you have read Chapter 8, "How to Get the Shows."

Ticket Price

This is the price of the ticket set by the promoter. This ticket price will have been derived from the promoter's show cost calculations. In some cases, the band or artist management may question a very high ticket price; it is very important to peg the correct ticket price for an act, especially in the early stages of their career. Charge too much for the tickets, and you will deter your prospective audience; charge too little, and neither band nor promoter will make any money!

Fee

The fee payment schedule is the most important schedule, so I am going to go over it thoroughly.

The fee payment schedule usually stipulates the following:

- The amount
- The currency
- The payment schedule

In our example, the fee is $300. (To keep things simple, I have not included any sales tax. In the UK, for instance, there is a sales tax called VAT that is added on to all goods and services, including the fees charged by musicians. I have not included such tax here for the sake of simplicity.) Don't worry about the "or 80% of door receipts after costs, whichever is greater" part for now. I will be explaining that in Chapter 9, "Getting Paid."

You should always get your fee paid in your home currency if you are performing abroad. This will help you avoid currency exchange fluctuations.

Also, *always* negotiate that your fee is "net and free of all local taxes." All countries (with the odd exception—Denmark and [soon] the Netherlands, for example) levy income taxation on their visiting workers, and music groups are no different. This taxation is administered by the relevant government department in each country. This means that any income you make in a country can be taxed, leaving you with very little left of your performance fee. Most countries require that the promoter deduct the taxation from your fee as soon as you earn that fee (that is, on the day you play); you cannot pay it retrospectively. If a gross figure is offered for a performance, then do the math quickly to determine whether you will make any money off the show at all. Stipulate that all hotel, transportation, and per diems (if paid by the promoter) are also net and free of taxes.

Each country sets its own rate of taxation for foreign artists. In Europe, this is currently between 15 and 30 percent, depending on the individual country.

Note: Artist Taxation: A Useful Guide A good reference is "Tax and Social Security: A Basic Guide for Artists and Cultural Operators in Europe," by Judith Staines. This is a very informative guide to the varying taxation rates for foreign entertainers performing in Europe.

You can download this guide, free of charge, from www.on-the-move .org/documents/TaxandSocialSecurity.pdf.

The fee schedule should also include any other non-cash compensation—such as hotels, flights, and other travel—that are to be paid for by the promoter/buyer.

As I mentioned, always try to get paid in your local currency. Obviously, this is not a problem if you are performing in a bar down the street, but once you start to travel you will be earning different currencies. You may also want to specify a deposit to be paid before the performance. This is standard practice, especially if the fee is greater than £1,000 ($1,500). If you do want a deposit, then indicate this in the fee schedule with the amount required—for example, 50 percent and a bank account for the money to be paid into. Most established booking agents will collect deposits on their clients' behalf; the money is held in "client accounts" and the funds are disbursed upon request. This practice also allows the agents to deduct their commissions first!

The sending of a deposit can be used as a contractual milestone—no deposit received equals no show. Always stipulate the date before which the deposit should be received; this date should ideally be two weeks before the actual show date.

The remainder of the fee should *always* be paid in cash. Make sure that is stipulated in the contract, and, obviously, never take a certified check. Getting cash on the night is a security measure because you may not be able to track down a promoter who has given you a bad check once you have left town after the show.

In our example the sending of a certified check for the deposit is acceptable. It is a safer way to send money than sending cash in the post, and you can make sure the check has cleared before you perform the show. In practice, most promoters will simply initiate a money transfer for the deposit.

We have also stipulated that, in the event that the promoter cancels the show, we get to keep the deposit. Obviously, a promoter will only cancel a show as a very last resort and would attempt to reschedule the show as soon as possible. In that case, a scrupulous agent would keep the deposit in his account until the show was rescheduled.

Production Requirements

The production requirements clause in the contract will detail sound, light, staging, and catering requirements. This section will usually refer the promoter to the "rider" section of the contract. If these requirements are not detailed in the contract rider, then you may see something similar to this:

PA & LIGHTS

The Promoter agrees to provide and pay for a first-class PA (Public Address) System and a First Class Stage Lighting System as well as experienced technician(s) as necessary for use by the Artist for the duration of this Contract. The specifications for such PA and Lighting System will be advised by the Artist not later than fourteen (14) days prior to the performance.

Description of Special Stipulations

Are there any time or financial considerations specific to this engagement? In our example, we have stipulated that the logo of the band is not to be used in conjunction with any advertising or sponsorship without the artist's permission. The promoter will obviously want to promote the show and will use the band's name and logo in all advertising. The main purpose of this clause, however, is to prevent unscrupulous promoters and club owners from using the act's name to promote other events, such as after-show parties or radio appearances, from which the act themselves will receive no income. It is a very common occurrence for clubs near major concert venues to advertise an after-show event, such as "the official Millions of Americans after-show party! Half-price entry with your Millions of Americans concert ticket!" Audience members are tricked into going to the club, in the mistaken belief that they will see the band socializing. In reality, the band will be on a sleeper bus and traveling overnight to the next show.

It is difficult to police this kind of exploitation, but a contract clause that highlights this issue and refers to the penalties involved will hopefully prevent the promoter of the show from organizing an event without the band's permission and using the band's name and logo to make him extra cash.

We have also included clauses about our right to sell merchandise without having to pay the venue or promoter any commission. Many, many venues will charge you to sell your own merchandise, taking up to 25 percent of your money. (You will learn more about this hideous practice in Chapter 7,

"At the Show.") Although the promoter often has no control over merchandise commissions because he or she is simply hiring the venue, it is worth putting in this clause.

The promoter/buyer should study the contract carefully and sign and date it to signal his or her acceptance of the terms. By signing the contract, the promoter is saying, "Yes, I agree to provide all the conditions necessary for the performance of x on such date at such time for such amount of money."

If the promoter doesn't like something or disagrees with the terms, he can either contact the agent to try to renegotiate, or simply put a red line through the relevant clause and return the contract. This red line signals the promoter's refusal to comply with that section of the contract. A good agent would then, on receiving any amended contract, try to renegotiate the deal and get the promoter to accept all terms unconditionally.

When a contract is signed, dated, and returned to the agent, the agent should pass copies on to the manager or artist and to the artist's tour manager. As a tour manager or artist, you should travel with copies of all the contracts for the tour and you should have already studied them in order to pick up on any problems or disputes the promoters may have.

Should you have a contract for every show you do? Yes! As well as being a legally binding document in case of dispute, the contract also serves as a tool that enables promoters to forewarn you/the touring party of special circumstances at any particular venue. For instance, a well thought-out contract should at least try to state what time the promoter wants you to perform. I have been in situations where I have subsequently found out from speaking to the promoter that the artist's performance time was scheduled for 2:30 A.M. on the day after the date already given to me by the booking agent. I had already made extensive and expensive travel arrangements to get the artist and crew to a performance due on the evening before! This information was not in the contract, and it was only when I called up to check on technical information that I learned this.

Will you get a contract for every show you do? Probably not, especially when you are just starting out. Never mind, get in the habit of asking for one or supplying your own anyway. I take it you are serious about your career and making the best income you can from each performance, right? Then start issuing your own contracts! Study the example printed here; you can download an editable version from www.the-tour-book.com. Simply amend the relevant details, such as the promoter/buyer name and the show date, time, and fees. Even if you just issue a page that says, "You, Mrs. Bar Manager, agree to pay me in CASH the fee of x when I perform in your bar on the xxth of x. Sign here," you will be protecting yourself from potential nonpayment problems.

> "An exhilarating live show, small or large, is the beating heart of this industry. Playing live is of paramount importance, can earn a considerable proportion of the act's income, and is a way for performers to develop their art, rather than just knock out carbon copies of their records."
>
> —Matt Willis, CEC Management. Clients include the Eighties Matchbox B-Line Disaster, the Others, the Rakes, and Ben Folds.

The Contract Rider

You will know the term "rider" in relation to the food, booze, and red M&Ms that bands are given in their dressing room (as in "where's the rider?" and "that bastard support band drank all the rider"). However, the term "rider" refers to every aspect of the band's touring needs, from truck parking spaces to humidity onstage. Whereas the contract serves as an agreement that is particular to an individual performance, the contract rider is an agreement for every performance to which the act is contracted, regardless of any other consideration. It "rides" with the contract, hence the name.

The rider basically says, "For us, the artist, to do a really good show, we really need the following items, and you, the promoter, have to supply them at your own cost."

The following is the contract rider for Millions of Americans, a four-piece band who are traveling with five crew members. Again, notes and explanations follow the contract rider.

The rider is attached to a specific contract and is to be treated as part of the contract. It is *not* just a list of drinks! I will now explain each part of the rider; refer back to the contract here as needed.

MILLIONS OF AMERICANS EUROPE 2007

THIS RIDER FORMS AN INTEGRAL PART OF THE CONTRACT (#1234) TO WHICH IT IS ANNEXED.

CAST & CREW
Millions of Americans are 9 people:

4 x band

1 x TM/FOH engineer   Andy Reynolds
Contact: T: +44 (0)7762 551886   E: andy.reynolds@tourconcepts.com

1 x Driver   D. River
Contact: T: +44 (0)7777 12345   E: sprinter@merc.com

1 x backline technician   C. Himp
Contact: T: +44 (0)7777 98765   E: chimp@hotmail.com

1 x lighting engineer   Ms. L. Ampy
Contact: T: +44 (0)7777 90909   pulsarrules@aol.com

1 x merchandise seller   S. Wag
Contact: T: +44 (0)7777 00700   isithereyet@yahoo.co.uk

Millions of Americans are NOT traveling with a monitor engineer. The purchaser agrees to supply one sound engineer(s) who is capable and willing of mixing monitor sound for Millions of Americans, at no cost to the artist.

Cast and crew will travel together in one (1) vehicle as listed below. This vehicle also contains all the backline and lighting equipment.

PREPARED BY ANDY REYNOLDS - TOUR MANAGER
T: +44 (0) 7762 551886 T: +44 (0)870 126 5960
Email: andy.reynolds@tourconcepts.com

THIS RIDER EXPIRES AUGUST 30th 2007
PAGE 1 of 5

1. ACCESS AND EQUIPMENT

The Purchaser agrees to provide and pay for 2 (TWO) able bodied and sober persons to assist the Artiste with the get in and get out of the Artiste's equipment. The Purchaser also agrees to provide 1 (ONE) runner with own reliable transport.

The Purchaser agrees to allow access to the venue/performance space at a reasonable time as specified and agreed by the Artiste's Tour Manager. Artiste reserves the right to supplement certain sound and lighting equipment after consultation with the Purchaser; in such cases the Purchaser will provide and pay for a fully qualified electrician and provide and pay for all necessary sound and lighting operatives necessary to assist in installation of supplementary sound and lighting equipment.

2. PA and LIGHTS

See separate technical rider for Artiste's specific requirements.

Millions of Americans are carrying their own In Ear Monitor system (IEM). This operates on 832.700 MHz (EBU CH 66) and can be altered between 830 to 866 MHz. For full details please see attached technical specifications and/or contact Andy Reynolds on +44 (0)551886 or email andy.reynolds @tourconcepts.com.

Millions of Americans are carrying their own lighting system, which will complement the existing venue lighting system. For full details please see attached technical specifications and/or contact Ms. L. Ampy on +44 (0)7777 90909 or email pulsarrules@aol.com.

3. PARKING

The purchaser agrees to ensure parking space for:
1x Mercedes Vario band splitter van VRN # STA 456
This parking space should be adjacent to venue load in and be secure and free of cost to the Artiste.

4. MERCHANDISING

The Purchaser agrees to allow the Artiste sole right to erect stands for the sale of merchandise, in a clean and well lit area, at no charge whatsoever to the Artiste.

5. GUEST LIST

The Artiste reserves the right to admit up to 25 guests free of charge and this will not prejudice the Artiste's fee. Purchaser agrees to confirm numbers of Purchaser's own guests with Artiste's Tour Manager before opening the venue to the public.

6. SETTLEMENT

The Purchaser agrees to provide all documentation relating to the Artiste's performance for the inspection by Artiste and Artiste's Tour Manager. This documentation including but not limited to pre - sale ticket reports, show cost receipts, on night ticket sale reports and tax exemption submissions should be available at time of settlement, usually one hour before completion of Artiste's performance. The Purchaser agrees that all relevant show costs should have corresponding receipts and that failure to provide original receipts will result in corresponding cost to be null and void.

PREPARED BY ANDY REYNOLDS - TOUR MANAGER
T: +44 (0) 7762 551886 T: +44 (0)870 126 5960
Email: andy.reynolds@tourconcepts.com

THIS RIDER EXPIRES AUGUST 30th 2007
PAGE 2 of 5

7. SECURITY

Purchaser agrees to provide and pay for adequate numbers of reliable and reputable security personnel with clearly marked apparel and identification. Such personnel should report to designated security manager who in turn follows instruction from Artiste's Tour Manager. Purchaser agrees to coordinate with security manager and Artiste's Tour Manager regarding particular security arrangements, in particular pit crew etiquette and instruction.

The Purchaser shall guarantee proper security at all times to ensure the safety of the Artiste, auxiliary personal, instruments and all equipment, costumes, vehicles and personal property during and after the performance. Particular security must be provided in the areas of the stage, dressing room, and all exits and entrances to the auditorium, mixing consoles, and Artiste merchandising stalls.

Security protection is to commence upon arrival of the Artiste on the premises, until equipment is re-packed into transportation and Artiste personnel have left the premises.

Artiste will provide laminated passes that shall be sole accreditation valid on day of Artiste's performance. Artiste's Tour Manager will approve and issue sticky passes for all non-touring personnel. The Artiste reserves the right to refuse any accreditation issued by Purchaser or venue.

8. SUPPORT/OPENING ACTS

The Artiste reserves the right to approve and or amend support/opening acts. The Purchaser agrees not to add other acts other than those approved by the Artiste in writing.

The Artiste reserves the right to dictate the running order of the show and the acts appearing therein. The Artiste reserves the right to advise or amend any music, film, or performance relating to the Artiste's performance including but not limited to intro music, play on music, after show DJ's, and video compilations.

9. CATERING AND HOSPITALITY

The Purchaser agrees to provide the following:

Clean and hygienic toilet and sanitary facilities, including 2 (two) showers with hot and cold water available all day. If these are not available within the venue/performance area, arrangements must be made at a local hotel (or other) facility.

Dressing Room (band)
This room must be clean, well lit, furnished and lockable and in a secure area. 220v outputs and sufficient furniture for a minimum of eight (8) people. Adequate climate control or heating control in winter months is essential.

2 x large trash/rubbish bins.

Twenty (20) large, clean towels with soap required from sound check time.

Oil lamps, incense, candles, drapes, and flowers are all welcome and should be included to improve the ambience of the environment.

PREPARED BY ANDY REYNOLDS - TOUR MANAGER
T: +44 (0) 7762 551886 T: +44 (0)870 126 5960
Email: andy.reynolds@tourconcepts.com

THIS RIDER EXPIRES AUGUST 30th 2007
PAGE 3 of 5

Support Band Dressing Room (TBC)
As above (see separate rider for catering/towels, etc.).

Production Office

A secure production office that can be locked with telephone, desk, chair, Ethernet/CAT 5 cabling, and/ or Wi-Fi connection (please supply access codes, network keys, etc), RJ111 phone sockets, and 220v power will be required wherever possible.

Please provide the production Tel/fax numbers ASAP in advance.

Crew Room
As band (no mirror required) — 10 (10) towels and soap at load in.

Catering
At load in time (13.00) for 5 people (crew plus driver[s]):
Constant hot tea and coffee set up (with biscuits, etc.)
Bottled still mineral water (Volvic, Spa, or Evian)
Assorted Coca-Cola (no Pepsi!), Dr. Pepper, etc.
Assorted fruit juices (cranberry, orange, apple, etc.)

From 16.00 (4PM) band dressing room (drinks on ice):
8 x fresh vegetarian sandwiches (or sandwich ingredients plus bread)
24 x good quality local/imported bottled beer
20 x I litre still mineral water (Volvic, Spa, or Evian)
Assorted soft drinks, fresh OJ, apple juice, cranberry juice, Cokes, etc.
1 bottle of good quality local wine
1 x litre bottle quality vodka (Stoli, Findlandia, Moskosavoya, etc. NO ABSOLUT!)
Constant tea, coffee, and hot water set up
Lemons and honey
Tissues, chocolates, and chewing gum assortment

At 18.00 (6PM) main meal time for minimum eight (8) people (including 2 vegetarians)
A covered dining table in a clean, smoke free, and warm location (not the dressing room) with metal cutlery, appropriate crockery, and condiments. Some band members may elect to eat after the show and this facility must be available. Drinks should be re-iced as required.
NOTE:
A hot, nutritious meal is always preferable. Should there be no alternative, a buy-out of £10/€20 per person is acceptable. Please check with the Tour Manager in advance.

PREPARED BY ANDY REYNOLDS - TOUR MANAGER
T: +44 (0) 7762 551886 T: +44 (0)870 126 5960
Email: andy.reynolds@tourconcepts.com

THIS RIDER EXPIRES AUGUST 30th 2007
PAGE 4 of 5

Food:

Individual place settings with assorted local breadbasket

Choice of starter (hot and cold) plus large fresh washed mixed salad bowl with dressings.

Hot choice of three entrees with vegetables, not limited to:
Vegetarian option (can include pasta)
White meat/fish option
Red meat option

Sweet dessert course

Please leave some empty boxes in the dressing room to pack items at the end of the night

After show bus supplies:
Hot local take out specialty or pizza (1x vegetarian, 1x other)
10 x sodas

PREPARED BY ANDY REYNOLDS - TOUR MANAGER
T: +44 (0) 7762 551886 T: +44 (0)870 126 5960
Email: andy.reynolds@tourconcepts.com

THIS RIDER EXPIRES AUGUST 30th 2007
PAGE 5 of 5

Cast and Crew

In my experience, the cast and crew section is the most important part of any rider. This lets the promoter exactly who he is dealing with. In this example, Millions of Americans are playing at the Fleapit in Sheffield, a 350-capacity venue. Millions of Americans will be nine people, which include the four band members, and they are traveling in one van with their equipment, which includes some lighting equipment. An experienced promoter would expect this for a signed, national touring act at this level. The promoter would be worried if Millions of Americans were advising they had eight crew members and needed parking for a sleeper bus and a 7.5-ton truck that was filled with PA and lights!

I have noted that we do not have our own monitor engineer. This gives the house/venue crew the necessary information to plan their day because they now know at least one of the sound guys will be mixing the stage sound for the headline act. If he does a good job, he may even get a full-time job with the band! I have also noted that we are carrying our own in-ear monitor (IEM) system. (See Chapter 6, "Equipment," for more information on IEMs.) We are not touring with our own monitor engineer, so it is only right and fair to give the venue/house engineers advance warning of this. It is not a huge deal, but some engineers may be unfamiliar with mixing for IEM.

Also note that I have specified the frequencies on which the IEM system operates. There will be a detailed explanation of this is Chapter 6.

When writing riders, make sure you detail exactly who is walking into the venue, what transportation you are arriving in, and what extras you may be bringing in, if applicable. Obviously if you are playing an Enormo-dome, it is understood that all PA, light, and video is being bought in!

Access and Equipment

Even though the band has its own crew, it is crucial that the promoter or venue also supplies some help. Remember the local crew I talked about in Chapter 2? Here they are, paid for by the promoter. We have also asked for a runner, the local crew person who runs around all day doing our essential shopping while we are stuck in the venue doing sound checks.

We also want to be able to get into the venue in a reasonable time to get set up and have a decent sound check. The times for this initial access will depend on the time that the venue opens to the public. This time is known as "doors." "What time are doors?" is one of the main sayings of any show day because that is the time when all sound checks have to be completed, lights must be focused, merchandising has to be set up, and security teams must be briefed. Based on the time for doors, the tour manager will work backward to establish a decent arrival/access time. I allow five hours for a small to medium-size band: two-and-a-half hours to load in, set up, and line check; and another hour for the headline band to sound check. This leaves an hour and a half for any support bands to do sound checks.

The term "load in" can refer both to the time the equipment loads in and to the physical access point of the venue. In other words, you can ask, "What time is load in?" and, "Excuse me, where is the load in?"

PA and Lights

Because the technical requirements vary from act to act, it may be useful to have an amendment to the rider that details the requirements. This is what we have done in our example, and you will see that specific section reproduced later in this chapter. Even though there is detailed information about the sound and lights in the separate technical rider, I have noted here that we are carrying some lighting equipment and have provided the relevant contact information for our lighting engineer.

Parking

As well as specifying that the promoter should try to sort out free parking for you, this section can also be used to detail the type and number of vehicles for the information of the promoter. Your production might be using trucks and sleeper coaches. These will need parking close to the load in of the venue and power. Sleeper buses can connect to mains electricity in order to run all the lights, sound systems, fridges, and so on that they contain. (This power is known as *landline* or *shore power*.) It is the promoter's responsibility to provide this power or to let the tour party know if there is no landline available at the venue. If this is the case, arrangements should be made to allow the bus to run its engines or internal generators.

Trucks do not necessarily need power when parked, but it always useful to have the truck somewhere near the load in of the venue!

Guest List

The guest list is the list of… er, guests—people who have been invited to the show and who do not need to pay. Promoters do not like guest lists because, obviously, they receive no payment for the tickets allocated to the guest list. It is important to have an agreed-upon number of guests, and this is specified here. You will need a higher number of guest list places in major music market cities, such as New York, London, Köln, and Los Angeles.

Settlement

I will be looking into the issue of settlement further in Chapter 9, but here we are stipulating that we need the ticket stubs, receipts, and any other documentation presented in a tidy manner, at a time that is convenient for the tour manager and promoter/promoter's rep. Common practice is that the box office (the place to buy tickets on the day of the event) will close about 45 minutes after the headline band has started to play. This prevents customers from demanding their money back if they are sold a ticket just as the band comes offstage! This timing also gives the tour manager time to complete settlement in a businesslike and relaxed manner before dealing with the band coming offstage.

Security

As you saw in Chapter 2, security is vital to the well being of the both audience and the production team. A good security team with adequate coverage of the venue and backstage areas costs money; an unscrupulous promoter may try to get away with inadequate numbers of security personnel.

It takes quite a bit of experience for a tour manager to judge what will and will not be effective in terms of security numbers, but common sense will dictate what level of coverage will provide a safe environment.

In terms of this rider, the tour manager is thinking about pit security and access to sensitive areas—front of house control, dressing rooms, and vehicles. Suppose the tour manager is working for a three-piece alt-country act; he would not expect too much moshing and crowd surfing at a show like that. However, if the tour manager is working for a five-piece rap-metal band, then he should anticipate a lot of crowd action, with numerous people trying to get over the barrier to stage dive. In this case, a decent tour manager will include some mention of this in the security section of the rider. He will need more capable but sensible security personnel in the pit than would otherwise be necessary. Obviously, the promoter should know this is the case anyway, because he booked the show in the first place!

Support/Opening Acts

Opening acts (or "support acts," as they are known in Europe) are usually decided long before the tour starts or the show takes place; support acts are chosen by the headline band themselves or recommended by the booking agent or management. There can be immense pressure from agents and promoters to get a band into an opening slot because a good sold-out major show is a great place for a young band to be seen. This means that occasionally the acts are added onto the bill, often without the headliner's knowledge or permission. Although it does not necessarily affect the headliner to have extra bands on the bill, it certainly affects the crew and the audience. The crew now has to deal with two or more extra acts, often on an already crowded stage.

Audiences also have to endure a lot more music at high volume than they bargained for. Most concertgoers pay to experience as much as possible, but having to stand through three unknown bands before seeing your heroes can be a negative experience, especially if the opening acts run over. Hence the clause about approving support acts. It seems promoters will sometimes lob anybody on the bill as a favor; I feel the headline act and tour should have some say in this decision.

I also always include the clause that I can "advise or amend any music, film, or performance relating to the Artist's performance, including, but not limited to, intro music, play on music, after-show DJs, and video compilations." After years of touring, I am now immune to the house sound engineers playing *their* heavy metal compilation at excruciating volume, regardless of what genre of live music is being performed.

However, I also have a good sense of how a show should run; a 20-year-old "New Wave of British Heavy Metal" compilation is not going to be part of the "theme" if you are a three-piece alt-country act. I therefore now keep an eye on what audience "walk-in" music is being played, what advertisements or cable channels appear on the screens in the bar, and especially what CD the house DJ may play as the band walks offstage.

Hospitality

Here we go—this is the list of drinks that we all think we know about.

Actually, although this is a fairly detailed rider, my main aim when writing a rider is to produce a document that lists:

- How many people are in the touring party

- Whether anyone in the touring party has any major dietary concerns

- What we really do *not* like within the given items of food, beer, and water

For me, this is what a rider should be. It conveys information about the touring party in a clear and sensible manner. A good rider should prioritize the information that may cause problems for the promoter, such as types of transportation, excessive numbers of people, showering facilities, and special equipment needs. The list of food and drinks is not that important unless, as I say, any member of the touring party has specific dietary concerns.

In the hospitality section of this rider, I have attempted to detail what I would like to see when I arrive at the venue. Most professional promoters obviously will try to make the visiting artists happy by agreeing to the stipulations of the contract and the contract rider. By the same token, promoters are trying to make money and are not going to build a brand-new dressing room for you, regardless of what your rider says!

I find that the one clause that needs attention is the one relating to showers and showering facilities. The use of sleeper coaches to convey bands and crew to the next show has led to the need for multiple showers at venues—

showers that can provide hot water all day for up to 30 people. Music venues are built to showcase music, not as washrooms; therefore, they are often lacking in adequate showering facilities. It may seem extremely un-rock 'n' roll to be talking about showers, but believe me, after a night on a sleeper bus, I would trade all the rock excess possible for a hot shower with good water pressure! You should definitely make sure the promoter agrees to check out whether the showers are suitable at the venue, and if they are not, to make alternative arrangements at a nearby hotel.

In this case, the members of Millions of Americans are traveling in a van and are presumably staying in hotels every night. I therefore would not be too concerned with the showering situation at the venue. However, if I was on a sleeper bus and knew that the venue had no shower, I would definitely make sure well in advance that the promoter agreed to organize and pay for two rooms at a local hotel. This arrangement is known as "day rooms" because the hotel rooms are usually booked for the day only— from 8:00 A.M. until 6:00 P.M. You can usually negotiate a reduced rate on the room, depending on the hotel. (A large hotel with 24 housekeeping staff can service and re-book the room for that evening after you have checked out—they will therefore give you a discount on the day room rate.)

It is also worth noting that sleeper coach drivers in the US expect a day room after driving overnight, whereas European bus drivers will sleep on the bus when it is parked during the day. You will have to book a day room for the driver anyway if you are touring the US. You can split the cost of this with the promoter and use the room for after-show showers.

Finally, I have included all relevant contact information. I have noted that the rider was prepared by me. Anybody from the promoter's or the organizer's office then knows to contact me directly in case of challenges or issues. I have also indicated that this rider should expire on a certain date. There is a common tendency for agents to keep out-of-date and irrelevant contract riders and technical specifications on file and keep reissuing these documents to the promoters. This practice is not necessarily the fault of the agents; bands and band tour managers not updating the agent with the relevant information is probably the culprit. Always copy your agent and management on the latest version of your rider and make sure all out-of-date copies are destroyed.

> **Note: Make Your Paperwork Temporary** Mark your contract riders and tech specs with an expiration date. This may be at the end of the year or at the end of the touring period. In this case I have marked the expiration for the end of August—the end of the festival season in Europe and a natural break in the touring year.
>
> Mark all input lists and lighting plots with version numbers, as in V1.01, V1.02, and so on. This is a practice from the software industry and ensures that the recipients of your documents are reading from the most recent version. For example, when talking through a document with a house lighting person, you could say, "I am referring to version 3.02 of our lighting spec here; is that the one you have in front of you?"
>
> Finally, note "replaces all previous versions" and add all relevant contact information for front-of-house (FOH), monitor, and lighting engineers.

Contract Rider—Technical Specifications

Attached to the contract rider will be the technical specifications the artist requires the promoter to supply and/or the items the artist may be bringing as part of the production. Following is the "tech spec" for Millions of Americans.

Figure 3.1 shows the input list and stage plan that go with the technical rider.

As you can see, I have indicated that this document is integral to the contract for this particular show. I have had occasions when a promoter has argued that the terms of the rider are not enforceable because the rider arrived separately from the contract. This is not true as long as the rider has a note that references the number of the contract issued to the promoter. It may be a load of hassle to keep writing the contract reference into your contract riders, but believe me, it is worth it!

MILLIONS OF AMERICANS EUROPE 2007

THIS RIDER FORMS AN INTEGRAL PART OF THE CONTRACT (#1234) TO WHICH IT IS ANNEXED.

The purchaser agrees to supply the following at sole cost of the promoter:

CREW
Competent and professional sound and lighting crew. The sound and lighting crew should be familiar with the venue sound and lighting system. Millions of Americans are NOT traveling with a monitor engineer. The Purchaser agrees to supply one sound engineer(s) who is capable and willing to mix monitor sound for Millions of Americans, at no cost to the artist.

STAGE POWER
8 x 220V 13 Amp sockets from same phase. Isolated distribution as main sound power.

PA SYSTEM
PA system should be minimum 4 way active stereo system capable of producing and sustaining 118dB (C weighted) at the mix position. Acceptable components include L'Acoustics V-Dosc, L'Acoustics L-ARC, JBL VerTec, d&b 402, EAW KF750/850/900, Turbosound Floodlight or Flashlight, Meyer MSL3/4, Nexo Alpha, Martin Wavefront, BSS, Carver, Crown etc. NO Peavey, NO old Martin, NO homemade boxes.

FOH CONSOLE
32 channel with 4 auxiliary sends and 4 band EQ with sweepable mid frequencies with 8 VCA/ sub groups is our minimum requirement. Acceptable makes are Digico D5; Innovason; Yamaha PM5000/ PM4000/ PM3000,PM2000; Midas H3000/H1000, XL4/XL3/XL200, Soundcraft Europa, Vienna, Venue, K2, 8000, Series 5 etc. NO Peavey, NO TAC Scorpion, NO Mackie.

FOH INSERTS AND EFFECTS
2 x 31 band third octave graphic EQ
4 x gates and 10 compressors - BSS, Drawmer, Klark Technik, etc.
1 high-quality DDL - Roland SDE3000, TC Electronics, etc.
2 high-quality multi-effects units - Yamaha SPX 900/990/1000, etc.
CD player
Cassette deck
Talk to stage
ClearCom or similar intercom system

PREPARED BY ANDY REYNOLDS - TOUR MANAGER
T: +44 (0) 7762 551886 T: +44 (0)870 126 5960
Email: andy.reynolds@tourconcepts.com

THIS RIDER EXPIRES AUGUST 30th 2007
PAGE 1 of 2

MONITORS

32 channel with 12 auxiliary sends and 4 band EQ with sweepable mid frequencies is our minimum requirement. Acceptable makes are Digico D5; Innovason; Yamaha PM3000; Midas H3000/ H1000, XL3/ XL200; Soundcraft Series 5; etc. NO Peavey, NO TAC Scorpion, NO Mackie. Minimum of 7 mixes - 3 downstage wedge mixes, one IEM (we supply) plus one drum fill and 2 side fill mixes. Each mix (except the IEM mix) should have dedicated 31-band third octave graphic EQ. Wedges should be two ways bi-amped and comprise double 12″ or double 15″, two wedges per mix position. Drum fill should be bi-amped with at least 18″ sub.

If monitors are from FOH board, then channel splits should be provided to enable separate pre-fade vocal channels with no compression.

LIGHTING

Basic generic lighting - at least 12 PAR 64's plus at least 4 floor lamps.

Millions of Americans will also be carrying their own lighting equipment, comprising:
1 x DF50 hazer
2 x MAC 500 moving lights
1 x power distribution system
2 x 2m Tri-Lite truss sections
Cable to suit

Full lighting plot TBA. MoA lighting engineer will advise on power and lighting console requirements.

PREPARED BY ANDY REYNOLDS - TOUR MANAGER
T: +44 (0) 7762 551886 T: +44 (0)870 126 5960
Email: andy.reynolds@tourconcepts.com

THIS RIDER EXPIRES AUGUST 30th 2007
PAGE 2 of 2

MILLIONS OF AMERICANS

INPUT LIST AND STAGE PLOT
EUROPE 2006

VERSION V1.04 EXPIRES AUGUST 30™ 2007- REPLACES ALL PREVIOUS VERSIONS

CH.	INSTRUMENT/ SOURCE	MIC/DI	2ND CHOICE	INSERT	MON CH.	MON INSERT	NOTES
1	KICK DRUM	SHURE SM91	SHURE BETA 52	GATE	1	GATE	
2	KICK DRUM	BETA 57A	SENN MD421	GATE		GATE	
3	SNARE TOP	WE SUPPLY	SHURE SM91		2		
4	SNARE BOTTOM	SHURE BETA 57	SHURE SM57				
5	HI HAT 1	AKG C451	CONDENSOR		3		STAGE LEFT
6	HI HAT 2	AKG C451	CONDENSOR		4		STAGE RIGHT
7	RACK 1	WE SUPPLY	SHURE SM91		5		
8	FLOOR 1	WE SUPPLY	SHURE SM91	GATE	6		
9	FLOOR 2	WE SUPPLY	SHURE SM91	GATE	7		
10	RIDE	AKG C451	CONDENSOR				
11	OH SR	AKG C414	CONDENSOR				
12	OH SL	AKG C414	CONDENSOR				
13	BASS BOOM	DI			8		FROM LAPTOP ON DRUM RISER
14	BASS DI	XLR	COM/LIM		9		DIRECT OUT
15	BASS MIC	SENN MD 421	RE20				
16	GUITAR SR DI	WE SUPPLY	DI		10		XLR FROM RED BOX
17	GUITAR SR	AKG AT4050	SENN MD 409				
18	GUITAR SL DI	RED BOX	DI		11		XLR FROM RED BOX
19	GUITAR SL	AKG AT4050	SENN MD409				
20	VOCAL SR	WE SUPPLY	SHURE BETA 58	COMP	12		
21	VOCAL CENTER	WE SUPPLY	SHURE BETA 58	COMP	13		
22	SPARE MICROPHONE	SHURE BETA 58	SHURE SM58	COMP	14		JUST IN CASE

MONITOR MIXES:

MIX 1: DOWN STAGE RIGHT	1 X BI-AMPED WEDGE	
MIX 2: DOWN STAGE CENTER	2 X BI-AMPED WEDGE	
MIX 3: DOWN STAGE LEFT	1 X BI-AMPED WEDGE	
MIX 4: DRUM RISER	2 X BI-AMPED WEDGE OR 1 X DRUM FILL WITH 18" SUB	
MIX 5: IEM	WE SUPPLY	
MIX 6: SIDE FILL STAGE RIGHT		
MIX 7: SIDE FILL STAGE LEFT		

PREPARED BY ANDY REYNOLDS – TOUR MANAGER
T: +44 (0)7762 551886 F + 44 (0)870 1265960
E: andy.reynolds@tourconcepts.com

Figure 3.1   The input list and stage plan that go with the technical rider.

Crew

We are asking that the promoter supply "competent and professional" crew. You may take it for granted that the venue will have sound, light, and engineers, but because assumption is the mother of all screw-ups, you should always stipulate that you require house people to run sound for you.

I have also made a note to inform and remind the promoter and house people that we are *not* touring with a monitor engineer, so we need the house people to be able to operate the monitor sound system for us. This was also detailed in the introductory contract rider document.

PA System

When producing this section of the rider, I will have consulted the band's FOH and monitor engineers. Sound engineers are professional trade people and therefore have their own likes and dislikes when it comes to equipment. A good engineer should also be aware of what equipment will best complement your particular style of music. Although PA system manufacturers strive for sonic excellence across the board, any experienced touring engineer will tell you that certain speaker and amplifier combinations sound better for certain types of music. Always consult your technical team or a trusted local engineer when compiling your tech specs.

Note that I have also specified what I really will not tolerate in terms of PA systems. The band is paying the engineer a lot of money to make them sound good; therefore, the engineer (in this case, me) should be able to cope with any sound system that may be provided by the promoter. However, there are certain components that I know from experience will not be up to scratch, and therefore I will avoid using them if at all possible.

I have detailed the inserts and effects I need; again, this is a wish list. If I *really* need a Roland SDE-3000 for a specific effect in a certain song, then I should consider carrying one on the tour.

I have also indicated that we are carrying our own in-ear monitor system. Remember that I advised the promoter earlier in the document that we are not touring with a monitor engineer. IEM systems are not difficult to set up, but some house/venue engineers may be uncomfortable or unfamiliar with the technology. It would also be unprofessional to ask a house or festival monitor engineer to cope with more than one IEM mix. If your band is working with one or more IEM mixes, then you should really be paying someone to travel with you at all times. You should check out the section on in-ear monitors in Chapter 6 for more details.

Input List

Attached to the technical specifications will be the input list. "Input" in this case refers to the sound sources that need "inputting" into the sound system. You may just be a four-piece guitar band, but did you mention to the venue/house sound person that you have a laptop computer that runs the drum loops you must have for the show? Or that the vocalist runs her microphone into an effects pedal and that she needs to hear both signals onstage?

Providing an accurate input list will ensure that any house/venue sound team will know exactly how many instruments you have on the stage, how many inputs you need to go to the sound system, how many DI (direct injection) boxes you may need, and how many monitor wedges/mixes you require. I will be going into a lot more detail about PA and monitor systems in Chapter 6, so do not worry for now. Pay attention, though, because I am going to teach you how to present your input list in a standard format that any engineer, promoter, or rep will understand.

As I said, the main aim of your input list is to convey to the venue, house engineer, festival stage team, or radio station the exact amount of audio sources you will be supplying to their sound system.

Imagine you are a singer/songwriter who plays an electro/acoustic guitar; the guitar has a built-in jack output. Your input list will therefore be:

- Electro/acoustic guitar—jack out, needs a DI box

- Vocal

But wait a minute. Say you are booked to do a session for a local radio station. Halfway through your recording session, you pull out your other "proper" acoustic guitar (the one with no jack output) and start to play your instrumental number. To amplify the guitar, you pull the vocal microphone down to point at the guitar. At this point the radio station engineer starts to freak out and runs into the studio. "What the hell are you doing?" is the polite translation of what she screams at you. "I always do this when I play this tune in clubs—is it a problem?" you reply.

Yes, it is a problem. Audio engineers strive for audio purity. Modern recording techniques allow for each instrument to be recorded separately, thus allowing for EQ and levels to be adjusted to suit the overall mix. This applies to live sound reinforcement as well. In our example, the radio station engineer will have used a really expensive, high-quality condenser microphone on your vocal. The engineer will have EQed, compressed, and added reverbs to your voice and adjusted the level to get the best sound into the recording device. With all that done, you yank down the vocal microphone and shove it into the sound hole of an acoustic guitar! Aside from damaging the engineer's hearing and the microphone's diaphragm, the sudden increase in sound level will make the acoustic sound really, really bad—the compressor will cut in, and the warm tones of your guitar will be squashed into a reverb-y mess.

Imagine if you did this in a concert! Imagine the cacophony that would result from the volume that a modern PA can produce! You may think you only have a guitar and your voice, but in this example you actually have three separate sound sources: your vocal, the guitar with the jack output, and the acoustic guitar. Going back to your input list, you should instead specify:

- Electro/acoustic guitar—jack out, needs a DI box

- Acoustic guitar—microphone

- Vocal—microphone

Given this new information, the engineer will be able to set the best microphones, EQ, reverbs, and compression for each of the separate sound sources. Ultimately, this will give you control over your sound and convey a more professional impression.

This is a simple example of what you should try to convey when producing an input list. Study the input list for Millions of Americans. To arrive at this list I visited the band at their rehearsal studios. I then simply went around inspecting the instruments and other sound sources and noted what elements needed to be amplified by the PA sound system.

When you have collected this information, your input list should show:

- The number of inputs needed into the sound system.

- The separate instruments and audio sound sources. Everything that needs to be heard through the PA needs either a microphone or a DI box. You should work with your audio team and specify what sound sources need to be heard and which microphones are preferable. In this case, Millions of Americans are touring with some of their own microphones, and I have specified this as such.

Note: **Stage Left and Stage Right** Stage right or left is expressed from the viewpoint of standing onstage and looking at the audience. Always try to use stage right and left descriptions when working in a music concert.

For each instrument or sound source I have indicated:

- **A channel number.** Having a channel number makes troubleshooting a sound-related problem easier. For example, you can say, "There is a buzz on channel 13," rather than, "There is a buzz on the bass booms." You may know what the bass booms are, but many house or festival engineers may not.

- **The name of the instrument or source.** Note that I have indicated *SR* for stage right and *SL* for stage left.

- **The preferred microphone or DI box needed.** You will find that there are some conventions when miking up sound sources in modern music production. Although there is a vast array of microphones to choose from, most engineers tend to work with a trusted few brands and models because experience enables them to predict exactly what results they will obtain. For example, there are certainly better microphones than the Shure SM58 dynamic microphone, especially for vocals. However, a combination of rugged design, fairly flat frequency response, and good feedback rejection make the SM58 an ubiquitous choice for vocals, especially with rock and pop bands. Notice as well that I have indicated that the output of the bass DI channel is a straight XLR out, no DI box needed. Much more "pro" equipment has XLR (also called "balanced") outputs these days.

- **A second-choice microphone.** I add a second microphone to my input lists out of a sense of completeness more than anything else. As I have mentioned before, if you really have to use a certain piece of equipment to create your show, then you should consider carrying it with you!

- **Insert.** Inserts are dynamic controls, such as gates, compressors, and limiters. They are "inserted" into the relevant channel rather than sent via an auxiliary. (Don't worry; there will be a more detailed explanation of this entire subject in Chapter 6.) In this example, I have asked for gates on some of the drum channels (this helps me produce a tighter drum sound) and compressor/limiters on the bass DI channel and two of the vocals. I do not need compression on the stage left vocal because this person does not tend to sing loudly or to shout.

- **Monitor channel.** Again, for the sake of completeness, I only list the instruments that are actually needed in the monitor mix onstage. This practice would be useful if two bands were sharing the same mixing consoles. Suppose, for instance, we were using a 24-input board. My input list has 21 channels, which means 21 of the 24 channels available on the mixing board would be used. If I do not share my channels, there will only be three input channels left for the support band. This means both bands would have to "share" channels; once we have sound checked, the board would be reset for the support band, which means I would have to mark down *all* my settings.

Wait a minute, though. Do I really need all these sources in my monitor mixes? (Do you want to hear the cymbals through the monitors?) By skipping the inputs that do not need to be routed to the monitor system, I can save on the number of channels. In this case I can slim it down to 13 channels for monitors, freeing up 11 channels for the support act. Both bands should be able to squeeze their inputs into the 24-channel board and will not have to share channels. This is a great tip for monitor engineers—poor old FOH engineers are faced with marking down all their settings for all their channels!

- **Monitor insert.** Again, I have specified which dynamic processors I require for the monitor sound.

- **Notes.** The drummer for Millions of Americans uses two hi-hats, and I have indicated where each hi-hat is. I have also noted where the bass booms live on the stage and that the guitar DIs are from the Hughes & Kettner Red Boxes on each guitar rig.

Note: My Tip for *Huge* Live Rock Guitar Sound Rock guitar? Hughes & Kettner Red Box DI, as well as a microphone? *Huge* sound? Absolutely!

As well as a comprehensive and explanatory input list, you should also provide a stage plan. A stage plan should merely indicate what instruments live where and what channels are grouped together. You can also indicate monitor wedge positions and where on the stage backline power is needed. You do not need pictures of guitars, crosses indicating where people stand, or 3D projections of the stage. I have seen many stage plans like this, and although they are very pretty, they are often confusing and irrelevant.

For the Millions of Americans stage plan, I have simply indicated stage positions of the instruments with notes on where to find the various channel numbers as indicated on the input list.

Finally, I have provided a quick monitor crib, which simply notes which monitor mix goes where, along with the fact that we have our own IEM system.

Note: Upstage and Downstage As we have stage left and right, we also have downstage and upstage. Downstage is at the front, nearest the audience, and upstage is at the back.

The technical specifications are there to give the promoter more information about what you are trying to achieve; the document is not intended to browbeat the promoter into supplying the best PA and lights in the world! Your show may totally depend on one specific piece of equipment—a specific tape echo unit or lighting effect. However, it is really naïve to expect that every promoter will be able or willing to supply this equipment, despite what any contract or contract rider stipulates. As I've mentioned a couple times already, if your show really depends on this one item, then maybe you should think about carrying it with you.

If you decide to carry specific items yourself, then make a note in your technical rider. I have done this with the Millions of Americans rider—there is a section detailing the lighting we are bringing with us into the venues. Again, this gives the local crew and organizers advance warning that we are bringing in additional equipment. Hopefully, the venue engineers will then contact us if they foresee any challenges or issues.

Obviously, the tech specs relate to the technical aspects of your show. Always consult with your technical team when compiling the specs or ask a local sound and light engineer to look over any specs you send out. You have my permission to copy the input list in this chapter, but it really may not be relevant to your equipment setup or style of music.

"Any artiste must be competent live if they're looking to sustain a career in this industry. The difference between a good sound in a rehearsal and good sound live is massive. Playing live is the only way a band gets tight enough to make it."

—Gerrard Phillips, A&R, Independiente Records

So that covers the main points of the contract rider. Any promoter or event organizer needs to study this document properly. The costs for the show are largely dependent on the requirements listed in the rider, and the promoter may not have seen these requirements when agreeing to the show and signing the contract.

If the promoter agrees to supply the demands as stipulated in the rider, then he signs the contract rider and returns it with the contract to the agent.

If the promoter sees a problem with something he cannot or will not supply, then he may call the agent to renegotiate or he may simply "redline" the clause/want/need in question.

The best riders list clearly the physical and emotional expectations of the artist and give the promoter exact information regarding the number of tour personnel and the amount of equipment that will be rolling into his venue.

Through years of experience, I have come to learn that riders are the bane of promoters' (and tour managers') lives. Due to ever-changing tour personnel and requirements, contracts are often sent with outdated or incomplete riders. The updated and late riders may contain items that significantly affect the promoter's ability to stage the show under the agreed-upon terms (and within his budget!). Remember, all items and conditions listed in a rider are supplied at the sole cost of the promoter.

Suppose a promoter has agreed to stage a concert in his 1,000-capacity club. He has agreed with the agent verbally to supply PA, lights, and catering, plus the fee of $6,000—fairly standard stuff. He calculates his costs as follows:

Hall rental	$500
PA	$400
Lights	$500
Security, etc.	$500
Catering	$300
Publicity, ticket print, etc.	$500
Performer's fee	$6,000
Total expenses	$8,700

Based on the stipulations stated by the agent, he calculates that if the show sells out, he will come out with $1,300 profit. He sets the ticket price at $10, so he needs 870 ticket buyers to break even. He receives, signs, and returns a contract from the agent and starts to publicize the show.

Then, as is the way, the contract rider turns up. Amongst other demands, the rider stipulates catering items totaling nearly $1,000. (Courvoisier is not cheap, you know!) Other clauses include the provision of Sony widescreen TV, an Xbox 360, and assorted sports-related video games. The promoter is now facing a rental charge of $500 to $600 for the night.

Suddenly, by supplying these items, the promoter's profit will vanish even if the show sells out! Now he is faced with a dilemma. He could supply these items and lose money, but keep the goodwill of the artist. He could supply these items but cut costs elsewhere. He could approach the agent and try to renegotiate the fee based on the revised rider demands. Or he could cancel the show.

Obviously this is just an example, but similar scenarios are played out in promoters' offices across the world on a daily basis. It is extremely important that agents have the latest rider information from the manager and tour manager before the contracts are issued. We will examine costs and budgets in more detail in Chapter 11, "Getting Onstage: Advanced Information."

> "[The importance of playing live] is paramount. The only way to build a solid faithful fan base is to be a great, consistent live band. Being an incredible touring band can keep you in pocket without a recording deal."
>
> —Alex Gilbert, A&R, Warner Bros.

How to Get Your Music on the Road

4 Getting Onstage: The Basics

"The live industry is going from strength to strength at all levels at the moment, and playing live is a key area for developing artistes to build a fan base. Other areas of the media, like radio, are tough to break into, so building a loyal following through touring is essential."

—Phil Catchpole, A&R Manager, Chrysalis Music Publishing

So, what do you want to do? If you are interested in working behind the scenes as touring crew, promoter, or booking agent, then you should perhaps move along to Part III, "Working in the Live Music Industry" (but by all means read this section as well!). If you are a performer, musician, or DJ, or if you are just curious about what it takes to get a show together, then this is the section for you.

I am assuming that, as a musician, you may feel that as well as achieving satisfaction from your creative output, there is a certain inducement for fame and riches. That is fine; if you strive to be the best at something, you should be rewarded. Your music (or someone else's) could well be a passport to fame, glamour, and wealth.

It is unlikely, however, that you will earn much more than a meager living initially from just selling CDs or just playing live, unless you are incredibly lucky. (Even in this age of television-based talent shows, such as *American Idol* in the US and *Pop Idol, Fame Academy,* and the *X Factor* in the UK, the winners have had to go through a long and arduous selection process, which is usually built on the back of years of trying to escape from obscurity. Overnight fame and fortune do not happen.) A combination of promotion tactics, including live performance, should provide you with an adequate living and may catapult you to superstardom.

The main point I will stress in this book is that tireless self-promotion is the only way to succeed, whether you want to be the next Bono of U2 or you want to run a simple cabaret band. As consumers, we are subjected to so many media and advertising choices that it is often very difficult to decide what film to watch, what restaurant to try, what car to buy, and what CD to check out. The fact that you are holding this book means that my team and I have persuaded you to investigate this book over any other you have seen. If you are serious about your music, you have to be prepared to market yourself, and I believe that live performance is an integral part of this marketing strategy. Fortunately, it is also the most enjoyable. I do not know any musician who does not enjoy the thrill of public performance.

I mentioned that it is unlikely that you will earn much more than a meager living initially from just one type of music reproduction. By this, I mean that you should have an eye to exploiting all forms of exposure. Play live, sell CDs, send MP3s, run a website. You may be the most talented singer/songwriter of this decade, but if you spend all your time and money just pitching to record company A&R people, then you are not going to build up an audience for your music. You may want to run the best party club band in the Bay Area, but if you do not give out business cards and flyers at your gigs, you will not get any more business.

Any act has to build up an audience; playing live is integral to this. Playing live in itself is not very lucrative, though, at least initially. However, selling CDs, T-shirts, and other merchandise can be very lucrative and can give you enough income to keep going as well as spread your name (see Figure 4.1). It is important that you investigate any opportunity for self-promotion and income based around playing live. I shall expand more on this in Chapter 10, "Marketing," but bear it in mind always when reading through the book.

Choices

I am going to give lots of examples of performance and music types in this book, most of them based on firsthand knowledge. I show no distinction between the smallest cabaret-type duo and platinum-selling

Figure 4.1 Concert merchandise can provide a healthy income for artists.

stadium rockers. If you are considering (or are already earning a living from) performing music live, then this information is for you.

Bearing that in mind, here are the kinds of musical performances in which you might be involved:

- Band, urban, or dance/DJ act, writing and performing original material.

- Tribute act.

- Cabaret and variety act, performing at weddings or parties on cruise ships, in casinos, at hotels, and so on. This includes solo pianists and vocalists.

- Street performer.

- DJ at weddings and parties.

- Club and festival DJ (not radio-based).

- Orchestral and big band.

- Orchestral and operatic vocalist.

- Theatre musician or theatre vocalist.

Obviously the list goes on. My experience is working mainly with original rock, jazz, dance, and DJ acts. However, I have also worked for cabaret bands, cruise ship entertainers, and solo singer-songwriters. I have worked on shows in stadiums, in pubs and bars, in arenas, at shopping malls, on cruise ships, on mountains and in fields (muddy or otherwise), at hotels, on rooftops, and at subway stations. I know what it takes to create a good live show regardless of the musical genre or venue. In this chapter, I am going to outline what I have learned from working on those shows and how you can apply it to get your show on the road.

Rehearsing

Whatever you do, it has to be right from the start. I have seen so many inexperienced bands adversely affect their chances of making an impact because they were under-rehearsed. Yes, they could play their songs properly. Anybody can do that, though, given enough time and money. There is a difference between practicing your instrument and rehearsing. The analogy I always use is that actors learn (practice) their lines, but they rehearse the show. Actors are confident with their individual parts and then are bought together by the director or producer to work up the parts as an ensemble piece, with each actor working together to create the show. You could adopt this routine as well. Think about how your show is going to work, beyond simply practicing the music for each song.

You need to practice your individual parts; only when you are totally confident with your performance can you look at the show as a whole performance piece. Practice your parts and rehearse the show. Have an objective or an aim in mind when you are rehearsing. I would suggest that every time you perform live, you need to:

- **Impress the audience.** Make them want to pay to see you perform live in the future. Make them want to buy any merchandise you may have for sale at the event. Impressing your audience is the most important reason for performing live in the first place!

- **Impress the promoter.** You need the guy to book you again, hopefully for more money or at a bigger venue!

- **Impress the A&R, publishing, or artist management people that may be at your show.** These are the people who ultimately will assist your career. You may eventually elect to do everything yourself and set up your own record label or publishing company, but you will still need the approval and industry recognition of the A&R and artist management people.

"Next it is important that I can see the band live and see a performance that is exciting and energetic if that's where the music is coming from, or that it draws me in. Doesn't even matter if the musicians aren't brilliant players, so long as they are putting their heart and soul into their performance. Sex Pistols [are] a great example. If all goes well, the band will be playing the same songs night after night, and if they look bored at their early gigs, it doesn't bode well!"

—Andy McIntyre, Director of A&R, Mushroom Records

To make these positive impressions, you need to make sure you utilize any public performance time to the maximum advantage. You may not be interested in becoming a rock star; you might be content just to play your music wherever possible. That's fine, but if you come across as under-rehearsed, your potential for future public performance will be diminished. I stress again, it is not just about learning the songs; the whole package is important. With that in mind, let's take some time to work out how to get your show on the road and to make sure the show has the most impact.

You need to rehearse your music and the show elements. Where can you do this?

Rehearsal Venue
Depending on the type of music you are creating, you might need to spend money on renting rehearsal space. As with everything, do your research. You should take into account cost, location, access, facilities, and storage (see Figure 4.2).

Cost
Most rock-type rehearsal studios are small businesses, usually run by musicians themselves. They will try to sell you blocks of rehearsal time

Figure 4.2 Modern rehearsal facilities can help you perfect your music, but at what cost?

with discounts for paying in advance. For instance, they might offer you every Monday and Wednesday night from 6:00 P.M. to midnight for 20-percent off the hourly rate. Think about it, though. Are you really going to want to rehearse that much? How much of the arranging, programming, or whatever can be done at home or somewhere else (for free)?

Work out how much time you are really going to need in this environment. Do not overbook. It feels very relaxed and creative to book a room for a whole week and saunter in and out when the muse strikes. However, this is a stupid way to waste money for anyone, established signed acts included. As a tour manager, I have seen ridiculous bills for time booked in expensive rehearsal rooms—time booked but not used by the band. My experience shows me that three hours at a time is the maximum anyone can truly be effective in a rehearsal situation. Book sessions of two to three hours, but allow time on both sides for arrival and setup/breakdown of equipment. You may end up saving a lot of money by only booking a couple of sessions before a show or event.

Location and Access

Rehearsal rooms are often in older industrial-type buildings that have been converted to rehearsal room use. Therefore, they tend to be in industrial sections of the city, either on the outskirts or in the city center. Consider access to the rehearsal rooms from both your home and the major roads into the city. Rehearsal rooms are great if they are situated right near your house, but if they are miles away from the nearest freeway/motorway, that will add extra time to your journey before and after every show or event to pack up and drop off equipment. Likewise, rooms that are locked after a certain time or have lots of stairs quickly lose their appeal—imagine lugging your gear into a cold, dark rehearsal studio situated up four flights of stairs at three o'clock in the morning! When choosing a rehearsal studio, always determine what floor the rooms are on, what access there is, and what time constraints, if any, there are for picking up or dropping off your equipment.

Facilities

You are in a band. You rent a rehearsal room with a state-of-the-art sound system. You turn up, plug in, and start to play. Boy, it feels great to practice at full volume with this incredible PA and lights! Did anyone mention that it is also really expensive?

Rehearsal rooms with state-of-the-art sound systems also have state-of-the-art rental prices. Do not waste your money! Think about what you need from a technical point of view and stick within those parameters. If your backline equipment is in reasonable shape, you should not need to amplify your instruments. Therefore, you will only need some way to amplify your vocals. The room you rent (or the system you buy) should be a small PA of 300 to 500 watts, consisting of a mixer, amplifier (or combination mixer amp), speakers, and microphones. This should be just enough to amplify the singers while the rest of the band plays through their guitar amps, bass amps, and so on.

Most budget rehearsal rooms (and a few expensive ones!) are run as small business, often with little profit margin. PA equipment in rehearsal rooms is often overworked and under-maintained. When inspecting a rehearsal room, ask to look at and listen to the equipment. Most rooms won't sound great; the equipment is often a budget brand. However, it should all be working. Check the mixer and amplifier for electrical safety. There should be no bare or exposed wires, and fuses (correctly rated) should be in place.

Next, listen to the system. (There is a detailed section on PA and sound in Chapter 6, "Equipment"; read up on that if you are not sure what you are doing.) You are listening for a full sound from both speakers. You will often find that the high-end frequencies—top end or treble—are missing because the speakers that produce those frequencies have been destroyed through misuse and lack of maintenance. If this is the case, you are in for a miserable rehearsal experience. Without the high end in the speakers, there will be no vocal clarity. This means you will not be able to hear yourself sing very well and you will often end up shouting or overstretching your voice, limiting your potential rehearsal time and maybe causing permanent damage to your voice.

Unfortunately, this lack of high end is very common in budget rooms such as the one shown in Figure 4.3 because the components are not capable of handling the abuse caused by inexperienced artists. However, there are limits, so do not put up with totally inferior sound. You may be happy with the cost and location, but check the maintenance policy of the rehearsal space.

You may be in a band using electronic instruments that have no amplification source of their own or are working to playback sources, such as a computer, DAT, CD, or mini-disk. In this case, the rehearsal room mixer or mixer/amp should have enough line-level inputs (usually 1/4-inch jacks) to accommodate your needs. You will also need Direct Injection (DI) boxes if the mixer or mixer amp is at professional level and only accepts XLR connections. You will need to check with the people running the rehearsal room to ensure that they can provide enough DI boxes for all your equipment.

You should also check to make sure that the room has enough working, safe, domestic-type power outlets. Inspect each outlet for burn or scorch marks. Scorch marks will tell you that there has been a problem

Figure 4.3 A small rehearsal room with a budget sound system.

in the past, which may have been caused by the room's power supply. Checking this may be hassle now, but it will save you grief in case of a grounding problem that could cause you or a fellow band member to receive an electrical shock.

Note: A Quick Lesson on Earthing (Grounding) Electrical Equipment Electricity naturally flows to the Earth, or to ground, through anything that will conduct electrical current. There are some substances, such as wood and glass, that are not good conductors of electricity. But electricity will pass through the human body, sometimes with fatal results, trying to get to ground. If your guitar amp, mixing console, or keyboard is faulty or has a shorted wire, for example, the electrical current may try to find another path to ground—and that path may be you.

That's why electrical systems should always be grounded. A safe path to ground for electricity is away from your body and confined within whatever piece of electrical equipment you're using. Unfortunately, a lot of audio equipment is deliberately ungrounded to avoid the dreaded "ground loop." Ground loop produces a very audible low-frequency hum and or a high-end buzz or "rizz." The simplest way to reduce ground loop hum is to remove the ground from one or two pieces of connected equipment. This is also the most dangerous remedy because your equipment is now not grounded. Should the equipment be faulty or introduced to water, you run the very real risk of fatal electrical shock.

A ground loop is common in any audio system containing balanced and unbalanced cables. In unbalanced audio cables (guitar cables, for instance), there is a single insulated core surrounded by a screen. The screen is grounded/earthed to prevent other electrical interference. However, in a system containing mains-powered equipment joined together by cables, the signal screens and main ground wires interconnect. As voltage flows through the screens, a difference is created between the two contacts of each cable, and signal contamination takes place—in other words, loud hums!

To break the loop, each piece of equipment should only have one ground current path between it and the rest of the system to which it is connected. As I mentioned, the easiest way to do this is to remove the ground from one or more pieces of equipment. It may be easy, but it also may be illegal and it is very, very dangerous.

Instead of removing the ground/earth from a system, disconnect everything and build up your system one piece at a time, checking for hum at every stage.

If, after connecting a particular piece of equipment, something starts to hum, then try the following:

- Use balanced cables in all connections.
- Take rack-mounted equipment out of its rack and/or place it in a different rack.
- Avoid running mains and signal cable side by side.
- Check to see whether equipment has a ground-lift switch. If it does, then use it!

If all else fails, you will have to buy or build some ground-lift cables. More on this Chapter 6.

Finally, check the lighting, heating, ventilation, and toilet facilities of the rehearsal venue. If your price range is in the budget category, then you obviously should not be too fussy; however, it is reasonable to expect a warm, dry room with sanitary conditions. If your price range is "no limit," then be careful about paying for hidden extras you may not use. Large rehearsal spaces can supply catering, transportation, and storage that may seem convenient, but these extras will be expensive. Better costs can be negotiated directly with the suppliers of these services. I tell the truth—I have had to pay £25 (approximately $48) to "rent" a £15 ($29) guitar stand for the day!

Many rehearsal rooms sell strings, picks/plectrums, cables, and sticks onsite. This is very convenient if you break a string, for instance, during rehearsal. It is also expensive. Large or small, rehearsal facilities do not have the purchasing power necessary to obtain volume discounts from manufacturers. They will buy at a higher price than the music instrument shops and therefore will sell to you at a high price. They will probably only carry a limited supply and have the most major brands. Make sure you have spares with you in rehearsal, just as you would for the show. Buy in advance and in bulk if possible; save yourself money!

Storage

In my experience the biggest potential money pit for a successful band is the cost of equipment storage. As a live, gigging band you may accrue a substantial amount of equipment over the years—equipment that is big and heavy. You may not need this equipment all the time, and therefore you will need somewhere to keep it all. I don't know about you, but I personally do not want this equipment in my house or my garage, shed, or whatever. For a start, your garage may not be secure enough or dry enough to store valuable and fragile equipment for a long period of time. So, what do you do?

You can store your equipment at your rehearsal space, if you have one. Most professional rehearsal rooms will charge you for storage of your equipment on the premises. Consider this carefully before parting with any cash. If you will be rehearsing regularly (and by this I mean at least three times a week, every week), then yes, you should consider en suite storage. The added time and money involved in picking up and dropping off the equipment for every rehearsal will be far greater than the storage costs. However, if you are only using the rehearsal room a couple of times a week or less often, then you should consider storing your equipment at home or in some other free, secure place. Chances are you will be taking your gear from home or wherever to your shows anyway. Why suffer the added time and cost of going via your practice space to pick up the equipment?

As I have said, in my experience the larger, more established bands are especially guilty of squandering money on storage. Wander around some of the larger rehearsal facilities in any major city, and you will see full lockups—these spaces contain not only backline equipment, guitars, and cases, but also band members' personal items! I personally have seen clothes, hi-fi equipment, sporting equipment, and even washing machines in the lockups of the acts for which I have worked. And these rehearsal room storage facilities are not cheap!

The lockup becomes a handy one-stop catch-all for the detritus of the successful band. I advise that, yes, a band should use the rehearsal room storage facilities while actually rehearsing there. However, large acts will often rehearse for a couple of weeks before going into the studio or before a major concert tour, but very rarely otherwise because they should be busy touring or in the studio! Therefore, when the band is on tour, in the studio, or resting, they can save a lot of money by consolidating the equipment and moving it all to a commercial storage facility. They will be able to negotiate better rates there, especially on long-term storage (six months or longer). Access is usually good with city center locations, and because many of these facilities are franchised chains, the insurance and safety are easily verified.

Storage of personal belongings and equipment is a big business at the moment—our newfound pastime of Internet shopping and bargain hunting means we do not have enough room in our homes, and the need for offsite storage has increased. You should therefore be able to rent a 35- to 50-square-foot space for about £30 ($60) per month. (Roughly 35 to 50 square feet is the equivalent of a full equipment van; 50 to 75 square foot is the equivalent of a room in an apartment.)

You should also study the insurance policy of your equipment. (You are insured, aren't you? You should go straight to Chapter 11,

"Getting Onstage: Advanced Information," if not!) Some policies may preclude the storage of equipment in areas other than your home or business address. And while you are thinking about insurance, it is always worth asking what insurance policy has been taken out by the rehearsal/storage facility.

Finally, on the subject of rehearsal venues, you may be a vocalist, a DJ, or a solo instrumentalist, in which case you are going to save a ton of money! As a solo player, you should be able to practice at home, in your bedroom or wherever. At some point you may feel the need to move into a "pro" rehearsal facility, but that should be when you have every element of your individual performance memorized and you need to rehearse "the show."

"An artiste can make the most impressive debut album ever, but if they can't back it up with a strong live performance, forget it."

—Jonny Simon, A&R, Vertigo/Mercury.

5 Preparation for the Show

"I wouldn't touch a band until I'd been blown away by their live show, regardless of what their recorded material is like or the apparent hype surrounding them. If the act can't impress at their shows, a crucial aspect of the whole strategy to build a fan base and sell records is lost."

—Jamie Graham, A&R, One Little Indian

You have found your rehearsal space and checked the cost, access, facilities, and storage. So you move in and start learning your songs, right? Well, yes and no. As I mentioned, it is not just about learning the song. Think of your gig or event as a play. You need to learn your lines but *rehearse the show*! Look again at what Jamie Graham has to say above. Study the other quotes throughout this book, all from industry insiders. They all say the same thing—your live show has to absolutely, positively be the ultimate showcase for you and your music!

Okay, but how do you achieve this?

From Rehearsal to the Stage

Obviously you should concentrate on learning your music. To do this, make sure everyone is confident and relaxed with the material and that you are capable of giving the best performance you can. When in the rehearsal space, set up in a circle so that everyone has eye contact with everyone else. Remember, this is the stage for concentrating on the music, not necessarily the show.

When rehearsing your music you should set up your equipment to make yourself as comfortable as possible; think about the best rehearsal environment possible. I recommend setting up in a circle with the singer(s) standing opposite the drummer. This positioning prevents the sound from the drums being picked up by the vocal microphones; drums are loud enough anyway without the vocal microphones amplifying them through the PA. Other band members should then complete the circle, bass players being next to the drummer and brass or string players being next to the vocalist. Do not worry about how you are going to set up onstage for the show; the positioning is not important right now. You need to get your music arranged and rehearsed!

Once arranged, you should all set good and comfortable levels on your individual instrument amplifiers. Start by listening to the drums on their own and adding in vocals through the PA until the voice sits comfortably over the volume of the drums. Then bring up the level on the guitar amps one at a time, adding bass amps, keyboards, and so on until everything can be heard but nothing is too loud or distorted.

The singer should take this preparation stage to warm up his or her voice. Advice from the numerous vocal coaches with whom I have worked indicate that at least 20 minutes of vocal exercises are necessary for a decent vocal performance.

When your positions are comfortable and you have set appropriate levels, you can practice your music. Having set up in a circle, you will now have the benefit of direct eye contact with all your band mates. Hopefully all the instruments levels sound balanced, enabling you to concentrate on playing together.

Turning Songs into Shows

After rehearsing your music, you should start thinking about the show. You may decide to do this in a separate session. No worries, as long as you are feeling confident with the music. If not, then keep practicing!

It is true that the rehearsal room is the best place to get together and discuss all the elements that make up your performance. Ask yourself and your band how you are going to achieve and exceed your own expectations, as well as those of your audience? Use this time to really explore the emotions that you are trying to get across; once you have identified your intentions, you are free to rehearse new ideas.

Figure 5.1 A typical purpose-built rehearsal studio. (Courtesy of Music Bank, London.)

I always recommend that any musical act watch itself in a mirror while rehearsing or, even better, film itself playing live and rehearsing. You can set up a video camera, perform your set—either in a rehearsal or at a show—and film it.

Note: Get It on Video Always tape/film your shows. However, do *not* ask a friend to hold a camera at the side of the stage. You want the audience's point of view, so you should set up the camera on a tripod at the back of the room or at the sound desk and set the camera to record a view of the whole stage. What you need to see on the tape is what your audience sees—you on the stage with no zooming or pans. This will give you the "warts and all" perspective of your performance.

When you have filmed your rehearsal or show, take the tape out of the camera and hide it. Do not watch the tape immediately. Wait a couple of days or even a week. Then sit down (with the rest of the band if you are not a solo performer) and view the tape.

Take my word for it, that initial viewing will be agony! The recorded sound will be horrible, and the lighting will be awful. The shot will be static and will be a million miles removed from the performance-type videos we see on cable music stations. However, we are not after an Academy Award for this tape; we merely want an insight into how the audience will perceive you and your performance. So, sit down with those tapes, show them to friends and family, and get real sense of how your show is coming across. If you find it painful to watch your own show, then think about how your potential audience will view your performance. Yes, you may be uncomfortable with seeing yourself "live." But if *you* haven't got confidence in your abilities, what impression is your audience going to have? As I said before, when playing out you need to impress the audience. They are the people who will pay to see you again in the future and will buy your CDs, MP3s, and T-shirts—but only if you impress them! Watch the tapes and study your performance.

When rehearsing for the show, you should prepare for the performance setting. Think about the environment you will be performing in and try to emulate that in the rehearsal space.

Note: Get Used to Tight Spaces You may end up supporting/opening up for a larger headline band. You may also find that by the time the headline band has set up its touring PA, lights, backline, and power distribution, the stage is full of black boxes! You will almost certainly end up with a thin strip across the front on which to try to set up all your equipment and find somewhere to stand while performing! If you are a "traditional" four- or five-piece band (in which the drummer usually plays behind the guitarists), you are faced with the choice of either no drummer for this show or a drummer placed on the extreme stage left or stage right.

My advice is to anticipate this situation. If you are really intent on playing large shows, then opening up for national touring acts should be your first priority—in which case the act of having to fit all your gear onto a postage stamp is bound to happen. Anticipate this by choosing to rehearse in this format, such as all musicians in a straight line across the front of the stage, with your drummer either far left or far right (see Figure 5.2). Determine who should stand next to the drummer for timing purposes (usually the bass player or other percussionists) and who can get away with being at the other end of the stage. Work out what instruments you will now need in your monitor mix (see Chapter 6, "Equipment") and make a note of them. Obviously you will need extra drums in your monitor wedge without your drummer immediately behind you.

So, as I keep stressing, simply playing your songs is not enough. What do I mean? Read on....

Elements of a Show

Music is communication. It is also entertainment. Audiences expect a professional and entertaining experience. So make your show professional and entertaining!

I am not referring to exaggerated dance moves, pyrotechnics, or other theatrics. These may indeed be applicable to your show. However, my experience tells me that the nuts and bolts of the performance are more important. These are:

- Set list and song order

- Intro/play-on music

- Instrument changes

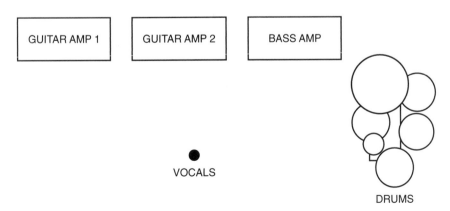

Figure 5.2 On a small stage, set the drums up to one side of the stage. The drummer should face across the stage and preferably be near the bass player for timing purposes.

- Speech
- Backup plan

Let's examine each of these points in turn.

Set List and Song Order

The *set* is the songs you will be performing; the *set list* is just that—a list of the songs in the order you have decided they should be played. Set list refers to both the order and the physical piece of paper written or printed out for everyone to follow (see Figure 5.3).

Talk to any established musician, manager, or agent about live song order, and they will usually agree that although it is one of the hardest things to get right, a good set list can make a concert and a bad one will ruin it. Set list order also causes the most arguments backstage between band members! You not only have to decide in which order you are going to present your material, but which material you are going to

SUPER FURRY ANIMALS
LONDON 08/04 2004 V.1.0

SLOW LIFE

MOTHERFOKKER

RINGS AROUND THE WORLD

GOLDEN RETRIEVER

GOD! SHOW ME MAGIC

DRYGONI

DO OR DIE

LIBERTY BELL

HELLO SUNSHINE!

RUN! CHRISTIAN! RUN!

CITYSCAPE SKYBABY

BLEED FOREVER

PICCOLO SNARE

SOMETHINGS COME FROM..

JUXTAPOZED WITH U

HERMAN LOVES PAULINE

PLAY IT COOL

INTERNATIONAL LANGUAGE

RECEPTACLE

OUT OF CONTROL

CALIMERO

Figure 5.3 A typical set list.

perform. This may be simple if you are just starting out and you only have a handful of songs, but obviously if you have a 20-year career and 200-odd songs to your name, then careful selection of material can be difficult!

My experience indicates that in the early days of your career, you are best off keeping set time short (20 to 25 minutes) and making sure you get your best songs in first. Any audience has a short attention span, so if you are opening up for a more established act, you should bear this in mind. The audience will be waiting for you to finish to make way for the headline act, or they may simply have wandered into the bar or club in which you are performing. Whatever the scenario, you need to keep your set short and effective.

Traditionally, bands save their best, most popular songs until last in the set, usually for the encore. However, you are not going to get an encore when opening up for someone else, and I would say that when you are starting out, you run the risk of your audience leaving before you even get to the end of your set! So, when deciding your set list, you should consider playing your really good stuff early on. Yes I know—*all* your songs are fantastic. I don't doubt it. You are obviously committed to your art and career; why else would you be reading this book?

Take some time to think about this matter of material, though. You must have a few songs that your friends, family members, and audience members have appreciated more than others in your set, right? These are the tracks with which you may want to end your set, so as to create a lasting impression. It won't work, though! As an unknown act, you need to wow your audience within the first couple songs you play. If you do not grab their attention right away, the audience will go to the bar, the other room, the hotdog stand, or the restrooms. This is especially true when you are opening up for a more established act—it is always better to play out your best songs early in your set. (Hopefully all your material is good, but some songs will always stand out.) Construct your set list to showcase at least a couple of those killer tunes within the first four songs. Think about it this way—if you grab the attention of the audience, they will stay with you until the end of your set.

Think very carefully about performing cover versions if you are an originals act. Why waste precious public exposure time on someone else's material? This is doubly true if you are playing to an industry house—for example, A&R people. They do not have time to hang around. A scout will traditionally see two to three acts in one evening; your version of "Rock On" by David Essex may be tremendous, but it does not say anything about you or your potential to create a career making original music.

You may be auditioning for a position in a band or for a talent competition, TV show, or similar event. In that case, you may be required to sing/perform an established cover. All the major talent search competitions (*X-Factor, Pop Idol, American Idol,* and so on) will predetermine a list of acceptable songs from which you may choose. Make sure you are familiar with the songs! It sounds like common sense, but it is amazing how many auditioned performers turn up with only scant knowledge of the songs they are asked to perform. It is your one really important chance to make an impression. Don't blow it!

As your career progresses, different factors determine the inclusion of material and the order. You may be on tour to promote a new album, in which case you obviously will want to play some of that new material. However, audiences have come to hear the songs they know and love, the "old stuff," as it gets called (as in, "They only want to hear the old stuff!"). The balance between established favorites (for the audience) and newer, more exciting songs (for the artist) takes considerable thought and practice. You do risk alienating your public if you choose to ignore the hits, but some artists find it quite demoralizing to realize their audience is only there to listen to the music they have heard before. I would say that you should never ignore or downplay the significance of those older songs if they have been successful. They are what bought the audience to you, they are money in the bank, and they enable you to continue your career. I'm sure Pete Townshend and The Who may be slightly uncomfortable singing "My Generation" these days ("Hope I die before I get old" sung by 60-year-olds?), but they continue to perform that song at every concert they give.

When you have determined your choice and order of songs, it is usually a good idea to write it down and make copies for all the musicians and crew involved. Try to use white A4/legal size paper and write clearly in black, broad pen. Red ink will disappear under stage lights! Try to avoid shortening titles or nicknaming songs. In the heat and confusion of the set, you may mistake one title for another. You will also confuse any crew or other personnel who are not familiar with the set. If you are using intro/play-on music, mark this as "intro" at the top of the set list. You would not believe how many times house sound engineers or lighting people have turned to me and asked, "Is this the first song?" during the band's walk-on music.

Note: Choose a List Master Make one person responsible for writing and distributing the lists. That way there is no confusion over this, and it is not left to chance. I used to get very nervous before performing, so I used to take responsibility for doing the set list to take my mind off the show. Now, as tour manager, it is my expected duty!

Make sure everyone involved has a copy of the set list before you hit the stage. Try to make sure everyone has seen and agrees to the set list before you make multiple copies. There have been countless times I have written out or printed multiple set lists, only to have to scrap the whole lot because of one change! Allow for all personnel involved when copying set lists—people usually anticipate one each for the band members and one each for all of the crew members. I also make lots of spare copies to put up in all dressing and changing rooms, at stage entrances and exits, and in catering areas and the production office. I also have copies for journalists, security personnel, merchandise people, and venue managers. The set list basically acts as a clock during the show—anyone with a copy of the set list can look at it and figure out where the band is in the set and work out how soon the band are liable to come offstage.

Note: Left-Justify Set Lists Do not center the words on the set list— justify the text to the left side of the page. This gives space next to the song title for musicians and crew to make notes about BPMs, guitar changes, and so on.

Intro/Play-On Music

The intro/play-on music is a short piece of music or sound that is played at the commencement of the act's set, usually coinciding with the house lights being dimmed and/or the curtain opening. I have a fondness for any type of play-on or intro music/event. I believe intro music shows a professional showbiz attitude that hopefully sets the tone for the rest of the performance. Remember, you are creating a professional and entertaining performance. Obviously with larger events, the intro music will be part of a carefully choreographed set piece designed to set the scene, but it also allows for the positioning of musicians, singers, and so on for a dramatic entrance.

Note: The Art of the Reveal Modern touring stage effects are adapted from techniques used in traditional theatre. Whatever the setting, the purpose of these effects is the same—to create a smooth transition from a cold, brightly lit room with a stage and an audience to a magical show. These transitions are known as *reveals*. Examples of reveals include:

- **Blackouts.** These are the most simple and effective form of reveal. All light on the stage is instantly turned off. When it comes back on, the performers are in place, ready to rock.

- **Kabuki drops.** Kabuki is an ancient form of Japanese theatre famous for, among other things, incredible use of reveals, using curtains and cloths suspended over actors and sets. On command these cloths fall away to reveal the next scene, almost like switching channels on TV. Many modern concerts now use kabuki drops. The most common example is to have a black kabuki (the generic name for any dropping cloth) between the performers at the front of the stage and an elaborate stage set at the back. The performers can play two or three songs in front of the kabuki and then, simultaneous to a big lighting effect, the kabuki can drop to reveal the huge stage set.

- ■ **Pyrotechnics.** Pyrotechnics (or *pyro*) works as a reveal by temporarily distracting the audience (with a massive bang) and covering the desired part of the stage with flames, sparks, and smoke. Used in conjunction with a blackout, pyrotechnics are an incredible form of reveal. A word of warning, though: Make sure your FOH engineer knows to mute all the microphones at the time of detonation. The sound of explosion being picked up by those microphones can destroy a sound system!

At its simplest level, playing a piece of music or sound at the top of the show can divert the audience's attention from the singers or musicians walking onstage, picking up instruments, fiddling around with microphone stands, and so on.

As always, check the venue's technical specifications before deciding to use intro music. Most venues will have CD players routed through the main house PA system, and certainly all touring PA systems will include CD players and possibly MiniDisc (MD) players and Digital Audio Tape (DAT) players, too. CD is the most popular format, so you should consider burning your chosen piece onto CD-R. Keep the piece short (two to three minutes); if it is a longer piece, then decide at which point it should be faded out when you are going to start playing. Agree with your own engineer or the house engineer if and/or when the intro should be started, stopped, or faded. Try to avoid having an intro that acts as a musical cue to your performance or is part of the first song in your set; CD players located at the front-of-house desk usually just go to the main speakers and are not routed to the stage monitors (see Chapter 6). It will be very hard to accurately hear any timing or pitching information on your intro if it is not being played through the monitors. Remember, intro music is just that. It can be very effective, but do not get carried away and try to make your intro too complicated!

Note: Be Creative with Your Opening Piece! "Ride of the Valkyries," the theme from *Thunderbirds*, the *Match of the Day* theme, the *Mission Impossible* theme, "An Ending (Ascent)" by Brian Eno … no, no, NO! These tracks have been used a million times by bands. Avoid them!

The choice of intro music to your concert is as individual as the music you have created, and I would be foolish to try to advise you about what you should use. However, in my experience, there are some things that work well—a remix of one of your songs; an orchestral or easy-listening arrangement of a current pop hit; some theme music from the latest computer game phenomenon; or Big Band, jazz, or show tunes.

Instrument and Costume Changes

During the course of your performance, you may have the need to change instruments or costumes. This may be a planned swapping of guitar (such as Fender for Gibson) for one song in order to vary the tone. It may be that the bass player and the drummer swap roles for one song. Or, as part of your performance, you change your costume for that big closing number. Whatever the need or reason, try to keep these changes simple and make sure you rehearse them! The theatre analogy still holds true here. A cast will have a technical and dress rehearsal after many a run-through to make sure they can incorporate all the prop, scenery, and costume changes and still get onstage in time to deliver their lines. It is no good planning a huge costume change for the last song in your set if it means keeping the audience waiting for five minutes!

As your career progresses and you are able to employ more crew and spend more money on costumes and set, then any changes during the performance can be incorporated and, increasingly, are expected. However, during the early days, please try to question the impact instrument or costume changes will have on the continuity of your performance. Swapping instruments on a small, cramped stage can be a difficult and time-consuming process. When you have located the "new" instrument, it must be checked to make sure it is still in tune. All this activity adds a delay to performing the next song and inevitably results in audience indifference.

Note: Separate Stands for Every Instrument You should always have separate instrument stands for all the instruments, as shown in Figure 5.4. This will prevent having expensive instruments leaning against amps or walls. Instruments are designed to be played; they are not much good at standing up unaided!

Try to avoid instrument changes wherever possible. Work out why an instrument change was thought to be necessary in the first place and

Figure 5.4 Have separate stands for all your instruments, and do not lean them against your amp or the wall!

seek ways to replace or avoid the change. Certainly swapping instruments among band personnel (such as the bass player and the guitarist swapping each other's instruments) should be avoided at all costs. This practice looks so messy and unorganized. Changing instruments is also fraught with danger—potential cable wrapping and tripping. And why, oh why, do bands insist on having different people playing the drums for various songs? As an audience member I pay to see music performed, not a bunch of people playing musical chairs onstage! Tell me, if you are changing drummers, why can't the first drummer play that song?

Work out the best way to perform your material without swapping instruments. Can the lead singer talk or introduce the band while you are changing guitars? Think about it—this is why you are rehearsing!

If you do need planned guitar changes to favor different tonal characteristics, then rehearse grouping songs in the set by the guitar involved—for example, all the Fender Strat songs together, followed by the songs that need the Gibson guitar. If two or more people sing lead vocals, then arrange for each person to sing his or her songs all together, or at least in batches of two to three songs at a time. Having this continuity gives the audience a focal point without unnecessary distraction. It also aids your crew, giving the front-of-house engineer more time to re-balance and re-EQ the replacement guitars and vocals over a series of songs.

Speech

I am constantly amazed at seeing the most natural, gifted, and articulate stage performers come up to an open microphone during a break in the performance and talk such utter drivel! Or a lead singer making an impassioned speech, only to have the drummer and bass player launch into the next song halfway through the speech, completely drowning her out!

Speech is like any part of the performance. You may be a talented and creative musician, but it does not necessarily follow that you are a confident and able public speaker—or that your band mates know you are going to launch into a privately rehearsed speech.

My experience leads me to believe that in-between song banter should be kept as short as possible and should be, to a certain extent, planned. Try not to mumble and try not to shout. You do not have to introduce every song, but it is a good idea to point out certain highlights, such as, "This is the new single; it's called 'The Black Hit of Space,'" or, "We have T-shirts and CDs for sale at the back of the hall." If you are an unknown/unsigned/newly signed act, make sure you let people know the name of your band at least twice during the set. Try to avoid talking or shouting over the start or finish of songs. When rehearsing your show, plan the breaks between or during songs for when your vocalist can relay information. Remember the tapes you made of your rehearsals? Watch them again. Can you understand the speech between songs?

Note: Proximity Effect Microphones will accentuate the bass/low-end frequencies of your voice. This is known as "proximity effect." The closer you place a dynamic microphone to your source, the more low frequencies will be picked up. This effect is great if you are miking up kick drums or bass cabinets. Proximity effect does not help speech, though. If you have a vocal microphone, such as a Shure SM58, close to your mouth and you mumble or talk quietly, your audience will only hear a subsonic rumble. Instead, raise your head up and speak slowly and loudly. If you have to shout for dramatic effect, then move the microphone away from your mouth by 30 centimeters at the loudest part. You can really destroy your hearing and that of your audience by bellowing into a microphone through a pro sound system.

Some people feel the need to fill the gaps between songs by talking. Nervousness may play a part here. Remember my advice on swapping instruments? A short speech is a good way to distract an audience while guitar changes are made. However, if you do not have anything to say, then do not say it!

Always, always plan your speech onstage. Even if you have a point in the set where you are going to improvise (based on your mood or the audience's), make sure you plan it. Every pro band I work for has this kind of planning on their set list—either specific speech or just an indication before a certain song that there will be talking from the band.

Short speeches are great if you have an interesting point or story about a song or an event. Just make sure the other band members know when these speeches are supposed to take place within the set.

Never, ever respond to hecklers. Try not to feel upset or enraged by their comments. You are onstage and you are entertaining. Arguments with members of the audience take away the focus from you and potentially alienate other members of the audience. Concentrate on wowing the masses and not on arguing with individuals.

Backup plan

Part of any good rehearsal should be planning what to do if things go wrong. Always have a backup plan. We're talking about your livelihood, so do not leave anything to chance. There are two potential disaster areas—instrument breakdowns and scheduling problems.

Instrument Breakdowns

While rehearsing and preparing for shows, make sure you have thought about spares and replacements in case an instrument breaks or fails during the performance. There are the obvious instances to take care of, and I have compiled a basic checklist here. As a working performer (and/or backline technician), you should make sure you have immediate access to the following items onstage:

- Instrument strings: Full sets with doubles of top strings e, b, and so on for guitar

- Extra plectrums/picks

- Drumsticks

- Snare drum head, batters, and snare

- Spare reeds

- Spare instrument and plug fuses: Examine your amp's instruction manual and determine what fuses are needed

- Extra batteries or spare power supply

- Spare cables/cords: Long and short

- Crosshead (Phillips) and flat-head screwdriver

- Pliers

- Flashlight/Mag-Lite

- Gaffa and PCV/PTFE tape

Make sure you have these items available for your performance. Make up an emergency/spares box, mark it clearly as such, and make sure it gets loaded onto the stage for when you perform (see Figure 5.5). A spares box is no good to you if it locked in your van, which is parked two blocks away.

If you are a guitar or bass player, try to have a spare guitar available, tuned up and ready to go. This is far better than stopping the set to re-string a guitar, even if you have to borrow a guitar from a friend or another band with whom you are performing. Drummers should try to have a spare snare drum and kick drum pedal because these are the items that tend

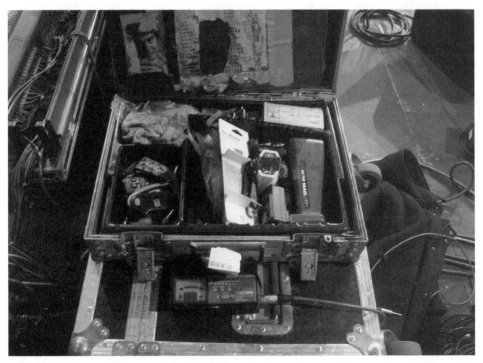

Figure 5.5 A sensible spares/tool box placed on a flight case with a guitar tuner ready for action!

to break first. Keyboard/sampler players should make sure all programming and sound data is backed up to at least two separate sets of media and that both backups are current and will restore properly.

While in the rehearsal space, make sure everything that you are going to use in the shows works properly. Check all electrical main cables for loose connections. Tighten up all internal connections and make sure you have plenty of fuses, both for main supplies and internal instrument fuses. Check all cables and connections for buzzes or hums, and make sure you have fresh batteries for all effects pedals, tuners, radio microphones, and so on. Obviously, do not forget to make sure anything you are using as an emergency replacement also works!

Note: Batteries Buy power supplies for your guitar effects pedals and tuners. Batteries cost a ridiculous amount of money and are *not* reliable. Luckily, there are many devices available today that are designed specifically to power your 9v stomp boxes (effects pedals), even if those pedals were not designed for use with A/C power. An example is the PA-9 from Godlyke (www.godlyke.com).

Try to anticipate any potential problems and how you will handle them. If you have a crew, discuss with them how replacements or spares can be gotten to you during a performance and what everyone's responsibilities will be in an emergency. I have seen musicians struggling with broken strings or collapsed stands while crew members stood at the side of stage simply because they were unsure whether they should come onstage. Obviously no one is to blame, but five minutes spent talking over these situations in the rehearsal room can save embarrassment onstage.

Computers onstage are now as common as guitar amps in modern music performance. Whether laptops running music sequencing software, hard disk recorders and samplers, or dedicated sequencing devices, you should make sure all data is backed up at least twice and that you also have a non-computer backup plan in case of a hardware breakdown. Computers do not really like traveling (even laptops), and I have spent many an hour in a cold venue on a Sunday afternoon trying to coax dead hard drives back to life. Have a duplicate of every machine and make sure your backups travel in separate cases from the main machines.

If you cannot afford separate standby machines, then devise another backup plan. The simplest and most foolproof audio backup (apart from doubles of all your computing hardware) is to record the audio output of the computer to DAT, MD, or CD while in the rehearsal space or recording studio. If worse comes to worst, you will be able to whack in your CD or DAT and continue your show. Obviously, you then need to make sure you have a dedicated CD, MD, or DAT player onstage and that it has outputs to the PA system in the same way as your computer/HD setup. This solution is a major compromise, but it is a solution. I have been in situations where we have used this kind of backup and managed to do a show and still get paid. The alternative was cancellation and no money!

When recording your audio output to a DVD, CD, or MiniDisc, you should try to separate individual songs or pieces with separate start IDs or track names. Your set may be one long, segued piece, but if you *do* have a failure onstage and your backup is one long audio track, you will have to fast-forward the backup to find the tune you were going to play next! This will not be a pleasant experience at high volume and will break the spell you may have built up. Having your audio as separate tracks also permits flexibility with your set list order.

If you are using sequencers to generate click tracks for drummers and percussionists, then an audio backup is difficult unless you bounce your computer output to a multi-channel tape machine, such as ADAT or DA88. If you do this, you could then have two tracks for the L&R main program and a third track for the click. However, you would have to have some way of quickly changing over the click source from computer/sequencer to the tape machine. I cannot help thinking that if you were going down this road, you would just use the tape machine anyway, and leave the expensive computers at home!

There are no hard-and-fast rules, and every act I have worked with has a different approach. The one thing they had in common was a secure and failsafe backup system!

One final note: When all else fails, leave the stage! It is far better to simply walk off and leave the crew, technicians, or responsible musicians to fix the problem than to stand there looking aimless and lost. Make an announcement such as, "We are having some technical difficulties and will be back in five minutes," and then exit. When all is fixed you can walk back on, looking like champions. If the problem cannot be fixed, you have at least made a dignified exit well ahead of time!

Scheduling Problems

When rehearsing and sorting set lists, try to anticipate the length of set you are permitted or expected to play. This is really important if you are opening up, supporting another act, or playing at a multi-act event, such as an open-air festival such as Ozzfest, Carling: Reading and Leeds, or Roskilde. Festivals operate on almost split-second timing; festival promoters are subject to very heavy financial fines if they run past an agreed-upon sound curfew. Bands performing at festivals are given a strict time to be onstage and offstage, with another set time for changeover (getting the previous act's gear off and their gear on). The promoter or agent will give you your set length well in advance, and it will be stipulated in your contract (see Figure 5.6). Make sure you work out how many songs you can fit into that time period and *never* take a chance of overrunning or squeezing in one more tune. You run the risk of having the power pulled on you, being pulled offstage, having your payment withheld, and being fined! It really is not worth it, especially because it will damage your reputation in an extremely competitive industry.

Bands do overrun, and an act lower down the bill than you may use up vital time. This time has to be clawed back somehow; otherwise, ultimately the headline act will have their set time cut. In this case the stage manager may inform the act due to perform after the offending band that they will have to lose a certain amount of time from their set. This may be you. Have you prepared for a possible change in your set? Five minutes is usually a whole song. Which song could you drop?

This presumes, of course, that you know about this problem before you get on the stage. You may be late getting onstage due to some technical problem during changeover. You could be only halfway through the set

HYLANDS PARK
Saturday 21st August

SITE ADDRESS	Hylands Park Chelmsford Essex CM2 8WF

SITE TELEPHONE NOS	PROMOTER PROMOTER FAX SITE OFFICE SITE OFFICE FAX

V Stage
SHOW TIMES

		Set Length (mins)
GATES OPEN	12.00pm	
BIG BROVAZ	12.25 - 12.50pm	25
THE DIVINE COMEDY	1.10 - 1.40pm	30
ATHLETE	2.00 - 2.40pm	40
PINK	3.05 - 4.05pm	60
FAITHLESS	4.30 - 5.30pm	60
CHARLATANS	5.55 - 6.55pm	60
DIDO	7.25 - 8.55pm	90
MUSE	9.25 - 10.55pm	90
CURFEW	10.45pm	

Figure 5.6   A typical festival running order. Notice that the changeover time between each act is about 20 minutes—all this and no sound check either!

when you spy the stage manager pointing frantically to the clock. Obviously this is not a situation you can plan for completely, but it is one you should be aware of when you are rehearsing and sorting song orders. Again, try to avoid having all your really big killer tunes together at the end of the set. If you are running short on time and you have to ditch a song on the run, then you will have to sacrifice one of your best songs. As I say, it is not a problem you can totally plan for, but bear it in mind if you are opening up/supporting someone else or when you are performing as part of a multi-act bill.

"In the current climate of limited radio and TV opportunities, [playing live] is a vital tool in building a profile around an artist."

—Mike Greek, booking agent, CAA. Agent for Alicia Keys, Franz Ferdinand, Red Hot Chili Peppers, Arcade Fire, Nine Inch Nails, the Dandy Warhols, and David Grey.

Contract and Rider

As you can see, there are quite a few elements involved in making sure that your show runs smoothly and that you maximize your time in front of an audience. While all this is going on, you really do not want to be worried about getting paid. This is where your contract comes into play.

It is easy to draw up and issue your own contracts and riders, as we saw in Chapter 3. When preparing for a show, you should always make sure you are covered in case something goes wrong, such as if you do not get paid on the night. If you do not have an agent to produce a contract for you, then you should draw up your own contract. Look at the example in Chapter 3, go to www.the-tour-book.com, and create or amend as necessary. As I said in Chapter 3, even if you just issue a page that says, "You, Mrs. Bar Manager, agree to pay me in CASH the fee of $X when I perform in your bar on xxth of x. Sign here," you will be protecting yourself from potential nonpayment problems.

Many promoters, bar managers, and venue owners will insist that a contract is not necessary. My advice would be to send a contract anyway. Make sure you send it as soon as the show is confirmed—call ahead and find out to whom a contract should be issued. Do not be put off if the bar manager tells you a contract is not necessary; simply explain that you would feel more comfortable with a written contract. Explain to the contact that you will send the contract in with a stamped, self-addressed envelope—all the recipient has to do is read and sign the contract and send it back in the envelope provided.

Try to avoid sending contracts by e-mail or fax. Receiving documents this way requires the recipient to take some action—he or she has to print out the e-mail or copy the fax and send it back. If a bar manager is not keen on signing a contract in the first place, he will be even less inclined if he has to print it out and send it back to you! So send your contract, recorded/guaranteed delivery if you can, printed and with a stamped, self-addressed envelope. Remember, all you are trying to do is produce a professional event and make sure you get paid for producing that event!

At some point you should also have written a contract rider, technical specifications, and an input list and stage plan. Be realistic when producing these documents. You really do not want to send off a four-page rider—you will appear both naïve and unprofessional. For shows in bars, pubs, or clubs, you should probably only produce a condensed document, such as the one shown in Figure 5.7

The kind of document shown in Figure 5.7, although not really a contract rider, gives the venue the basic information about the band. You would pass this to the venue so they have a quick overview of what you are all about. There is no point in stating your usual long list of demands (as in the contract rider in Chapter 3) because it is simply irrelevant to a small pub or bar. I have mentioned our IEM system, though, because we are not carrying our own engineer. We would therefore expect the house sound person to be able to set up and run the IEM system, under our supervision.

The input list is slimmed down because I am assuming there will be only a small vocal-type PA with a small mixer, which may only have eight channels. There is therefore no way to reinforce all the instruments with separate input channels for each. As such, I am going to concentrate on putting vocals in the PA. Standard practice is then to amplify the kick drum and maybe the bass guitar DI, as well as any line-level equipment, such as keyboards, decks, samplers, and computers, by putting them through the PA.

In the hospitality section I have added that we would like some water—I will probably have already spoken to the venue manager about this. Yes, we could ask for a bunch of beers and some food, but the costs of these would probably be deducted from our fee, and at this point in their career, Millions of Americans needs as much money as possible to be able to play more shows!

Always remember, all you are trying to do is present your band or act in a professional manner—one that conveys all the necessary information in a comprehensive and realistic manner. If you are in doubt about

MILLIONS OF AMERICANS
BAND AND CREW INFORMATION

CAST & CREW

Millions of Americans are 5 people:

4 x band
1 x merchandise seller

Cast and crew will travel together in one (1) LDV van with all their equipment.

Millions of Americans will be selling merchandise and would like a dry, clean and well lit area in which to set up the merchandise.

TECHNICAL INFORMATION

Millions of Americans are carrying their own In Ear Monitor system (IEM). This operates on 832.700 MHz (EBU CH 66) and be altered between 830 to 866 MHz. For full details please see attached technical specifications and/or contact Andy Reynolds on +44 (0)551886 or email andy.reynolds@tourconcepts.com

Millions of Americans have a backdrop, (1.8m by 1m) that they would like to suspend on the back wall of the stage.

CH.	INSTRUMENT/ SOURCE	MIC/DI	NOTES
1	KICK DRUM	SHURE SM91	
2	BASS BOOM	DI	FROM LAPTOP NEXT TO DRUMS
3	BASS DI	XLR	DIRECT OUT
4	VOCAL SL	WE SUPPLY	
5	VOCAL CENTER	WE SUPPLY	

CATERING & HOSPITALITY

Millions of Americans require:

12 X 50CL bottles of still water (Volvic, Evian or similar)

MILLIONS OF AMERICANS:
PLEASE CONTACT:
ANDY 07762 551886

Figure 5.7 A condensed version of a rider for use in bars and small clubs. It is designed to give information and not to make demands of the promoter.

an item in your contract or contract rider, do not include it without researching the implications or asking a more experienced person—me, for example! (You can e-mail me at book@tourconcepts.com.)

Safety

I do not want to come across as being like your mother, but *please* be careful up there onstage. Health and safety have come a long way since the '60s, but there is a still a lot of electricity in those cables and a lot of things to bump into or fall off (see Figure 5.8), so watch yourself!

From (sometimes bitter) experience, I have compiled the following dos and don'ts when it comes to stage safety:

- Never, never, *never* put drinks on top of amps, combos, or speakers, even if they are in sealed bottles or cans. Vibrations and human error caused by flashing stage lights, hazers, and so on will almost certainly cause those drinks to spill. The resulting mix of sugary

Figure 5.8 The reason you need to be safe—to enjoy your moment onstage!

liquids and electricity will be expensive, fatal, or both. *Do not do it!* If you have to take drinks onstage, then place them on the floor, behind and to one side of where you will be performing or working. The best place for drinks is on the front of the drum riser (if applicable), inside a shallow tray or a rack-case lid (see Figure 5.9).

- Close all butterfly catches on cases and push the butterfly flat against the case. An open butterfly clasp can result in a very painful and bloody wound if you rush past and catch yourself on it.

- Always ask before plugging anything into a mains supply. A modern stage has power outlets for a variety of functions, not just backline power. You could be plugging your Korg TRITON into the stage lighting power, an action that will result in a quick trip to the local music shop to buy a new keyboard!

- On a similar note, never unplug anything onstage without asking first. As well as causing huge audio "bangs" and damaging

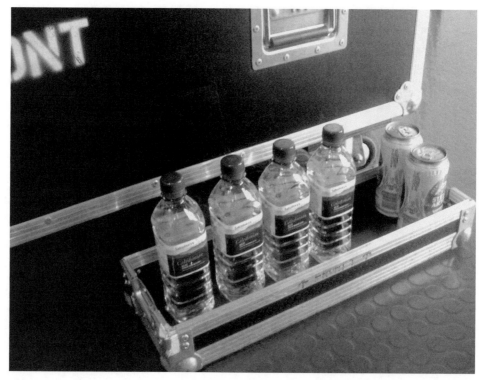

Figure 5.9 Place bottles and cans in a lid. If they spill, the fluid is contained in the lid.

equipment, your personal health will be threatened if the audio or backline crew gets hold of you.

- Look up. Working as part of a modern concert means that you will see lots of equipment "flown"—that is, suspended in the air (see Figure 5.10). Get in the habit of looking up when you first get on the stage, and try not to stand under flown PA speakers or lighting trusses or near truss ladders. Listen carefully if someone shouts, "Moving!" This means someone is lowering ("bringing in") or raising ("taking out") a lighting truss or a PA hang. Although bringing in or taking out a truss is a fairly slow and smooth action, objects have been known to become dislodged and fall during this time. There are also many cables that go from ground to the flown system, and these may drag across the stage as the truss is moving.

- Look down. As well as nasty, great big monitor wedges, there will also be raised stage sections with sharp corners and lots of cables. Get in the habit of marking corners of risers and platforms with strips of white gaffer.

Figure 5.10 A modern concert has more equipment above the stage than actually on it!

- Tape down your cables when you are sure everything is plugged in and working. Use a heavy gaffer-type tape, not masking tape. (You would not believe how many times I have seen this onstage. As well as being uselessly weak, masking tape is made of paper and will catch fire when hot.) Group cables together (avoiding mains cable with signal cable if you can) and keep them flat—in other words, side by side. Apply short sections of tape *across* the cable run, not along it.

- Avoid going barefoot or wearing sandals onstage. There are sharp corners, big boxes, and cables everywhere on a stage. Crew and other musicians will be lifting heavy equipment. Added to this, the stage may be dark and filled with stage smoke. Do you really want to risk your toes in this environment?

- Do not run cables that cannot reach and end up suspended between equipment or to the mains supply. Move your gear so cable can run along the ground, or borrow or buy a longer cable or extension cord.

- Never throw drumsticks into the crowd. If you must show your appreciation to the aspiring drummers in the audience, then walk forward to the lip of the stage and hand your sticks off to someone in the front row. A thrown stick can blind someone if it hits him in the eye.

- Likewise, never hand out bottles or cans of beer or soft drinks to the crowd. Many venues issue plastic glasses to the audience. You may be breaking the venue laws by introducing cans and bottle into that environment. You also run the risk of having the bottle thrown back at you.

- Watch your back. Lift gear from your knees, keeping your back straight. Hold heavy gear from the bottom, with both hands. Do not use the handles on the sides of your equipment cases—gravity acts upon the bottom half and makes the case twice as heavy!

- Never carry your drink with one hand and your gear with another. Put the drink down (somewhere safe), carry the gear, go back to your beverage, pick it up, and drink it—in that order.

- If you are a performer, do not climb on speakers or up trusses or cables without first checking with the stage manager, production manager, or sound and light technicians. You really have no idea how much weight these items can support, and you have no idea whether they are fixed in place. It's bad enough if you fall and hurt yourself—it will be worse if you and the speakers come crashing down on top of the audience. Also, bear in mind that after you have clambered up the truss or on top of the speakers, you have to get all the way down again and still look dignified!

- If you have to smoke onstage, watch where you place your finished cigarettes. The headline act may be using pyrotechnics, or someone may be painting a flight case or refilling a generator.

- Do not leave the lids of hinged cases open. The vibrations caused by loud music may make them fall shut, trapping someone's hands or severing a cable. Also, never let the lid on a hinged trunk drop when you are closing it—the place where the chest and the lid join is usually about the same height as a man's … well, you get the idea….

"The initial phases of setting a band up for both domestic and international live work are the most important for any band. Making sure you are working with the right agents and promoters. Ultimately, playing the right-size venues at the right ticket price is crucial."

—Colin Schaverien, Prolifica Management. Clients include Maximo Park, The Research, and Envelopes.

6 Equipment

The aim of *The Tour Book* is to give you a thorough guide to every aspect of the modern concert industry. Although it is extremely important and useful to know about contracts, safety tips, and the roles of the people with whom you will be working, none of that matters without the actual music. The music needs to be created, and in this chapter we will look at how this is done.

Although I have no idea what style or genre of music you are personally creating, I know you will use equipment to perform live. Some of this equipment is the actual instruments; other gear may include turntables and samplers, for instance. There is also the PA system used to amplify your sound for an audience, and maybe lights and video projections.

I have worked with many musicians and performers who are actually quite ignorant about their own equipment. I find this quite shocking; how can you hope to make any success for yourself if you cannot be bothered to understand the tools of your trade? And while I do not want to present the definitive guide to modern musical instruments, I can give you some general hints and tips about sound, PA systems, and your instruments (see Figure 6.1). Understanding these items will make you better able to communicate with performers and technicians and will make you appear knowledgeable and professional. It might also save you some money!

Sound: General Overview

Sounds that you hear as musical tones are made up of regular, evenly spaced waves of air molecules. The distance from the high point of one wave to the next wave's high point is called the *wavelength*. Sound waves travel at the same speed—about 340.29 meters (about 1,115 feet) per

Figure 6.1 Modern sound engineering equipment. Do you know what it does?

second. However, waves with a longer wavelength arrive at your ear later than shorter waves do. This frequency of waves (or cycles) is measured in Hertz (Hz). Hertz is a measure of how many cycles (wave peaks) go by in one second. Therefore, a 1-kHz tone means a wave with 1,000 wave peaks per second. The average human can hear sounds that range from about 20 to about 17,000 Hz.

This is all well and good, but when you are tuning your saxophone, you do not ask your piano player for 258.65 Hz. No, you ask for middle C. That's because in music, the frequency is known as the *pitch*. The shorter the wavelength, the higher the frequency, and the higher the frequency, the higher the pitch.

Great science lesson, but what does that have to do with getting your music on the road? Well, playing music onstage will bring you into contact with engineers and technicians who understand frequencies. They also often understand pitch. Many live touring professionals are also musicians, and they can speak both "languages." It therefore makes sense that you do, too. Suppose you are standing onstage and listening to the sound coming from your monitors. The sound is wrong to you. You say to the monitor engineer, "This monitor sounds wrong." How is she supposed to know what you mean? Is the mix of instruments wrong? Is the monitor too loud? Too quiet? Is the sound distorted?

To communicate properly, it really helps if you can convey your thoughts in a language that everyone understands. I know a monitor engineer who, while working with a very famous UK electro-soul band, was approached by the singer during the first song of the set and told, "The monitors sound very blue tonight." Is that a compliment or a complaint? What does a blue monitor sound like anyway? Obviously, it was important to the singer to convey her feelings, but did it give her technical team anything to go on?

Note: Feedback The most common scenario when a musician on-stage starts to think about sound is when feedback (a.k.a. *howl round*, *squeal*, or *screeching*) occurs. Feedback is a loop of sound caused when the output of a sound source is picked up by the same microphone that is being used to amplify that sound source in the first place. The classic example involves a vocal microphone and a monitor wedge. The singer's voice is picked up by the vocal microphone and amplified by the monitor wedge. As the vocalist asks for more of her vocal in the wedge (to hear herself better), the volume of the wedge starts to be picked up by her microphone. A loop then starts as the sound from the monitor is sent down the microphone, into the monitor, into the microphone, into the monitor, into the microphone....

You do not need to get an advanced degree in audio physics to talk to an engineer. Likewise, as a technician working with performers, think in musical terms when communicating a problem or idea. Having an understanding of the other person's perspective and language again will make you appear more professional and knowledgeable.

To get back to the aforementioned example, instead of saying, "This monitor sounds wrong," suppose you actually listen to the wedge and decide you can hear an odd sound in the monitor. Say to the engineer, "Hey, there is a low-pitched rumbling sound in this monitor." The engineer might say, "Okay, how low?" But at least you have given her a definition of a problem. Table 6.1 shows you the notes of a guitar and their corresponding frequencies. Keep a copy of this table with you and use it to work out the frequencies of any odd sounds you may hear during a sound check.

As well as hearing engineers and technicians talk about specific frequencies, you will also hear slang terms and buzzwords used to describe sound. Table 6.2 presents a list of commonly used sound terms ranging from low to high. These are not professionally accepted terms and they are definitely not official definitions for sound requirements. (As with any industry or profession, slang words can evolve, and given the often cheerful—that is, sarcastic and irreverent—nature of touring professionals, it is not surprising that we seem to have more than one way to describe an event or phenomenon.) However, use

Table 6.1 Frequencies and the Equivalent Guitar or Bass Guitar Notes

Frequency	Guitar or Bass Guitar Note
E = 41.20 Hz	E string on bass
A = 55.00 Hz	A string on bass
D = 73.42 Hz	D string on bass
E = 82.41 Hz	Bottom E string on guitar
G = 98.00 Hz	G string on bass
A = 110.00 Hz	A string on guitar
D = 146.83 Hz	D string on guitar
G = 196.00 Hz	G string on guitar
B = 246.94 Hz	B string on guitar
C = 261.63 Hz	Middle C on piano, C on B string of guitar
E = 329.63 Hz	Top E string on guitar
A = 440.00 Hz	Fifth fret of high E string
E = 659.26 Hz	High E string at twelfth fret

Table 6.2 Commonly Used Sound Terms

Term	Description
Chunky	Solid bass in the 80–90 Hz area
Balls	Has some real feel to it, 60–90 Hz
Boof	Bass at 100 Hz
Thin	Absence of bass
Woolly	Indistinct bass end, lack of high end
Punchy	Giving definition, 120–160 Hz
Knock	Can sound uncomfortable on kick drum and bass guitar, 160–350 Hz
Dark	General lack of high end
Rich	Falling off of frequencies above 400 Hz
Boxy	Sounds like being in a cardboard box; the sound has too much in the 250–450 Hz range
Honky	600–800 Hz Sounds like the "ow" sound when you say "honk" really loud
Nasal	Boosted at 1 KHz
Bright	Boost of frequencies above 2 kHz
Muffled	General lack of high-end frequencies above 2 kHz
Aggressive	Too much, 3–6 kHz
Sibilance	General hard "S" sounds, especially on vocals; excess of 5–7 kHz
Brittle	Lack of bass and excess of upper harmonics above 6.3 kHz

these terms—they may really help you describe your stage sound to a monitor engineer or perhaps communicate with a fellow technician.

The terms in Table 6.2 may be used when you are working with a monitor engineer during a sound check—in other words, when you are trying to make your stage sound comfortable. In the full flow of a gig, you will not be able to stop and articulate your thoughts to your monitor engineer, even if she *could* hear you above the sound of the backline and monitor wedges!

That's where a good set of hand signals can be useful. Use Figures 6.2 through 6.8 to get yourself tuned up in your wedge/in ear monitors (IEMs)—or to get someone else turned down!

Figure 6.2 Point to mouth. This means turn my vocal up/down in my wedge/IEM.

Figure 6.3 After indicating the instrument in question (vocal, guitar, and so on), you should then point up (more level in your monitor for this instrument) or down (less instrument level in your monitor).

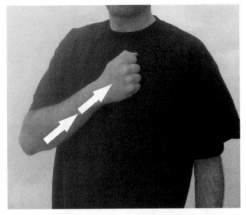

Figure 6.4 Fist on chest, then point up or down. This means more or less kick drum.

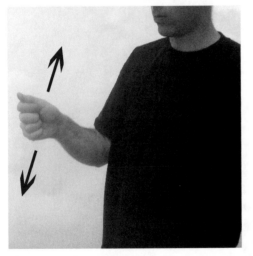

Figure 6.5 Downward fist. This means snare drum. Then point up or down. This means more or less snare drum.

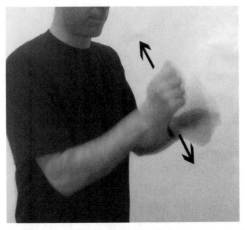

Figure 6.6 Two clenched fists. This means hi-hat. Then point up or down. This means more or less hi-hat.

Figure 6.7 Two hands doing circles. This means DAT, computer, backing track up or down.

Figure 6.8 One hand circle, then point up and down. This means turn my whole mix up or down, please.

PA Systems: A Very Basic Guide

National touring and recording acts do not need to buy a PA system. The costs of trucking, storing, maintaining, and crewing even a mid-size PA is prohibitive to all but the most successful of bands. Even if you are in the mega-selling category, it probably would not be a wise business decision to purchase your own PA and hire full-time crew unless you then rent out the system when you do not need it. (Pink Floyd did exactly that from 1971 until 1984, building up an impressive stock of touring PA equipment. They would use that for PA for their own concerts, leaving their crew to rent it out between tours.)

No, the way forward is to rely on in-house systems and your own crew, and rent when the venues get too big. I mention this because a band I once toured with persuaded their management company to let them buy a monitor desk because the very successful multi-platinum act with whom they had just toured had one.

Note: Your Own PA System If you are a professional or a semi-professional cabaret or club band, then owning and running your own PA is vital. A small but powerful system capable of handling vocals, keyboards, and drums will cost in the region of $1,200. When buying a personal PA system, think about the following things:

- Get a mixer with enough channels to accommodate all the various instrument input channels you may be using now and in the future. A couple hundred dollars extra to give you 24 input channels as opposed to 16 may be a significant investment for the future. Factor in stereo keyboards, stereo playback machines, and extra/guest musicians when working out how many inputs you need.

- Avoid combination mixer/amplifiers. A great idea in practice, mixer/amps are all-in-one packages with the amplifier needed to power the speakers integrated into the sound mixer. All inputs and outputs are connected to the same device, which saves time, space, and money. This is great until something breaks, and then you have lost both your amp and your mixer. Buy a separate mixer and amplifiers for your system; upgrading and replacing will be much easier.

- Separate bass enclosures. Most compact personal PA systems utilize two full-range speakers to handle the complete frequency range. Limitations in budget and speaker technology mean that these speakers will not be very loud and, more importantly, they will not be able to reproduce significant amounts of low end.

The music you are playing may not need ultra-heavy bass, but at high volumes the *lack* of bass will result in a thin, harsh sound. Your paying customers will not enjoy this, which means you might not get paid and you will almost certainly not get recommended to their friends, family, and colleagues.

Instead, you should go for a system with separate (sub) bass speakers. This will be more expensive, and will need more amplification. But think about your audience and what they are expecting from you. As an entertainment professional, you should invest in this kind of system as soon as you are able to; you will earn your money back very quickly.

The PA (public address) or SR (sound reinforcement) system (see Figure 6.9) is divided into four main parts: the stage box, the FOH control, the monitor speakers (and control desk, if applicable), and the FOH speakers.

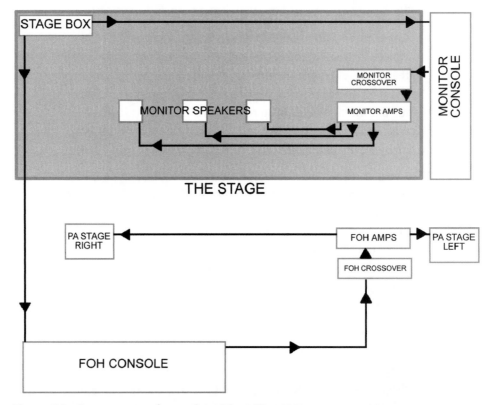

Figure 6.9 Components of a modern PA or SR system.

All PA systems are designed along the same lines, whether they are small systems at your local clubs or massive stadium line-array systems. Understand this, and you will be better able to help yourself if you are confronted with a problem onstage.

Stage Box

Sounds from your instruments and the vocals need to be amplified by the PA. To do this, you need to place microphones at each instrument source. The microphones are then plugged into the PA via the FOH mixing desk. However, if your desk is at the back of the hall, you will need some pretty long cables to reach from the stage to the FOH desk!

This is where the stage box comes in. The stage box is connected to the FOH desk via a multi-core (also called a *multi* or *snake*) cable that runs to the FOH desk. The multi takes the microphone signals from the stage to the FOH desk and brings back the final mixed output from the FOH desk to the FOH amps and speakers, which are generally either side of the stage, facing the audience. The stage box also splits the microphone signals from the stage and takes them to the onstage monitor system (if there is one).

A stage box can be located on a wall, on the floor, in racks at the back of the monitor system—wherever is most convenient for the stage audio crew. There may be several sub-stage boxes running to various parts of the stage as well. Keep an eye out for the stage box(es), and try not to block them in or cover them with your bass amp or keyboard rig. When in doubt, ask.

FOH Control

At the FOH control position, you will find the mixing desk, equalization, and effects and dynamic controls.

FOH Desk

The function of the FOH desk is to bring all the various instrument sources together so they can be mixed to create the sound the audience hears. Figure 6.10 shows a typical modern FOH desk. The desk is divided into many separate input channels, a grouping section, and an output section.

Figure 6.10 A modern FOH desk. This is a Midas Heritage 3000. (Courtesy of Midas Consoles.)

Each microphone signal arrives at the desk via the multi-core and goes into its own input channel. Each input channel consists of an input gain, an equalization section, an auxiliary section, and an output fader. The volume and equalization (EQ) of each instrument can be adjusted by the engineer using these controls on each input channel (see Figure 6.11).

Groups of channels—all the drum channels, for instance—can also be grouped together for ease of operation. For instance, if you want to turn up the volume of all the drums, you would have to grab all the individual drum input channels faders—kick drum, snare drum, hi-hats, toms, and so on—and move them at the same time. However, by assigning all the 10 drum inputs to a group in the grouping section, you adjust the overall level of all the drums by moving one fader. Finally, all the individual and group input channels go to the output section, usually run in stereo, and are sent back via the multi-core to the amps and speakers facing the audience.

Figure 6.11   The individual channel strips of a live sound desk. You can see clearly the faders along the bottom.

FOH Equalization

Located in racks next to the desk (or in the software of digital desks) is the main or system EQ (see Figure 6.12). There will usually be two channels of EQ—one for the left stereo output, and the other for the right—as well as the EQ on the individual input channels. The engineer will use this system EQ to overcome any acoustic anomalies or shortcomings in the PA system for the whole of the mixed sound.

FOH Effects

The FOH engineer also has the option of adding effects to the individual instruments to enhance the sound or to create a special effect. The individual instrument channel can be sent (routed) via a control on the desk called an *auxiliary* to a dedicated effects processor to add the following effects to the instrument source:

- **Reverb.** This simulates the natural reverberation as heard in a large empty space, such as a church or an empty concert hall. Reverb is used to add ambience to an instrument or vocal.

Figure 6.12 A modern FOH rack containing system EQ, effects, and dynamics.

- **Echo.** This is a series of repeats of the original sound. Echo is also known as *delay*.

- **Pitch shifting.** The original sound is recreated at a different pitch to either produce a "Mickey Mouse" (pitched up) or a growling (pitched down) effect.

- **Harmonization.** This is a subtle form of pitch shifting that can thicken and add richness to vocals and strings.

As I mentioned, the effects are created by dedicated effects processors—either stand-alone devices or multi-processors capable of creating all the effect types listed previously. Look again at Figure 6.12; the middle rack contains processors by Eventide, Yamaha, TC Electronics, and Lexicon.

FOH Dynamics

As well as effects, the engineer may use dynamic controls to help regulate and control the instrument sources. The two common dynamic controls are compressors/limiters and gates.

Compressors. In an ideal world, all the sound sources from the stage would remain at a reasonable and constant volume level. But in reality, musicians playing live get excited, scared, or tired, and their playing ability changes. A vocalist may start to shout during an audience clap-along section, or a guitarist may turn up his volume to make himself heard. A good FOH engineer will keep her hands firmly on the output faders of the instrument sources that tend to vary in volume—vocal, for instance. However, with 48 channels to attend to, it is not practical to have a hand on each fader; instead, we use compressors.

Compressors act by limiting the output of an instrument signal, regardless of the increase of signal input. If a vocalist starts to shout, the compressor will detect the amount of increase in the signal strength (measured in decibels, or dB). The compressor then will reduce the output of the signal. The amount of this reduction (known as *compression*) can be set by the engineer as a ratio. The ratio is expressed as x:1 and basically says that for every x amount of dB rise in volume on the input, the output volume will rise only by 1 dB. For instance, at 10:1 compression, a 10-dB input rise will be only 1 dB louder to the audience.

Compressors are set in a circuit on the channels that usually require it—typically vocals, bass guitar, brass instruments, and keyboards.

Gates. Gates act just as their name suggests—they open to allow sound through, closing again when the sound has finished. With so many microphones and so many (often very loud) sound sources on a modern concert stage, there is bound to be spill—in other words, sound from another instrument being picked up a microphone. This spill leads to coloration of the instrument sound and makes mixing more difficult.

Gates can cut down on this spill by only allowing sounds above a certain dB threshold to pass through; anything below the threshold is cut off. Obviously, when the gate is open, all sound (not only that of the primary instrument source) is allowed through. However, once that primary sound has stopped, the gate closes, and the microphone is effectively turned off. Gates work best with sharp, transient sounds, such as drums, because there is a clearly defined attack and decay to the signal. Gates are often patched into toms, for instance, to stop the toms from ringing with unwanted harmonic overtones after being struck. (In fact, this is an engineer's quick fix; ideally, the drums and drum heads should be tuned properly to prevent ringing overtones.)

I mention gates and compressors only because during sound check, the FOH engineer will often ask the musicians to play the instrument repeatedly in order to "set the gates and compressors." So now you know!

Monitor Speakers and Control

Not all PA systems have monitor speakers, and the ones that do may not necessarily have a monitor desk. Confused? Don't be; it's all quite simple.

A monitor system is a set of speakers designed for the performers onstage to hear themselves. You may have thought that with huge piles of amps and speakers facing the audience, plus the guitar amps and cabinets onstage, there would be no danger of musicians not being able to hear what they are playing. Although this is true to a certain extent, the sound onstage can be very indistinct, causing confusion for the performers. Remember what I said in Chapter 4 about rehearsing? In the rehearsal room, it is convenient to set up in an arrangement so every musician can hear every other musician in the band. This arrangement is almost certainly not applicable on a concert stage. Stage monitor systems therefore have been developed to keep pace with the demands that modern music production puts on performers.

> **Note: The Beatles at Shea Stadium** In August of 1965, there was a famous performance by the Beatles in front of 53,275 screaming (and I mean screaming) fans. The vocals were amplified by the stadium's house PA system; there were no microphones on any of the instruments, and definitely no stage monitoring system! The concert film clearly shows the four musicians constantly looking around at each other, unable to hear themselves above the noise of the audience and desperately trying to stay in time and tune. The Beatles did not know any different, but there are not many performers who could comfortably put on a similar show today!

Monitor systems today are composed of the controls to send/route the input signals from the stage to monitor speakers, and then the speakers themselves. As explained earlier in this section, the various microphone and instrument sources are plugged into the stage box, and the sound signal is then split and sent to the FOH control and to the monitor control. Each instrument source on the stage is capable of being routed back to the stage to be heard by any or all of the musicians.

Ideally, each musician will have his own monitor wedge speaker placed in front of him or will have an in-ear monitor (also known as an *IEM*—more on these later on in this section). The individual instrument input signals arrive at the monitor desk and then are routed by the monitor desk engineer to the corresponding monitor speaker, or *mix*. Go back and look at the Millions of Americans technical specs in Chapter 3. Look at the input list in the "Technical Specifications"

Figure 6.13 The view of the stage from the monitor board. Note the set list (on the desk)—one day a desk will be built with a space large enough to place a set list without it covering up vital controls!

section of their contract rider, and you will see that I have specified the monitor mixes we require for the band. The mixes correspond to a stage position or an individual musician. Therefore, if the guitarist needs kick drum in his monitor (monitor mix 1 – downstage right), the monitor engineer goes to the kick drum input channel on his desk. He quickly locates the auxiliary control that is routed to mix one and adjusts that control to send more of the kick drum input into mix one.

As you can see, every instrument can be sent to any musician onstage via the monitor desk. The vocalist may want to hear only himself on his monitors, in which case the monitor engineer will send just that vocal input to the center mix. The monitor engineer can also send that same vocal input to any of the other wedges, side fills, or drum fills onstage.

Note: **Monitors from FOH** In a small PA system, such as a bar or club system, the signal will not be split from the stage box to a separate monitor control; the signal goes only to the FOH desk. The engineer can then use auxiliary controls on each input channel to send the signal back to the stage for the musicians. This obviously is not an ideal situation for the FOH engineer—she not only has to mix the instruments for the FOH sound for the audience, but she also has to try to create monitor mixes for the musicians onstage. This is problematic because any adjustments in input gain, EQ, or compression of instrument inputs at the FOH will affect the instrument sound heard by the musicians onstage. This is why the very words "monitors from FOH" on a venue technical specification will often cause dismay for touring engineers and musicians.

Although modern monitor speakers and amps are often capable of superior audio reproduction, they also have limitations. The volume and amount of bass a wedge speaker can produce is obviously no match for the FOH amps and speakers. Please do not expect earth-shattering levels of kick drum or bass guitar from a wedge containing a single 12-inch speaker. Try to think of the wedges as adding definition to the sound already on the stage, not replacing it.

In-Ear Monitors

In-ear monitors (IEMs) are the latest solution to the complex stage monitoring requirements of modern concert touring (see Figure 6.14). Developed in the late 1980s, IEMs were originally conceived by a front-of-house engineer, Chrys Lindop, touring with Stevie Wonder. The idea of IEMs is to replace the bulky floor wedges and side fills with a small wireless device that is worn by the performer. Earpieces connected to the device deliver the monitor mix directly to the ears of the musician; the musician can then adjust the volume of the overall monitor mix himself.

The use of IEMs not only gives control back to the performer, but it also helps to create lower stage volumes and a more immersive experience for the musician wearing the IEMs. The volume the performer needs for his monitor mix is lower in IEM earpieces than the equivalent wedge volume; the mix is more direct and gives more of the audio information the performer requires. The earpieces can be custom-made to fit the ear of the individual performer; therefore, they help to block out all other stage

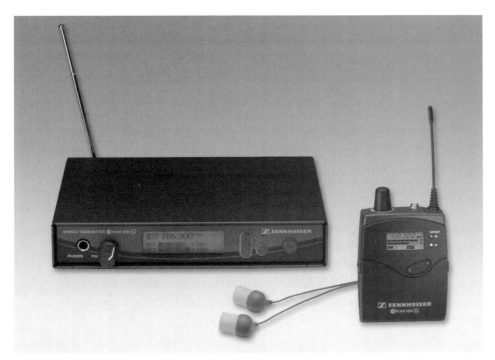

Figure 6.14 A modern IEM belt pack and earpieces (right), shown here with the transmitter unit.

sound. A modern IEM mix is often in stereo, and a good monitor engineer can have a lot of fun setting up a mini-FOH mix for each musician, with stereo reverbs, compression, and all the other FOH tricks!

In practice, the IEM mix is set up just as a wedge mix. The mix outputs of the monitor desk are connected to the IEM transmitter (instead of an amp and a wedge speaker). The transmitter uses UHF technology to broadcast the mix to the performer's belt pack. This is obviously much less hassle than trucking and setting up lots of wedge speakers and amps. In fact, an IEM system for the average four-piece rock band can be flown as hold luggage on almost any airline, ensuring that you have perfect monitor sound at any dodgy festival appearance your agent may have booked you into!

IEMs used to be the preserve of mega-rock stars and multi-million-selling country rock stars. Prices have fallen, though, and technology has improved, making professional-spec IEM systems available to all performers for $275 to $500.

Note: UHF Transmitters and Licenses IEM systems are composed of a transmitter and a receiver. The receiver is worn by the musician (along with the earpieces). Modern wireless microphone systems are also composed of transmitter and receiver; in this case, the microphone is the transmitter. In all cases, the sound is sent via UHF electromagnetic microwaves using set frequencies (between 300 MHz and 3 GHz). These UHF frequencies are also used by TV and in the two-way radios used by the police and emergency services. The allocation of the various frequency bands is very strictly controlled for obvious reasons. You cannot just start cranking your monitor mix on any frequency you want! Therefore, you should check to make sure your equipment is licensed for use. Even though the manufacturer has set pre-installed frequencies within the unit, you still need to have a license to operate. Licensing information is provided by the FCC in the US, by Spectrum Direct in Canada, and by Ofcom in the UK.

Bass players and drummers traditionally like to feel the low end of their instruments onstage. High-quality instrument amplification and huge drum fills can fulfill that desire, but in-ear monitoring systems (coupled with larger stages) have caused problems for monitor crews trying to provide an adequate amount of bass. These technicians obviously want to keep the performers onstage happy, but knowing how excessive low frequencies can ruin a stage sound, they are not keen on pumping massive amounts of bass through the side fills or drum fills.

The answer is thumpers. A bass driver (speaker) is fitted to the drummer's seat/throne/stool. This is connected to the outputs of the monitor desk via a power amp as usual. The kick drum signal is sent to the thumper as a regular monitor mix. However, instead of hearing a monitor wedge or a drum fill, the drummer "feels" the low-end frequencies of his kick drum throughout his entire body. This thumping has the effect of cleaning up any unwanted low end on the stage (and it looks better for the lighting/video crew!). Bass players can feel the same benefit by standing on a small platform with bass drivers fixed underneath it. This kind of direct bass monitoring gives a more precise monitor sound to the musicians.

Note: A Monitor Engineer Speaks Paul Myers, monitor engineer for The Hours, Fun Lovin' Criminals, and Joan Armatrading (among others), says, "Mixing for in-ear monitors is a lot harder for a monitor engineer as it is so precise. But because it is so hard, it actually makes [mixing] easier because you are not relying on the quality of the [monitor wedges] you are given. IEMs really work for bands that are still playing 300- to 1000-capacity venues and cannot afford to take their own sound production with them because they get the same quality of sound in their monitors every night."

Many musicians who have performed for years using wedges are very reluctant—indeed hostile—to the thought of using IEMs. The closeness and detail of the sound coupled with the apparent sense of isolation is disturbing for many musicians who are used to a loud stage sound. My view is that IEMs are very beneficial to a modern performer—the sooner you start to use them, the better.

The Instruments

The instruments of modern music performance are usually thought of as the various physical musical instruments—guitars, drums, keyboards, woodwinds, samplers, brass, and percussion. In my opinion, we also must include the human voice as an instrument.

The following sections are my guide to understanding, care, and maintenance of the basic instruments found on today's concert stage.

Vocals

The voice is the primary means of communication for human beings. In music, the vocal performance often conveys the emotion of the song. Broken instruments can be replaced or mended, but it is very difficult to repair a singing voice that has been damaged through overwork or abuse. As the singer or vocalist, you owe it to yourself to take optimum care of your voice—it is your career and your livelihood.

Most of the voice-related problems I have encountered are caused by the vocal folds (commonly known as the *vocal cords*) being neglected and then overworked. Your vocal cords are two small muscles at the base of your throat that vibrate and create sound when controlled breath is passed through them. Usually, the vocal cords are smooth, without any irregularities on the vibrating borders. Causing the cords to vibrate too hard by shouting, yelling, speaking, or singing too much causes friction, and a "bruise" will develop on the vibrating edge of the cords. Over time, the bruise will be replaced by fibrous tissue, which becomes larger and eventually appears as a soft or hard white nodule.

The symptoms of these nodules, or *nodes,* include a quivering in the voice (especially in the higher registers), hoarseness, an inability to sing high notes, and a breathy or husky speaking voice. The nodules can be corrected by completely resting the voice for two to three weeks and then undertaking training and speech therapy to correct the vocal behavior that caused the nodules in the first place. Surgery may also be necessary in extreme circumstances.

Obviously, with a lot of today's music genres, a rough singing voice and the inability to sing high notes are not a problem—modern rock music almost demands it, for instance. However, continuing to abuse your vocal cords by singing with nodules eventually could lead to laryngeal cancer. Think about your long-term career: Do you still want to be singing in 40 years? If so, then you need to look after your voice now!

My tips to help maintain your voice (and your general health) are:

- Always drink plenty of water! Water is good for the whole body, not just your vocal cords. (Health experts and doctors recommend you drink eight large glasses of water [2 liters] per day.) If you do not drink enough water, your body will dehydrate, and your voice will suffer damage as the cords dry out.

- Always warm up! This is even more appropriate to sound checks in cold, empty venues. You should have a set of warm-up exercises for your voice. Do not strain yourself, though; just get loosened up nicely. My experience tells me 20 minutes of mild breathing, humming, and *la*-ing before sound check and again before the show will keep your vocal folds and your neck muscles in great condition.

- Avoid air-conditioned environments. Put a clause in your hotel requirements that your room should be on a lower floor, where your hotel room windows may be opened. Switch off the A/C on the bus or in the van and open the windows.

- Humidity helps. Inhale steam in a non-humid environment. Portable steam inhalers are now available in any good department store or online. If you cannot afford one, then boil a pot of water on the stove and remove it once boiled. Place your head over the steam and place a towel over your head and the pot. Breathe deeply with the towel still over your head.

- Don't smoke (anything). The middle of a lit cigarette can reach 700° C (or 1292° F); imagine what that temperature will do to your vocal cords! Even if you do not smoke, you may be subject to secondhand smoke from your crew or your fellow band members. Try to avoid this secondhand smoke because it can also dry out your cords.

- Caffeine and alcohol will dry out the protective mucus on your vocal cords, so try to avoid both for at least two hours before the show.

- Rest your voice totally on the day of a performance. Limit all interviews and promotional activities to a total of 20 minutes.

- Do not scream or shout during sound check.

- Work with your monitor engineer to get the best stage monitor sound possible. You are less likely to strain your voice if you can hear yourself and the other instruments clearly onstage. Invest in an IEM system as soon as you can—this will definitely help you to get a good, clean stage monitor sound.

- Don't strain. Change the key of songs if necessary.

- Avoid all dairy products before a show, especially if you have a cold. Colds can produce an excess of mucus; dairy foods have been also been known to produce extra mucus. The two together will have you sneezing, coughing, and spitting in no time!

- Do not use over-the-counter sore-throat sprays. These sprays will numb the pain and lead you to believe you can still sing well, even with a raging sore throat. You will feel less pain after applying one of these sprays, but once the spray has worn off, your throat will feel worse. Also, you will have done even more damage to your vocal folds because you could not feel any pain. You are better off buying a bottle of glycerine instead. This will coat your vocal cords and ease speaking and singing, but it will not disguise any pain you may feel.

Vocal Microphone Technique

Microphone technique describes the art of how to hold your microphone, how to treat it, how to sing into it, and what you should or should not do with your microphone onstage. Good microphone technique gives you years of strain-free singing and reduces the threat of feedback—both major priorities for any touring performer.

How Your Microphone Works and How You Should Hold It

How to hold your microphone—sounds pretty obvious, right? You just kinda pick it up, and there you are, right? Actually, no. Learn how your microphone works, and you will learn how to use it to your full advantage.

Microphones work by converting sound into electrical energy. The sound waves are captured by a very lightweight electrical component called the *diaphragm*. When you sing into the correct end/side of a microphone, you are singing into the diaphragm. You cannot see the diaphragm because it is protected by a mesh or grille.

Figure 6.15 show a Shure SM58 microphone. Although many critics would argue it is not the best microphone in the world, the simple, rugged construction of the SM58 coupled with above-average frequency reproduction makes it almost ubiquitous in modern music concerts. You can see the large round grille; inside is the capsule containing the diaphragm.

Most stage microphones you will encounter in rock touring, such as the SM58, will be the dynamic type (as opposed to condenser, capacitor, electret, or ribbon types). Dynamic microphones are relatively inexpensive, require no electrical power to operate, and are usually built from a few robust parts. A dynamic microphone can survive the odd accidental drop every now and then without suffering too much. This makes dynamic microphones ideal for both budget recording and live

Figure 6.15 The Shure SM58 microphone—the standard of rock touring microphones.

performance. Don't go deliberately throwing or dropping your microphone, though, unless you own it outright and can afford to replace it immediately.

Microphones also have pickup or polar patterns that dictate the amount of sound they will pick up from various directions. An *omni-directional* pickup pattern means the microphone will pick up all sounds from any direction, which is great for natural-sounding outdoor-location film recording, but not so great for miking onstage with guitar amps and drums producing high-level volume.

Pickup patterns for modern stage microphones are usually more selective, only picking up sound from a certain direction. This pickup pattern is known as a *cardioid* type because a graph of the microphone's pickup sensitivity is approximately heart-shaped. You can see these patterns in Figure 6.16.

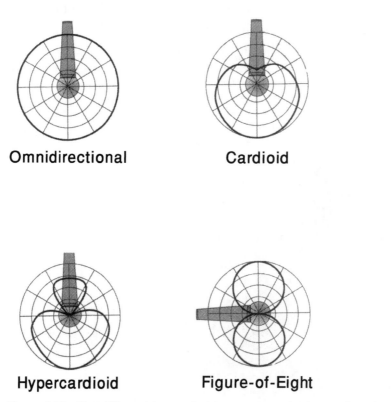

Omnidirectional   **Cardioid**

Hypercardioid   **Figure-of-Eight**

Figure 6.16 The different types of pickup patterns in stage microphones.

You can see from Figure 6.16 that the cardioid pattern picks up most of its sound mainly from the front of the microphone and is less sensitive to sounds from the rear. This makes the cardioid pattern ideal for live music sound reinforcement because placing a cardioid microphone in front of a sound source (Marshall amp, snare drum, vocal, and so on) will result in other stage sounds being excluded by the microphone. This is especially useful for vocal microphones. The sound coming from the monitor wedges on the ground will be directed into the back of the microphone and therefore will not be picked up.

Be careful, though, if your microphone has a hyper- or super-cardioid pickup pattern. As you can see in Figure 6.16, hyper- or super-cardioid microphones are more sensitive to sound sources from directly behind, making their use as vocal microphones dubious in high-monitor-level applications.

That's how a microphone basically works. So how does that help you to hold the darn thing? Well, by knowing about pickup patterns, you will understand what happens if you hold the microphone too close to the grille or you cover it with your hand.

By enclosing the grille (and therefore the capsule) of the microphone in your hand, as shown in Figure 6.17, you will alter the pickup pattern of the microphone. Sound will be funneled into the microphone's diaphragm through the small gap in your hand. The diaphragm, which works by sensing the differences in pressure between the front and back of the capsule, will be confused, and the directional characteristics of the microphone will change. Yes, you will achieve a higher volume from the microphone, but you also will increase the risk of feedback. In fact, feedback is more than likely to occur because you will be boosting the very frequencies that are more likely to be produced in a feedback loop. Instead, hold the microphone halfway down the barrel, making sure that no part of your hand touches the grille.

Microphone Technique
Good microphone technique involves not only handling, but also knowing the correct way to sing into the microphone.

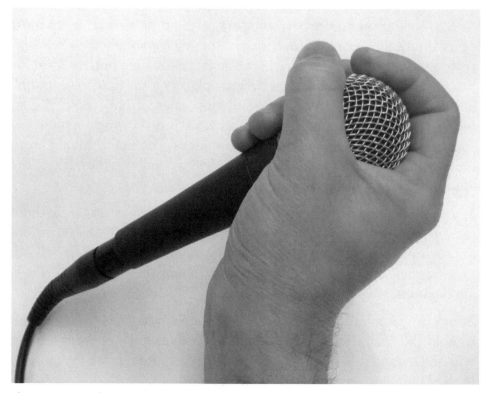

Figure 6.17 Bad microphone technique—do not place your hand on the grille at the end of the microphone!

Look again at Figure 6.16. Imagine trying to get maximum volume for your vocal from the microphone. It makes sense to concentrate most of your power into the part of pickup pattern that will reproduce the most frequencies, which involves singing directly into the front of microphone.

Also, keep an eye on the distance between your microphone and your mouth. Too close, and you run the risk of filling the diaphragm with spit, which will destroy the diaphragm's sensitivity, leading to a muffled sound. Too far, and the reproduction of your voice will be compromised as the microphone starts to pick up stronger sounds from the sides. Ideally, your microphone should be two to three inches from your mouth and not touching your lips.

If your singing performance involves a vast range of volume—such as low mumbling up to emo screaming during the same song—then think about moving your microphone away from your mouth during excessive shouting/screaming parts. This will help keep the perceived volume of your vocal on an even level without compressors. This, in turn, will help your sound engineer to better place your vocal in the mix, as well as prevent damage to the microphone's diaphragm. Take a look at the some of the more established vocalists of our time, such as Frank Sinatra and Aretha Frankin. Observe how each constantly moves his or her microphone away from the mouth during loud vocal passages.

Be careful with excessive microphone movement, though—this can cause a fluctuation in tone. Cardioid microphones have a characteristic called the *proximity effect,* which results in bass frequencies being boosted when the sound source is very close to the microphone's diaphragm. This is very useful for adding a rounded tone to a vocal and can be used for great effect. Obviously, the proximity effect will stop as soon as you move the microphone away from your mouth, causing the tone of your voice to constantly fluctuate. Experiment with the optimum distance between microphone and mouth while trying to avoid fluctuations in tone and volume.

Microphone Care and Maintenance

Never intentionally drop or throw a vocal microphone. The impact will warp and distort the diaphragm, which will reduce the frequency response of the microphone. The resulting sound of impact can also cause system damage to the PA. Microphones are also rather heavy objects and can cause real damage when hurled at audiences or other band members.

The microphones used in modern concert touring, such as the Audix OM series or the Shure SM58, have a detachable grille that protects the microphone's capsule from damage. You can remove this grille and clean it; I strongly recommend you do so as often as you can. Simply unscrew the grille, lift it off the main body of the microphone, soak it in boiling hot water, and dry it thoroughly (with a hairdryer if possible). Put the microphone somewhere safe when you do this—the capsule is now unprotected.

You also can simply spray the grille with a disinfectant spray—again *after* removing the grille from the microphone and storing the microphone safely. (I believe there are some dry-on-contact disinfectants on the market in case you cannot remove the grille from your microphone. However, I have never tried one of these, so I advise caution.)

Tape Up That Cable

Your microphone may become unplugged while you're running around the stage, giving your best performance. This is a common byproduct of a frenzied stage performance, and most vocalists and stage crew resort to simply taping the microphone to the cable, wrapping tape around the end of the microphone and the XLR connector, as shown in Figure 6.18.

Figure 6.18 A bad way to tape up your microphone cable.

Taping up the microphone in this way will certainly prevent the two from becoming detached, but what happens if either the microphone or the cable stops working during the show? The two are now bound together with duct/gaffer tape, which is extremely strong in the first place and gets stronger the more tension you put on it? I have witnessed many a road crew trying to separate a microphone from a defunct cable onstage, during a song, and in a hurry. Not many of those crews were successful!

To avoid this, do not tape the microphone directly to the XLR connector. Instead, lay the cable along the body of the microphone with the connector pointing away from the grille (see Figure 6.19).

While holding the two tightly, pull enough cable downward that you can snap the XLR connector into the bottom of the microphone (see Figure 6.20). Allow a tiny amount of slack, and then place *one* wrap of duct/gaffer tape around the cable and the body of the microphone (see Figure 6.21).

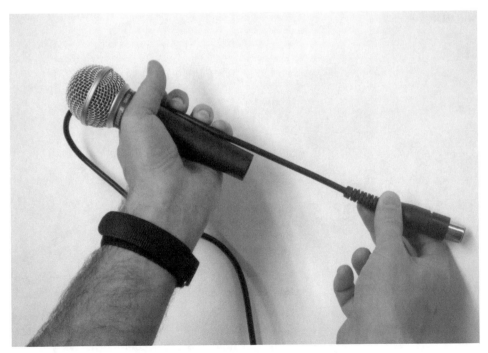

Figure 6.19 Prepare the cable against the microphone body.

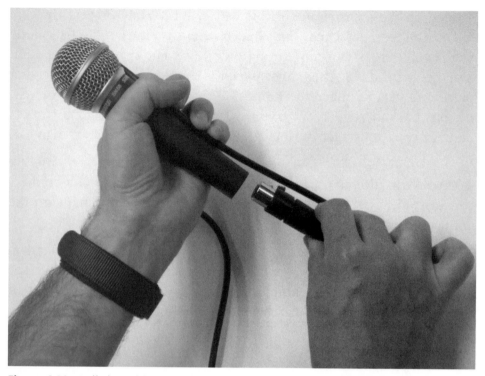

Figure 6.20 Pull the cable away from the grille to give you enough slack to connect the XLR.

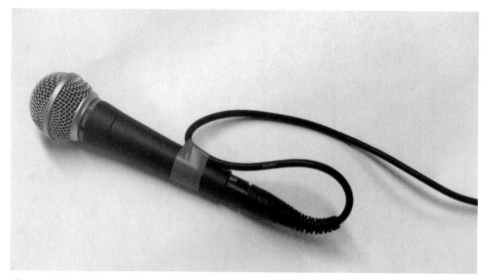

Figure 6.21 Wrap gaffer or PVC tape to hold the cable against the body of the microphone.

If the microphone becomes wet or damaged, you can simply discon-nect from the cable and pop another microphone onto that same line. Yes, you will have the original broken microphone dangling, but at least the vocal will still be going down the same channel (with all the EQ, dynamics, monitor levels, and effects still in place).

If the cable fails, you can simply disconnect the microphone from the cable and cut through one wrap of duct/gaffer tape to free the micro-phone. Then pop the microphone onto a spare cable (a *line*), and you will be set to go. This is far better than struggling with ever-tightening duct/gaffer tape!

Obviously, the total pro approach is to have a spare microphone specified on your technical rider's input list. (See Figure 3.4 in Chapter 3.) This should be an identical microphone to the main vocal microphone and should be sound checked, EQ'd, and in easy reach of the vocalist and/or the monitor engineer (see Figure 6.22). You still may have to tape the microphone up, though, depending on the vocalist's performance style.

Figure 6.22 A spare microphone, tested and placed downstage between the wedges.

Guitars and Basses

You or someone in your band probably plays the guitar. You probably know that there are many books, magazines, and websites out there dedicated to guitar playing, but I would like to share with you some hints and tips about how to select and use your guitar on the road.

Types

My number one piece of advice is to think about the style or genre of music you are attempting to play and pick the right guitar or bass. At the moment, you may be learning on a guitar or starting to work together as a band, but your instrument may not suit the type of music you are creating.

You may be going for some genre-defying new form of music, but if you are basically working in a certain accepted music type, then perhaps you should follow tried-and-true methods. Certain combinations of guitars and amplifiers work better for certain modern production sounds, so do your research. Look at your favorite players in that genre and emulate their gear.

Table 6.3 details some examples of famous guitars and their respective genres.

Note that amplification is needed in the case of the Fenders, Gibson, Rickenbacker, and Jackson because they are solid-bodied electric guitars/basses.

Guitars: Care and Maintenance

Your success and fortune depends on your guitar or bass, and you expect that hunk of steel and wood to be playable night after night. However, modern touring can be pretty rough on equipment and people alike; you should learn how to make sure your instrument will be in perfect condition, no matter what the schedule might be.

Case. Get a case for your instrument when you buy it! I have seen too many guitars wrapped in towels, T-shirts, or thin air rolling around in the back of vans. And guess what? You get to the next show, and your guitar has no neck!

Table 6.3 Famous Guitars and Genres

Guitar Make and Model	Type	Musical Application
Martin Dreadnought	Acoustic	Jazz, folk, country and western, alt-country
Takamine G series	Electro acoustic	Jazz, folk-rock, country and western, alt-country
Fender Stratocaster	Electric	Blues, light rock, country and western, indie, new wave
Gibson Les Paul	Electric	Heavy blues, heavy rock, jazz
Fender Telecaster	Electric	Country and western, indie, rhythm and blues, new wave, alt-country
Jackson/Charvel	Electric	Heavy rock and metal
Fender Precision	Electric bass	Jazz, blues, rock, country and western
Rickenbacker 4003	Electric bass	Rock, new wave

Buy a case for your guitar, even if it is a padded gig-bag. Better still are the hard fiberboard cases sold by most guitar shops. This is a vital investment for touring.

You should invest in a full-flight case when you start to do serious traveling involving vans, trucks, and crew (see Figure 6.23). Sorry to say that other people will not treat your prize "axe" as well as you do, even the crew you pay. Big, heavy, and expensive flight cases will protect your guitar totally for life on the road. Don't throw away that old gig-bag, though—it will be very useful for getting your guitar up to your hotel room after the show!

Strap Locks. Earlier I told you about microphones and their cables getting separated during a concert performance. Well, I am sure you are also familiar with guitars/basses falling off their straps. It can be embarrassing (at best) and expensive (at worst) when this happens, so don't let it happen! Buy some good-quality strap locks for *all* the guitars you will be taking on tour. Make sure you buy the same type of

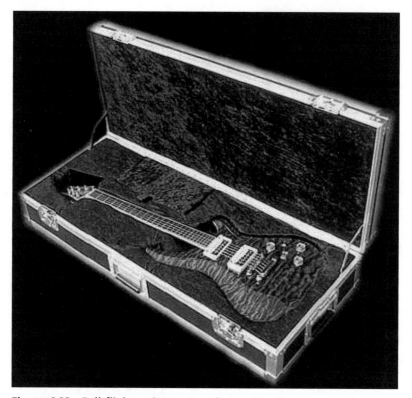

Figure 6.23 Full-flight guitar cases. They are really heavy, so buy one only when you can employ a backline tech!

system for each guitar, so you will be able to keep wearing your favorite strap and swap guitars.

Note: Stinky Straps Leather and cloth guitar straps absorb sweat. Sweat smells after it dries, and after a good two- to three-week tour, your strap will smell really bad. That smell will permeate your guitar case as well your nicely cleaned stage wear. To prevent this, you should buy nylon washable straps and wipe them down after each performance, washing them thoroughly in clean, hot water after every five to six shows.

Wrap Your Cables. While on the subject of guitars, straps, and cables, make sure you get in the habit of threading your guitar cord through your strap to prevent it from pulling out of the jack socket (see Figure 6.24).

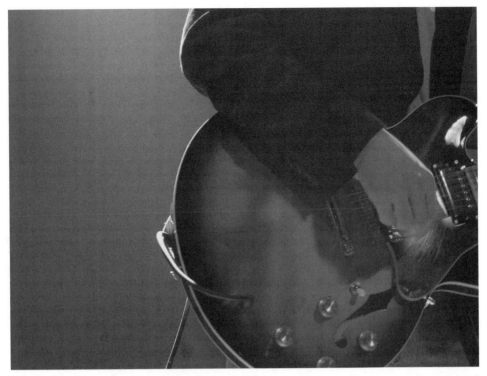

Figure 6.24 Pass your guitar cable inside your strap and then plug it into the output of the guitar. The cable is now supported, and this lack of tension will help to prevent the cable from being disconnected during your performance.

Transmitters. Using a UHF wireless guitar system (see the "In-Ear Monitors" section earlier in this chapter for an explanation on UHF transmitters and receivers) obviously frees you from the peril of your guitar cables becoming snagged or disconnected. To recap, the guitar signal goes straight from your guitar, via a short cable, into a transmitter that sends the signal to the receiver, which is plugged into the input on your amplifier. The transmitter can be put in your back pocket or, better still, fixed to your guitar strap (see Figure 6.25).

Problems arise when you and your strap get sweaty. The sweat can find its way into the transmitter pack, causing it to short-circuit and stop working. I have some pretty ingenious ways of preventing this from happening. Positioning the transmitter high up the strap, so it sits on the user's shoulder when worn, can work well but looks unsightly. The modern touring consensus is to have the transmitter right down at the bottom of the strap, in a place where the strap has no contact with body.

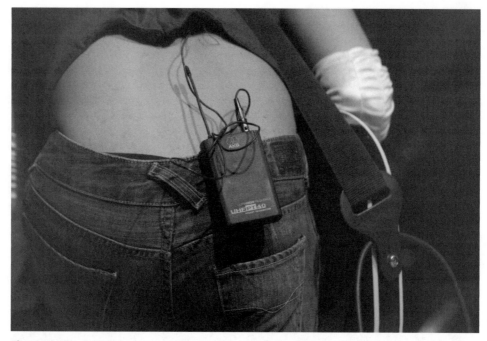

Figure 6.25 A UHF instrument transmitter pack, in this case for guitar.

I have also seen transmitter packs (and other items of gear) wrapped in toweling or sweatbands to prevent sweat from entering the unit. Think about this, though. Toweling is designed to absorb water/sweat. It then holds that water within the cloth. If that cloth is wrapped around your delicate transmitter, you run a greater risk of the sweat getting into your unit!

Strings. Another sweat-related problem: Human sweat can corrode (oxidize) and possibly dissolve metal surfaces with which it come into direct contact. This includes your guitar strings! Your fingers and your picking/plectrum hand will leave sweat on the strings, which will corrode them and cause their tone to dull. You may have the budget to change strings for every show on your tour, so you may not be concerned about this. However, the sweat left on the strings after the show will run onto the tuning pegs, bridge, and saddle of the guitar, potentially corroding them as well. Unless you want to remove the strings after every show, you should always wipe down your guitar strings thoroughly after performing, preferably with a lint-free cloth. Pinch the cloth in your fingers and then run your fingers up and down each string in turn.

Strings also become dull in tone due to the buildup of dirt and skin particles. Wiping them clean (as mentioned a moment ago) is a great preventative move if you are more budget conscious. Many guitarists—and especially bassists—also advocate boiling strings periodically to restore tone and brilliance. In my experience, I find this does restore some tone, but the restoration does not last. You will get maybe two to three days of playing before the strings will lose their tone again.

As I mentioned in Chapter 4, you should consider buying your strings in bulk. The initial outlay will be great, but your cost savings per string/packet will significantly outweigh the hassle of having to boil strings to keep your tone!

Transporting Your Guitar

As well as being your passport to success, your guitar (or bass) is your pride and joy. Have you considered what will happen to your instrument when you start to tour extensively and perhaps employ a road crew to take care of your stage equipment? How will it travel?

Vans and Trucks. Guitars in cases are small, thin packages that you can wedge into all sorts of spaces when packing your van or tour truck. The danger is that your guitar will then be placed upside down or resting neck down. For a one-off journey this will not be so bad, but after a two- to three-week tour in cold temperatures, you may start to experience tuning stability problems (or worse).

Avoid ground transportation problems by clearly marking your guitar case, using white gaffer/duct tape, with "Top" and "This Way Up." If you are not responsible for packing the truck, then explain your concern to the crew and ask them to observe the instructions of your labeling.

Airplanes. Unless you can afford to buy a seat for your guitar, you will have to place it in the hold of the aircraft when you fly. A non-pressurized hold can reach a low of $-40°$ F. At that temperature, the metal parts of your guitar will contract. The strings, being thin, will contract more then the truss rod or the wooden neck. This puts an enormous strain on the neck, so always loosen the strings of your guitar or bass before putting it into the hold.

Amplifiers and Speakers

While on tour, I constantly see mistakes and misunderstandings regarding guitar amplifiers. The following sections detail the most common ones.

Resistance, Impedance, and Ohm's Law

Stay with me; we have a bit of math here. Ohm's Law states $V = I \times R$, where V is voltage, I is current, and R is resistance. We'll deal with resistance here as it concerns the relationship between your guitar amp and the speaker cabinet. If your guitar or bass amp is of the combo type (the amplifier and speaker are housed in the same box), you really do not have to worry about Ohm's Law. If you have a separate guitar head (amplifier) and speakers, then you should get a grip on Ohm's Law.

The speakers in a cabinet offer an electrical resistance, known as *impedance,* to the outputs of your amplifier. This impededance is measured in ohms; most speakers offer resistance at 8 ohms. The outputs of your amp are rated in ohms, specifying the impedance load at which the amp can operate—for example, this amp can deliver 100 watts at 8 ohms. Amplifiers are designed to work best at specified impedance; the amp and speakers should operate at the same ohms. An impedance mismatch in an amp can result in damage to the amp; it may even burn up.

So how does this affect you in practice? In a standard amp and cab setup, the output of the amp will match the impedance settings of the cabinet—in other words, the amp will be rated as delivering 100 watts at 8 ohms. No problems there. Suppose, however, that you are opening for another band and you agree to use their cabinets, saving you having to truck your own cabinets. How do you know your amplifier will be suitable for the cabinet you are borrowing?

Most amplifier heads offer different ohm outputs, and in modern guitar cabinets there are only three real possible choices of impedance—4 ohms, 8 ohms, or 16 ohms. If you are using a single cabinet, it is pretty obvious that the amp should be set to the same impedance as the cabinet—for example, 4 ohms for a 4-ohm cabinet, 8 ohms for an 8-ohm cabinet, and so on.

If you are using two cabinets of the same impedance, you divide the impedance of one cabinet by the number of cabinets being used. So for two 8-ohm cabinets, you would set the amp to 4 ohms; for two 16-ohm cabinets, you would set the amp to 8 ohms.

Another common situation would be two cabinets rated with different impedances, such as one 16-ohm cabinet and one 8-ohm cabinet. In this case, you should set your amp to 4 ohms. Always try to switch your amp to half the value of the cabinet with the lowest impedance. The impedance should be correctly matched because it is vital to the correct and safe working of any amplifier.

Tone

Another common problem is the inability or lack of understanding about how to recreate the fabulous guitar tones of your musical heroes. It is true that with digital "modeling" amplifiers, you can get almost any sound out of any guitar, but, as I mentioned in the section about choosing the right type of guitar in this chapter, you should really do some research to establish which amp/speaker combination suits the musical genre in which you are involved.

Relying on awesome digital effects or modeling will not help you if the final output stage, your amplifier, is underpowered or unsuited to creating the tones you need. A 4×12 cabinet will physically push a lot more air than a 1×12 combo amp. Even if you can recreate the sound (distortion and so on) of the tone you are looking for with digital effects, the sheer lack of power of a small amp will still mean that your sound will not be right.

EQ

Setting the guitar/bass amplifier EQ for playing live is crucial to obtaining a good sound. Remember that every tweak you make to the EQ will be accentuated by the PA system, possibly to the detriment of your sound.

When setting your EQ and tone, make sure your ears are directly in line with the speaker cabinet. Many guitarists set their EQ with the amplifier on the floor and the sound projecting into their knees! Obviously, you are not going to hear a lot of definition from the cabinet if it is pointing at your knees; the tendency then is to add more high mids and treble to brighten the sound. Now put a microphone in front of this cabinet, run it through a large PA system, and imagine the results. That's right; the sound will be excessively bright, almost painful at high volumes.

Bass players make the same mistake with low-frequency boosting. In a cold, empty venue your bass tone will sound slightly weak. (See Chapter 7, "At the Show," for a full explanation.) Again, the tendency is to boost the low end to compensate for this apparent thinness. However, then the bass frequencies will be further accentuated by the PA system. As well as leading to an indistinct or wooly sound, you face further problems as all that extra bass rolls around the stage, being picked up by all the other microphones.

My advice is to put your cabinet up high or, failing that, leaning back with the speakers pointing toward your ears (see Figure 6.26).

Figure 6.26 A typical guitar rig. The two Fender Twin amps are placed as high as possible on upturned flight case lids. The Ampeg bass rig is placed right next to the guitar amp—maybe too close? And, despite my warnings, someone has placed three cans of soda on the bass amp head!

If you play bass, try to place bass cabs as far back as possible or stand as far in front of them as possible. Get your body and your ears in line with the speakers, and then begin to listen to your tone and EQ. This is so important and something I cannot stress enough: Your ears have to be in line with the speakers! That way you can accurately judge the EQ and the volume of your rig.

Always remember, an amp on the ground will fire directly into the face of the audience. It may not seem loud to you, but it will be pretty darn loud to anyone standing in front of it!

Avoid over-EQing your sound; remember, the PA will accentuate the highs and lows of your sound (see Figure 6.27). I always make sure all the guitar amps onstage have there EQ in a "flat" (i.e. not boosted and not cut) position. If I am setting up the equipment for a bass player will I actually "roll off" (decrease) the bass frequencies on the amplifier; I find it tightens up the stage sound and the FOH engineer can always add the bass back using EQ from the DI box on the bass.

Figure 6.27   The EQ settings on a guitar amp. Notice they are all fairly flat—there is no excessive cut or boost.

Note: DI Box for Bass It is a convention of modern live sound engineering that electric bass guitars are reproduced through the PA by both a microphone and a DI (*Direct Injection*) box. The microphone is used to capture the amplified sound from the cabinet. The DI is used to take the natural sound (well, the sound from the output of the pickups) of the bass. The microphone and the DI sources are then mixed together by the FOH engineer to create a smooth but powerful bass sound. (The two inputs are put out of phase with each other to prevent the frequencies being cancelled out.)

If you are a bass player, you may not have come across this technique before, and setting up a DI box with your rig may confuse you slightly. Don't worry, though–this is how it works. The DI box basically splits the signal from your bass guitar; one signal is sent, via XLR cable, to the stage box or mixing desk, and the other is sent via a "link" lead to the input of your bass amp as normal. You simply plug your bass into the input on the DI box and make sure the link cable goes into your bass amp or the input of your effects chain, tuner, or whatever.

Amplifier Spares

Once you have purchased an amplifier you are totally happy with, then spend a little time and money making sure your rig is in disaster-proof condition.

Fuses and Tubes/Valves. Check the manufacturer's user guide and the back panel of the amplifier and note the type and rating of all the internal and external fuses. (This includes any fuses in the power supply or power cables.) The internal fuses are especially important. Also, check the type and number of any tubes/valves the amplifier may use. Purchase as many of the fuses as you can afford and try to buy at least one replacement valve. Keep all these spares in some kind of cushioned box and carry it with you on tour.

Allow tubes time to cool down before moving. This especially true if the amp will go straight from a hot stage into a cold truck and will be bounced about all night. Try to leave moving the amplifier until the last possible moment. (This is difficult, I know, with local crew herding you off the stage!).

Power Cables. Power cables fail—sometimes the fuse in the plug will blow; sometimes the strains and stresses on the cable will cause metal fatigue in the copper conductors. Whatever the reason, your mains power cable failing is the most common cause of your amp not working while on tour. I have seen many a guitar amp in pieces during sound check, only for the poor tech to discover a faulty power cable or fuse!

Get in the habit of checking the internal connections of the plug on your power cable and keep a good supply of (correctly rated) fuses. Make sure all the screws in the plug are tight and that strands of conductors are not touching other metal parts. Finally, buy a spare power cable, make sure it works, and carry it with you. (Detachable mains power cables are called *IEC cables,* not "kettle leads." Please!)

Audio Cables. The weakest connections in your audio signal chain will be between your instrument and your amplifier and between your amp and its speakers. Consider upgrading these cables to higher-quality cables and connectors as soon as possible. Look for Van Damme, Klotz, or Monster cable and Neutrik connectors. You can buy these cables premade in a pack or, if you really want to learn a skill and save a ton of money, you can make cables yourself. To do this, you need to learn to solder (see the following section for more on this) and buy the components. Buying a reel of good-quality cable and the connectors is fairly expensive, but it will allow you to create custom-length cables, repair old cables, and sell pre-made cable to your band mates!

Learn to Solder

Soldering is not difficult, it just takes practice. Learning to solder means being able to make your own guitar and speaker cables and, more importantly, repairing connections in amplifiers, foot pedals, and electric instruments.

There is a bewildering array of soldering equipment on the market, but for on-the-road use, you basically only need a simple electric "iron." Do not buy a so-called "soldering gun"; these are high-voltage machines for use in other specialized tasks. Look for a kit that contains an electric soldering iron rated between 25–50 watts, a stand, some solder, and maybe replacement tips for the iron. Another really handy purchase is one of those "helping hand" tools used by jewelers and hobbyists to hold tiny parts.

Soldering is basically creating an electrical connection between two metal parts by attaching them together with a third metal part—the solder. It follows that the better the soldering, the better the connection. The solder itself is an alloy (mixture) of tin and lead, typically 60-percent tin and 40-percent lead, which melts at a temperature of about 200° C. (Lead is poisonous, and you should always wash your hands after using solder.) Solder comes in the form of thin, very pliable wire.

To make a simple guitar cord, you need to prepare the guitar cable and the two 1/4-inch (or *jack*) connectors. The cable used for a guitar cable contains two conductors running the length of the cable—one that carries the cable and one that acts as a conductive "screen." The screen conductor has either a braided or an aluminum covering. In both cases, you need to prepare the ends of the conductors by stripping away any covering to reveal about 3mm of bare wire.

The conductors then need to be joined to the appropriate part of each of the jack connectors, which are the tip and the screen (see Figure 6.28).

Figure 6.28 The tip and screen connectors of the guitar jack with the guitar cable.

Heat up the soldering iron, unscrew the barrel of the connectors, and push them onto the cable. Once the connector has been soldered to the cable, you will not be able to get the barrel on again, so do it now!

You now need to "tin" the ends of the connectors and the conductors. *Tinning* coats or fills the wires or connector contacts with solder so you can easily melt them together. To tin a wire, apply the tip of your iron to the wire (or connector) for a second or two and then apply the solder to the wire. The solder should flow freely onto the wire and coat it. Be careful not to overheat the wire, because the insulation will start to melt. Once you have tinned both parts, you are ready to solder them together.

The trick to making a good solder joint is that less is more—less heat, less solder. You want just enough heat for the solder to wet the surface, but not enough to damage components. Hold the wire onto the appropriate connector and apply the iron. It is important to hold the pieces of the connection completely still while the solder cools. Any movement can cause a poor solder joint. It only takes a few moments for the iron tip to heat the components so that the solder flows evenly over the metal. A cold solder joint is dull and has a crusty or crystalline appearance. A good solder joint is shiny, smooth, and strong.

Once you have made the joint, you should inspect it and try to avoid the urge to blow on it—this causes impurities to adhere to the cooling solder. The good thing about soldering is that you can easily undo a joint by simply heating up the solder and gently pulling the cable from the connector.

If all looks good with both joints, then locate the barrel of the connector and screw it back on.

As I said, soldering is not difficult, but it does take some practice. Start with broken cables and connectors and see whether you can repair them!

Drums

Although drumming is considered by many people the most rudimentary of musical skills ("Hey, you hit things for a living?"), modern drum manufacturers definitely have kept abreast of technology, both in the manufacturing of the shells and hardware and also in the application of electronics, such as samplers and triggering devices. The following sections describe some tried-and-tested drum hints and tips.

Cases

Yes, I know, I'm off on my case rant again. Drum shells are pretty delicate, despite the fact that you hit them to make a sound, and they can be subject to warping when dropped unless they are well protected. This warping makes it difficult to fit a head (skin) onto the shell and even more difficult to tension the head correctly. A badly tensioned head will constantly sound wrong, producing unwanted overtones and ringing.

On a health and safety note, dropped or damaged shells can splinter very badly. Get some good cases, especially for your hardware (also known as *traps*).

When you start to tour in larger venues, you or your crew may be tempted to invest in an all-in-one drum trunk that will hold all your shells, snares, and cymbals in one massive case on wheels. These cases are great for packing into trucks and pushing in and out of arenas, but they are an absolute pain in the butt for anything else. Suppose you are doing some TV show or radio session or you are simply trying to store your drums. Is there really going to be enough room for this monstrous case?

I once worked for a band whose drummer invested in a custom-built case, and it was a problem everywhere we went. It was so big that two blokes could lie on it side by side; it was like a king-sized bed! And because it contained all his shells, cymbals, and hardware, it also weighed a ton. The crew had to take all the drums out of the trunk and carry them into the venue at nearly every show on tour, leaving the trunk sitting by the side of the truck. Drum trunks—waste of space and money!

Heads

The sound of the drum is a combination of the resonance of the drum shell and the tone of the head when it is struck. You should buy drums based on the sound of the resonance of the shells, but remember that your choice of head and the tuning of that head will alter the overall impact of the most resonant shells.

I have heard and seen some pretty interesting tuning methods for drum heads over the years. All these theories and methods just go to show that there is no hard and fast rule about changing and tuning drum heads. As in anything involved with music, the most useful tool is your ears. Do your research and find out what your favourite players use to get their sound. Use your ears when experimenting, and remember that the sound of your drums will project out to other people in the room. What sounds good to you may not sit well with the tones of the other instruments.

Cymbals

As with drum shells, there is some irony in the fact that, despite being huge lumps of metal that you hit, cymbals are quite delicate and do not travel well. Lack of tone and even cracking will occur if you do not store your cymbals properly while on tour.

Cymbals get quite warm under hot stage lights. Give them time to cool down before slinging them into a cold truck.

Keep the plastic bags in which your cymbals were packaged; place each cymbal in its own bag before putting it back into the case. This will prevent the cymbals from rubbing together during transit, which may rub off any coating.

Put your cymbals in the passenger compartment of your van or in the bus, not in the trailer or the hold. The extreme temperatures in the hold or truck will cause metal fatigue, which will exacerbate cracking.

To clean or not to clean—the jury is out on this one, but, as with guitar strings, I would advocate wiping down the cymbals with a dry, lint-free cloth as soon as possible after the show. Try to handle the cymbals with that same cloth when you pack them away.

Hardware

The hardware of your drum kit—the stands, pedals, and clamps—should last for years if cared for properly. Heed my advice about metal fatigue, though: Hardware is subject to the same heat stresses as your cymbals. Buy a proper hard-shell hardware case and line it with blankets or cushions. The aim is to minimize the stands banging against each other during transit.

Do not tighten the locks when packing up your hardware—at least not to show setup standards. Simply collapse the stand and leave the locks at very loose finger-tightness—it is a massive waste of time and effort to tighten them all the way up and then un-tighten them when you next set up.

Seat

Invest in the best drum seat or stool (also known as a *throne*) you can. Although you will not actually spend that much time sitting on the seat (one hour for sound check and 90 minutes maximum for the show per day), the time you do spend on the stool involves fairly extreme physical conditions. You may not agree that you are experiencing extreme physical conditions, but think about every show you play. Chances are you will be playing under hot stage lights, your body will be confined to a stooped or slouched position, and you will be subjected to high sound volumes. Your body, and especially your back, will be subject to strain, so don't you think you should take care of yourself?

Invest in a stool that will support your backside and the tops of your thighs properly. Make sure it has plenty of padding, it is stable (in other words, it does not wobble around when you play), and preferably it has a backrest. When you found the ideal stool, adjust the height of seat so that your thighs are parallel to the floor. Learn not to slouch by training yourself to keep your back pressed against the backrest. Back pain is a drummer's most common enemy; don't let it happen to you!

Drum Carpet

Modern drummers need a drum carpet—a piece of fabric placed on the stage on which the drummer places his kit. Basically, a drum carpet stops the various drums and stands from sliding away from the drummer during the show. I have toured for nearly 20 years now. I have probably spent half of that time either asking venues whether they have a carpet we can borrow or arranging to buy drum carpets. I don't know what it is, but we touring people just do not seem to be able to retain the information in our brains and remember that the drummer needs a drum carpet!

With this in mind, it is probably not worth spending a lot of your money on the more professional drum carpets out there. All you need is some fairly heavy dark carpet, preferably with a foam-type backing. Office carpet is fantastic and can be bought off the roll for next to nothing. The foam backing will stick to almost any stage, and the surface will give ample hold for the drum and cymbal stands.

Computers, Electronic Keyboards, and Samplers

I have grouped computer, electronic keyboards, and samplers together because for me (and for most touring people), they simply scream "backup!"

I mentioned backup and alternative methods of getting the show together in Chapter 5, but it is worth repeating here: Make sure you have reliable and tested backup for your data, songs, and sounds! You can buy a 2-GB USB memory stick for $50 or less. There are online backup services for computers, and a CD-R costs a couple of cents. There is simply no excuse for not backing up your data!

Once your data is backed up, make sure you can restore from the backup and that you make copies of it. Give one copy of the backup to another (reliable) member of the tour party and keep the other copy away from the device to which it pertains. (If the bus burns up, you do not want the original device and the backup to both be on it, do you?)

Here are my other hints and tips for computers, electronic keyboards, and samplers:

- As soon as you can afford it, buy or rent a UPS (*uninterruptible power supply*) unit. In the case of mains power failure, a UPS unit will provide power to anything that is plugged into it.

  Typically, a loss of power onstage will cause all devices to turn off instantly. Of course, many modern music devices, such as hard disk–based computer systems and samplers, require a proper shutdown procedure to protect the hard drive. If the power just fails, then damage to the hard drive may occur. Other devices will also suffer, especially if there is an intermittent flickering or surge of the mains power; this is common at outdoor festivals, where power is supplied by portable generators.

A UPS will continue to provide power for a time period limited by the capacity of the device. Most UPS units also incorporate some kind of mains-power surge protection. Look for a unit specified for home computer use. These will typically give you 10 to 20 minutes of electricity after the main power has gone—more than enough time to safely back up and power down your rig.

■ Always disconnect mains extension cables and external power supplies units (also known as PSU or "wall warts") from your computer, sampler, or keyboard before you plug into the stage power. I have seen and heard some pretty impressive—and ultimately expensive—bangs when gear has been plugged into the mains power. More often than not, the mains cable or external power supply is at fault, caused by a short circuit, water damage, or another problem. Nonetheless, if a cable or PSU fails, it will probably take out the computer, sampler, or whatever else is connected to it. Get in the habit of connecting power cables and external PSUs first, and then plug into the appropriate device.

Turntables and DJs

DJs and turntablists are common parts of any modern concert, either as part of the band or by supplying warm-up/support music (see Figure 6.29). However, a turntable setup can still cause problems at a show or festival for a variety of reasons. Turntablists and DJs have pretty bad reputations among most touring sound crew—the common perception among crews is that turntablists and DJs are ill prepared and ignorant. Prove that you are different by following my advice.

Headphones

Carry your own headphones! It sounds obvious, but I would not be stating the fact unless I had to. You need headphones to DJ properly, but many DJs have turned up without headphones as support acts or at festivals I have worked on, and they then ask to borrow some! As well

Figure 6.29   A DJ is a common sight in modern bands.

as being completely unprofessional, asking to borrow some headphones assumes there will be some available. What if no one has headphones to lend you? In any case, most touring sound engineers (myself
included) refuse to lend headphones to DJs.

Mixer

Buy a mixer with XLR outputs. It will save you and the sound crew
time and effort. If you cannot afford a mixer with XLR outputs, then
buy some RCA (phono) to 1/4-inch jack cables and connect those to
the mixer outputs. Then the sound crew will only have to connect DI
boxes to your 1/4-inch cables. This saves a bit of time and, more
importantly, it shows you are trying to work with them to achieve a
professional result.

Mixer Levels

It is the oldest trick in the book: You start with your levels low on your
mixer during sound check, let the FOH engineer set a nice loud level
for you, and then you crank your mixer level right up for your set. This

makes you sound really loud and impressive, right? Actually, no. Sound crews are extremely knowledgeable about this trick, so they will always insert a compressor over your mixer output channels. (See an explanation about compression earlier in the "PA Systems: A Very Basic Guide" section of this chapter.) The more you increase your level, the more the compressor will limit the output. It does not matter how much you turn up; the volume will remain the same. What will happen, though, is that the compressor will remove all the dynamics from the record, squashing everything into a stodgy mess. You will also distort the inputs on the FOH and monitor desks. The end result is that you will not sound loud and impressive—just the opposite, in fact.

Work with your engineers during sound check. Set the output levels of your desk at one notch below maximum, and set the input gain for each deck or CD so it is not distorting—in other words, it is not in the red zone on your meters. (Figure 6.30 shows the input level meters of a modern mixer.) Then ask the engineer to set your stage volume. If

Figure 6.30 A modern DJ mixer. The input levels can clearly be seen at the top of the unit.

you need it louder in your wedge, ask, and she will turn it up for you. The audio quality will be preserved, and you will definitely sound loud and impressive.

Bass Feedback

Bass feedback for turntablists is always problematic. It is caused by the bass frequencies being picked up by the needle cartridge and amplified back into the PA system or monitors. This feedback is usually at about 80 to 110 Hz. Most DJs will panic and turn down their levels until the feedback goes away, but there are several more precise ways to combat the problem. First, avoid excessive EQ and gain. Do not crank the bass controls on your mixer and set your gains so they are not showing red on your meters. Have all the tone controls set flat—in other words, not boosted and not cut. Remember, less is more.

Work with the monitor engineer to cut out the most common frequency, such as 100 Hz in your monitor wedge or fill. Place the monitor on a case or stand so it is nearer to your ears, and make sure the wedge is not touching any part of the DJ table or stand.

Make sure the turntable is as isolated from bass frequencies as possible. I have seen a variety of methods of doing this—foam under the turntables, tennis or squash balls cut in half under the turntables, and even suspended turntables. I personally always use two paving slabs under each turntable. It is a major pain to tour with a bunch of paving slabs, but I very rarely get bass feedback from my touring turntablists.

Ears

I have saved the most valuable and important instrument until last— your ears. True, ears do not actually make any sound, but without your hearing it will be difficult to create or appreciate music. (I know Beethoven was deaf, but I am sure he would have preferred not to be— genius or not.) Look after your hearing. Invest in some good musician-friendly hearing protection. All good musical instrument shops sell inexpensive earplugs. If you cannot afford rated hearing protection, then at least buy a pack of disposable foam plugs. I recommend the type shown in Figure 6.31. (Do not get the wax-based ones. They are basically a ball of wax. I don't know about you, but I really do not need to put more

Figure 6.31   Disposable earplugs—get some now!

wax in my ears.) Make yourself wear your hearing protection at rehearsals, in performance, and when going to other concerts or nightclubs.

Excessive volume helps to cause adrenaline in human beings. The adrenaline makes you excited and gives you the buzz of playing onstage. Many musicians complain that hearing defenders cut down the excitement they feel onstage. Get into the habit of putting in your plugs at least 20 minutes before starting rehearsals or your show. This will help you get used to the change in volume and will stop you from taking the plugs out because you don't feel the buzz.

7   At the Show

"Leave rock-star attitudes at home and listen to the in-house engineers; it's their job to help you. And don't overplay."

—Neil Campbell, promoter

Remember me telling you that I used to be in bands myself? Well, a couple of those bands did quite well, and one in particular had a great manager who got us onto some pretty impressive opening slots.

I will never forget the weeks of anticipation following the announcement that we had one of these fantastic opening shows. My band mates and I spent hours and hours re-recording our cassette backing tracks, discussing our stage moves, and posing in the rehearsal room. (Hey, it *was* the '80s!) The sense of excitement and possibility filled my every waking hour: "We are opening up for [*insert name of über-selling indie/alternative band here*]! The crowd will love us, and we are going to get signed to MegaGlobal Records for a million quid!" All I could think about was a huge stage to perform on and a room full of people who were ready to be entertained and impressed.

Notice my thoughts were not full of sound specifications, lighting plots, parking, and stage curfew times. Did it matter? Oh boy, did it ever matter!

As a band, we had no concept of how a show works—the whole mechanism of line checks, sound checks, and so on. I remember turning up late at one of London's premier large-capacity music venues and immediately being hassled by a big sweaty bloke dressed in black, requesting information about our setup, input list, and monitor requirements. I mean, what the…?

BIG SWEATY BLOKE DRESSED IN BLACK (A.K.A. **BSBDIB**): Spike, house sound crew. You're late. You got an input list for me?

Us: A what?

BSBDIB: Input list. Y'know, what you got? Drums, bass, guitars, and vocals—that kind of thing. You got one, or you just wanna tell me what you got?

Us: Well, there's the cassette player, and then Leslie, sings and...

BSBDIB: Whoa. Stop right there. Cassette machine. Is it on XLR or jacks?

Us: Er, um, wait a minute...er, I, well, that is....

BSBDIB: Jesus H. *Big sweaty bloke dressed in black stomps off. Returns 10 minutes later.*

BSBDIB: I've looked at the multi, and you got eight channels left. You reckon you can fit it in that? I ain't got time to p**s about, so that's it.

Us: Er, multi? Channels? Er, not quite sure what you mean...

BSBDIB: For the love of.... Just get yourself onstage sharpish when this lot finishes their sound check, and don't go moaning while you are doing it!

Obviously our manager was good, but not *that* good. None of us had the experience necessary to make sure that the promoter and/or venue had our input list and stage plot, even if we *had* known what an input list and stage plot were. That is why the big sweaty bloke dressed in black came to us looking for information that he needed to work out how many microphones, DI boxes, risers, and monitor mixes he had to supply. We could not supply this information, so we diminished ourselves completely in his eyes. Faced with this incompetence from the artiste (us), the BSBDIB decided that he was not going to the extra trouble of re-patching the system to give us the maximum amount of inputs into the sound system; we would get what was left over, and that was that.

As it turns out, eight input channels were more than adequate because we were a three-piece band using a cassette machine and two synthesizers. However, the problems continued. The saga of providing mains power, outputs from the cassette machine, and the monitor mix would probably fill a book—suffice it to say, the band and the house crew were not the best of friends by the conclusion of the sound check. ("Anger check" would be a more honest description!) That was just the start of the evening! Did I mention our difficulty in getting our vehicle anywhere near the venue for load out? Or us forgetting to get paid?

How could we have avoided that situation, and how can you avoid making the same mistake that I made? Now, of course, I know exactly how a shows works and what I can expect from any individual or at any particular point in the day. Obviously, this knowledge comes from years of experience. You may not have the experience, but I can certainly give you some of the knowledge.

Following here are examinations of two typical show days—one in a small pub/club–type environment, and the other at a larger theatre or arena show. The diaries are written from my perspective as a professional tour manager. As you read through them, try to picture yourself in the role of tour manager, band leader, or promoter. Study the activities and the times that they occur. The level of preparation and *continuous* work that goes on throughout the day may surprise you.

You will also begin to appreciate why sound checks appear to take so long. Have you ever sat through a headline act's sound check and wondered, "Why is the band not onstage making music, and why is it taking so long, anyway?" After you read this chapter, you will understand why. A sound check may appear to be a haphazard affair, but usually there is hard work going on. The level of hard work may surprise you. However, if you are serious about your career as a musician or a backstage worker, you will need this level of knowledge, anticipation, and readiness for hard work in order to succeed.

Show Diary #1
Millions of Americans at the Flea Pit in Sheffield
Date: Saturday, April 25

Country: England

City: Sheffield

Venue: Flea Pit

Status: Headline

Capacity: 350

Ticket price: £6.50

Millions of Americans is on its first headlining tour of the UK. After three years of playing local bars and clubs, coupled with the odd prestigious opening slot in London and intense self-marketing, the band signed a deal with MegaGlobal Records late last year. Millions of Americans then toured nationally a couple of times, opening up for more established bands in 800- to 2,000-capacity venues. By reading *The Tour Book,* the band learned how to be friendly, professional, and prepared for these support slots. With a mix of this knowledge and sheer hard work, the band won over the hearts and minds of audiences and promoters alike.

During this time, the band also recorded its debut album, which is being released next month. To prime its audience for this release, the band's booking agent has booked the band its first headline tour. Figure 7.1 lists the dates, cities, and venues.

Because I worked for the band previously, I was again approached by the band's management to act as tour manager. The band members are still in the early stages of their career (they have no real income apart from record company advance money!), so I agreed to work as FOH engineer as well as being the tour manager. I was not amused, however, when, having agreed to perform two jobs for only one and a half times my normal wage for performing one job, I was asked to budget for carrying lights and a lighting engineer to work on the tour! I will explain more about this in Chapter 8, "How to Get the Shows."

On Saturday April 25, the band and crew will roll back into Sheffield, the band's hometown, for another show at the Flea Pit. Millions of Americans has played there a number of times, but usually opening up for other acts. This will be the band's first appearance in Sheffield as a headline act at a national touring venue.

Millions Of Americans Headline Tour Spring 2007

DAY	DATE	MONTH	COUNTRY	CITY	VENUE/ACTIVITY
WEDS	**15**	**APRIL**	**ENGLAND**	**MANCHESTER**	**ACADEMY 3**
THURSDAY	**16**	**APRIL**	**ENGLAND**	**PRESTON**	**THE MILL**
FRIDAY	**17**	**APRIL**	**SCOTLAND**	**GLASGOW**	**KING TUTS**
SATURDAY	**18**	**APRIL**	**SCOTLAND**	**DUNDEE**	**READING ROOMS**
SUNDAY	19	APRIL			TRAVEL/OFF
MONDAY	**20**	**APRIL**	**ENGLAND**	**LEEDS**	**COCKPIT**
TUESDAY	**21**	**APRIL**	**ENGLAND**	**BIRMINGHAM**	**BARFLY**
WEDS	**22**	**APRIL**	**ENGLAND**	**BRISTOL**	**FLEECE & FIRKIN**
THURSDAY	**23**	**APRIL**	**WALES**	**CARDIFF**	**BARFLY**
FRIDAY	**24**	**APRIL**	**ENGLAND**	**OXFORD**	**ZODIAC**
SATURDAY	**25**	**APRIL**	**ENGLAND**	**SHEFFIELD**	**FLEA PIT**
SUNDAY	26	APRIL			OFF/TRAVEL
MONDAY	**27**	**APRIL**	**ENGLAND**	**LONDON**	**MEAN FIDDLER**

Figure 7.1 Millions of Americans tour dates.

This is a band and crew with a lot of shows under their belt, but they are still green when it comes to the real world of touring. In a situation like this, what can the band, the crew, and you expect? To explain and educate, I have presented a typical tour day in a diary of sorts. In the diary, you will meet all the various personnel I have described so far and see how the hypothetical situations I have described actually become relevant once you are on the road.

9:30 A.M.: Good Morning!

Being a professional tour manager, I advanced all the shows for the tour a couple of weeks ago with the production manager at TKN Concerts (and the other tour promoters). During that advancing process, I requested a 2:00 P.M. equipment load in at the venues on the tour wherever possible. (This load-in time could be a lot later, but we are carrying lighting equipment, which takes considerable time to set up.) A 2:00 load in will give me and my crew ample time to load in our equipment, set it up, line check, test the lights, and be ready for a full band sound check at 5:00 P.M. From the advancing process, I know that doors are at 7:00 P.M. or 7:30 P.M. for the whole tour, giving the band one hour to sound check and still allowing time for the support acts to get their gear onstage and get a (quick) sound check.

Millions of Americans played in Oxford last night, and after the show, the band and crew stayed in an Oxford hotel. I know that the distance between Oxford and Sheffield is 228 km (142 miles) and should take about two and a half hours traveling at 80 kilometers per hour (50 miles per hour), which is all the Mercedes Vario packed with nine people, lights, and full backline is capable of. I also know that traffic on the highways will be light on a Saturday at lunchtime, but the weekends are typically used for construction work, so we may encounter delays. With all this in mind, I have calculated that we should leave Oxford at 11:30 A.M., and, being an experienced tour manager, I have informed the band and crew that we are leaving at 10:30 A.M.!

At 9:30 A.M. I give all the touring party their wakeup calls, stating what the present time is, what time we are leaving, and how much time that gives them to be in the lobby ready to leave: "Morning, this is Andy. It is now 9:30. We are leaving at 10:30, which gives you one hour to get downstairs. Don't be late!"

10:45 A.M.: Depart Oxford

Band and crew finally leave the Oxford hotel, 15 minutes later than the Tour Manager Time (TMT) bus call, but working in real time we are still early. Another day on the road!

1:15 P.M.: Arrive in Sheffield, Drop Off at Hotels and Homes

We arrive in Sheffield nice and early, so I instruct our driver, Dan, to drop the band members at their respective homes and hotels, and then we will proceed with the crew to the venue. I have not booked a hotel for the band members tonight because this is a hometown show, and the band members all still live here in Sheffield with the exception of the guitarist, who has moved in with a music TV channel presenter in London and therefore has a hotel room for tonight. As we drop all the band members, I inform them that sound check is at 4:15 P.M. ("4:15—do not be late!"). Obviously this is TMT, but I never tell anyone that! I usually ask the band whether it wants to be picked up from the hotel, or, if the hotel is close enough to the venue, I inform everyone that

I will walk over and escort them to the venue for sound check. In this case the band is in its hometown, so its members can bloody well make their own way to the venue!

I also ask the merch guy, Steve, to come directly to load in with us, even though he is not needed until much later.

1:55 P.M.: Arrive at the Venue

We arrive at the Flea Pit and observe that the venue and/or promoter has blocked off a parking space outside the load in for the venue for us. I requested this specifically because I know this part of Sheffield and I know that on a Saturday afternoon, every available parking space will be filled with cars parked by shoppers. (This is usually true of any town or city.) A good venue knows its environment and can predict when parking will be a problem.

2:00 P.M.: Load In at the Venue

Dan maneuvers the van into the parking area, and I jump out and locate the load-in door and attempt to get it open. In most venues you do not load in through the main public doors. There often is a separate entrance for gear, usually a set of fire doors that lead directly to the stage, into a backstage area, or onto the dance floor.

Note: Be Polite! Never, ever kick the doors to alert the staff inside. If there is no bell/buzzer, then rap on the door with your knuckles/ Maglite/Leatherman/Gerber/keys or wander around to the public entrance and see whether that is open. Kicking doors is just plain rude, and I have seen it result in more than one shouting argument between venue staff and visiting productions!

The house crew (who is doubling as the local crew; see Chapter 2 for an explanation of local and house crew) meets me at the load-in doors to help us load in our gear. The load-in doors for the Flea Pit lead directly onto the dance floor in front of the stage. With the help of these people, we load in our backline, lights, and merchandise. Luckily,

Figure 7.2 The backline is loaded into the venue. Note each piece is laid on the floor; the gear is not piled up on top of each other.

the load in is a flat push from the van to the floor in front of the stage. We push in all the gear and leave it in its respective cases in front of the stage (see Figure 7.2).

During the load in, I try to direct the gear to its appropriate place to save having to move equipment again over large distances. Carting equipment left, right, and center after it has been loaded in is a massive waste of time and energy. We call this stupid activity *double handling,* and we try to avoid it at all costs. To this end, I have marked all of the equipment cases with the following information:

- Name of the act (Millions of Americans)

- Contact telephone number (management office or home) in case of loss/theft

- Brief description of contents: Fender Strat Blue Spare, LX Tut, Production Spares, and so on

- Location: Up Stage Left, Monitor World, LX – Front of House, and so on

Note: Mark Your Cases Cases often are spray painted with a stencil to mark the name of the act, the telephone number, and so on. However, cases are expensive and do not depreciate much in value if left unmarked. Your best bet is to mark cases with strips of white gaffer tape and then write the band name and contact info on that. This tape can be removed easily, allowing you to swap the function of the case and/or to sell your cases if necessary.

If you are working in a tiny 350-capacity pub, I agree that there will not be much strain in double handling and the like, but if strangers are helping you to load in your equipment (whether they be experienced local crew or new crew members) and/or you are working in a much larger venue or festival, it will help everyone involved if all the equipment is clearly marked to indicate where it should "live" in the gig.

Note: Use a Taxi A sensible idea is to use a large item with wheels as a "taxi" for heavy items you need to move over long distances. It amazes me, though, when people carry equipment cases and then dump them on top of other items. Someone will have to lift that case off again! Place everything on the floor, guys!

2:20 P.M.: Meet the Staff

With the load in completed, I establish who is responsible for house sound and lights and introduce myself. This is a small venue, so all the sound and lighting equipment has been permanently installed; the house crew is there to maintain the equipment, to provide the microphones and stands we ask for, and to operate the equipment if we do not have our own engineers. I explain that I am the FOH engineer and that we have no monitor engineer. I ask if the sound people have received our technical specifications, input list, and stage plan. Often this is a redundant question because the house sound and lights people usually have asked you for your lighting plot and input list by this point in the day anyway! Remember what I said in Chapter 3 about information not reaching the right people? We will look at the reasons for this in Chapter 11, "Getting Onstage: Advanced Information," but always be prepared for the fact that the house technical staff may be working off an outdated and inaccurate technical specifications list or may not have received one at all!

I supply the house sound people with an updated technical specifications list. (I have several copies printed out in my day folder—a three-ring folder with divisions that contains all the signed contracts returned from the promoters, plus copies of our contract rider, tech specs, input list, rooming lists, and per diem sheets. It is great having everything on your laptop, but it is even better to prepare printed copies to whip out in a hurry.) I remind the house crew that we are carrying our own lights—this is a big deal in a venue this size. I introduce my lighting person, Lisa, to the house lighting person and then ask Lisa how long she needs to set up. Lighting always gets set up first because it usually goes up in the air above everything else. Once the lighting is rigged up in the air, then the stage and PA wings will become clear. Lisa replies that she will need about 45 minutes.

2:30 P.M.: The Lighting Equipment Gets Rigged
Having gotten the lighting people working with each other, I tell my backline person that he has about 45 minutes before he can load to stage. I also make sure that Steve, the touring merch person, is confident that all the merch is loaded in and in a secure place. The merch person does not really have to start work until about an hour before doors, but I do not want him wandering off into town, leaving the entire stock of band T-shirts, CDs, and DVDs lying around on the floor of the venue. Having satisfied myself that Steve has stashed away all the merch (either leaving it locked up in the van or in a tidy pile somewhere), I give Steve directions to the hotel and remind him to be back at 6:00 P.M.

2:40 P.M.: Park the Van
I quickly run out and make sure that Dan, the driver, has secured the vehicle and that we are okay to stay parked in this space until load-out time. It may also be necessary to use our tour vehicle to go and pick up the band from their homes/hotel, and I make a mental note to check with the promoter's rep that we can have this parking space again if we happen to leave it before the end of the night.

2:45 P.M.: Meet the Promoter's Representative

I wander off to find the venue or promoter's representative. Although we are in a relatively small venue, Million of Americans are tipped for great things, and a couple of national promoters have become involved, even at this early stage. Tonight's show is being promoted by TKN Concerts, who are based in London. The Flea Pit does promote its own shows and also will hire out the venue, especially to more established and reputable national promoters. Remember that it is unlikely that the main promoters at TKN Concerts will attend tonight's show themselves; TKN has therefore sent up a representative who will be my main contact for the evening.

2:50 P.M.: Set the Day's Schedule with the Promoter's Representative

I find the rep, Sarah, in the dressing room surrounded by supermarket bags, busily unpacking the food and beverages that make up our catering rider. Sarah ordinarily would be here at load-in time, having stopped at the supermarket beforehand. However, she got lost on the new one-way system and, on arrival at the venue, found the local crew was busy loading in our gear! Sarah therefore had to wait for the "locals" to load in our backline and lights before they could give her a hand unloading the catering rider into the dressing room.

I agreed with Sarah during my pre-production advancing that we should cut down the amount of food on the rider because this is a hometown show, and the band can go home before sound check. However, I asked her to make up the difference in cost with extra booze because I know the dressing room will be full of friends and family after the show. Sarah then gives me my buyout money. Remember the clause in the contract regarding the promoter supplying catering? As well as the dressing room/hospitality food and drink, our rider stipulates a hot meal or a buyout. In this case, it is easier and cheaper for TKN to give us the buyout, so Sarah hands over £90 (9 × £10) and makes me sign a receipt for the sum received.

Sarah and I discuss a bit of business, namely how the show is selling. Sarah informs me that the show is nearly sold out. She does not have the exact figures, but she will call for updates from the office. Off the top of her head, she thinks it has done more than 300 in advance. It is a Saturday night show, so there should be a good walk-up (people buying tickets at the door) and therefore it should sell out easily. This is good news for three important reasons:

- A sold-out show makes the band and, more importantly, the promoter very happy.

- If we sell out, we will break percentage. More on this in Chapter 8, but basically, we will get more money than the guaranteed fee for tonight's show. Woohoo!

- A packed, hot and sweaty venue sounds a lot better than a cold, empty one!

Sarah asks me whether I know anything about the opening band for this evening, and I tell her it has been on the last four days of the tour and is easy, both technically and emotionally, to deal with.

We then have a quick chat about times for the evening. Doors have already been agreed as starting at 7:30 P.M., and all live music has to be finished at 10:30 P.M. to allow the venue to be cleaned and turned around into a club for the evening. Working backwards, we agree that Millions of Americans should start at 9:00 P.M. The band's set is currently about one hour and ten minutes, but this is a hometown headline show, and anything could happen! Therefore, I have built in a bit more time just in case.

The opening band, firstname.lastname, is a three-piece, and it does not have much equipment. The stage is quite deep (the distance from the front of the stage to the back wall is quite large), so Millions of Americans will be able to leave all the band's backline set up after sound check, enabling the support band to set up in front. This means we only need 20 minutes for changeover (the time needed to remove the support band's equipment after it has performed). (Standard changeover time to a headline act is 30 minutes.) The timings for the evening will be as shown in Figure 7.3.

Sarah informs me she will type up, print, and post all the signs displaying these times. She will post them in each dressing room, in the hallways backstage, and at the entrance to the stage, and she will

T.K.N
Concerts

Millions Of Americans

Saturday 25th April. Flea Pit, Sheffield

19.30	Doors
20.10 – 20.40	firstname.lastname
20.40 – 21.00	Changeover
21.00 – 22.30	**Millions of Americans**
22.30	Live music curfew
23.00	Load out finishes

Figure 7.3 Timing for the show, prepared by the promoter's rep. Look out for these signs and make sure you know what time you are supposed to get your gear onstage and offstage, as well as what time you need to be out of the venue!

give one each to the house monitor, the FOH, and the lighting engineer. She will also print extra copies to give to the venue manager and security/door people.

Note: The Last Train It is always tempting for bands to go on as late as possible, just in case a few extra people turn up or so that the audience is really drunk by the time the band plays. Always bear in mind, though, that your audience has to get home, often by public transportation that stops running at a certain time. It is no good to go onstage and see everyone leave to get the last bus!

Why would the security people need the timings for the show? Well, during a show there will be natural times when the crowd is moving around more than at other times. After the support band has finished, there may be a natural rush to the bar and/or bathrooms. Similarly, when the headline act finishes, a majority of the audience will flock to the band's merchandise stall (hopefully) and/or the cloakrooms and the exit. Therefore, it is extremely useful for the house security and stewards to be prepared for these mass movements so they can get extra staff in place for these times. Likewise, the stewards suddenly may be aware that the music from the stage has stopped before the proposed finish time. Without the show timings, the stewards would not know this proposed finish time and might not investigate if all the music stopped.

Providing clear and accurate timings for everyone involved behind the scenes at a show is a very necessary procedure.

Note: Set Times and Running Order Always put start *and* finish times when you write up times for the show. Each band's set time and changeover time should be clearly marked. You can even put the amount of time in parentheses, such as "8:10–8:40 (30 mins.)," to reiterate the strict running schedule. I have seen show times printed up with no finish times or changeover times indicated, and every band on the bill thought it had an hour onstage and were pretty disappointed when it got pulled offstage after 30 minutes, the correct stage time.

Now that we have discussed times, Sarah reminds me about the strict curfew and the need to get all our gear loaded out before 11:00 P.M. Because there is no load out possible from the stage, we are faced with the dreaded "disco load out"—in other words, having to hump our gear out through the crowd! This is a time-consuming and fairly hazardous procedure. There will be loud music, flashing lights, drunken people, and heavy equipment in big square boxes that have sharp corners. Not a good combination!

As well as the normal backline equipment, we also have lights that will have to be de-rigged and lowered onto the stage. Obviously, we will do as much as we can to clear our equipment before the club reopens at 11:00 P.M., but it will be a hell of a rush. I make a mental note to make sure the support band has all its gear either loaded out or out of the way when we come to load out. There is nothing worse than ripping all your gear offstage, only to find that the other acts on the bill have their equipment piled up everywhere, blocking exits and packing-down areas. A good discipline is to get all your gear offstage the moment you finish playing. Do not sit in the dressing room for five minutes or go the bar to see your boyfriend—get your stuff offstage, packed away, and, if possible, loaded out into your vehicle. Then you can totally relax, knowing you have all your gear accounted for and safe. You will have the rest of the night to socialize, especially if you're an opening act. Do not incur the wrath of the other bands and crews by leaving your gear onstage or blocking access points—especially if you are the drummer; drums take up a lot more space when assembled than guitars or bass amps.

Note: Think about the Load Out before You Load In! I always think about the end of the show as soon as I get loaded in. What time does the show finish? Where do empty cases go, and can I get at them to pack down? How can I get my gear out of the venue if I am with an opening act? Who is going to pay me, and where will that person be when we have finished performing? Can I get my vehicle close to the load out before the headline act loads out? It may seem premature to think about the end of the show before you or your band have played a note, but this kind of thinking marks you as a professional team player.

3:15 P.M.: The Backline Equipment Gets Set Up

Having checked in with the promoter, sorted out catering, and agreed to the running order times and other matters, it is time for me to head back into the hall and check that the lights are rigged and that the backline is being loaded to the stage.

I go back to the main hall of the venue and see that Laura has finished rigging the lights and is in the process of running cables to the FOH lighting desk. Because the stage is now fairly clear, I give Charlie, the tour backline technician, and the local crew a hand getting the band's equipment onto the stage. Like most touring acts these days, Millions of Americans has several guitars, each used in specific songs. This requires Charlie to string and tune each guitar, keep them all tuned, and hand them to the relevant player at the relevant point in the set. To keep all the guitars safe and accessible, Charlie has a *toast rack*—a multiple-guitar stand—that he places on a flight case and wheels to the side of the stage (see Figure 7.4). This area is now officially guitar world, and it is Charlie's own personal fiefdom. It might be the Millions of Americans show, but it is Charlie's stage!

When the majority of the backline has been un-cased and moved into position, I start setting up the drums. I have agreed with Charlie that I will set up and tear down the drums each day just to save a bit of time, even though Charlie is the backline tech and I am already doing two jobs.

3:30 P.M.: The PA Equipment Gets Set Up

Charlie continues to cable up the amps, run out pedal boards, and tune guitars ready for sound check. I get together with the house sound guys, and we discuss which microphones we will use on specific instruments. I have specified certain microphones on my input list, but, as I've mentioned, this is a wish list, and the venue may not have the microphones I prefer. (I actually prefer the microphones that most engineers prefer, such as Shure SM58s, because they are workhorses and they get the job done with minimum of work from me. And the venue is more likely to have them!)

Even though we have stipulated certain technical demands on our contract and rider, I am an experienced professional with a "let's make this work" attitude, rather than a "the world owes me a living, and I will shout and scream until I get my way" attitude. I have said it before: If you *really* need Equipment X to make your show work, then you should buy Equipment X or rent Equipment X for the show/tour and take it with you to the next show at the end of the evening. If you cannot afford to rent it, buy it, or truck it, then make sure you discuss exactly what

Figure 7.4 A toast rack guitar stand. Toast racks are more suitable for your guitar technicians to keep multiple guitars ready; they do not really work when placed on the performance area of the stage because they take up too much room.

you need with the promoter/promoter's rep and technical crew at least two weeks before the show. I routinely work with a couple of acts that have very complicated stage setups with numerous monitor mixes. We cannot afford to take a monitor system with us at the present time, so I make a lot of lengthy phone calls to discuss and arrange exactly what I need on the day. In most cases, I am supplied with a good working compromise. I know that this would not be the case if I just turned up on the day and started pointing excitedly at my technical rider, screaming, "We have to have 10 mixes, it says here!"

3:40 P.M.: Prepare the FOH Console and Outboard Equipment

When the microphones have been approved, I give the sound crew a hand setting up microphone stands and placing them in position. We have to wait 10 more minutes for Charlie to finish setting up the backline, so I take this chance to prepare the PA system. This involves marking up the inputs, flattening off the EQ and crossovers, putting gates and compressors into the appropriate channels or groups, and EQing the system. (Refer to Chapter 6 for an explanation of sound and sound equipment.)

Note: Label Your Equipment and Your Desk Properly Please use appropriate technical or descriptive language when marking up a desk, a piece of technical equipment, or even a flight case. You may find it amusing to mark up your desk inputs with nicknames for the equipment or band personnel as a way to relieve the boredom or as part of some touring in-joke. Think about this, though: If you get food poisoning after sound check, or you get stuck in an elevator as the show starts, or you have your watch still set to your local time and you are two hours late (all true events I have witnessed), then someone else will have to leap in and start to mix the show. Will that person be able to decipher your handwriting, let alone your "codes?" I always assume someone else will need to work out what I have prepared and label my desks, guitar amp settings, and flight cases accordingly. A box labeled "Jam sponge and custard" is pretty useless to everyone.

4:00 P.M.: EQing the PA and the Monitors

The monitor engineer and I work on ringing out the monitors—in other words, altering the EQ to get the wedges as loud as possible before they start to feed back. I also cable up the band's IEM system and check to make sure it is working properly. When I am happy with the stage sound, I run back to the FOH position and EQ the PA speakers for the room.

Lisa, meanwhile, has finished patching her desk into the house system and is happy that she has control over the system. Although it would

Figure 7.5 The view from FOH after sound check—the lighting director (LD) now gets some quiet time to program the lights.

be ideal for Lisa to have a dark, quiet stage when she begins to program her lights, on this kind of tour we are all working in the same time period, so she will have to program as we are sound checking (see Figure 7.5). This means she will be deafened by loud ringing out and sound check sounds, and the band and sound crew occasionally will be plunged into darkness as Lisa programs the various lighting states for this evening's show. (Cue shouts of, "Can we have some light onstage, *please*?") I always try to build in some light programming time each day; ideally, sound checks for the two bands will be completed by 6:45 P.M. so Lisa has some quiet time to program before doors.

4:15 P.M.: Line Check

The sound crew and I do a line check. Charlie is onstage and he hits, strums, and presses each piece of equipment to make sure that it is working, that the microphone or DI box that is connected to it is working, and that we have signals into both the FOH and the monitor desk. When we are confident that every input is working, we have a "full house." It is time for the band's sound check.

4:25 P.M.: Time Out!

"Whoa, time out! Time *out*!" I hear you cry. "It's 4:25 already! You have been here since 2:00 P.M., and it's only *just* time for the band sound check? This is crazy!"

You may be right. Certainly, it does seem like a long ordeal to get a couple of guitars plugged and a sound system working. Consider this, though. If you were employing a crew to help you present a professional show, if you were working for a band or a venue and you desired a fulfilling and permanent career in the industry, then wouldn't you work this diligently, anticipating everything and painstakingly troubleshooting and preparing every aspect of the show? I think you know the answer!

4:30 P.M.: Sound Check

The band members, working on 4:15 TMT for sound check, have arrived and have found their way to the dressing room (the DR). They are in good moods because there is no promo (promotional activity) scheduled for today. That means no interviews at the venue or elsewhere. The musicians in Millions of Americans are not a lazy bunch and are obviously keen to do any promotional activity requested of them. However, the tour is nearly over, and any interviews done today would not be published until next week—far too late to publicize the tour or the new album. Therefore, the band has had extra time to relax today, and they really appreciate it.

I meet the band in the dressing room, check that all is well with them, and inform them that the stage is ready for sound check. It is good practice to have a set time when the artist gets onstage; it can be very frustrating for both artist and crew if musicians keep wandering onstage and offstage during setup and line check. I do not mean to disrespect my artists, but in my experience, sound checks go a lot more smoothly and quickly when the crew can just get on with it, making sure all is ready before the artist takes the stage.

Sound check progresses. I already have a good idea of levels and a few basic sounds from doing the line check. My priority for a decent sound check is to make sure the band is comfortable with its onstage sound and that levels from backline amplification are not too high. With this in mind, I take each player in turn, asking each to play while I adjust the gain and EQ for each relevant channel. I may ask the player to turn up or down or to brighten or dull his or her sound, or maybe to move closer to the microphone to get a better result without resorting to excessive EQing or gain. Remember in Chapter 2 when I explained that there is no magic with live sound? A bad-sounding instrument will still sound bad through a state-of -the-art PA system, only louder. It is important to get the source sound right.

Note: Keep Your Eye on the Engineer A good sound check is all about communication. Players should *always* keep an eye on the FOH engineer. FOH and monitor engineers should have access to microphones that can be heard through the monitor wedges and IEMs. This system is known as *talk-to-stage,* and it makes life much easier—well, easier than shouting over a drummer in full flow from a FOH mixer 20 meters away!

Having set good levels for each of the musicians and any samplers and hard disk recorders onstage, I turn off the FOH system to allow the band to set its monitor levels. A good monitor engineer will have already dialed in levels as I was setting my levels and will have put vocals in the appropriate mixes.

Turning the FOH speakers off gives a bit more clarity to the stage sound and enables the musicians to have a clearer idea of what the stage sound will be like when the room is full and warm.

I allow the players to get their monitor sound together and then request they play a song together. At this point, neither the band nor I, as FOH engineer, should expect super fidelity sound. I know what the difference is to the FOH sound in a cold, empty room, and therefore I will not take ages trying to recreate the sound of the band's latest album onstage in a Sheffield pub. I will, however, use my experience to set up a rough starting point for the sound, knowing I will be able to judge the sound more accurately later.

Note: The Physics of Sound Checks and Why They Can Sound So Bad! So why does the performance sound so different at sound check than it does at show time? Physics plays a large part. (Bear with me—this is very important!) The speed or velocity of sound in air is approximately 344 meters per second, 1,115 feet per second, or 770 miles per hour at room temperature of 20°C (70°F). The speed varies with the temperature of air, such that sound travels slower at higher altitudes or on cold days. Also, in a cold room, the sound waves will refract (bend) downward as they travel away from their source. Therefore, in a cold, empty room, you will have the sound waves slowing down and dipping in height as they reach into the room. For the high-end frequencies, this causes a lack of clarity and direction. For the low frequencies, a dampening occurs more than usual. The result is a smeary, bass-light mess. Add in the highly reflective walls, floors, and mirrors in a bar or club, and suddenly you can see and hear why sound checks often sound so awful!

4:50 P.M.: Sound Check Continues

I have individual and ensemble levels and sounds for each of the players, and they have an acceptable monitor sound with which to work. The band then plays two songs together for the sound check. I listen carefully to any instrument or frequency that really sounds misplaced or lacking, but I basically concentrate on making sure the band are getting a good monitor sound onstage. By the end of the second song, the sound is getting there. I ask the band, "Are you okay up there?" I get the usual, "Yeah, s'pose so" mutters and grunts. (Heh, heh, only kidding!)

I then ask the band to play the parts of any songs that have different instrumentation—for example, an acoustic guitar or a different vocalist. I concentrate on the major changes here; I do not check each electric guitar change! I also do not need to check the whole song—just a verse or chorus will do. Remember, the crew and I have already line-checked all the instruments, and Charlie played them all for me before the band arrived. However, it is always beneficial for the FOH engineer to hear instruments *in situ*.

Finally, I ask the band to play the first song of that evening's set. This is really important. Everyone needs a starting point when starting to play onstage, mix the FOH sound, or make sure the monitors sound as they were in sound check. As I explained before, the sound of the venue and the sound onstage will change dramatically after sound check and before the show. By playing the first song of the set last in your sound check, you are doing as much as possible to ensure the starting sound of the set will be as close to a good sound as possible.

When the intro song is finished, I thank the band, inform them to please wait for me in the dressing room, and then begin the process of noting all the settings on the mixing desk, effects units, and dynamic controls. This is known as *marking up*, and unless you are using digital desks, it is a lengthy but necessary process. Every knob and fader on the mixing desk that has been used in sound check should be noted and marked down.

Note: Amusing Anecdote Many years ago, I was mixing FOH sound for a young local band that was supporting a national touring act. After sound check, I watched the headline act's FOH engineer pull out a cassette-based dictation recording machine and read out all the relevant settings from his desk into the machine: "Kick drum gain 11 o'clock. No high-pass filter. Treble plus 3, mid high 3.5k cut 2dB...." I thought this was so cool! I had not been touring long, but I was already sick of marking up desks. This looked like the easy way to do it! My admiration later turned to amusement, however, when I watched the same engineer trying to recall his settings during changeover. The club had a house DJ system, complete with DJ, who was cranking the indie hits of the day at full volume during each changeover. The hapless FOH engineer had his cassette machine pressed hard against his ear, but he still could not hear what he had recorded earlier!

5:15 P.M.: Marking Up the FOH Console, Striking, and Spiking

While I mark up, Charlie (our fantastic backline technician) takes all the guitars and puts them away, either in their cases or back in his toast rack. No one should leave anything from the front line of the stage (guitars, pedal boards, small amps, and so on) out after sound check. The risk of breakage or theft is too great; it's not worth the risk. Leaving things out also presumes that all the other acts for the evening will work around your setup. And presumption is the mother of all f**k-ups.

Charlie then takes a roll of electrical/PVC/PTFE tape in a bright color and spikes the stage (see Figure 7.6). *Spiking* means marking the placement of all the amps, pedal boards, monitor wedges, and microphone stands for the band. Charlie coils up all the instrument cables neatly, working from the downstage back to the amp or DI. He then takes the tape and marks the corners of each pedal board and monitor wedge with two pieces per corner to create an L shape. The idea is that when the item is struck—in other words, taken away—it can be replaced *exactly* by matching the corners to the relevant spike marks. Obviously

Figure 7.6 Stage spiking marks showing the replacement position for effects pedals. Spiking is used for anything placed on a stage that is subsequently struck (removed). The spike marks should indicate the exact position of the item before it was struck. By using the spike marks, you should be able to exactly replace the item in its original position.

this is easy with large, square items, such as pedal boards, guitar amps, and monitor speakers, but how the hell do you spike a microphone stand? And why would you want to?

How? Place three pieces of tape at the end of each of the microphone stand's tripod legs, in an inverted U shape, surrounding the tip of the tripod leg.

Why? Remember our lighting person, Lisa? As we sound check, she is busy focusing, aiming, and programming lights to create the evening's show. During the day she will aim various lighting fixtures at various points on the stage. As human beings move about onstage (we are not in a large enough venue or in a strong enough financial position to have "follow spots"), Lisa needs to aim at certain objects, such as microphone stands for singers, pedal boards for guitarists, and so on. Now that she has spent all afternoon focusing her lights to create fantastic looks for the band, it would be pretty daft if we struck all the gear and then replaced it for the show in random positions, as space permitted! The lights would be pointing to areas of dead stage and/or shining in the performers' field of vision.

Note: Check before You Move That Amp! If you are going to move something onstage—your amp, microphone stand, or monitor wedge—*please* check that it has not been spiked first. If it hasn't, then please ask your crew/the house crew/the other band's crew whether it is okay to move or adjust the position. If it *has* been spiked, again *ask*! If lights have been focused on your position for the show and then you move one meter upstage, you will be in darkness! Remember, everyone is working together to create your show, whether you are a crew person, a promoter, a T-shirt seller, or a performer onstage.

As Charlie is spiking and striking, the house sound guys also swing into action. During the time we took to set up and line check, the support band, firstname.lastname, arrived and loaded everything onto the dance floor in front of the stage. Having read *The Tour Book*, the band knows to assemble as much of its equipment as possible on the dance floor or side stage—set up the drum kit, de-case and assemble the guitar amps, and get the guitars out of the cases. The house sound guys have also checked with band members and discussed their input list and stage plan.

5:30 P.M.: The Millions of Americans Sound Check Is Finished. Next!

We have finished our sound check and tidied away all the guitars, pedal boards, and other loose items. Charlie has closed all the cases and stacked them somewhere sensible—in other words, not in front of a doorway, a fire escape, or any cupboard that needs to be accessed. If there is no room in the venue, then Charlie will put the cases back in the van if it is still parked outside. That would be a terrible idea tonight, though, because we have the dreaded disco load out. (A disco load out is a load out through a venue that continues as a nightclub or disco after the live music performance. It involves pushing heavy equipment that has sharp corners through crowds of dancing people. The club will be lit with flashing lights and strobe lights and filled with stage smoke. All in all, it's a dangerous and trying way to move your equipment out of a venue.)

Once the tidying is done, I ask Charlie whether he is happy that the stage is clear, and I make sure the local crew people are ready for the support act to take the stage. *Always* ask someone before starting to load your equipment onstage. There are always numerous little jobs to be done once a headline act leaves the stage after sound check, and you will not be made to feel very special if you unceremoniously dump your bass amp onto the stage as the backline techs are trying to spike the stage or coil cables.

Note: Leave Your Equipment Turned On Do *not* turn off your amps, pedal boards, and keyboards after sound check. Leave them powered up and on standby if possible. Why? There are many reasons, the most prominent one being that in the heat of a hurried changeover, you may simply forget to turn your amp, effects rack, keyboard, and so on back on. It seems improbable to you now, but I have seen it happen. Leave it all switched on. It saves time and worry later.

5:40 P.M.: The Opening Band Loads Their Equipment for Sound Check

I leave instructions with the members of the support act that they need to be finished with sound check by 6:45 P.M. and that because it is a disco load out tonight, they need to leave all their cases and equipment stored somewhere accessible for after their set. This gives them an hour, which, as anybody will tell you, is not a great deal of time to get all your equipment onstage, set up, miked, and cabled, and then to perform a couple of numbers. Also remember that the local crew will have to re-patch the mixing boards, moving wedges about and trying to keep notes about what they have changed. However, an hour is better than 15 minutes, which is what you usually will be allotted! (If this is the case, then please remember my advice and set up as much of your equipment as you can before taking the stage.)

5:45 P.M.: Set List and Guest List

I hurry back to the dressing room to catch the band; I need a lot of information from them, and the sooner I get it, the better. First, we need to establish the set list for the night.

An established touring act probably will work out a set list for the entire tour while still in rehearsals. That set will be performed in the same order on every night of the tour, with all lighting effects and instrument and costume changes becoming second nature to the artists and crew. However, it may become apparent that some songs just do not work live, or that the set is too long (or too short), so songs may be added, dropped, or swapped around for particular shows.

In the case of Millions of Americans, we do have a tour set list, but the band likes to change things around on a show-by-show basis. I always keep a copy of last night's set list printed out and show it to the band when asking them to arrange tonight's set. As I've mentioned before, there is usually one band member who is more in charge of compiling the set list than the others. It is supposed to be a democratic decision, but after many years of the band working together, the decision seems to get left to the one person.

The band agrees to the changes, and I ask them to mark the changes on the copy I have with me. I will type it up and print it out later, but I now need to sort out the guest list. This is a hometown show that is close to selling out. Therefore, there is a restricted number of guest tickets available for the band and crew to give away to friends and family. Being a top tour manager, I anticipated this problem some weeks ago and have, on every day of the tour so far, asked the band members to compile their guest list for tonight's show. I informed them of the allocation (we have 30 places available) and have kept on them to sort out this list well in advance.

Guest lists are a pain in the posterior for everyone involved. Promoter, promoter's rep, tour manager, the band themselves—everyone is affected. No one likes to refuse a band member a guest list ticket, especially for a big important show like a sellout hometown gig. However, you do have to be realistic. Health and safety regulations and common sense dictate there is only physical space for so many people. The financial workings of a modern show also dictate that you cannot invite the world and their wife in for free. It may be *your* show, but you and the promoter need to make as much money as possible out of every show. It demonstrates very poor awareness of the system to promise all of your family and 15 of your friends free tickets for your show without first checking or discussing the numbers involved. This is why I have been reminding the band about the allocation for tonight's show—I don't want anybody to feel let down or embarrassed.

Note: Using Guest List Tickets to Boost Your Career Artists I work with often complain that their management or record company gets their hands on the band's guest list passes and tickets before the band members do. This is especially true of festival tickets and passes. Although I can see the band members' point of view, I find this complaint to be short-sighted. I will explain why.

Your management team is presumably working hard to promote you and your music. Part of this promotion involves getting tastemakers and pundits to see you play live and to meet you in person. Because you are all working on a tight budget, it obviously makes sense for the management team to use all means at its disposal to ensure free entry for these VIPs. And this means using your guest list places. Obviously, there should be some advance discussion about the allocation of passes and tickets, but consider this: Giving guest list tickets to your mate Dave, whom you have known since you were a kid, is all very nice, but Dave is not going to help further your career much, is he? (He probably does not even pay for your music, because you give it to him anyway!) Wouldn't it be a greater use of the guest passes if that hip journalist from *Spin* got in for free and had access to your dressing room, where you could ply her with free food and drink and impress her so much that she would write a really good review of your new album?

Yes, it is annoying if your management/leader/record label takes all the festival passes without telling you or assumes that they can use the guest passes on your behalf. It is even more annoying when you find out that the management/label personnel are using your passes to get *their* mates in! In the case of festival passes, always make sure that your contact information (or your tour manager's contact info) is with your booking agent and the promoter, rather than with your management or label. The agent usually will send out any festival passes or pass requests directly to the contact he has on his system—in other words, your management—because that is who he usually deals with. Contact your agent and make sure all passes and so on come to you. That way, you can sensibly allocate the passes, bearing in mind the point I made about your mate Dave!

Finally, record companies are supposed to buy tickets to use for promotion of their artists. The label will contact the promoter directly and buy 20 to 100 tickets, which will be given to journalists, DJs, retail staff, and other taste-makers. At an average of £10 a ticket, this can be a considerable expense to the label. Recently, I have noticed a trend involving labels buying fewer tickets and then trying to use the band's guest list to ensure free entry for the "important" people. Look out for this practice! Although you obviously are trying to maintain an honest and productive relationship with your label, you need to point out that they have a duty to spend money on promotion for the mutual good (contract terms permitting).

6:00 P.M.: A Chance for Band and Crew to Relax

The set list and the guest list are sorted. The crew had no guests and probably would not have been able to get anyone into the venue tonight anyway! The band is now free to relax for a while before the show. Ordinarily, I would take this opportunity to run the band and crew back to the hotel (or go and check in if we did not get a chance before arriving at the venue). As I mentioned, though, this is a home-town show, so the band members have their own homes to go back to, apart from the guitarist. I ask the band what everyone is doing and check with Charlie, Dan, and Lisa to see whether they would like to go to the hotel now. Dan says he has been already and he wants to eat. Charlie wants to eat as well, but would like to pop into the hotel to dump his bag and freshen up. Lisa is still programming and will be working right up until doors; could one of the crew grab her some food to go? Our guitarist says he'll walk back with Charlie and then go on to eat. The other band members also want to eat, and they know a great Thai place around the corner. This is all fine with me and fairly standard stuff, so I hand out the band and crew buyout money to each person (making sure I keep a note in my Black Book) and tell them to be back at the venue at 8:00 P.M. at the latest. Charlie quickly checks the timings list that Sarah has placed on the monitor board and informs me that Dan and he will be back at 8:30, as changeover is at 8:40. (Dan has being helping out with setup and changeover because he is trying to become a more experienced backline technician.) I make sure everyone has their laminates on them for when they return, and I head off into the production office.

6:05 P.M.: The Production Office

This is the first chance I've had all day to set up my laptop computer, printer, and filing case. Setting up my space in the production office usually is my first job on arriving at the venue, but because I am also employed to take care of sound for the band, I tend to be pretty busy working on the stage after load in.

The production office at the Flea Pit is actually quite large and pleasant. I find that venues tend to look after visiting productions a lot better these days, providing clean and warm backstage facilities that encourage bands and crews to return. In this case, the production office has more than enough desk space for Sarah and me to set up our various laptops and printers, and we have a telephone each. And there is a large photocopier in the hallway. More importantly, the production office is at the back of the venue and upstairs, as far away from the PA system as possible!

I amend and type up the set list and make about 20 copies. I then fill in my guest list template with the names for tonight, print that out, and hand it to Sarah. Sarah is responsible for taking the guest list to the box office at the venue entrance and making sure all the appropriate access passes are given out to relevant guests. This has to be done before doors open at 7:30 P.M., so I make sure Sarah has the list well before then. Because the dressing room and backstage areas at the Flea Pit are so small, I have limited guest access to these areas. The venue turns into a club after the show, and I'm sure most friends and family of the band will hang around for a drink or two in the club anyway.

I have from now until about 8:00 to try to get my admin work, accounts, and schedules up to date. This can be a very productive time for me as a tour manager, especially because most of the associated UK offices have now closed, and the phone is not ringing every five minutes!

6:45 P.M.: Please Stop Making That Noise!

I go back into the venue and help the support band, firstname.last-name, finish their sound check with the cheery instruction, "Oy! Get off the stage!" Lisa is still programming her lighting for tonight's show and now will have a nice, quiet stage on which to fine-tune the various scenes she has programmed.

Steve (our merch guy) has returned to the venue after depositing last night's takings into the band bank account and has set up a display at the back of the venue, near the entrance/exit. (The merchandise operation is a really important part of touring today, so I have devoted a whole section to it in Chapter 9, "Getting Paid.")

7:15 P.M.: Preparing to Open the Doors

Charlie pops back into the venue with Lisa's food and then heads off to the hotel. Lisa has finished programming her lights, and I take a last look around the venue to make sure we have not left any cases lying around or any other valuables at FOH. The venue door staff, bar staff, and security people all have arrived, and the venue is bustling

Figure 7.7 The venue prior to the doors opening.

with activity. I pop a CD of carefully chosen music into the FOH CD player and adjust the volume to create an acceptable walk-in environment. One last check, and I go back to the production office to inform Sarah that we are ready to open the doors if she is (see Figure 7.7).

7:30 P.M.: The Doors Are Open!

Sarah has taken the guest list to the ticket office and has given the all-clear to the venue manager. The venue doors are open to the public. The venue staff is taking care of customers, and I can get back to the production office and do some more work. I have about 40 minutes before I need to make sure the opening act gets onstage. I finish off my accounts and send the rest of my e-mails.

8:05 P.M.: Making Sure the Support Act Is Ready to Go

I go downstairs to the DR and inform the members of firstname .lastname that they are due onstage in five minutes. Obviously they are ready and prepared to go onstage anyway, being the good, professional support act that they are, but it does me and them no harm to keep with tradition and give them the time check. The one time I do not swing by their dressing room to remind them will probably be the one time they are still in the pub next door! Besides, the band are really excited about playing tonight because it is a sellout for Millions of Americans, and the venue is more than half full already.

8:10 P.M.: Hey! There Is a Band Onstage!
Firstname.lastname hits the stage. I make my way to FOH to check the sound and the atmosphere in the venue, and I also make sure that Steve is okay at the merch stall. I try never to forget about my merchandising people and to make sure they have drinks and that I can take over for 10 minutes every now and then if they need a bathroom break.

8:30 P.M.: Preparing for Changeover
Things are getting busy backstage. Charlie and Dan have returned, and Charlie is preparing for changeover. We only have 20 minutes to get the support band and all its equipment off the very small stage and all the Millions of Americans frontline equipment back on. This is a small venue, and storage space and access are at a premium. Charlie is at his workstation at the side of the stage, busy tuning and checking the guitars and basses. Meanwhile, I am gathering set lists (giving one to each crew-member) and getting towels and water ready to put onstage.

Note: Choose Your Moment! If you are going to approach the TM, the backline crew, or the sound and lighting techs of the headline band, please make sure you don't do it during changeover time. This is *the* busiest and most stressful period of the touring day, and basically you will get 1) yelled at or 2) ignored.

8:40 P.M.: Hurry Up, Hurry Up!
Firstname.lastname finishes, bang on time. The band members quickly troop offstage and head into the dressing room. Unfortunately, no one in the band gets to chill out for long because they have to get back onstage to get their gear off. We have no dedicated local crew to

help with the changeover, so it really is up to them to get their equipment out of the way as soon as possible. Charlie and Dan from the Millions of Americans crew do what they can to help, but ultimately your gear is *your* gear, and you should never assume that someone else will be kind enough to pack your gear away for you.

Because the stage, dressing room, and backstage area are full of people and equipment being passed about left, right, and center, I use this time to go FOH and reset my desk, effects, and dynamic controls. Obviously this is a sold-out show and the house is full, so just getting to FOH can be an ordeal. Having made it there, I really do not want to go back and forth too many times, so I make sure I have everything I need with me. I then reset all the desk controls, working off the notes I made earlier. When I finish this, I push my way back through the crowd; collect the towels, water, and set lists; and start to set them out for the act. By this time Charlie should have most of the stage reset, the local house guys will have set the microphones, and the stage should be a bit calmer.

Note: Whose Job Is It? It is always worth specifying early on who is responsible for setting out the set lists, towels, and water. I, as tour manager, have always seen it as my responsibility. I know some backline techs who like to do it, probably because they have a closer working relationship with the musicians and they may know a specific preference of set list position and so on. Whoever does the job, though, make sure they always do it! Never assume because you have not put out the lists that some else has. I have heard, "Where are the set lists?" from bands onstage too many times....

8:55 P.M.: Five Minutes to Go

Time is running out in the changeover. Although the timing is not super strict (we are the last band on, and the set is a good deal shorter than two hours), it is a professional courtesy to stick to a schedule, especially if it is you who organized it! The stage is reset, Charlie has checked that he has sound from all the instruments, Lisa has repositioned her lights, and I have put out set lists (stuck to the floor in front of the performers and slightly to the right), water (*never* on top of amps or cabs), and towels (folded on top of the cabs or placed on the drum riser). We still have to do a final line check, though, so I fight my way back through the crowd to FOH position. Lisa is already there with her set list, making last-minute adjustments and notes. After making sure Charlie is onstage and that the house monitor engineer is at his position, I start to call out the instrument channels in turn. Charlie hits, strums, or presses the appropriate button, and the monitor engineer and I make sure we have a signal just as in the sound check. The complication now is that the house is full and pretty loud with music and talking. To overcome this barrier to communication, I use a microphone from the FOH board that is routed into the stage monitors. I can talk to Charlie and the monitor engineer onstage, calling out, "Kick drum, snare top, snare bottom," and so on, and working through the input list. I also wear my headphones, and if there is a problem, Charlie can talk to me down the main vocal mic, which I have selected to be in my headphones. In this way, we can establish that we have a correct and full signal into both desks. When this is finished, the band can hit the stage!

9:05 P.M.: Millions of Americans Is Onstage!

One final check, and I flash Charlie with my Maglite to signal that we are ready. Because I am at FOH, Charlie is going to put the band onstage for me—in other words, tell the band members that the technical crew is ready, the stage is set, and they should get ready to go on now. Lisa tells her house crew person to dim the house lights, and I quickly start the intro music CD. The crowd cheers loudly, and after a minute of the intro music, the band strides onto the stage. This is the moment we all have worked for all day—seven hours of teamwork and concentration!

9:45 P.M.: No More Tickets

The box office is closed now, and any money taken on the night is tallied into the final figures and presented by the venue manager to the promoter's rep, Sarah. Sarah then compiles those figures into the figures she has for costs and profit. Meanwhile, with the crowd mostly watching the band, Steve takes advantage of the lull in activity, starts to tidy up his merch stall, and does a quick tally of shirts sold and money taken.

10:15 P.M.: Encore!

Millions of Americans finishes the main part of its set and leaves the stage to thunderous applause. The band members run off to the dressing room, exhausted and soaked in sweat. Charlie, equally soaked in sweat, takes their guitars and hurriedly retunes them for the encore. He has about five minutes before the band reappears and crashes into the first of a three-song encore. The band members pride themselves on giving a special performance at every show they do, but it seems the excitement of the hometown show has given their energy an even greater lift. It has been a great show, and every member of the band and crew feels a unique sense of accomplishment and pride about what we have achieved here tonight and on the tour as a whole.

10:30 P.M.: Hurry Up (Again)!

Those feelings of pride and excitement are quickly forgotten by the crew, though—we have some real work to do now. The crowd is baying for more songs, but I cannot have the band performing past the live music curfew, so I signal for Lisa to turn up the house lights and I put on some music over the PA system.

Note: Let the Audience Know the Show Is Finished Audiences can be very ignorant about the fact that the show is finished. In my experience, you will always get a handful of people who will shout and plead for more songs. As a performer, you should try to resist the urge to play more songs just because someone asks for them. If you have worked out a really good set and played a good show, then know when to finish—stick to your set list plan. I always think it looks really unprofessional when acts keep coming back onstage, especially if the crew thinks it's time to go home and they start packing up the gear!

Signal the end of the show by making sure that the house lights go up in full and that you put on some music over the PA, preferably a genre or style of music completely opposite the style of the last act. I always find some ultra-fast 1920s or 1930s jazz clears alternative rock fans away pretty quickly!

10:35 P.M.: Great Show; I'll Be Back in a Minute...

I run back to the dressing room to check to make sure the band is okay. I also am able to ensure that the members of the band get 10 minutes to cool down, towel down, and change before hordes of well-wishers, friends, and family burst into this tiny space.

10:40 P.M.: At the Merchandise Stall

The crowd has flocked to the merch stall. The difference a great show has on the overall merchandise sales never ceases to amaze me, and now Steve's little table is mobbed. To maximize sales, Steve has arranged his T-shirts, CDs, and other items in easy-to-reach piles and boxes. Money is changing hands at a considerable rate, and happy customers walk away with big ads for the band on their backs!

10:45 P.M.: Pack It All Away; We Do It All Again Tomorrow

Onstage, the house sound and lighting crew are putting away mics, monitors, and stands. Charlie and Dan have removed all the frontline equipment, guitar pedals, and such just as before, following the sound check (see Figure 7.8). They then collect all the guitars out of the toast racks and wipe down the strings before putting the guitars in their road cases. Cymbals and stands are taken off the kit, leaving the shells to be cased. Time and space are at a premium, so cases are brought onto the stage, where they can be filled and then pushed onto the dance floor, out of the way. As soon as a suitable space has been cleared, Lisa can get a ladder and start to take down the backdrop and the lighting fixtures she flew during the setup.

I do what I can, removing towels and drinks from the stage, putting away guitars and other small items. In the lid of each case, we have put an inventory of what should be in that case. It is easy to assume you have packed everything away, but it is easier to have a list and work off that. We also have a load list for the van. I have found that, in practice, one person should be in charge of packing the van. Over a period of shows, that person can develop "the pack"—the best way to get an extraordinary amount of gear into a small space. Having one dedicated person to administer the pack also cuts down on the potential for forgetting an item. However, we do have a list and a diagram in case our dedicated packer—in this case, Charlie—is ill or otherwise indisposed.

Figure 7.8 The backline crew tears down the gear, starting with any equipment placed downstage.

The packing away is well in hand, so I go up to find Sarah, the promoter's rep, to do the show settlement and to get paid. Sarah has all the figures ready for me, printed out on a spreadsheet. The show did sell out, so the settlement is fairly easy to calculate. I double-check the spreadsheet, and Sarah counts out the cash. A deposit has already been made by TKN Concerts to our booking agency. Therefore, I am picking up the remainder of the guarantee plus a split of the profits. (I will explain all of this in great detail in Chapter 9.) I count the cash and make a note of the amount collected in my notes, taking a copy of the settlement figures from Sarah. I then go find Steve at the merch stall to make sure he is okay and to give him a hand packing up.

10:55 P.M.: The Load Out

We are almost ready to load out. All the lighting equipment and the backdrop (don't forget the backdrop!) has been packed away and placed next to the load-out doors. The local crew has finished putting away the house equipment. Members of the crew are now available to give us a hand with load out. Dan arrives with the van (I sent him to get it 10 minutes previously), and we quickly load out.

11:05 P.M.: Make Sure the Van and the Gear Are Safe

The gear and merchandise are loaded, and the back door of the van is slammed shut, marking the end of another 10-hour day. We, the touring crew, thank and shake hands with the local crew, and we arrange to meet back inside for a beer. First, though, we need to make sure the van is safe parked here or that, if not, it is moved somewhere else. Because Dan wants to perhaps have a beer later and not risk drinking and driving, he volunteers to drive the van round to the hotel, park it in their car park, and walk back. I agree that is a very sensible thing to do, and then head back inside myself.

11:15 P.M.: The End of the Day

Inside, the venue has been transformed into a club and is slowly filling up with people. It is difficult to imagine that only 30 minutes ago, this place was a heaving rock show. I duck into the dressing room again to check that all is okay. The entire band is still there, joined now by the crew; everyone seems to be having a jolly good time. It has been a great show, and, better still, we have a day off tomorrow!

Ordinarily after a show, we would travel back to the hotel or perhaps drive to another city. In that case, I would have collected all the spare food and drink from the catering rider and made sure it got packed in the van. In tonight's case, I left it all for consumption, and now, 45 minutes later, most of it is gone! Because we are not traveling and most people know how to get home or to the hotel, I do not really have to organize transportation home or wakeup calls for the morning. I grab a beer and find a nice comfy chair....

Conclusion

Phew! Reading Show Diary #1 will give you an idea of an average day for a modern touring band. Okay, so not all bands play cutting-edge metal music like Millions of Americans, but the touring rigmarole is still the same. I personally have toured with a 24-piece jazz band, and my touring days were exactly the same as described in the Show Diary #1.

I am trying to convey the amount of preparation that goes into the shows, even before the tour starts, and the hard work needed to actually make a show work. You also have seen what each person does at a show and how these various people work together. Finally, notice in Show Diary #1 that the band, Millions of Americans, has surrounded itself with a competent and able crew, which is paid to do a great job day after day. The band is not afraid of hard work and it is totally capable of setting up its own guitar amps and drums. Modern touring goes beyond being able to play your songs and drive to the next show, though, and extra technicians and other crew are needed to maximize the potential of playing live.

The Etiquette of Sound Checks I always advise the bands I work for to pick two of their songs to play for sound check. This is really important for two reasons. First, a consistency of sound and presentation is created if the band plays the same two songs for every single sound check. I have lost track of the number of times I've had to ask a band onstage to please play something I know. I don't mean I don't know the band's material. But musicians are (hopefully) always writing and adapting their material. Because the only time they actually get to play together (apart from during the main performance) is during sound check, most bands see sound check as an opportunity to write, jam, or rehearse new material. So as soon as I ask them to play something, the band launches into the "new" song with players coming in and dropping out all over the place. Because the material is unfamiliar, I have no reference points.

As I keep saying, *sound check is not a rehearsal.* (I will remind you of this fact over and over during the course of this book.) Please do not even think about trying to rehearse at sound checks, especially if you are trying to create something amazing for that night's performance. Sure, you might be getting an hour to sound check every night on tour, but bitter experience has shown me that the one time you really need an hour at sound check, perhaps to write a new part or rehearse an old song for a radio session, that will be the one time when the bus will break down on the way to the show, or the bass amp will stop working for the whole sound check, or the musicians in the headline act will decide they are going to rehearse for their radio session for the next day! Just as most experienced recording musicians and producers do not try to "fix it in the mix," a touring band should never rely on sound check time to rehearse.

The second reason for planning sound check songs and parts is to create discipline. Sound checks can be a fiasco for many reasons, including treating sound check as a rehearsal. (See, I told you I would be reminding you!) Given that many musicians move straight from a comfortable, familiar environment (a recording/home studio or a rehearsal room) onto a cold and bad-sounding stage, it is not surprising that sound checks end up in a never-ending cycle of adjustment, then listening, then adjustment, with despair and anguish thrown into the mix. I am sure that given long enough, *any* stage sound or room can sound good. However, a band usually does not have an inordinate amount of time, and, as I explained earlier concerning sound waves and physics, the sound will not really improve until the rooms fills up with hot, sweaty, music-loving people. Therefore, it is important to accept these parameters early on in your career as a musician and/or crew person.

Always endeavor to carry out sound check as efficiently as possible. Don't rush or skip sound check if you can help it. At the same time, it is good discipline to restrict the number of songs you play at sound check. Basically, if you and your crew cannot get it together at the small club/theatre level in three songs, then something is wrong!

There is other etiquette and good practice to observe. Vocalists should always warm up before sound check, just as they would before a performance. Sing at three-quarters of your usual volume so as not to "blow" (ruin) your voice. If shouting/screaming is part of your vocal technique, then you should check one shout or scream so the FOH engineer can set the appropriate compressors and limiters. Do not shout at your full capacity and do not repeat more than three times. You do not want to blow your vocal cords for the show!

Always play the first song of your performance set as the last song for sound check. This will leave all the settings in place for that first song when you perform later. Of course, the sound will change with people in the room, and other bands may be using the same mixing board, but at least you and your sound crew will have a fighting chance of getting your sound mixed as it should be.

Finally, bands: Always thank the FOH and monitor engineer at the end of sound check. Sound crew: Always thank the band for its time and patience.

"Get a good tour manager and soundman straight away."

—Gareth Dobson, Drowned in Sound management

Show Diary #2

Millions of Americans did not always have the means to hire a crew to help them. Like countless bands before them, the members of MOA spent years driving themselves to shows in a cheap rental van, often sitting on top of their own gear. Lack of finances dictated driving back to their hometown after each show or arranging to sleep on friends' and fans' floors. Even after signing with MegaGlobal, the band members still did not have a great deal of money to spend on touring and continued to do all the driving, carrying, and merch selling for themselves.

They also made mistakes—lots of them.

In this second diary, I will describe in much more detail how a larger tour operates, what the functions of other crew and personnel are, and how a young, emerging act fits into this highly professional environment.

Millions of Americans Opening for Your Material Story at Brixton Academy, London

Date: Tuesday, December 12

Country: England

City: London

Venue: Brixton Academy

Status: First Opener

Capacity: 4,700

Ticket price: £25.50

Two years before Millions of Americans did its first headline tour, it was already being touted as the next big thing. Thanks to the band's booking agent, it was given opening slots for many prestigious acts. One of these shows was performing as the second opening act (first on stage of a three-band bill) to Your Material Story, the (then) darlings of the US rock scene. Your Material Story had just completed a sold-out tour of Britain and was finishing the tour off with a show at one of London's premier venues, Brixton Academy. Millions of Americans, on the other hand, was still playing shows in large pubs and small clubs.

Booking Millions of Americans onto larger concert bills enabled the band's management and booking agent to put Millions of Americans in front of hundreds more people than they had previously played to, and also helped give the band the confidence and ability to perform on larger stages.

Playing on a large stage in front of another band's audience is a true test for an upcoming act and clearly a goal for the team surrounding Millions of Americans. If you can win over another band's audience, then you are really doing something right.

It was not all smooth sailing for Millions of Americans, though, as you will see.

7:00 A.M.: Arrival

Your Material Story performed last night in Manchester, which is only 200 miles away (about four hours' driving distance). However, the two trucks and three tour buses are already here, parked outside the load-in bay of the venue. Inside the buses, the band and touring crew are sound asleep in their bunks. Modern touring is set up for overnight transportation of people and equipment. The huge amount equipment used for sound, lighting, video, stage, and set means that load in and setup take at least five hours. If you want to be ready for an artist's sound check at 3:00 P.M., then you need to start pretty early! Hence Your Material Story and the band's production team traveled overnight from Manchester and arrived in good time to grab parking spots directly outside of the venue (see Figure 7.9).

Figure 7.9   Brixton Academy in London, a 5,000-capacity venue.

7:45 A.M.: Local Crew, Runners, Catering Assistants, and Rigger Arrive

As you saw in the table of venue types in Chapter 2, a venue the size of Brixton Academy will not have a sound or lighting system permanently installed. Therefore, there is no full-time venue crew to look after the sound and lighting equipment or to assist with load in and load out. In the case of a large production tour, such as Your Material Story's, the sound, lights, video, stage, and set are hired by the band and transported from show to show, along with the necessary crew to set up and operate the systems. We still need someone to help us physically load it all in and out again, though, so, as you also saw in Chapter 2, the artist's contract specifies that the promoter agrees to supply locally hired crew to help with the unpacking, loading in, setting up, packing up, and loading out of all the equipment—in this case, two 40-foot trucks. (Actually, the tractor and trailer unit is 54 feet long, but the trailer that has the gear in it is 44 feet long. That is a lot of space to be filled with equipment!) The show also requires a rigger who is responsible for preparing the suspension points, motors, and hoists needed to suspend (or *fly*) the lighting, video, and PA systems in the air.

The number of local crew needed for a show call is always calculated in multiples of two, the theory being that it takes at least two people to lift or push an equipment case. This tour is a *two-truck tour* (the tour has two trucks!), and the production manager for Your Material Story, Chris, has asked each promoter to provide 12 local crew for the load-in call and 14 for the load-out call. These strong and capable people are now assembling at the loading dock of the venue for their 8:00 A.M. call.

Meanwhile, members of Millions of Americans are still at their homes, fast asleep.

8:00 A.M.: The Load In
The production manager for Your Material Story is in charge of 23 touring crew:

- Two caterers supplied by the catering supply company

- One FOH sound engineer hired and paid by the band

- One monitor sound engineer hired and paid by the band

- Two sound system technicians supplied by the sound system supplier

- One drum technician hired and paid by the band

- Two guitar and bass technicians hired and paid by the band

- One keyboard technician hired and paid by the band

- One lighting designer/operator hired and paid by the band

- One video operator hired and paid by the band

- Two lighting system technicians supplied by the lighting system supplier
- Two video systems crew members supplied by the video system supplier
- One wardrobe/dressing room assistant hired and paid by the band
- One security person hired and paid by the band
- Two truck drivers supplied by the trucking company
- Three tour bus drivers supplied by the bus company

As well as these people, there are two merchandise people, the tour manager, and the five band members, bringing the total touring party to 31 people. The caterers and video systems and lighting systems crew will be needed at load in, and the production manager will make sure they are awake and ready. The load in can commence when all the relevant touring crew and local crew are assembled and ready.

To keep 31 people happy and well requires that they eat properly. Leaving the venue to find food is impractical because the whole crew is busy pretty much all day, and often good food is a long way away! Therefore, modern touring takes its kitchens and cooks along for the ride. Catering equipment, cookers, fridges, coffee machines, cutlery, crockery, and food are all built into flight cases and trucked around with the rest of the equipment. This morning (as with every load in), the catering equipment is loaded into the venue first, and the caterers begin setting up the equipment and preparing the first meal of the day—breakfast. They planned menus and shopping lists last night, hopefully maintaining an interesting but nutritious diet for the band and touring crew.

One runner already has been given a pre-shop list (usually listed in the contract rider) of food needed by the caterers to cook breakfast for the crew. The runner has gone to buy what is needed. Back at the venue, the locally hired catering assistants will work with the touring caterers, doing food preparation and lots and lots of dishwashing.

8:15 A.M.: Rigging, Video, and Lighting

Back at the load-in dock, Chris, the production manager, is supervising the load in, directing the boxes being wheeled into the venue to their respective places. There is no point in unloading everything into the venue at once; it would simply fill the load-in bay and cause an immense log jam of cases. The production manager, working with the crew boss of the local crew, makes sure that each respective department of the production (video, lights, and sound) has the space they need to get their work done before the next department starts to get loaded in. Truck #1 contains catering, rigging, lighting, and video equipment; this is unloaded first.

Nothing can be achieved in a modern production without the motors and the rigging being put into place. The rigger is already in the roof void preparing the points. These are the points in the roof or on the ceiling beams from which the chain hoist motors can be suspended in order to raise the lighting trusses, the video screen, and the speaker boxes into the air (see Figure 7.10).

Below, on the stage, there is an immense amount of activity. The various lighting truss sections have been laid out on the floor and are being assembled by the local crew, ready to be hoisted up into the air. Once assembled and attached to the chain hoists, the trusses will be raised to chest height in order for the touring and local crew to attach the various lighting fixtures to the truss. The video crew has rigged the screens to the chain hoists and has instructed the local crew to connect the power and signal cables.

Figure 7.10 Truss section showing lamps attached and motors in place.

9:30 A.M.: The Runner Returns

The runner responsible for the catering supplies returns, his car full of groceries for the day. Remember, the food needed for cooking breakfast was already organized; this food is for lunch and dinner.

10:00 A.M.: PA System

With rigging, lighting, and video setup well underway, Chris signals for the PA truck to be opened up and unloaded. Meanwhile, the caterers have almost finished preparing breakfast and have set out hot and cold food and drink for the touring crew.

The promoter's rep, Barry, has arrived at the venue and opened up the production offices. The promoter, TKN, has promoted most of the shows on this tour, and Barry has been able to travel with the band on one of the crew buses. He is now setting up his laptop and printer in the production office. Barry arranged with the venue to have 40 bath towels ready for crew showers, and the truck and bus drivers already have taken advantage of the clean showering facilities. Chris also has his computer, as well as touring cases containing paperwork and other supplies that he shares with the tour manager. These all have been loaded into the office by the local crew. Barry and Chris briefly discuss the schedule for the day and agree on the timings shown in Figure 7.11.

Barry says he will double-check this with the tour manager, Kristen, when she comes in, but both agree that these timings will work for now. Barry then sets to work organizing the signage and timing sheets for the day. The runners make themselves known to Barry, and he takes their cell phone numbers and prints them on a runners list, which he pins up in the office.

10:30 A.M.: The Support Band Starts Its Day

Meanwhile, 170 miles north in Sheffield, the various members of Millions of Americans are beginning to wake up in their respective homes. They have agreed with Dan (their mate with a van) that they will leave Sheffield no later than midday to get to London in time for their sound check. Even though the band signed to MegaGlobal Records earlier in the year, they still do not have access to really good tour support from the record label, so they do not have a professional tour manager. Dan

T.K.N Concerts

Tuesday 12th December

Show times

15.00	Sound check - Your Material Story
16.00	Set up and sound check - Terrible Mistake
17.15	Set up and sound - Millions Of Americans
18.00	Dinner
19.00	**Doors**
19.20 - 19.50	Millions Of Americans
20.05 - 20.30	Terrible Mistake
21.00 - 22.45	**Your Material Story**
23.00	Curfew and load out.

Figure 7.11 The timings for tonight's show. Notice the rep has made the important times bold and also specified how much the onstage time should be for each band.

has been working as tour manager and learning really well, but the band members feel they would like to hire someone else as soon as possible. They feel Dan does not have the experience of the larger shows and that too many mistakes are being made. In the meantime, the band's manager has been working with the booking agent and supplying Dan with the necessary load in, sound check, and show times.

Note: A Long Day Please remember that some people started working on the show long before you even got out of bed.

11:00 A.M.: Promo

Your Material Story has some promo organized today at a record megastore in the heart of London. Kristen, the tour manager, woke them up about an hour ago, and now five slightly dazed young men emerge from their bus and, accompanied by their security guy, climb into a car sent by the record label. The schedule supplied by Kristen means that they will be back at the venue by about 2:00 P.M.

11:50 A.M.: It's All Up in the Air

Back at the venue, the PA system has been loaded in, set up, and flown in the air (see Figure 7.12). The system crew checks the PA, usually by running a test signal through the system. This signal is called *pink noise,* and it is designed to give the same energy across all audio frequencies. (It sounds like a sustained whooshing sound.) By pinking the system, the PA crew can check its various components by listening to the output from each speaker. This checking is done with the PA system suspended just a foot or so off the stage; it is a bit pointless to fly it all the way up in the air and then do a check. If the PA is not working, you will have to bring it all the way down again!

After being checked, the PA is raised to the correct height and made secure. The stage is now clear of flight cases, so the local crew has been able to set up the small platforms, known as *risers,* for the drum kit and the keyboards. The sound system crew has placed the monitor wedges in the approximate positions needed. It has also run cables and mains power across the stage. Remember, the band's actual equipment has not been set up yet, so there is no point in placing monitor wedges all over the stage. The sound crew can build the side-fill and drum-fill speakers, though. Side fills are placed stage left and stage right, facing each other, and the drum fill is built on top of a wheeled sub-bass speaker. This can be placed directly behind the drummer in

Figure 7.12 A typical flown PA system.

order for him to be able to really "feel" his kick drum when it is struck (see Figure 7.13).

Note: Side Fills Side fills are designed to supply more power and volume in the monitor system than the wedge speakers. With that in mind, use them with care. The fact that they face directly across the front of the stage means that their sound will often travel straight into the downstage vocal microphones. This can cause feedback problems and a lack of clarity in the onstage sound.

Figure 7.13   A drum fill monitor stack. This will be placed directly behind the drummer, much to the annoyance of the lighting engineer! Drum fills tend to be large and tall; any lighting from behind the drummer will show this huge lump as a stark silhouette.

12:00 P.M.: Programming and Backline

The band's own lighting and video operators are busy fine-tuning the programming for tonight's show. This includes focusing two massive follow-spot lights that have been placed up in the balcony and that are used to highlight key members of the band at appropriate points in the performance. The bus and truck drivers will be paid in cash (in addition to their normal wages) to position and operate the spots. The crew supplied by the lighting and video suppliers is redundant for a while (unless they have major repairs or maintenance). They take this opportunity to grab a shower and some lunch and to have a nap. Having your "home" (the tour bus) parked right outside the venue is a great thing—you can go and climb in your bunk anytime you have a spare moment!

Meanwhile, the local crew is helping the four backline technicians set up the band's stage equipment. Compared to two trucks full of PA and lights a few guitar amps is nothing, but the band's backline crew still appreciates the help. Once the backline has been set up, the sound system crew can start to place the microphones and monitor wedges.

Julie, the monitor engineer, will ring out the monitors—that is, adjust the volume and equalization of each monitor wedge on the stage to obtain maximum volume from each wedge without feedback. Unfortunately, the only way to do this is to stand onstage and speak or shout into each microphone for what seems like an eternity!

Note: One Two, One Two, Testing, One Two… Ringing out the monitors is potentially hazardous to your hearing; if you do not have to be onstage during this process, then leave the room.

1:00 P.M.: Cut the Locals

Local crew is contracted out to the promoter on an hourly basis, usually with a minimum on-call time of five hours. Obviously the promoter does not want to pay extra for the crew if he can help it, so after five hours, Barry checks with Chris to make sure the local crew can be dismissed for the morning. Chris then checks with the head of each department to make sure they no longer require any local crew. If this is the case, then the majority of the local crew will be dismissed ("cut") until that evening's call. Some crew will be selected to stay on for the duration of the day to help assist with loading in merchandise and equipment belonging to the opening bands; in this case, just two crew.

1:15 P.M.: The Support Band Is on the Road

The members of Millions of Americans have loaded up their van and left their hometown. Through a combination of bad planning on Dan's behalf and total carelessness by the band, they are running late already. Dan is really worried about getting stuck in rush hour traffic as they hit the outskirts of London. The band members are also worried. This is the biggest show they have ever played. They know they have rehearsed every aspect of the show—the songs as well as the performance—but they still are feeling anxious. There was a problem at last night's rehearsal with one of the guitar amplifiers. The band members are not experienced in maintaining or fixing their equipment, and now they can't help feeling that they should have taken the time to fix the problem then, instead of assuming it will be okay today.

Note: The Chance of a Lifetime Every show is important; some shows are just a bit more important than others.

1:30 P.M.: All Quiet

The local crew has been cut, and the venue is strangely quiet. The lighting, video, and PA systems are all flown and secured, and the stage is starting to resemble a proper rock show. The backline crew is onstage, still setting up the band's backline equipment. The lighting designer/operator (LD) is fine-tuning the programming of her show. The lighting show has been designed in advance and is mainly computerized, with a digital desk commanding lamps that contain motors for movement. However, the difference in venue heights and widths means that the lighting fixtures have to be manually adjusted each afternoon in order for their light beams to hit the correct part of the stage. This process is known as the *focus*, and it will occupy the LD for the rest of the afternoon.

The video crew has tested the screens as well as the control equipment, and the crew is happy that it is all working well. Because the content shown on the screens is already recorded and edited, the video crew has little to do now apart from maintenance. After that, it is time for some lunch and perhaps a shower and a nap.

In the catering area, the tour chefs and cooks have served up a bewildering assortment of soups, cold dishes, and snacks for the crew lunch, and there is now a line forming outside the catering room.

The sound crew is still working with the band's backline technicians to place microphones, wedges, and cables. The band's FOH engineer wants to start line check at 2:45 P.M. in order to start sound check at 3:00.

2:00 P.M.: Setting the Scene

As lunch ends, the caterers begin to prepare the dressing room and the hospitality supplies. Amy, the wardrobe and dressing room assistant, helps the local catering assistant by placing ice in cooler boxes and then filling the cooler boxes with the various beverages on the rider for the headline and support bands. Although the promoter has agreed to supply the food and drink necessary for the show (by signing the contract and contract rider), it is cheaper and easier for the promoter to actually give the headline act the catering money directly. The caterers are then given this cash, and they use it to buy the supplies for the support acts as well as the headliners. Therefore, it is the caterers who supply (and clean up) the dressing room catering rider for the support bands.

Note: **Make Friends with the Caterers** Always make friends with the caterers on a tour or event. This is especially true if your show deal does not involve you getting fed. Caterers are responsible for working out how much of the overall catering budget they can spend on each of the support acts' drinks and dressing room snacks. Be extra nice to the touring caterers, and you may get a few more beers or an extra bottle of wine at the next venue!

2:25 P.M.: Where Are the Showers?

The five band members of Your Material Story have returned from their promo commitment. Kristen shows them around the venue, pointing out the dressing rooms, the catering areas, and the showers. As well as dressing rooms, the venue is large enough to have space for dedicated band practice/tuning rooms. The members of Your Material Story are young musicians and passionate about their art and their musicianship. The individual members practice their instruments whenever they can, so rooms are set up for them at each venue so they can practice their parts during the day.

Note: Save Water—Don't Shower Taking a shower is very important to anyone who is touring on a sleeper bus. If you ain't on a bus, then don't use a venue shower without asking first! Touring personnel have a show to put up and have little time to be waiting in line for a shower.

2:30 P.M.: Still on the Road

As the show setup in London continues according to schedule, Millions of Americans is far from being on schedule. A combination of a late start, a slow van, and bad traffic has contributed to the band being at least two hours from the venue at this point. They were told to be there at 4:00 P.M. for a 5:00 sound check. Dan estimates that they will now arrive closer to 5:00. He debates whether to call ahead and let the YMS people know, but decides he'll call when he has a more accurate arrival time.

2:45 P.M.: Line Check

Dave, Your Material Story's FOH engineer, arrives at the FOH mixing desk. The band's monitor engineer and the backline techs are ready onstage to start line check. Remember, this is not the full sound check, but a preparation session to ensure that all the instruments have the correct microphones and DI boxes attached to them and that all those microphones and DI boxes are connected to the right inputs on the mixing desks. Dave calls out the instruments using a microphone that is connected to the PA system and routed through to the onstage monitor speakers (see Figure 7.14). The backline techs then hit, strum, press, or sing into each microphone as necessary. Dave and the monitor engineer, Julie, check each input on their respective mixing desks to make sure that the right instrument is coming up the right channel

Figure 7.14 The FOH engineer begins the sound check process.

and that the signal is at full strength and is not distorted, hissy, or in any other way impaired.

When each channel has been checked, Dave may ask for a crew member to actually play the instrument in a performance style, and then he will listen to that instrument through the PA at full volume. Your Material Story has been on tour for a week or so now, though, and the various instrument and desk settings have been pretty much set during that time. Dave and Julie both know through years of touring experience that they will only need to adjust a few specific levels to get a decent sound, especially in the sound check. There is little point in tweaking and adjusting for hours—the equipment will behave in the same way as it did at last night's show when the venue is warm and full.

3:00 p.m.: The Sound Check

Kristen has brought the band members down from their dressing and practice rooms and onto the stage. The backline techs have done final checks on the instruments, and all the lines (channels into and out of the FOH and monitor desk) have been proven to work. It is time for sound check. Your Material Story has been touring professionally for about three years now, and members of the band know that the idea of a sound check is to become accustomed to the different venues, making any adjustments in stage volume for the backline equipment or stage monitors, and to play through a few songs in order to give Dave and Julie a chance to check all their settings.

Sound check is not a rehearsal or a songwriting opportunity. (I told you I would remind you of this!) With this in mind, the band works its way through four or five songs, stopping only to give directions and suggestions to band members or crew. The songs are all part of tonight's set, and there is no practicing or writing of parts or songs.

Even still, to the casual observer the sound check seems like an unorganized shambles, despite the band and crew's professional approach and years of experience. This whole thing started at 8:00 this morning, and the band is only just doing a sound check!

3:30 P.M.: Still Stuck in Traffic

The members of Millions of Americans have managed to make up some time and are nearer to the city, but are now stuck on the outskirts in very bad traffic. The band is scheduled to arrive at the venue in 30 minutes, but it is at least an hour away! The band members are really nervous now. Dan already warned them (from information given to him by the manager) that there might not be time for a sound check anyway, even if they were on schedule. This is a big show for the musicians in Millions of Americans, and it is inconceivable that they might blow their big chance by being late. The thought on everyone's mind is, "Oh, why didn't we set off on time?"

Note: Add an Hour I always add an hour to any estimated travel time. No one will be upset if you arrive early.

3:45 P.M.: Opening Bands

Terrible Mistake, the tour's opening act, has arrived at the venue and its musicians are setting up their equipment with the help of the local

Figure 7.15 The local crew pushes the opening band's equipment onto the stage.

crew who are still on call (see Figure 7.15). The musicians assemble as much as they can, especially the drum kit. There is no point in waiting to set up everything while actually onstage—this just wastes time. Terrible Mistake has played on every date of the tour so far. The band members are label-mates and friends with the band members of Your Material Story, so it was deemed appropriate for Terrible Mistake to be on the bill; the promoters really did not have a say in the matter. Your Material Story's booking agent did the deal with the promoters, and it was only for this London show that TKN, the promoter, felt it necessary to add a third band. TKN were specifically looking for an act that would be able to draw at least 250 people, and Millions of Americans fit that bill.

As I mentioned, Terrible Mistake has been on the whole tour so far, so the band is pretty used to the routine of this tour. The band is traveling with its own tour manager and FOH engineer, and the crew for Your Material Story is helping out with fixing and tuning guitars wherever they can, mainly as a special favor to a young band who also happens to be label-mates with the headline act! This courtesy even extends to trucking Terrible Mistake's equipment. A deal was done by Terrible Mistake's tour manager with the Your Material Story production manager before the tour started. This deal means Terrible Mistake did not need to hire an expensive van with a trailer or cargo space for its gear, thus saving the band money.

The FOH engineer for Terrible Mistake is not too pleased tonight. Usually Terrible Mistake is first to perform onstage, so all the settings for the show can be set and then left after its sound check. Tonight, however, there will be another band (Millions of Americans), so for the first time on this tour, Terrible Mistake's engineer will have to chart (write down the settings for) his desk after sound check. This also means that the sound will not be perfect for the first couple of songs in Terrible Mistake's set tonight. The engineer will try to write down all his settings and recall them as accurately as possible, but mistakes happen, and, besides, the backline equipment will have to be struck after Terrible Mistake's sound check to make way for the opening band.

Note: Sound Check and Performing Order Bands sound check in reverse order to that in which they are booked to play. The headline act will do sound check first, then the band next below them on the bill, and so on until the first band to perform sound checks last. This prevents having to change settings, microphones, and stands too many times during the sound checks and changeovers. This is why it is doubly important to have a running schedule well ahead of the concert day and to make sure you are not late for your arrival, load in, and sound check. You may have no sound check at all if you are late and you miss your slot.

4:10 P.M.: Next Sound Check!
Your Material Story has finished its sound check. The band members troop offstage and back to their dressing room. A TV interviewer and film crew are upstairs from one of the national music programs. The

program is interviewing the band for an upcoming TV special, so it needs a fair amount of access to the band.

Onstage, the techs are putting guitars back into toast racks, removing pedal boards from FOH, and tidying up cables. The drum tech places a black cloth over the drums, and the guitar techs place other black cloths over the amplifier cabinets. As well as offering a slight protection from liquids hurled from the crowd, this black backdrop creates a more neutral backdrop for the opening acts.

The PA sound crew have already prepped the various microphones, stands, and wedges they are going to use for the opening acts, and they wait patiently to set these once Terrible Mistake has set up its gear. Even before the tour, the FOH engineer for Terrible Mistake emailed an input list to the PA company, so the systems crew knows exactly what it needs to provide for this band.

Your Material Story's own sound crew, Dave and Julie, are not really employed to take care of the opening acts, so after making sure that all their settings are saved or marked down, they are free to relax until changeover.

4:30 P.M.: Still Stuck in Traffic

The members of Millions of Americans are about 15 minutes from the venue, but they are still stuck in bad traffic. Dan has been worrying about calling the venue; he wants to let the staff there know that he and the band may be late, but he does not want to appear unprofessional or disorganized. In the end, Dan decides to be sensible rather than allow his pride to get in the way, and he makes the call to the venue's promoter listed in the information that Millions of Americans' manager gave him. Dan is a bit surprised because the telephone number for the venue is a Manchester number; he was expecting a London telephone number because they are playing at Brixton Academy in London. He calls and asks for the person listed on his information sheet, only to be told that the person is on vacation and will be back next week. Dan is really confused now—he is calling a Manchester telephone number for a London show, and the person organizing the show is on holiday? This cannot be right, can it?

> **Note: You Know Better** Learn the roles and responsibilities of each person involved on a tour. This shows respect and an interest in the industry in which you are involved. Your sound checks and shows will go a lot better if you take the time to know who is doing your monitor sound or lights.

4:55 P.M.: **Where's the First Band?**

Terrible Mistake has set up, its equipment has been miked up, and its musicians are proceeding through their sound check. One of the PA system crew is operating monitors for them, but because Terrible Mistake has been on the entire tour, the engineer has a good idea of what the individual musicians need in their stage monitors. This knowledge means it does not take the engineer too much time to get the band's stage sound dialed in. This leaves some time for the two engineers to plan what they need in the way of microphones and monitor wedges for the opening act, Millions of Americans. Or it would if they had received any information about the band and their technical requirements. The engineers have received no input list, despite repeated requests.

The touring system engineers have asked the production manager, who has asked the promoter's rep, who in turn talked to the office and tried to get the promoter to contact the artist's management through the booking agent, but to no avail. The engineers do not even know how many musicians there are in Millions of Americans, what instruments they play, or what style of music they perform. (However, it is a safe bet that the band will play some sort of rock or metal, given the style of the other two acts!) Unfortunately, with limited time and microphone stock available on the tour, the two engineers will have to be pretty brutal when it comes to setting up this opening act. In other words, the opening act is going to get what it gets, not what it really wants. Besides, they are late, and that is the worst crime of all.

> **Note: Respect** Being late is the worst crime of all for a young band or crew. You are forcing people who may have already worked an eight-hour day to hang around even longer.

Word of the late arrival has also reached the production office. The production manager, Chris, has decided that his crew needs to have its dinner break at 6:00 P.M., no matter what happens. If the opening band turns up soon, it might get a chance for a quick line check, and that's all.

5:15 P.M.: You've Had Your Chance

Dan and Millions of Americans have finally arrived at the venue, but they have no idea how to get in or where to load in their equipment. After driving around the block, they finally spot the trucks and buses parked at the load-in bay. Dan pulls over and shouts to the band to unload all the gear so he can go off and park the van. The boys in the band immediately jump out and start hurriedly pulling heavy amps and cabs onto the sidewalk, but frankly, they are a bit bemused—why the hurry? "It's only 5:15 P.M., and we are not onstage until 7:30," is the common thought. "Why is Dan panicking, and why do we have to rush?"

Note: **Wasting Time** Driving around a venue or trying to find a parking place can take 20 minutes. You might only have 30 minutes for sound check....

The band members haul their gear into the loading bay and onto the stage, walking straight past the local crew who are still on call, as well as the sound system techs who have been patiently waiting for them. Luckily, the local crew and the PA guys realize that these "kids with guitars" must be the opening act, so they quickly approach the band to sort things out. The local crew grabs the remaining backline and brings it into the venue.

The PA techs start to interrogate the musicians to establish whether they have a FOH engineer. Upon learning that the band does not have an engineer, the questions become about the band's lineup, input list, and stage positions. With some helpful explanations and suggestions from the PA guys, the band and the PA crew work together to enable the sound crew to provide a basic microphone and monitor setup.

Note: The Non–Input List Explanation A sound engineer needs to know how many sound sources there are in your setup—how many guitar amps, how many vocalists, what kind of outputs your DJ mixer has, and so on. If you do not have an input list for the engineer, then try to describe these sound sources instead.

Meanwhile, Dan has managed to find a parking spot several streets away for the van. He discovers that the band has left the merchandise (T-shirts and hoodies to sell) in the van, so now he has to lug a heavy cardboard box all the way back to the venue. Added to this, his mobile phone is ringing constantly; the manager, record label, and booking agent are all calling with guest list requests and schedule updates.

6:00 P.M.: The Concessions

Your Material Story has a licensing deal with a professional merchandising company (see Chapter 9), which has supplied two merchandisers to go on the tour and take care of selling the vast range of clothing and accessories that are branded with the Your Material Story logos. These people do not need to be at the venue until late in the afternoon, so they do not ride on the tour buses. Instead, they have a van and stay in hotels overnight. Arriving at the venue each afternoon at about 5:00, the two merchandisers immediately find the local crew and use them to load in the boxes of merch from the van, as well as any other merch that may have been carried in the trucks.

Lightweight professional display stands can be used for the T-shirts, and now the two merch people are busy putting up and creating an attractive display. The company merchandisers will not actually get behind the stands and sell the merch, though. As is common with most venues, Brixton Academy charges visiting productions a concession fee for all merchandising sold in the venue. For this, the venue agrees to supply people to actually sell the merch, presumably to keep an eye on actual sales. To create an accurate picture of total sales, all stock must be accounted for, and a total figure must be agreed upon between the tour merchandisers and the venue. Therefore, the stock is checked and counted by a venue representative before the doors open to the public.

Meanwhile, the catering area is filling up with the Your Material Story band and crew, all of whom are hungry and eager to relax. Dinner is served at 6:00 each day by the tour caterers, and it is the last proper meal of the day for people who will be working until 1:00 the next morning.

6:10 P.M.: Dark Stage

Millions of Americans has finished setting up its gear, and all the microphones are in place. It has taken quite a long time because there is little usable space onstage, and the PA people do not have sufficient equipment to provide the band with dedicated microphones and wedges. The two PA guys had to borrow microphones, stands, and wedges from the Terrible Mistake setup and re-patch various cables to make the new setup work. When that was finished, a quick line check was performed, and actual sound check began. Now, however, time has run out, and Chris, the production manager, has come down to the stage and ordered the PA guys to have a break and go for dinner.

Members of Millions of Americans are furious. They cannot understand why they can't have a full sound check! Everything is set up, and now some guy is telling them that the sound guys are going for dinner? Can't that wait a bit longer?

After a bit of shouting, it is patiently explained to Millions of Americans that the sound guys are not from just around the corner; they travel with the tour. They have been here since 8:00 A.M., rigging, flying, testing, and running this system. They will be here until 11:00 P.M., and then they will have to take down the whole lot again and pack it into trucks. If the PA guys do not take a break now, they will probably not get a chance again until 1:00 A.M. Besides, Millions of Americans was late. "You are either here for sound check or you are not. It's as simple as that," says Chris. Chris also informs them that they need to get up to the production office to get their passes and to hand in any guest lists—now!

Note: Know Your Place You have no rights as an opening act; you cannot expect a sound check even if you have an agency contract. If the headline act has overrun or if you are late arriving at the venue, it does not matter; the doors to the venue still have to open at a certain time, and the show has to finish at a certain time.

The lighting crew and the band's lighting designer have been relaxing during the various sound checks. They then made sure they were first in line for the evening meal because they can use this "dark stage" hour to do final focusing and programming of the lights.

6:15 P.M.: T-Shirts—How Much?

Dan has managed to struggle back to venue, carrying his rapidly collapsing box of merchandise through the back streets of Brixton. Like the band members in Millions of Americans, Dan has no idea where to gain entry to the venue, so he staggers around the block with his box. The streets around the venue are already packed with fans lining up for entry, as well as police, security personnel, and scalpers (also known as *ticket touts*). Dan finally collapses back at the main public entrance and explains to a venue security person who he is and what he is doing. Obviously, with no entry ticket or pass, the security people do not have to admit him, but luckily they take pity on him and direct him to the merchandise concessions in the venue foyer. Here, Dan spies people hanging up shirts and unpacking boxes. He quickly introduces himself and asks whether he can sell his T-shirts here as well.

After some time, Dan is introduced to one of the tour merchandisers, who is still overseeing the count-in and display of the Your Material Story merchandise at the three venue merch concession stands.

DAN: Hi, I'm Dan. I'm with Millions of Americans; we are playing tonight.

KEV (TOUR MERCHANDISER): Unlucky mate. What can I do for you?

DAN: Er, well, we would like to put our shirts up here and sell them. Please.

KEV: [Laughs] Well, you can't put them on my stands [merchandising display boards], mate. The band has done a licensing deal with my company, so they get sole use of these boards. Besides, we've got so many designs I've filled all my space. You should have been here earlier; we could have sorted something out.

DAN: So I can't sell my shirts here?

KEV: You can sell what you like, mate, but you need to sort it out with the venue. It's a concession, so everything has to go through the venue. Nothing to do with me, mate. Sort a deal out with them, and I'll see if I can free up a bit of space for you. How many designs you got?

DAN: Designs? Er, I dunno. I've got this box of T-shirts to sell and some CDs....

KEV: No mate—how many *different* sorts of T-shirts you got? You know, have they all got the same thing printed on 'em and are they a girls shirt, a regular T, and a hoodie? You know, stuff like that.

DAN: Oh, I see. Well, it's the same picture, but on two different types. We have a black T-shirt and a hoodie. The shirt is in small, medium, large, and extra-large, and the hoodie comes in...

KEV: Yeah, whatever. So you got two designs—a T-shirt and a hoodie. Okay. The venue will charge you for each shirt you sell, and you cannot sell less than my shirts.

DAN: But Millions of Americans is a new band. We are bound to sell fewer shirts than Your Material Story!

KEV: [Confused] What? No, I mean you cannot sell your shirts for less money than the Your Material Story shirts!

DAN: Oh, sorry. How much, then?

At this point, Kev explains the prices, and Dan nearly passes out. Your Material Story is charging nearly five times the price of the Millions of Americans shirts! Who is going to pay that much for a shirt from a relatively unknown band? And if they *do* sell anything, Millions of Americans will have to pay some of that money back to the venue! "This is absurd," thinks Dan. No wonder concert merchandise costs so much.

Dan turns to approach the venue rep to negotiate a deal. As he goes, Kev offers one last piece of advice.

KEV: Oh yeah. If you and your band really want to make it big, make sure your guys get to this merch stand straight after they play and meet the kids.

Dan has no idea what Kev is talking about, and he stomps off to sort out his ludicrous merchandising deal.

6:20 P.M.: The Promoter's Rep

Kristen, the tour manager, is in the production office (see Figure 7.16). She has collated all the various e-mail, fax, and telephone requests for guest list tickets for tonight's show and is entering them into a spreadsheet. Kristen needs to get this completed and handed to Barry well ahead of the doors opening because Barry then needs to print and authenticate the various passes and make sure he gets the whole lot to the box office before the doors open. Obviously, for a show like this, the promoter will cap the guest list tickets (usually at the contract stage), but even so the total number of free tickets and passes will reach the 100 figure. That means a lot of passes and envelopes to prepare, and it is unfair to leave it until the last minute. Therefore, Kristen and Barry are working furiously to prepare everything well ahead of doors.

Figure 7.16 A typical touring production office. This is the nerve center for the tour, but only for one day. Good use of flight case as a seat as well!

Note: Don't Leave It until the Last Minute! If you are trying to get guest list places or free tickets for a concert, get those names on the list at least before lunchtime the day of the show. This applies to you especially if you are performing or working on the show. The number of guest list places for a show is allocated very early on in the contract negotiation process. Once this has been contracted, a good tour manager will work throughout the tour to get a clear indication of all guest ticket demands, especially for the major city shows, such as London, New York, Paris, Köln, Berlin, Toronto, Sydney, Tokyo, and so on. On the specific show day, the tour manager and promoter will want to finalize the proposed number of free tickets and passes as early as possible, at least 30 minutes before doors. The list then can be printed off, passes can be printed, and the whole lot can be delivered to the box office or guest list entrance at FOH. It is a huge pain for the tour manager to add names and passes to the list after the guest list has been sent to FOH and the doors are open. Therefore, if your name or the names of your guests have not been added to the list before the doors open, they probably will not be added!

6:25 P.M.: The Guest List

Following polite instructions from Chris, the production manager, the musicians from Millions of Americans have found their way to the production office. Knowing they have to sort out their guest list, the band members file into the office and ask whom they should speak to. Kristen, the tour manager, points them to Barry, who is the promoter's rep. Barry first introduces himself, informing the band that he is the person they should deal with all night, as he works for the promoter. Barry then asks the musicians how many people they are. "Pardon?" says the band.

Barry patiently explains they need passes for access to the stage and their dressing rooms, and he needs to know how many passes they need. Luckily, the band remembers Dan and tells Barry they will need a total of six passes. Barry grabs passes from his production case, authenticates them, and hands them to the band. Then, counting out some cash, he looks at the band. "Okay," he says. "Here is your buyout money." The musicians in Millions of Americans have no idea what "buyout money" is, so when this guy starts giving them £10 ($18) each, they figure it must be a mistake. Barry explains, again very patiently, that as part of the contract and contract rider negotiated by the Millions of Americans agent, TKN Concerts is contracted to supply food and drinks to the band. Because it is easier and a standard concert cost for the promoter to give the cash than to supply a hot meal, TKN is now handing over £10 ($18) to each member of the Millions of Americans cast and crew.

Finally, Barry asks the members of Millions of Americans whether they have a guest list for him. The members of Millions of Americans are very familiar with the process of guest lists, having gigged up and down the country for the last two years. Dan had previously informed them that their free ticket allocation would be 10 tickets, so the band has prepared a list, which they now hand over to Barry.

6:35 P.M.: The Support Band Dressing Room

The musicians in Millions of Americans are in their small but very comfortable dressing room. They are overjoyed to see an assortment of crisps/chips, dips, veggies, and fruit laid out for them, as well as loads of beer plus a bottle of spirits, drinks on ice, and lots of new plastic cups. "Wow, this is the *big* time," they think to themselves. The band has no idea that this has all been sorted out in advance by their agent issuing a standard contract rider.

Dan has also made it to the dressing room and, although he is very stressed and nervous, he is glad to see the boys in the band looking happy. "Might be a decent show after all," he think to himself.

6:45 P.M.: Security Briefing

Forty-five security staff have been hired by the promoter for tonight's performance. They have been sourced from a reliable and fully licensed specialized event security company, and now they have arrived at the venue. Already briefed by their team leaders, the staff allocated to be stationed in strategic areas—especially the pit and backstage areas—are further briefed and introduced to the touring production key personnel—the artist's head of security and the tour manager. During this extra briefing, the security personnel are given a brief background about the type of music, crowd behavior patterns, use or restriction of alcohol, restriction to professional pass-holding photographers, and other important crowd and artist safety considerations.

Note: Photographers' Restrictions—First Three Songs, No Flash

"First three songs and no flash" is the catch-all restriction applied to professional photographers given passes to take photos from the pit (the space in front of the stage between the stage and the crowd safety barrier, if there is one). This basically means that after three songs, the photographers must exit the pit and take no more photos. They also cannot use a flash while taking photos in the pit.

What is the reason for this? It's simple. After the first three songs, your artist will have become hot under the stage lighting and may have become sweaty and disheveled. It's not a good look for a national newspaper or magazine. Also, most musicians onstage are playing some kind of instrument that usually requires them to look down at their instrument (guitar, bass, keyboards, strings, and woodwind, for example). Whereas the lighting rig will be focused to shine on the musicians from above and behind, if you are studying your fret board and some photographer blasts you from the pit with her mega-camera flash, you may become slightly distracted.

Beside, photos taken with flash look lousy.

6:55 P.M.: Time for Doors

This is a sold-out show; tickets are no longer available, especially "on the door" (at the venue box office) and have not been for several weeks. Despite this fact, a growing number of young fans have been lining up outside the venue since midday. These are the real die-hard fans that have come to embrace the true spirit of concert-going—meeting their friends and sharing the unique experience of the music. Fueled by fast food and cheap alcohol, the ever-growing line of fans is cheerful and good-natured (see Figure 7.17).

It will soon be dark and cold; rain is on its way. It is very important to the venue and the promoters that the audience members are admitted

Figure 7.17 The reason the circus is in town—a line of adoring fans who have waited all day, even though they have tickets.

as soon as possible. Barry, the rep, checks with Kristen to make sure the production is ready for the doors to open. The guest list has been delivered to the box office and the hired venue security people have been briefed by Kristen and the band's security person. Kristen checks with Chris, who in turn checks with the various department heads to ensure that all departments are ready for the doors to open.

When making a venue ready for the audience, the following points need to be considered:

- All flight cases and cables are cleared from the auditorium.

- All lighting trusses and flown PA systems are secured and safe.

- The lighting crew have finished programming and have lit the stage with a decorative "walk in" look.

- The merchandise teams have finished preparing the merch stands and are ready for the sudden influx of (hopefully) paying customers.

Chris gets the okay from all departments, makes sure the PA systems guys have put on some suitable music, and then gives the okay. The doors are open!

7:15 P.M.: Hi, Is Everything Okay?

Millions of Americans is due onstage at 7:30 P.M. It is now 7:15 P.M., and the band is pretty nervous. They have been unable to relax, especially when confronted with a stream of well-wishers trooping into their small dressing room. The guests are from the band's record company, their booking agent, and their manager. They make up a substantial part of the band's guest list, which kind of annoyed the band because they wanted some of their mates to be able to get in for free as well.

The band's guests ask about the band's sound check (which obviously produces a few strong words) and help themselves to the beer and soft drinks supplied as part of the band's rider. Dan realizes too late that the five small bottles of water he was going to put onstage for the musicians have now been drunk! And, he realizes that the towels, also destined for the stage, were used by various band members for washing and mopping up beer spills. Dan makes a mental note to hide those items away in good time in the future.

Note: Hide It Away Hide anything that you will need later onstage. Towels, water, other stage drinks, set lists, clean T-shirts—whatever needs to go onstage will almost inevitably get used before actually getting placed onstage, either by the musicians themselves or by their multiple guests. As tour manager, responsible band leader, or crew person, please work out what needs to go onstage, ask the promoter for it directly on arrival, and hide it away. (Ideally, you should specify these supplies in a separate section of your catering and hospitality rider.) Even then, you are not assured that your precious stage supplies will remain unused. I've had a couple of memorable occasions when, while I was waiting at the side of the stage for the previous act to finish, a musician coming offstage has grabbed a towel off my pile, toweled himself off, and thrown my towel on the floor!

Meanwhile, in catering, the chefs and catering assistants have finished serving dinner for the band and crew and have packed away most of the equipment and food. The catering assistants have been washing up all day, but they have finally finished. The chefs sit down for a well-earned break. Soon they will finish off for the evening—preparing sandwiches and snacks for the load out—but for now they can catch a breather. The caterers do not even have to plan tomorrow's menu because this is the last night of the tour. Next week, they will be out on a different tour with a different band.

7:20 P.M.: The First Band Is Onstage in 10 Minutes

There is a knock at the door of Millions of Americans' dressing room, and Chris pokes his head into the room, informing the band that they have 10 minutes before stage time. With so many people in the room, the message does not get to all the musicians immediately, but with Dan's help, the five performers start to extricate themselves from their guests and make their way downstairs.

Dan now has another "too late" thought. There are a number of people in the band's room—he and the band have to get onstage, and this room is full of the band's personal belongings as well as the remaining booze. Not that the band are a bunch of alcoholics, but it would be nice if there was a beer or two left for when Millions of Americans finishes its set. However, with very little time remaining, Dan really cannot do anything about this situation, other than worry and make another mental note to be aware of this situation for next time.

7:30 P.M.: Millions of Americans Live Onstage

The five members of Millions of Americans are now at the side of the stage, waiting to go on.

BASS PLAYER (TO DAN): The sound guy has got the intro tape, hasn't he?

DAN: What? What intro tape?

BASS PLAYER: Dude, we always have the intro tape! You know, it's on a CD in the guitar cords box. Ah, man—did you not sort it out?

DAN: Er, well, no. I was busy with merch and stuff. I...

BASS PLAYER: [Stomps off after lots of swearing and mumbling]

Note: Sort It Out in Advance In my experience, the last-minute additions to a show—intro tapes, complicated light show requests, and so on—ruin a big opening slot for a young band. Rehearse your material and your show, and play it as you rehearsed it.

At this point, a man comes up to the band and asks them whether they are ready to perform. He is the venue stage manager (working directly for the venue), and he is responsible for turning off the house lights to signal the start of the band's performance. (The *house lights* are the main auditorium lighting for the audience; modern concert and theatre convention dictates that they are dimmed or turned off for any performance, which helps accentuate the production lighting but also raises excitement in the audience.)

The venue stage manager is working with Chris, the touring production manager, to make sure all is set with the production and the performing acts. Chris has already made sure that his PA and lighting guys (if applicable) are at their stations, and now he just needs the final word from the venue stage manager. On being asked whether they are ready, the musicians say yes, and the stage manager turns around and presses a switch that turns off the house lights.

The crowd erupts into applause.

The members of Millions of Americans stand rooted to the spot.

Dan realizes that some of the musicians are still expecting their intro music to be played over the PA. He shouts at them to get onstage, and the young musicians walk out onto the dark, empty stage. The guitarist and bass player strap on their guitars, turn on their amps, and start to tune up their guitars. The touring lighting systems person, who is running the lighting for the opening acts, is expecting the band to start playing, so he brings up a bright wash. Suddenly, the five musicians in Millions of Americans are illuminated, tuning and fiddling around with their guitars, in front of at least 1,000 people.

Note: Pack 'Em In The bigger the venue, the longer it takes to actually admit the audience. Admitting 1,000 (or more) concert-going people into a venue can take up to one hour. If your stage time is scheduled for soon after the doors open, then you will not be playing to the full house. Up to three quarters of your audience either will be lined up to get in—security and ticket checks—or will be interested only in seeing the headline act and so will not arrive in time for the opening acts. You will not be allowed to go on later unless the organizers or promoters have built in lots of extra time to allow for delays.

Dan is now having an acute stress attack. This is the biggest show of the musicians in Millions of Americans' careers so far; they only have a 20-minute set time allocation, and they are using up at least five minutes of that set time tuning up their guitars! Dan does not have that much experience, but he was told by the band's manager about the importance of making sure the band adheres to their given set times. Stories of dark, grumpy people dressed in black and given the title of "stage manager," dragging young bands offstage if they overrun their allocated stage time, are filling his mind. "Get on with it!" he yells.

The musicians finally finish tuning up and launch into their first song. Meanwhile, the audience has become restless and therefore indifferent. Modern audience's expectations of a show today are of a seamless rock 'n roll professional experience—bands erupting onstage in a blaze of light and thunderous sound. The sight of five guys (however cute) fiddling around onstage has not impressed this audience one bit, and the musicians in Millions of Americans now face an uphill struggle if the band wishes to engage, entertain, and ultimately impress their new audience.

7:50 P.M.: Thank You and Goodnight!

The musicians in Millions of Americans are having a miserable time onstage. Yes, this is the biggest show of their career so far (although none of them views it as a career at this point—it is their dream), but it has not gone well. Multiple factors have contributed to their unhappiness—being late to the venue, having no sound check, having no one to really look after them or explain to them the situation, then having no intro tape and a totally empty venue in which to perform. To make things worse, the sound onstage is awful; the faulty guitar amplifier cut out during the last song, and the audience (what there was of it) was completely indifferent.

Note: The Audience Does Not Know An audience wants to be entertained. They do not need to know that you were late, you have technical problems, or you cannot hear yourself onstage. Never inform your audience of these matters—you will not get any sympathy.

Having given it their all and now being thoroughly exhausted, the musicians from Millions of Americans troop offstage, thinking of nothing except getting upstairs to the dressing room, having a couple of cold beers, and relaxing for the evening. However, as they start to walk off, the band members are shouted at by Dan, the venue stage manager, and Chris, the production manager. The two local crew members who have been contracted to help with changeovers are already pulling apart the drum kit and bringing it offstage. The shouting is directed at the band to ask them to help get their *own* equipment offstage—do it now, or no one will be responsible for where their expensive equipment will end up. The musicians get back onto the stage area and start to wrap up cords and cables, only to be told to get all the gear offstage as soon as possible—it can be tidied and put into cases later!

This may seem a heartless way to treat a band that has just come offstage, but remember, unless you pay individual crew members to take total care of your backline equipment, you need to get all that stuff offstage right away. Don't put it all in cases and coil cables on the stage; simply disconnect everything from everything else and carry it offstage or, if there are stagehands/local crew, indicate to them that it is ready to be taken offstage.

The vital point here is that every minute you spend onstage packing away your equipment is a minute lost for the local crew and the following act getting their equipment onstage, ready for their performance. You might not care after your show finishes, but one day you will be following an opening act, and you will want as much time as possible to get your equipment onstage and line checked and to ensure that all your backline and monitors are in place and working properly.

The backline equipment for Millions of Americans is carried offstage and placed, in as tidy a fashion as possible, in a corner of the loading bay. The two local crew then run back to the stage to assist the backline techs for Terrible Mistake, the next band, to get its gear onstage. Because most of this other equipment is still onstage following sound check, it is just a matter of helping to rearrange a few monitors and push around guitar worlds. Having done that, the local crew then returns to the Millions of Americans musicians to see whether they need help packing down and loading out their gear. This offer of help is gratefully received, and the local crew set about dismantling the drum kit and putting away guitars for the band.

Dan is there as well now, and he suggests that he could perhaps go and get the van from the parking place and load the gear straight out as soon as it is packed away. The local crew agrees that is a very good idea, but they only have another five minutes to do this; the stage loading doors cannot be open when a music performance is taking place. Dan knows he cannot get the van back to the venue in that time, so he and the local crew agree to convene when the next act comes offstage at 8:30 P.M.; they can load out the Millions of Americans equipment then.

Note: Use the Crew If stagehands/local crew are provided, use them and use their knowledge.

8:05 P.M.: The Dressing Room—Post-Show

As Terrible Mistake takes to the stage with a huge audience cheer, the members of Millions of Americans file wearily into their dressing room. They know it has been an awful show. The band feels that so many things went wrong today. The musicians realize they really do not understand the whole process of playing live in a venue this large. Each band member feels that there seemed to be people everywhere, all day, who were telling the band what to do, and yet ultimately no one was there to guide them. They feel that they ended up with a terrible stage sound, playing to an empty venue.

The band mentions all this to their manager and booking agent, who have now entered the room. The two professionals are keen to respond, sensing that the band, instead of blaming others, blame themselves for being under-rehearsed and unprofessional. This is a good sign, and, unfortunate as it may be to have a bad show, the fact that the band are seeking answers at this early stage bodes well for their career. The manager and the booking agent make some suggestions and recommendations to the band and inform them that the audience reaction for Millions of Americans was actually quite favorable; the band should not be discouraged. This view is reinforced when two members of Your Material Story also poke their head around the dressing room door, saying, "Awesome show, guys!" and giving a more encouragement.

Note: Embrace the Moment You may have had a terrible show. Do not sink into despair. Embrace the opportunity. Can you learn from the experience?

Dan enters the room at that point. He heard a couple of the band members from Terrible Mistake mention that they were going straight to the merchandise stand in the foyer as soon as they finished playing to "hang with the kids." Dan remembers what the tour merchandisers said earlier about this as well and realizes he has seen bands do this before—stand at the merch stalls, signing fans T-shirts and getting people to subscribe to the mailing list. Dan now tells the musicians from Millions of Americans to grab a beer and a pen and get to the merch stand—now! Wearily, the band members agree. After the encouragement from Your Material Story and their own team, the guys know that getting out there with the audience is a good thing and may just salvage a bad evening.

8:30 P.M.: Changeover

Terrible Mistake is finishing its set, and the sound, lighting, video, and backline crews for Your Material Story are preparing for changeover and the headliner's set. The FOH sound systems and lighting system crews are already at their respective FOH and stage controls, along with the FOH, LD, and monitor engineers for the band. With a full house such as this, you really cannot waste time trying to push your way through the audience, so the technicians who work FOH made their way out in good time to be ready for the changeover. At the side of the stage, the backline technicians for Your Material Story are also waiting, making last-minute tuning adjustments to the guitars and radio systems.

Immediately when the support band walks offstage, myriad people swarm to the equipment. The local crew starts to tear off the drums, guitar and bass cabinets, and amps, assisted and directed by the Terrible Mistake backline techs. The sound system crew takes away all the microphones, stands, and DI boxes, as well as the extra monitor wedges. They then tidy up any microphone, speaker, and mains power cables that are left to save time later and to ensure a tidy, safe stage for the headline act. (While Your Material Story performs onstage, the sound system guys will use the local crew to pack the gear used for the opening acts.)

The stage is fairly clear now, so the backline techs are able to take off the protective covers and start to check their individual instruments. When this is finished, Dave, the FOH engineer, starts to call the line check. Again, he can talk to the techs onstage through the monitor wedges.

As line check takes place, Chris walks around the stage, putting out towels, water, and set lists for the band. The backline techs already have taken set lists for themselves and the musicians, but Chris tapes down the lists that are positioned downstage by the monitor wedges. He has already ensured that lists have gone to the FOH positions.

Millions of Americans' driver and acting road manager Dan has collected his van and parked it at the loading dock. The local crew have finished changeover and loading out Terrible Mistake's equipment and are now bringing out Millions of Americans' equipment. Dan packs the gear in the van as the local crew brings it out to him. He then gives the two local crew members a Millions of Americans T-shirt each as a way of saying thanks and also to spread the word about the band. Hands are shaken and thanks are said, and Dan drives off again, hopefully to reclaim his parking spot.

Note: Spread the Love The musicians, crew, promoters, booking agents, managers, and venue staff you meet during a show day can directly influence your career. Do whatever you can to make sure they have a positive impression of you.

Two of the truck and bus drivers are making their way up to the balcony to the follow spot positions. Once there, they will put on headphones that will put them in direct communication with the LD. The LD will give the operators cues during the set; these cues are instructions as to which band member to follow, which type of light beam they should set their follow spot to produce, and which (if any) colored "gel" the operators should apply.

Julie, the band's monitor engineer, has finished her onstage checks and has taken the musician's IEM packs upstairs to the dressing room. The band is used to putting on their own packs, but it is a professional courtesy to make sure everyone is happy with the cables and earpieces. This is the final act of the changeover, and now Kristen can radio down to Chris to inform him that the band is ready. Chris acknowledges the stage is set and that Kristen should bring the band down. He then lets everyone know they have five minutes, and half of the crew disappears to the toilets—90 minutes is a long time if you need to urinate!

9:00 P.M.: Ladies and Gentlemen, Live on Stage... Your Material Story!

It is show time! As the band waits at the side of the stage, Chris gives the word again to the stage manager, and the house lights go down. The video and lighting operators, also given a cue by Chris, start the short video film that the band is using as its walk-on introduction. The show has started (see Figure 7.18)!

Figure 7.18 The opening of the show, as seen from the crowd.

Even though a full sound check was performed in the afternoon and all the equipment has been checked and re-checked, the crew of Your Material Story is not complacent. The FOH and monitor sound engineer work hard during the first couple of songs, making the necessary audio adjustments to compensate for the difference in sound that results from a full, hot, and sweaty house. The backline techs are equally watchful during these first couple of songs, concentrating like hawks on each musician. Everyone in the crew wants a good, professional, and entertaining show for the 4,500 people who have paid to get in tonight. The last thing that should happen is technical breakdown or missed cues. Yes, things happen, but as the crew say, "It's funny, y'know—the more we practice this, the more luck we have!"

After four songs, Dave at FOH has re-balanced the various levels to compensate for the different acoustics of the room and is getting a pretty solid sound together. It helps that the guys in the band rehearse regularly, can really play, and spend a *lot* of money on their equipment. Therefore, as far as Dave is concerned, the sound the musicians make themselves is pretty polished and pre-mixed—all Dave has to do is balance the various elements. Meanwhile, onstage, Julie has tweaked the musicians' individual monitor mixes and settled into the performance. This does not mean she can relax, though. As you saw in Chapter 6, monitor sound in modern concert performance requires an infinite amount of flexibility and manipulation—manipulation that can only be achieved using digital technology. This is why Julie has different individual monitor mixes for nearly every song in the set stored in her digital desk (see Figure 7.19).

9:30 P.M.: Can You Sign My Shirt?

The musicians in Millions of Americans, on the other hand, are now relaxed and happy. They managed to get to the merch stand in the FOH foyer just after Terrible Mistake took the stage and, following the performance earlier, were instantly recognized by hundreds of audience members. Therefore, they have spent the last hour chatting

Figure 7.19 The digital lighting desk, seen here during the setup.

with new fans, posing for photographs, and signing shirts, arms, and other body parts. As well as helping the band members recall the reason they are in a band in the first place, getting close to their audience has given the musicians a good feel for how the music of Millions of Americans reaches a potential new audience. It has also helped the band to sell a few Millions of Americans T-shirts (see Figure 7.20)!

10:15 P.M.: Settlement

Barry and Kristen are preparing the evening's figures and any cash that Kristen may need to take away with her. Barry collected the ticket report from the venue box office a while ago and already has ticket figures from the various other outlets because they closed earlier in

Figure 7.20 The merch stand after the show.

the day. This event sold out weeks ago, so the settlement has been fairly easy; Barry just needs to go through all the agreed show cost figures with Kristen. Kristen is not picking up cash this evening because this is the last night of the tour, and she worked out sufficient cash flow to see her through any expenses needed. The cash balance for tonight's performance will be transferred by the promoter straight to Your Material Story's agent on the next working day. That money will be disbursed by the agent to the band, via the band's management company in LA.

With the settlement completed, Barry is basically free to relax for a while. Show etiquette demands that Barry is in place and available until the production loads out of the venue; this means he will be here until at least 12:30 A.M. Meanwhile, he can have a beer and watch a bit of the show.

10:30 P.M.: Local Crew Evening Call

The 12 local crew members needed for the load out have arrived and are crammed into a crew room deep in the bowels of the venue. (There are 14 on the call, but remember, two crew are here already as "stop-ons.") Chris and the "locals" crew boss make sure everyone has turned up and then allocates people to the various tasks needed to load out. These are:

- Backline: Four people, then moving onto lighting
- PA: Four people
- Lighting and video: Six people

Each member of the local crew is given a T-shirt, colored to indicate which "department" he will be working for. They wait patiently for the concert to end.

10:45 P.M.: First Encore

Your Material Story has finished the main part of the set and the musicians have come offstage, ready for their encore. The backline techs are scurrying around the stage, picking up used water bottles and items thrown onto the stage by the crowd. They tape down loose cables and recheck the tuning on guitars and drum heads. Anything that is not needed for the remaining songs of the set is put aside or packed away—all to save time in the load out.

The story is the same in catering. Everything that is not needed has been packed away in flight cases, ready for load out. Plates of sandwiches, pizzas, and hot snacks have been prepared and placed on the tour buses for the band and crew. Even though the tour ends after tonight's show, the buses will be going out to the airport to drop the band and US crew off for an early flight. There is no point in booking a bunch of hotel rooms that will only be occupied for three hours, so Kristen is using the buses again tonight. The crew and band can party a while at the venue, shower up, and then head out to London's Heathrow airport in the early hours of the morning, while traffic is still quiet.

The only people who cannot start packing away yet are the merchandise operators. As soon as the band's set ends, 4,500 people will start exiting the venue. Many will gather around the merch stalls, trying to decide whether to spend their return train fare on a T-shirt. Unfortunately for the merch operators, there is no way to predict the demand, so they wait patiently for the concert to end.

10:55 P.M.: Thank You and Goodnight!

Your Material Story finishes an amazing set. The crowd goes wild and, in order to press home the point that the band is not coming back onstage, Chris cues the stage manager to bring up the house lights. Dave at FOH puts on some soft music, and the crowd begins to file out of the auditorium.

It's now time to get the whole PA, lighting, video, backline, and catering equipment packed down and loaded into the trucks. The stage is now a flurry of activity. The local crew report to their relevant touring systems people and are given the first of many jobs. The systems guys themselves are not slouching, though—they are in the thick of it, organizing empty cases and putting away the smaller items. The load out goes in the exact reverse order of the load in, so the stage has to be cleared before the lighting truss can be bought down. The backline techs for the band direct their local crew to bring up flight cases and pack them in the right order. The full cases are then wheeled into the loading bay, and the local crew is set onto another task.

The PA can be dropped from its flying position to the front of the stage without too much being cleared away. Already the rigger is in the roof, undoing the safety cables and preparing the motors on the chain hoists for use. As you can imagine, there is the potential for accidents as cables and ropes are dropped down by the rigger, and this is not the kind of place you should wander around in if you are not 100 percent alert—in other words, stay away if you're drunk!

Note: Stay Away from a Stage during Load Out If you do not belong onstage during load out, or you do not know what you are doing when you are there, please stay away! Don't be tempted to cut across a stage on the way back to your dressing room or show your friends what is happening—the crew people are in a hurry and they are tired. There are also too many people and too many cables, cases, trusses, and ramps for it to be absolutely safe

---

11:15 P.M.: The Merchandise Stands

There is now organized chaos at the merch stands—the venue concession people are selling T-shirts, hoodies, posters, and pins at an alarming rate. The tour merchandisers run around frantically, making sure the right merchandise is available at each of the two stands. Merchandise sales are hugely important to a modern rock band, but the fans cannot spend money if the merchandise is not available, so the team is desperate to keep the stands well stocked.

The venue staff is keen to get the audience outside as quickly as possible, so there is a great deal of shouting as venue stewards "encourage" fans to exit, often while the fans are still trying to buy a shirt. By 11:20 P.M., the foyer is empty of the audience and the tour merchandisers and the venue concession people can start the process of counting the remaining stock and figuring out the money (see Figure 7.21).

11:30 P.M.: The After Show

The members of Millions of Americans are now in the Your Material Story dressing room, having been invited in by the Your Material Story band members. The young musicians from Millions of Americans are slightly over-awed but, remembering the lesson of the day, they seize the opportunity to give thanks, be polite, and hopefully make friends.

Figure 7.21   Go home! Well, you cannot stay here!

The dressing room is packed with well-wishers, friends, and family of Your Material Story and, more importantly for Millions of Americans, music industry professionals.

Dan, the tour manager, waits patiently in the corner, sipping a non-alcoholic beverage. He still has to drive the band back to their home-town, some three hours away, and he would dearly love to get going. However, he appreciates that this kind of networking opportunity is vitally important for the band's—and therefore his—career. He also still has to collect his shirts and any money due from the venue merch people.

11:45 P.M.: The Load Out

The load out is in full swing. The backline has been loaded out, and most of the PA has been dropped to the stage. Chris oversees the oper-ation, ensuring as rapid a load out as possible while still guaranteeing everyone's safety. His team has been up since 8:00 this morning, and even with an afternoon nap, the sheer physical nature of the work means that people tire easily.

Chris also has another set of logistics to consider. This is the last night of this leg of the tour, and all the hired equipment, PA, lights, and so on have to be returned to the suppliers tomorrow morning. As well, the band's backline is made up of equipment brought over from the States and equipment rented locally. This all needs to be separated and packed differently. Usually, packing the trucks is a straightforward affair because the packing has evolved over the last couple of weeks of the tour. Now, however, Chris has to start all over again, making sure the right equipment goes on the right trucks in order to be dropped off in the correct order the next morning.

The last day of a tour is always the most difficult.

Note: End-of-Tour Parties The proper end-of-tour party is always on the penultimate show night. That way, the crew has a vague chance of attending whatever event has been organized. The load out on the last night means a considerably greater amount of work because PA, lights, staging, backline, and catering equipment have to be sent back to the appropriate suppliers.

11:50 P.M.: Back at the Merchandise Stall

Dan is talking with the venue concession people, trying to sort out a deal. Dan is supposed to pay a percentage of his total shirt sales to the venue. Fans have bought five shirts, which is pretty good given that the shirts were sold at full price and the band are relatively unknown. Having the band come down to the merch stand after their set definitely helped to make those sales. However, the thought of then having to pay 15 percent plus sales tax of the shirt sales to the venue is a little galling. Dan pleads his situation with the venue, and they let him off the fee but ask him for a free shirt. Dan weighs this option and decides the goodwill involved outweighs the loss of a shirt, so he agrees.

12:15 A.M.: On the Way Home

Dan has finally asserted his authority and made the band leave. He made sure they said goodbye properly to everyone, especially the promoter and promoter's rep. More free shirts were given out ("Maybe next time we should have stickers," thinks Dan), and the band climb back into their van. It has been a long and eventful day. The musicians in Millions of Americans still have a lot to learn but have overcome some major hurdles today.

12:30 A.M.: The Venue Is Closed

The Your Material Story load out is nearly finished. All the lighting is now down on the ground and put into the flight cases to be packed onto the trucks. The rigger has dropped the motors for the chain hoists out of the roof. Catering is all packed up, and the local crew is working in teams to load up the two trucks.

By 1:45 A.M., the truck doors are slammed shut. Everyone shakes hands with the locals, the odd beer is handed out, and the local crew is dismissed for the evening. The tour crew head onto their buses for the short ride to the airport.

The venue stage manager checks the auditorium and the stage for any left items and switches off the lights (see Figure 7.22). There is another show loading in at 9:00 A.M. tomorrow, so he wants to get home as soon as possible.

Figure 7.22 The end of the day. It all starts again tomorrow.

8 How to Get the Shows

The *Tour Book* is about playing live. So far in this book you have learned about contracts, technology, technical terms, and who does what at a modern concert. None of this matters, though, if you do not go out and actually play some shows!

Before you get all excited and rush to book shows left, right, and center, you need to ask yourself two questions:

- Why do you want the gig?
- Do you have an audience?

To help explain the reasoning behind these questions, I want you to read an example of one of the hundreds of e-mails I receive every week, this one from a guy who we'll call "Brad":

> Hi, my name is Brad. I am in the bass player in my band. Basically, my band is trying to get support slots on tours with more established bands—not massively successful artists, but bands that were recently in the same situation we are and are now attracting attention. We have no manager and we are releasing our CD with our own money. I have been checking into the possibility of touring through Europe. We have done some research and think Europe may be a good idea for us. Can you please send information that can help us to calculate our costs for a tour that consists of 40 shows in 60 days? How much do we get paid and how is that calculated? What about promotions and advertising? Will the music press do articles on us to help in the promotion? Basically, how much is it going to cost us out of pocket to come and tour Europe? We as a band don't want to worry about anything except playing, so most likely we would want someone to set up and take care of everything for us, so all we have to do is get up there and play. This tour would be the debut CD release tour and would continue on into Asia, Australia, and back to the US. Thanks for your time and have a great day.

Thank you, Brad. Now, let us have a good look at what you are proposing....

Why Do You Want the Gig?

Ask yourself this question: Why do I want to play this particular show or tour? In my experience, too many bands try to play live at too early a stage in their formation, perhaps exposing their lack of development and their weaknesses to potential audiences and industry taste-makers. Far too many acts also think they can just hook up a coast-to-coast tour (refer to Brad's e-mail) with no audience, promotion, or even a CD release!

To get on a larger show, you have to reach and impress booking agents and promoters, as well as the other acts on the bill and their managers— before you even get the chance to ask for a show. Brad is trying to get slots on these larger shows, but he has no audience and no release. Perhaps Brad should think again and ask himself why exactly he wants to tour or to perform opening slots for national touring bands. He does not mention wanting to thrill audiences or give the crowds want they want. Brad's motivation is not based on entertaining anyone—his idea of playing shows is purely to advance his career. Which is pretty silly when he has never even played outside his own state before!

Read Brad's e-mail again. Are your situation and attitude similar to Brad's? If the answer is yes, then maybe you also need to spend to time examining why you want a gig.

Playing live may get you noticed by an A&R scout or artist manager and, if you play the larger shows that Brad is so keen about, you may get to reach 200 to 500 people in one night. However, especially with those larger opening slots, the audience will quickly forget about you— probably before the night is over. Your hard work will have gone to waste if you cannot impress and connect with your audience.

On a more positive note, playing live will improve your ability as a musician, singer, DJ, or band and will build your audience. The more shows you do the better, especially if you play lots of shows around a more important showcase or opening slot.

> "Playing live is absolutely the best way to hone your craft, confidence, and ability."
>
> —Adam Saunders, Helter Skelter. Booking agent for the Darkness, Squarepusher, Belle and Sebastian, Capdown, and many more.

With this in mind, perhaps approach your initial shows as a way of testing the water of your music/musicianship and also as a way of having a good time. In other words, play shows to entertain people, not to get signed.

If you get offered a show at whatever level, think about the offer in context, beyond the initial excitement of having a show. As Sam Heineman (former director of international touring/international marketing for Sony Music Entertainment) says, "If [a show] doesn't make sense, don't do it." Examine the potential of the show in terms of building an audience, how much money it is going to cost, the time off your day job, what taste-makers may be there, and how much you are going to enjoy the show. In our previous example, Brad wants to play 40 shows in 60 days. Why? It would be a hell of a schedule even if he could afford sleeper buses and a full crew. Forty shows in sixty days is a pretty tough schedule. Worse still, his band has no audience and no CD to promote. Therefore, he has no fans to play to and will waste his time and money sitting on top of his own equipment in a rental van, slowly grinding his way along to the next completely empty and non-paying show.

I will say it again: Touring is expensive. To give you an idea of how much it costs to tour, consider this: A two-week club tour of the Midwest for a four-piece band with two crew members, a van, and a trailer will cost $8,000 to $12,000. That money is just for basic wages, transportation, gas, and hotels. That's for no frills and a lot of miles (see Figure 8.1).

	Price per day/unit	Days/multiplier	Multiplier	Amount	Notes
WAGES					
Tour Manager/FOH engineer	$120.00	14	1	$1,680.00	Tour Manager gets paid for each day of the tour
Backline crew person	$80.00	12	1	$960.00	Backline person only gets paid for show days
Crew day off	$10.00	2	1	$20.00	Backline person gets $10 a day on days off
ACCOMMODATION					
Band	$50.00	13	3	$1,950.00	3 twin rooms at $50 a night
TRANSPORT					
15 Seat Passenger van	$150.00	15	1	$2,250.00	Total includes pick up and drop off days
Fuel		15000 miles		$1,205.67	
Trailer	$25.00	15	1	$375.00	
Parking	$5.00	14	1	$70.00	Just in case!
BACKLINE					
Equipment consumables	$200.00	1	1	$200.00	Spare strings and replacement, batteries, sticks etc

GRAND TOTAL:	$8,710.67

Figure 8.1 The cost of 14 days of touring in a van and trailer around the Midwest. Scary, isn't it?

At the other end of the scale, I recently managed a full-production tour of theatres and arenas. The band I was working for has been going for nearly 15 years and has sold a bucket-load of records all around the world. The tour's basic production equipment is housed in two 40-foot trucks packed with PA, lights, video, and set. They also have two sleeper buses for the band and crew—a total of 29 people. There are only five band members, but we also had four session musicians and 20 touring crew. That tour cost an average of $15,000 (£7,700) per day.

Can you imagine paying $15,000 to play one rock show? That is the reality of modern touring. And that total cost per show is assuming you are capable of playing headline shows in big theaters and stadiums.

Think about Brad's e-mail. I asked you whether you have the same attitude as Brad. Now, after seeing how much it costs to tour, you should really be asking yourself, "Why do I want this particular show?" Why on earth would you want to spend a huge amount of money and x number of days of your life touring around and playing to no one?

If your answer is, "I want to entertain people," then you are probably on your way to making a career out of live music. Music is entertainment, and you should not forget that. Yes, you may get noticed by an A&R scout or artist manager, but please do not forget the people in the room—ordinary people who have paid for concert tickets and may also buy your T-shirts and CDs. My advice is to learn to entertain people first and think of the business second. Concentrate the impact of your initial live performances. Play really good shows in front of small crowds. You don't have to put on a cheesy performance to entertain an audience, just be sincere. The small crowds you play to initially will probably be your friends and family—the harshest of critics. Always videotape your performances (see Chapter 5) and view the resulting footage. Discuss the performance and musicianship with your band mates, friends, family, manager, studio owner—whoever. Negative comments about the show should not be dismissed outright; if the comments are valid, what can you do to improve?

I have worked with many local/young bands who complain to me that, although they can get shows in their hometown bars or clubs and play pretty much any day of the week (which is great), their audience numbers remain the same or even dwindle. My advice about playing lots of small shows to hone their craft falls on deaf ears because they want to get to the next level quickly. I accept this is a valid point, but as I always say, if your audience numbers are not growing, you are not capable of sustaining the interest of the audience. Your aim is to make every person at the last show you performed think, "I am going to the next show by this band. I will bring all my friends to that same show and post about the band online to tell everyone how completely incredible they are. I am going to buy their T-shirts and CDs and download their music and join their forum and go to their MySpace site and, and, and...."

How you make your audience feel like this is up to you. I can advise you on performance skills (Chapters 4 and 5) and marketing (Chapter 10, "Marketing"). Please read these chapters and see what advice and strategies best suit you and your music. Obviously, you have to remember that not every person in your audience is going to feel like coming to your next show, buying your CD, or telling their friends about how fabulous you are. You should not feel too bad about that fact.

You do need to worry if no one wants to come to your next show, buy a CD, or recommend you to their friends. Your fan base will not increase if people do not want to come to your next show, no matter how many shows you play.

So, if by some fluke or carefully considered strategy, you get offered an incredible opening slot for a huge national touring act or a chance to tour around the country, what would you think? If you are Brad, you would probably not give it a thought and you'd hit the stage. You'd play the show or the tour. But then what happens? Well, that depends on whether you have an audience.

Do You Have an Audience?

"Bon Jovi had released three albums and played 500 shows before they broke [into the big time]."

—Doc McGee, manager for Kiss, Bon Jovi, and Motley Crue

Can you draw a paying audience into your shows? Once you can draw a crowd, can you sustain those numbers at every show you do? Never

Figure 8.2 Playing for an audience.

underestimate the importance of a consistent draw; solid audience numbers mean you are reaching people and entertaining them, and they want to come back for more. Promoters only want one thing—a guaranteed amount of ticket sales for any given show. Can you honestly approach a promoter and say that you can guarantee *x* number people at *every* show you do? Look again at Brad's e-mail. Brad's band has no audience, so what bar or club owner is going to give them a gig?

Concentrate on the ticket-selling potential and audience-pulling power of your act. This may mean forgetting about taking your shows to the next level for a significant amount of time. Build yourself up as a quality act, and the promoters and record labels will come to you. It is far better for your career to play two or three shows a month for six months and have 100 people turn up for every single show than it is to play one show in front of 2,000 people and then not play another show for six months. There is no fast route to the top. You are the best band/artist in the world (yes, you are!), but has anyone else heard of you yet? No one has heard of Brad's band, yet there he is, planning a full European, Australian, and Asian tour!

Make sure you captivate your audience, no matter how small, at every show you play and in every set you perform. Compel your audience to come to your next show by being professional, good-natured, and well-rehearsed, both to the audience and to the behind-the-scenes workers. (Read Chapter 7 again for a reminder about how your band and crew should act in order to maximize the exposure that playing live brings.) It does not matter whether you are playing to 10 or 1,000 people, you should still act professionally. In fact it is more important if you are playing to 10 people! Those 10 people are at least there to see you, so treat them with respect and get them to spread the word for you. This involves some marketing. I will be detailing marketing techniques in Chapter 10.

To illustrate my point, here is the story of a band. This band is no better or worse than a million other bands trying to make a career in the music industry; the difference is that this band worked hard to maximize their appeal to existing and potential fans. The band is called Capdown.

Capdown was formed in 1998 and immediately signed to Household Records from London, England. Household gave them a very small amount of money to record an album, and that was it. There were no living expenses and there was no tour support. There was also no marketing or promotional budget, so Capdown's chances of selling any records was going to be pretty slim. Realizing that they were going to be very poor, the band decided that they might as well play gigs every day rather than stay at home and starve. (One member of the band did not have a home anyway, and two others were living with their parents on minimal state benefits.) The record label put them in touch with an agent—Ian Armstrong at Hidden Talent booking agency—who specialized in "DIY" bands and worked to get them shows. (See how this works? Even with a label deal, the band still needs a booking agent to secure them shows.) These shows were very, very small shows in pubs and bars in England, initially playing to 10 people or fewer. Nonetheless, the band jumped at the chance to be playing live and did not have ambitions to move to any other level at any time in the near future. They were happy to gain an audience and to strengthen their position as a band that could play well live, draw fans, and make promoters money. Jake Sims-Fielding from Capdown says that the band's "good nature" and the fact that they were "an easy band for people [promoters] to put on" meant that they became the perfect opening act. Jake estimates that in 1999 and 2000, Capdown played 250 shows a year, visiting 12 different countries. The average fee for these performances was £30/$50, although many shows were performed for nothing. The band traveled in their own regular van, with no crew, and slept on floors in fan's houses in each city. All the time, the word about Capdown was spreading.

The band continued to tour, and their success increased. Jake mentions that once the debut album came out, promoters and fans alike were even more impressed with the act and began to take them more seriously. At this point, the band began to sell merchandise at their shows, which added to the daily income. As Jake says, "The effect of selling five albums a night if you are making £3/$5 each off them can make all the difference." Their positive relationship with promoters was also paying off. The band had always limited ticket prices for their shows to an average of £5/$8 as a way of appealing to potential fans. After selling out the MDH in Manchester (capacity 700) but only netting £500/$800 for themselves, the promoter very kindly advised them that the band was actually doing itself out of money and that they should raise the prices slightly!

Today the band is going from strength to strength. They have signed with a new agent who has a more international appeal. Capdown now tours with a sound engineer and a technician. They sell more than $3,000 (£1,500) of merchandise per night on their own Internet mail-order site. At no point have they moaned about getting to the next level. They have concentrated on gaining an audience and then capitalizing on their appeal to strengthen their appeal with their audience.

It has not been all smooth sailing. Capdown plays a particular kind of music that attracts a particular type of fan, and their move into the big time has led to criticisms of their integrity. Jake is quick to defend the band from accusations about selling out, saying, "You realize that all these people from these big companies are still individuals, and if we can respect them and work with them, then that's what it's about."

Although they are based on strong values and integrity, at the end of the day Capdown wants to have a career (see Figure 8.3).

Figure 8.3 Jake Sims-Fielding of Capdown. (Photo by James Sharrock, courtesy of *Kerrang!*)

The Booking Process

Hopefully, by now you have thought about why you want to play shows and what audience draw you may have. It is time to approach the promoter and get yourself some gigs!

Researching and Targeting Venues

Do some research into the different types of venues in your town or state. Think about how your band is going to fit into that environment. Some venues are known to audiences as featuring a certain genre of music or audience type. Your town may have a bar that books deep-house DJs and targets a young club-type crowd. There might also be a local House of Blues type of venue that books blues-based rock bands, as well as alternative bands. Both are considered to be cool places to go and check out music. Each venue's music booking policy attracts a certain audience type. Will your band's music really fit in a particular venue? For instance, an alternative rock band based in New York should not try to get a gig at Birdland (a famous jazz club), but would probably approach Arlene's Grocery (a small alternative-rock venue).

You probably know your hometown venues from attending shows there yourself, but it may be harder to judge your appeal to audiences at out-of-town venues. Look at the venue's website or local newspaper ads. Check out what other acts are playing and what kind of bands are being billed together. Ask your friends, your fans, and other bands about their experiences performing at or attending a venue. Venues can get terrible reputations for a variety of reasons. The only effect of these reputations, as far as you're concerned, is that audiences may tend to stay away.

The other factor to bear in mind is the size of the venue. Of course, it would be great to play in a nice 2,000-seat theatre, especially if you are opening up for a national touring act. Remember, though, that it takes quite a long time for 2,000 audience members to get into venue. By the time they all decide to enter the gig, you may have already played and be out in the street, packing your van.

Be realistic and keep it small. Work out how many people are likely to show up for the show, halve that figure, and book a gig to hold that number of people. I am serious. You are better off with people standing in line to get in and the people inside being packed like sardines than you are having your audience saying to their friends, "It was great, but there was nobody there," because you were persuaded to play in a venue too big for your draw. You have to make your audience perceive that you are incredibly successful, and playing half-empty rooms is not the way to do that.

Always think of your audience. This is probably the only time in your career when you will be able to think directly of the people paying to see you. Thinking about your audience is an investment for the future. You need them, so take care of them. You should ask yourself whether your audience can get to the show. More importantly, can they get home again? What kind of public transport is there? Does the venue have lots of car parking? Is the venue in a relatively safe part of town? Is the beer cheap? Does the venue charge for tap water?

When you do start to tour nationally, be aware of the "small and out-of-the-way venue syndrome." Basically, a promoter, a friend, or your booking agent will try to persuade you that you should play some really small venue in a remote town somewhere. The idea is that, because nothing ever happens in this town, a touring band turning up will somehow unite the townsfolk, and they will all show up for the concert. The venue will be packed, and everyone will be happy. Of course, the reality is that it will cost you an arm and a leg to get to the town in the first place. The lack of any local paper, magazine, radio station, or large-scale promoter in the town will then mean there is no promotion for the show. Finally, the number of people who do want to attend will be proportional to the town's population—in other words, not many. Be wary of this type of show—if it seems too good to be true, then it probably is.

My final advice when researching venues is to avoid the "club night" show. Nightclubs that do not normally feature live music (such as disco/dance venues) and their promoters may offer bands slots during a themed club night, often in a smaller room or on a corner stage in the same venue. Ms. Promoter can offer this kind of show to a band without an audience draw because she does not have to worry about losing money on the deal; the club will be making money from entry, coat check, and drinks anyway. To the band, the lure of these shows is that the place is always packed on a Friday/Saturday night, and hundreds of people will see them. (At least, that's what Ms. Promoter tells the band.) The promoter will make money and a bit of prestige by promoting local talent, regardless of how it turns out.

The reality for you as a band is that people have paid good money to drink and dance, not to see live music. Audiences can be quite adverse to live music, seeing it as an invasion of their good times. The upshot is that you face a hostile crowd, you suffer a bad sound, and you end up playing to nowhere near the number of people you were promised.

Who Books the Shows?

In Chapter 2 I explained promoters and promoting; I also explained the differences between in-house and outside promoters. Research the promoters before you start firing off demo CDs to the venue. Does the venue have an in-house promoter/booker? Or does it rely on outside promoters? Look again at my venue examples in Chapter 2.

- A small bar, pub, or club will usually have an in-house promotion team, often the owner or a long-term employee. You should be able to find out who these people are through telephone research and then approach them directly.

- A larger venue may attract outside promoters who merely hire the venue and its facilities for each show. You will be able to tell by looking at the show posters and website of the venue. Look for "*Somebody* presents ...," where *somebody* is a big local or national promoter, such as Live Nation. There may still be a local intermediary based at the venue, but the contract will be issued by the national promoter. You will therefore need to have a huge audience draw or a booking agent in order to get a show at one of these venues.

- Chain venues, such as House of Blues and Barfly, may have a national promotions team that works with other independent promoters to book the shows. This way the chain can book a successful act into each one of its regional venues as a full tour or as part of a larger tour. Again, you will probably need to have a huge audience draw or a booking agent in order to get a show. It is always worth trying the actual venue manager, though—he or she will be able to tell you where all booking inquiries should be made.

- I get lots of e-mails and phone calls from bands starting out who want to get on a large festival bill. Again, do your research. Go to any festival and observe the acts on the bill. You may look at these bands and say you have never heard of them, and that you and your band could/should be up there instead. That may be a fair point, but let me tell you something now: Even the bands at the bottom of a main stage running order will have a label deal, a major booking agent, or a substantial audience draw—or all three. Do not waste your time trying to pitch yourself to festival organizers...yet!

The Approach

Pitching your music/band to venues and promoters in order to get shows is exactly the same as pitching your music to a record company, a publishing company, or an artist manager. There are rules and conventions, and your career will be affected by the mistakes you make by not following these rules and conventions. Pitching your music to industry professionals is fraught with the potential to make mistakes, so the next few sections will cover a few guidelines in case you do *not* know how to approach people with your music. These guidelines also include information specific to the live music industry.

Identify the Key Contact

Salesmen and saleswomen talk about key contacts within a company or organization. These key contacts are the people with the job titles and responsibilities who will be more useful to you when trying to sell goods or services to that company. When trying to sell your band to a promoter, you need to identify the key contact. Remember what I said in Chapter 2 about promoters, the promotion company staff, and promoters' reps? (If not, then go back and reread that part of Chapter 2 now—it is very important.) Many, many people work in a club or a national promoter's office, but only one or two people can actually place you on a bill for a show. Your job is to identify the decision-maker within the organization—that is, the person at the local bar, out-of-town club, or national promotion company who actually decides what bands are going to play and how much they should be paid.

The best tool you can use to identify key contacts is still the phone. Yes, you will be able to establish broad contact details using the phone book, music business directories, and the Internet, but you have to ensure this information is up to date and relevant to you. Get the number of the bar, club, or office and call them up!

Note: We Keep Pretty Strange Hours.... Live music is largely a nighttime activity, and the workers in this industry keep pretty strange hours. Trying to contact bar or small-club owners during conventional business hours may be difficult; most venues are shut down during this time. There is also little point in trying to call when the club or bar is open—a combination of workload and noise may prevent anyone in the venue from answering the phone. The best time to contact a bar or small-club promoter is about an hour before the club or bar opens.

You should always have an objective in mind when making a business telephone call, especially if that call concerns your career. I understand you may be uncomfortable calling on the phone. E-mail and instant messaging have grown to prominence in business communications, so many people are no longer used to making business-type calls.

You should be aware, though, that all promoters, artist managers, record label A&R people, and booking agents are bombarded by e-mails, most of which are unsolicited. These e-mails are not exactly spam, but they are sent without permission or without relevant contact to the recipient. The volume of unsolicited and untargeted e-mail that modern music industry professionals receive per day means that in order to make an impact, you will have to make contact in a unique way. In a bizarre turn of events, the modern reliance on e-mail now means that the humble telephone call really makes a difference when you are making that unique contact.

Try something along the following lines when calling a pub, bar, or club.

You: Hello, I am trying to find out who is responsible for booking the acts that play at your pub (or club or bar). Could you tell me who that is, please?

Person on Phone (P.O.P): Yes, that is Paul Romoter.

You: Thank you. I'd like to send Mr. Romoter some material. Is this the best address to send it to?

P.O.P: Yes. He has his office here. (Or, perhaps, "No. He is based at _____ ," or "He works from home.")

At this point you should ask for the correct spelling of the key contact's name and the full address of the club or other office/home. Note that you do not waste time trying to tell the person on the phone who you are, the name of the band, the fact that you want a gig, and so on. You just need to get the information that is going to help you, and you need to get it as efficiently as possible.

You: What would be the best number to call Mr. Romoter at, please?

Make a note of the number. Repeat it back to the person on the phone to make sure it is correct.

You: Finally, does Mr. Romoter have an e-mail address, please?

P.O.P: Yes, it is _____ . (Or, perhaps, "I'm sorry, I do not know," or "I cannot give out his e-mail address.")

You: Okay, thank you. (Thank the person in either case.)

Getting an e-mail address is very important for obvious reasons, but do not instantly send off an e-mail. Instead, you should call the key contact to try to establish the format he or she prefers when receiving material.

You: Hello, is this Paul Romoter?

P. Romoter: Yes it is.

You: Hi. I got your number from the Flea Pit. I'm looking to book some shows for my band and I'd like to send you some of our music. Would you prefer a CD, or can I e-mail you an online link?

Take note of the kind of language you should use here. You are not asking whether you may send the key contact some music; you are asking him how he would like to receive the music. This is important because you are not presenting a question. If you ask, "Can I send you some of our music," the contact will answer either yes or no—and you really do not want him to answer no!

Note: Physical versus Electronic—How to Send Your Music Many music industry professionals (me included) have gone off receiving CDs and now prefer to listen to music online, through a link to a dedicated website or via a MySpace, PureVolume, or even YouTube page. Tom Hopwell, booking agent for Primary Talent International, says, "I'd really advise all bands to get a website. Not having a site can be a real downer as [we] cannot access information." Put the relevant URL for your website or MySpace page (such as www.YourPageAtYourSite.com) on all the e-mails and letters you send out. Keep the music file sizes available on your site as small as possible, but not so small that the audio quality suffers. And never, ever send MP3s or WAV files as e-mail attachments! You run the risk of having your e-mail rejected by spam filters when you attach any kind of large file, such as an MP3. This should only be done after you ask the recipient for permission.

The Pitch

You now have the key contact at the venue who is responsible for booking the shows. You need to send your contact the music and the information about your band that will persuade him to book you. As I keep mentioning, any promoter you approach will want to know that you can sell tickets and that your audience is going to buy lots of drinks, food, or coat-check tickets while in the venue. The type of music you play may leave the contact cold personally, but if you can sell out the venue or add 250 ticket sales to a show, then they will book you…period. You may not be in that position now, but your blurb (the content of your e-mail or letter) still needs to make a serious impression on your potential promoter or booking agent. This applies to your webpage or MySpace site as well. The following two sections provide my top tips for pitching you and your music more effectively.

The Musical Content

1. Do not include any more than three tracks. This applies to both CDs and websites, but it is especially true for a CD. Either your listener will be hooked after listening to three tracks, or he will pass on your material. Either way, the decision will be made before the listener reaches the end of the third track. Putting 12 tracks on a demo is a waste of your resources (copying time, label printing, and so on) and the listener's time. Think about it: If you hear a song you do not like by a new band, do you immediately ask to hear another song by that band? Of course not.

2. Put your best song first. Do not save the best until last. Even if your listener likes the first track, she may not have the time or inclination to check out the last track. Open up with your killer tune—if it really is your best song, then you will have to stand or fall by that track.

3. Never submit a cover or tribute song—unless you are a cover or tribute band! Presenting someone else's song in a demo is a massive waste of time and opportunity; it tells the listener absolutely nothing about you or your music. Don't do it!

The Blurb

Your music is your most important offering to the prospective promoter, booking agent, or A&R person. However, it is very rare for any industry professional to take the music in isolation. They will want to know about you, your history, your current status, and your future plans. You need to convey your situation and your plans in words.

The temptation is to write your life story to convey how passionate you are about your art. This degree of detail is not necessary and in fact is a complete waste of your time. Instead, you should introduce yourself and your music in the most concise way possible.

The information you present is known as the *blurb* (like the description of a book on its back cover). It should follow these guidelines:

1.   Keep it brief. The key contact needs to know a bit about you, and that's all. She does not need to know where you and your fellow band members met, how long you have been together, where you went to school, or that your mom thinks you are going to be the next Dave Matthews Band/My Chemical Romance/Beyonce.

2.   Never apologize for the quality of the recordings. If you are ashamed of them, don't play them for anyone. How can you motivate someone to see you as a serious artist when you start by defending your own material?

3.   Give stats. How many shows have you played? How many people do you usually draw? How many CDs or tracks have you sold? How many people are on your MySpace site? How many forum members? What radio play do you have?

4.   Name drop. What other bands or acts have you played with or opened for?

5.   Provide testimonials. Do you have a glowing review or e-mail from a music industry professional or a well-established band? I am not talking about press reviews here. I mean a short quote from someone with authority in the industry—maybe a reply from a record company to you, praising your music.

6. Keep press reviews short. Your prospective booking agent or promoter does not need to see a copy of every review you have ever received. Simply take one or two relevant sentences from each review and create a one-page summary. For example, consider this uncomplimentary review. You would not send this to a promoter or booking agent.

> "Are you just the same?" the band repeatedly inquires on their second track, "Same."
>
> Somewhat ironically, as it happens, because there's not a riff, a melody, or a sudden change of tempo on here that you haven't heard before.
>
> There's the stuttering drive of Lostprophets, the handcrafted temperance of Incubus, and the precision vocal quicksteps of Linkin Park. Mainstream alternative is no longer a contradiction in terms but, by Christ, they do it well.
>
> The sound is huge, the production razor-sharp. And the songs are so well designed and delivered—guitar-fueled aggression replaced by soaring melodies just where you might expect—that they could have been factory-made.
>
> —Paul Travers, *Kerrang!* magazine, August 2005

This is not a positive review. However, by using only a couple of sentences from this bad review, you end up with this very concise and exciting glimpse of the potential of this band:

"There's the stuttering drive of Lostprophets, the handcrafted temperance of Incubus, and the precision vocal quicksteps of Linkin Park.... The sound is huge, the production razor-sharp."

—Paul Travers, *Kerrang!* magazine

7. Be honest. Tell the contact you are not ready to headline large shows, but you can bring a crowd for a support slot.

8. Give a timeframe. Are you available for shows now? Or are you looking to play as part of a tour in a couple of months?

9. Finally, make sure your contact information (e-mail address and home or mobile phone number) are on every item you send out or list online.

List all this information as concisely as possible. Ideally, you want to get it onto one side of a legal/A4 page with another page for press clippings.

Following is an example of a concise yet informative cover letter. The content could be used in e-mail as well.

Dear Mr. Romoter,

Further to our telephone conversation, I have pleasure in enclosing a CD of material by Millions of Americans.

Millions of Americans are not in a position to headline out-of-town shows, but would consider any suitable support slot at your venue in February, March, and April next year.

Anyway, have a listen and see what you think.

Some facts:

- The album *Caucasian Male* is available in all major chains in the UK and via mail order in the US (Casket Records/Plastic Head Distribution).

- Millions of Americans supported 30 Seconds to Mars on four dates of their recent UK tour and have opened up for such acts as All-American Rejects, The Academy Is…, Capdown, Bleeding Through, Cute Is What We Aim For, and Taking Back Sunday.

- After the last UK tour (May 2007), Millions of Americans sold 480 albums (*Caucasian Male*) at retail and 70 albums at four shows.

- The promo video for "Black Hit of Space" has been picked up by Scuzz and MTV (*120 Minutes* and *Headbangers Ball*).

- The website (www.millionsofamericans.com) now has 400+ visitors a day, of which 100 are returning (source: Statcounter.com).

(continued)

- There are 5,280 Millions of Americans mailing list subscribers (source: YourMailingListProvider.com).

- There are 720 forum members on www.millionsofamericans. com, posting 8,000 posts—an average of 15.8 posts per day.

- The new download single, "What's It to You?" will be released on February 5th.

- The video for "What's It to You?" will be released at the same time.

- The full UK tour will take place Feb through March 2008.

I will call you in a week.

Many thanks,

Andy R.

Do not worry about flashy color photographs or expensive CD covers. Photos and videos can be hosted online—just provide links to these in your e-mail or relevant URLs in your letter. Have one photograph somewhere in the literature, though. You cannot assume that everyone has the time to go on the web, or even access to it.

Do spend money on good-quality photocopies for the letters and CD cover/inlays. The copies do not need to be in color, but make sure the text is legible, especially for contact information.

The CD should be in a plastic or paper wallet. These are less bulky, cost less to buy and post, and are less likely to get damaged in transit. If you do send CDs in the full jewel case, then heed the words of George Howard of Rykodisc.

"Take the damn shrink-wrap off the CDs before you submit them!!"

—George Howard, A&R Manager, Rykodisc

Always target your key contacts before sending out or e-mailing the letters. Any band with an eye to a career wants those big opening slots on shows with national touring artists. I get many e-mails every month from bands asking how they can get on shows or tours with major artists. I'll say it again: Unless you know the headline act,

their management, or their booking agent, you are going to have to appeal to the promoter, and the promoter will not be interested unless you can pull in enough people to help sell out his or her show. Unless you have a fanatical (and very large) following, you do not stand a chance of getting one of those national shows. Assuming that you can will mark you as naive and unrealistic.

> "You are going to have to start with low-profile slots for little money and work your way up to higher-profile support slots. Be friendly, honest, and efficient to work with, and stick to whatever you agree with promoters. Stay in regular contact with the [promoters], build relationships, and you'll get some cool gigs."
>
> —Vuz Kapar, promoter, Vman Events

The Follow-Up

Do not just e-mail off your message or letter, sit back, and expect the key contact to ring you immediately. In fact, be very suspicious if a promoter does contact you right away. Either he is not very busy (which means he is not very good at promoting) or he is going to offer you some kind of pay-to-play deal.

Note: Pay to Play In my experience there are two types of pay-to-play deals. The first one is when the promoter (say, of a small club or bar) allocates you a certain amount of tickets for your show. You go away and sell as many as you can. You get to keep any money you make from the ticket sales above a certain agreed-upon amount. I have no problem with this type of deal. Obviously, you have to check the agreed split point, but if you really want the show and you think you can sell the tickets, then there is nothing wrong with this kind of deal. You can work hand in hand with the promoter to make the show a success. The harder you work to sell the tickets, the more money you make, and the more people will see your show!

The second type of pay to play is one in which you are charged a flat fee to play at a venue. You have no idea how many people will show up—if any—and you have no chance of making any money for the performance. Avoid this kind of deal at all costs!

Your e-mail or letter should be followed up by a phone call. Wait about a week, and then call up your key contact.

YOU: Hello Mr. Romoter. This is Andy from a band called Millions of Americans. I sent you some of our material last week. I'm calling to make sure you received it.

P. ROMOTER: Oh yes, I remember the CD. It's not really what i'm looking for right now, and I do not have any slots free for a couple of months.

YOU: Okay. Well, would it be okay if I call you back in two or three weeks, and we can discuss a suitable show for Millions of Americans then?

P. ROMOTER: Sure.

YOU: We have some other shows coming up soon. Do you mind if I send you the details of these shows? Perhaps you would like to come and check us out for yourself?

P. ROMOTER: Okay. Please e-mail me the details, and I will see whether I can send someone along to one of your other shows.

Your final remark indicates to the key contact that you are capable of getting other shows elsewhere. Maybe this promoter is missing out on something?

Another approach might be like this:

You: Hello Mr. Romoter. This is Andy from a band called Millions of Americans. I sent you some of our material last week. I'm calling to make sure you received it.

P. Romoter: Uh, I'm not sure. I get hundreds of CDs every week.

You: I appreciate that, Mr. Romoter. Well, obviously I sent you some material in order for my band to get a show at the venue *xxx*/opening up for *xxx*. Can I send you a quick online link by e-mail right now, and then call you back in 30 minutes or so?

This approach will have a yes or no response. You just have to make sure you have your webpage or MySpace site up and working properly and that you can send that e-mail link immediately if the promoter says yes.

If you get a yes response, then make sure you do call back when you are supposed to. Be brief, do not waffle, and be honest!

You: Hello, Mr. Romoter. This Andy from Millions of Americans calling you back as arranged. Did you get a chance to listen to the songs from the link I sent you?

P. Romoter: Yes, I did. They're okay, but not really my cup of tea.

You: Okay, I understand. Well, obviously I am still looking to book a show for my band, Millions of Americans, at your club. We are not capable of headlining our own show at the moment, but we would love the chance to open up for another band sometime. Shall I drop you a line again in a month and see what might be available?

P. Romoter: Sure.

You: Great. We are also playing a couple of shows next week/month, and I'll send you the details of those. Thanks for your time.

In this case you have come away without a show, but you have not been refused outright. Building a relationship is the important issue here. Even the smallest of promoters will have contacts or will be contacted by label scouts, booking agents, and other promoters, all of whom will be looking for new talent and the next big thing. By being upfront, honest, and businesslike with the promoter, you are not only trying to get shows for your band, but you are also creating a network, without even really trying.

Remember me telling you about all the bands who contact me saying, "We want to get to the next level. We have played all these small-town shows, and we want national touring shows?" You probably feel the same way. Imagine though, just for a moment, that you are the promoter who has been working with you and who has booked you into his venue. How would you feel, after taking a chance and booking a band into a venue, if they turned around and said, "You're too small for us now; we want something better?" Would you be inclined to book them again? Or would you think, "Well, best of luck. There

are plenty of bands around here who *do* want a show in my bar. Just don't come grovelling to me when you can't get your big out-of-town shows!" I know that's what plenty of promoters go through, and it just goes to show how shortsighted musicians can be. Someone takes a chance on promoting you and your music, and you turn around and say, "No thanks, it's not good enough for us?" Build those relationships—don't knock them down!

> "It is pretty hard, really, for a band to get those big opening slots—this comes when you get signed or get a good agent. It is best to just build a good local following, but be careful not to overkill. If you are good enough, the fans will come. It should snowball from there."
>
> —George Akins, promoter, Rock City, Nottingham

Other Strategies

The one key aspect of playing live that you should always keep in mind is that you are trying to maximize your exposure to new audiences and to existing fans every time you play a show. Obviously, this is why every band that e-mails me wants to play in front of 2,000 people as opposed to 20. In that scenario you are getting maximum exposure for minimum effort. This is true, but there are other strategies you can adopt that will have similar effects on your exposure.

Double Up

Your band may have a small following. You could probably draw 50 people to every show you play in your hometown. However, suppose you are aware that your fans are suffering from attendance fatigue—they will turn out, but they are finding it harder and harder to remain committed. Your fans are yearning for you to play bigger and better venues. You want to make the leap as well, but you cannot convince bookers or promoters at larger venues to book you.

This is the time to double up! Look for a band who has a similar-sized following or appeal and arrange to do a show together. You probably know such an act right now. Why don't you book your own show together? You may have to hire a venue and promote the show yourself, but at least you can give your audience a fresh incentive to see you.

A variation of this theme is to look for your favorite national touring band or a band you know from out of town and arrange a show for them—with your own band as the support act! This can work very well at the 50 to 250 capacity level. The fees demanded by an act at this level will not be prohibitive, and, if you approach them directly and not through their agent, you may be able to offer them a reduced fee as a favor. This kind of show is not to be undertaken lightly, though. I am always very wary of the "fan as promoter" syndrome. You will have to work extremely hard to make a show like this work. You are now acting as a promoter as well as everything else you may have going on in your musical or personal life. And do not forget, you still are going to have to get up there and play!

You will see how to create budgets and book shows in Chapter 11, "Getting Onstage: Advanced Information."

Play for Free

I warned you about paying to play. Why pay money to play? Actually, there are times when paying to play or playing for free may get you that extra bit of exposure. If you are totally confident in your abilities, you may want to organize a free show—in other words, no entrance charge for the audience. Think long and hard before you do this, though. It will be very difficult to charge that same audience for shows in the future!

A more sensible "free show" policy is to play out in front of captive, like-minded audiences. For instance, depending on your musical style, you may be able to perform acoustic versions of your songs. If you can do this, then think about getting out and finding crowds to perform to. An obvious example is at a show of a national touring band who you admire. You can't do this onstage in the venue, though—you won't get that kind of show, as we have discussed. Instead, play to the line outside the venue—this is a like-minded crowd who will be cold and waiting for the show. Set up and entertain them! Give away pins, stickers, or flyers as well. You have to make sure a prospective fan knows the name of your band.

You could go even further and play to the headline band in their tour bus. The UK band the View famously ended up being invited onto the bill of that evening's show after performing their songs to the lead singer of the headline act, Babyshambles, during the afternoon. They simply stood outside the tour bus and played, making sure they had a CD of their material to give away to the band as well. This led to a frenzy of A&R bidding and, eventually, a record deal.

DJs and turntablists are also in a great position to reach crowds through "free" shows. Nearly every pub, cafe-restaurant, record shop, modern clothes outfit, and coffee bar seems to have a turntablist tucked away in the corner, creating the necessary vibes for the shoppers. Do your research on the stores or bars that attract the people you think would appreciate your music. Most organizations have publicity and events departments, and a bit of telephone research should get you the relevant contact details. Follow the steps outlined previously to contact the key person and simply offer to DJ for free. A gig like this is a great form of exposure. It also means you can test out new tunes and mixes in front of a captive audience. When you get the gig, just make sure you have an ample supply of your own CDs/mix tapes for sale and that your name and website are clearly displayed.

Radio and TV

Play on national radio stations and syndicated TV shows is the ideal to which any act aspires. Despite the downturn in traditional CD sales and the popularity of the Internet to market and distribute music, record labels still rely on the traditional exposure of national radio to help break their artists. To do this, artists and labels employ specialized promotional departments or companies. These companies pitch or plug their client's latest single or album to the producers at the major stations and to the major shows, hoping to get airplay.

At the top end of the market (national radio and syndicated TV), plugging is seen as a specialized activity in a highly competitive area. There are too many records (31,291 different albums were released in the UK in 2005 alone), too few major stations, and not enough airtime! This specialization also obviously comes at a price. Paul Ungar, a music lawyer and industry observer, calculates that a major label will "release your record in one or two regional markets and spend about 20 G's on radio promo."

Interestingly, as the top end of the market becomes saturated, the outlets for music in the middle and bottom markets are increasing. The advent of broadband Internet and the resulting increase in connection speed means that radio has branched out onto the Internet, with thousands of stations available via web browsers. Digital radio is also becoming the norm, especially in Europe. All of this has left the existing regional and smaller radio stations crying out for content (music, interviews, and special reports) that will help differentiate them from the majors and from the plethora of Internet-only and digital stations. This differentiation comes by specializing in local content, and this is where you can gain exposure for your act.

By doing your telephone research as detailed previously, you can make sure your CD is on the desks of the station's music programmer and the producers of the applicable shows. Contact these people and offer to play a studio session or record some exclusive tracks. It is vitally important to tie this in with other promotional activity. Radio stations are like any other marketing medium—there needs to be a story around the event. Are you just about to play a big support show, or are you releasing your debut album? You stand a better chance of having a studio session offered if you have another notable event to publicize as well. If you can't get a session, at least you should be able to get some radio play and perhaps organize a ticket giveaway competition for your next show. Remember, local stations need local news. You supply them the news, and they can supply you with the exposure.

Other media channels hungry for content are the cable and satellite TV stations. Stations are seeking to differentiate themselves by offering niche programming. There are already a number of music-only MTV-type stations dealing in specific genres of music. Primarily showing promo clips, these stations also often feature live concerts, band competitions, and interviews. Can you record a show to a professional standard and have the station show it? Do they do outside broadcasts (O.B.'s) of local events? If so, would they like to come and film your show for broadcast?

If you do secure a TV or radio performance, make sure you are registered with a royalty collection society, such as ASCAP, BMI, or, in the UK, PRS. You are eligible for performance royalties for radio and TV play, and the collection society will collect those royalties and pay them to you. In the UK, for instance, you can earn £50/$110 for three minutes of airplay on national radio and £190/$494 for three minutes on a commercial TV station. For more details on ASCAP, BMI, and PRS, check out *All You Need About the Music Business* by Donald S. Passman.

> "What can unsigned/emerging bands do to get those "big" support slots? Make friends with the headline band."
>
> —Saunders, Helter Skelter. Booking agent for the Darkness, Squarepusher, Belle and Sebastian, Capdown, and many more.

9 | Getting Paid

"Sure we worry about the cost of touring. We just make sure we get paid a lot for each show we do."

—Chris Gaylor, drummer, The All-American Rejects

In Part I, I detailed the amount of money generated by live performances— $14.5 billion in 2005. In this chapter I will tell you where this money comes from and how you can get your share of it.

Fees

The majority of the money earned in the live music industry is from performance income. The audience pays the promoter money in exchange for the opportunity to see you perform live. The promoter then stages the concert in order to make money. You then charge a fee to the promoter for your services—in other words, performing your show. "Fees" or "the fee" is the industry-standard term for the amount of money you get paid when you play a concert (see Figure 9.1). The amount you can charge is usually dependent on how many tickets you can sell. The trick is to maximize that income by getting the best price per ticket that you can. Obviously, it is difficult to predict how many tickets you will sell for any given show, so how do you work out what to charge?

A show will have certain costs that must be paid for by the promoter. (You will also have costs associated with performing the show, but for the sake of clarity, I will not include them in this section. You will find out more about this in Chapter 11, "Getting Onstage: Advanced Information.") Once those costs are paid, the promoter will have money left to pay the performers. To work out what to charge, you need to figure out what the costs of the show will be and how much money the

Figure 9.1 Filthy lucre—make sure you get paid for your hard work.

promoter will need to break even. (The break-even point is the amount of money needed to pay back all the costs; anything left over will be profit.) If you can gauge those costs with reasonable accuracy, then you will have a ballpark for setting your fee. It is absolutely vital that you understand how these show costs are calculated. If nothing else, you will know when you are being ripped off!

Imagine you get offered a show at a bar that holds 100 paying customers. The ticket price is $1 (hey, let's keep it simple!). If 100 people show up and pay to see you, you will make $100, right? Wrong!

First, the promoter/bar owner will want to make some money from the event. Second, there are fixed costs that need to be paid, such as venue hire, door staff, sound engineers, equipment hire, tickets, and flyers.

Ticket sales	100	Ticket Price	$1.00	Total sales	$100.00

ITEM	COST
Venue hire (venue staff etc)	$5.00
Venue sound engineer	$10.00
Poster ads	$5.00
Newspaper ads	$5.00
Door staff	$20.00
Opening Act	$10.00
Total costs	$55.00
Total profit	**$45.00**

Figure 9.2 The show costs for 100 people in a bar at $1 per ticket.

Third, not everyone will want to pay or will be expected to pay. Taking these factors into consideration is the basis for calculating the potential profit for the show.

Suppose in our "100 people in a bar" scenario, the bar owner offers you $20 when she books you to play a show at the bar. You know that $100 is coming through the door from the ticket sales, so you obviously ask her for more money—say, 80 percent of the profits. The bar owner, in a display of tenderness not usually associated with her profession, sits you down and explains the financial situation to you. Even if all 100 turn up and pay, she will only make $45 profit, $20 of which she is willing to give to you. Figure 9.2 shows her calculations.

"Now let's be more realistic," says the kindly bar owner. (I told you to use your imagination!) "I really doubt 100 people will show up. It is a Thursday night, and there is another concert at the Enormodome that same evening. Besides, you want to invite those radio station people you told me about and the guys from the local press—that is 10 free tickets right there."

"I need 55 people to turn up and pay," she continues. "After that, I will have a profit. Let's say that 70 fans turn up and pay. There will only be $15 profit to split between us. Are you sure you still want 80% of the profits?" (See Figure 9.3 for a breakdown.)

	Ticket sales	70	Ticket Price	$1.00	Total sales	$70.00

ITEM		COST
Venue hire (venue staff etc)		$5.00
Venue sound engineer		$10.00
Poster ads		$5.00
Newspaper ads		$5.00
Door staff		$20.00
Opening Act		$10.00
	Total costs	$55.00
	Total profit	**$15.00**

Profit to promoter (20%)	*$3.00*
Profit to you (80%)	*$12.00*

Figure 9.3 The potential profit if only 70 people show up—not much!

I don't know about you, but I would probably take the $20 offer!

When negotiating an offer for a show, you might not be able to determine the promoter's show costs, and therefore you will not know whether you are getting a good deal. The amount of money the promoter has to pay out to put on a show should not really be any of your concern. However, when negotiating a deal, it pays to have all the facts. Based on what I am telling you here, you will be able to estimate quickly and make a decision. For instance, if the bar owner charged $20 a ticket and still wanted to give you only $20 for your performance, you could do some pretty quick calculations and determine whether you are being ripped off.

First, always establish the saleable capacity of the venue—that is, how many tickets can be sold. In the bar example, finding out that 100 tickets could be sold for $20 means potential revenue of $2,000! You also know (through researching the venue) that the PA and lights are already installed in the bar, but there may be a bit of advertising to be bought, and the bar owner may have to pay for a security/door person. There is no way any of this will cost more than $300, so, based on what you know about the potential income, you know that someone is going to make a load of money—and that person should be you and your band! Armed with this knowledge, you could go back to the bar owner and realistically ask for a fee of at least $200.

Guarantees

The "100 people in a bar" scenario shows basically how performance fees are negotiated by promoters and booking agents the world over. In this case, the promoter is offering the artist a guarantee—a fixed amount of cash for the show, regardless of how many people actually buy tickets. Obviously, the bar owner is not a very good businessperson because she will lose money on the deal at $1 per ticket unless she sells more than 75 tickets. That is not your problem, though; you know you are going to get paid and that the agreement is realistic.

Most of the fees you command in the early days will be guarantees, unless you promote your own shows. In fact, for a lot of shows you do—especially those big opening support slots—the guarantee will be pitifully small. The standard fee paid by a national promoter to an opening band on tour is still $50 to $100 (£50 to £100) per show. It does seem crazy when you are playing in front of 5,000 people to only get $50, when you could probably make $150 promoting your own bar show! The promoter of the national show or tour, however, will be treating your fee as another show cost—a cost he is trying to minimize.

For a headline act, the guarantee is worked out in much the same way as the "100 people in a bar" scenario. The costs are worked out, and a sensible payment to the acts is decided based on the figures. Figures 9.4 and 9.5 detail the realistic figures for a small-capacity show with two different ticket sales figures.

If I were the promoter in this case, I would offer $500 as the guarantee for the artist. How did I arrive at this figure?

You can see from Figures 9.4 and 9.5 that if the show totally sells out (300 tickets in Figure 9.4), then the total sales would be $3,000. The show costs are $1,130, so the profit would be:

$3,000 (sales) − $1,130 (show costs) = $1,870

To work out a sensible guarantee, I look to pay 30 percent of my potential sellout profit as a guarantee. In this case, 30 percent would

300 capacity venue

Ticket sales		300	Price	$10.00	Total sales	$3,000.00

Venue hire	$250.00
Venue sound engineer	$80.00
Venue lighting engineer	$80.00
Poster ads	$100.00
Newspaper ads	$40.00
Ticket print	$70.00
Door staff	$160.00
Opening Act #1	$100.00
Opening Act #2	$50.00
Catering as per rider	$150.00
Towels	$50.00

Costs $1,130.00   Break even   163

Guarantee 30% of total profit ($1870)

$617.00 $500.00

Total Costs $1,630.00

PROFIT $1,370.00

Figure 9.4 See how much money you would make on a sellout 300-capacity show!

be $617. To make it easier (and less of a risk), I round that figure down to a nice $500. That is the guarantee I will offer to the band.

"Wait a minute, though," I hear you say. "Five hundred dollars seems a bit cheap considering the promoter stands to take in $3,000 in ticket sales." That may be true, but the promoter is promoting music to make a living and has to factor in all the variables that may prevent him from making money. Let me explain.

Modern concert convention dictates that the promoter takes 20 percent of the show's profits and the artist takes 80 percent. In a total sellout scenario (refer to Figure 9.4), the promoter would have no problem paying the artist the $500 guarantee. However, look at the numbers for Figure 9.5, in which the promoter ends up selling only 200 tickets. In this case, the profits are:

$2,000 (sales) − $1,130 (costs as before) = $870

That is a big difference—$1,000, to be exact! Now I am less able to pay a big guarantee. In fact, the $500 offered seems pretty sensible.

300 capacity venue

Ticket sales		200	Price	$10.00	Total sales	$2,000.00

Venue hire	$250.00
Venue sound engineer	$80.00
Venue lighting engineer	$80.00
Poster ads	$100.00
Newspaper ads	$40.00
Ticket print	$70.00
Door staff	$160.00
Opening Act #1	$100.00
Opening Act #2	$50.00
Catering as per rider	$150.00
Towels	$50.00

Break even   163

Costs $1,130.00

Guarantee 30% of total profit $1870 $617.00 $500.00

Total Costs $1,630.00

PROFIT $370.00

Figure 9.5 This same show has not done so well. Luckily, your contract specifies you will receive a guaranteed payment—well done!

This is how the guarantee will be worked out. The promoter will also factor in weather, opposing events, and the popularity of the band when deciding the guarantee, but he will usually look to 30 percent of the total potential profits as a starting point.

Percentages

Look again at Figure 9.4. If you sell out—that is, all 300 tickets get sold—there will be $1,870 profit. Your contract stipulates a guarantee of $500. That means the promoter will walk away with $1,370, and you will get only $500. Hey, that ain't right! Luckily, there is a system in place to counter this potential unfairness.

Remember the show contract from Chapter 3? That contract contains the following clause:

> For a salary of: £300.00 plus PA/lights + catering or 80% of door receipts (after £1,116.43 costs), whichever is the greater.

That clause basically says that if the artist sells a lot more tickets than anyone expects, he or she will get a share of the increased profits as well. In our example, the artist will walk out with $1,496 if all 300 tickets sell. However, if less than 175 tickets sell, the artist will still get the guarantee of $500. If less than 163 tickets sell (the break-even point), then the promoter will lose money!

I hope these examples give you a clearer idea of how concert fees are determined. It is extremely useful to work out the potential sales of every show you do, as well as how much money everyone is making. With this knowledge, you would be able to go back to the bar owner in our "100 people in a bar" scenario and advise her to raise her ticket prices to $5!

As your career progresses, you may not actually ever need to use this knowledge, but I would advise you to keep a sharp eye on the amount of money being charged on your behalf and how much money you actually make from your performances. The deals may be worked out by the promoters and your booking agent, but there is one area of the operation with which you should always be concerned—the price of your tickets.

Ticket Prices

Ticket prices are the cause of much concern in the modern live industry. Many feel that concert tickets are too expensive, and that is *not* just the opinion of the ticket-buying public. Marek Leiberberg, based in Germany, runs the seventh biggest concert promotion company in the world. He feels that the unrealistic demands of artists and their agents have sent ticket prices spiraling. "They have no shame," he says of certain bands and artists. "Until the mid 1990s, €50 [$60] was the highest price most artists would charge for their concert tickets, and they were artists of the calibre of the Rolling Stones. Today, Robbie Williams won't go below €70 [$80], and Madonna recently charged €192 [$200]. Even a pop band such as Pussycat Dolls won't set foot on stage for anything less than €45 [$50] a ticket."

Mick Jagger of the Rolling Stones, on the other hand, disagrees. "Pricing a concert ticket is very different from pricing a Lexus or toothpaste. It's more like a sports event. And you are prepared to pay the market price? So if U2 or Madonna costs $100 (I'm making these up), you don't want to be charging $200. I try to keep ticket prices within the market price range." According to Pollstar, the average ticket price for the top 100 US tours in 2005 rose to a record $57, compared to $52.39 in 2004. The average ticket price for all concerts has gone up nearly $7 since 2003. But if there is so much concern, why are ticket prices rising?

Historically, ticket prices have been set by the promoter based on the expected show costs and market forces. In other words, are people willing to pay a certain amount for this artist's concert? Charge too much for a ticket, and people might not show up; charge too little, and you will make no profit. Once a ticket price is agreed upon by the agent and the band, the promoter arranges the show and pays the artist a share of the profits. If an artist's contract rider stipulations are extensive—and therefore expensive—the show costs will increase. In this case, the promoter will try to persuade the artist to reduce the cost of the rider stipulations. If he is unsuccessful, he will have to reduce his other show costs and/or increase the ticket price. It is usually easier to raise the ticket price than to reduce other show costs.

At the same time, many artists are creating their own concert production companies and are arranging and marketing their own tours, only using existing promoters for expertise and assistance in organizing and staging the actual shows. This gives artists a greater share of the concert revenue and allows them to set ticket prices to maximize revenue. The first act to do this successfully was the Rolling Stones for the Steel Wheels tour in 1989.

Before this tour, the Rolling Stones used a booking agent in the same way as every other band. The agent would contact local promoters in each city or country to set up shows for the tour, as we saw in Chapter 2. Individual deals had to be made with each promoter. The tour agent then had to collect $250,000 here and $400,000 there from promoters during the tour.

One such promoter was Michael Cohl. Cohl is a Canadian promoter who, while promoting a Rolling Stones show, had a run-in with the Stones' touring director/booking agent at that time. After that incident, Cohl realized there could be a better way to make the tours work for both the Rolling Stones and himself. He approached the Stones with a plan: He would work for the band directly and would book the entire tour himself, dealing with the venues directly and cutting out the local promoters. He would pay the band an agreed-upon figure up front and then split the profits with them. He also looked at other money-spinners, such as corporate hospitality and sponsorship, in order to maximize the exposure for the Rolling Stones at each concert. The whole package would be run directly by the band (through him), so there would be no need to pay percentages to third parties.

Luckily for Cohl, his plan worked. The 1989 Steel Wheels tour was a benchmark in modern touring, both artistically and financially, grossing $260 million worldwide. Many artists today seek to emulate that level of production and earning potential. Madonna, U2, and the Red Hot Chili Peppers, among others, have formed their own touring corporations, booking shows directly into venues and squeezing every drop out of the revenue opportunities available. The main revenue is obviously from the tickets, hence the increase in prices.

It could be argued that the increase in ticket prices is reflected in the staggering spectacle of modern concerts and that today's audiences demand this increased level of set, sound, lighting, video, and costume production. My fear is that artists with a lesser draw may be swept up in the high ticket pricing trend and may alienate their potential audience by appearing too greedy. I would advise keeping a firm eye on the prices you charge for your shows and making sure you understand the implications for you, your audience, and the bottom line.

Note: Festivals and Fees The modern outdoor festival presents a unique challenge to a band and its agent: How do you quantify how many people have actually paid to see you? The modern festival-goer looks for an "experience" and is rarely drawn by individual acts—an obvious fact due to the staggering number of tickets sold for major festivals before a lineup is even announced! Therefore, a band's fee is not directly tied to tickets sold; indeed, the stature of the band and the nerve of the agent will dictate how much money the promoter will pay. And they pay a lot! The headline act at each night of the Carling Leeds and Reading festival in the UK gets $1,947,000 (£1,000,000) per act; the top two stars at the Rock Am Ring festival in Germany earned $5,100,000 (£2,760,000) between them.

Merchandise

Merchandise sales (T-shirts, hats, badges/pins, stickers, CDs, and posters) is the lifeblood of any touring band—signed or unsigned, major label or DIY (see Figure 9.6). For instance, a hot young act can easily sell $1,000 to $2,000 of "merch" a night on tour, even if they are only playing 350-capacity rooms for $200 a night. A band such as U2 will sell $16 (£9) of merchandise to every single audience member on their tours. At a lower level, selling three CDs a night can provide a tank of gas for your van. (Merch is also known as "swag" in touring circles, but in my experience the term *swag* relates to the crew-only merchandise—satin tour jackets and limited-edition crew shirts.)

The best part of selling your merchandise is that, as well as making you money, your customers are then advertising your band when they wear your shirts or put your stickers on their schoolbooks. "Bands as brands" is a serious point of discussion at the moment; modern music stars are

Figure 9.6 A merchandise display.

launching their new clothing lines, perfumes, and guitar models every day. That brand exposure is then utilized by large companies to help promote other products. I will talk more about this in Part IV, "The Future," but right now you should know that if you are serious about getting your music on the road, it is vital to get your merchandising operation sorted out from the start.

Having said all that, I have seen some absolutely dreadful tour merch over the years, and I work with professional, high-profile acts. Merch seemed to be a last-minute thing for a lot of the bands I worked for. It seemed as if two weeks before the tour, someone would say, "Oh, we better have some shirts to sell," and *presto*—500 completely inappropriate T-shirts would be printed. No apparent thought would go into the designs, the prices, or the potential audience for the shirts, and you can bet that at the end of the tour, the band still had 300 of these rubbish shirts left!

You are in a different situation, though. Building up your career step by step means you are better equipped to think about the realities of making money from your music. Done correctly, tour merchandising will both create a highly profitable income and provide a unique opportunity to raise brand awareness. If done incorrectly, you will waste a *lot* of cash and have a lot of moldy merch in your garage after each tour. Pick and market your products carefully, just as you do with your music. The following sections detail some of my hints and tips for successful merch selling.

Products

Your music is based on a gut instinct, so if you want to remain an individual creative talent, perhaps you should not analyze or research the music you create too much. The exact opposite is true of anything associated with your merchandise. Tour merchandise consists of tangible products. Your fans will judge these products, regardless of how good they think your music is, so if your T-shirts are too small or your baseball caps look ugly, your fans will not buy them. Go to shows and look at what other bands are selling. Look at what you, your friends and band mates buy when you go to shows. Look at your audience. Ask your younger brothers and sisters. Then think about what products you are going to create.

T-Shirts

T-shirts obviously are the first thing people think about when talking about band merchandise. Because it is the most common product type, a bewildering range of options for T-shirt types and styles has evolved in the touring merchandise industry.

Do you recall Dan, our hapless tour manager and merch seller from the tour diary in Chapter 7? Remember how he was quizzed about how many designs and the like he had? You need to figure out the same. You may have one actual "look" of shirt—such as a new logo and album picture on the front—but how many variations of that shirt will you produce? For instance, if you play any type of rock (metal, speed, classic, thrash, nu-, heavy, alternative, and so on), a black shirt with your logo/album artwork on the front and the tour dates on the back has always been considered a classic shirt type. Audience demographics have changed in the last 20 years, though, and the average rock fan is no longer a large male. ("Large" can refer to either height or beer gut size.) These days, rock band fan shirts should always come in a "skinny" or "girls" fit, as well as in medium and large sizes. You should also still print extra-large shirts, but not too many; they simply do not sell in the numbers they once did. People may be getting fatter, but they certainly do not like to be reminded of it when buying tour merch. So you've got one design printed on a girl/skinny size, a medium, a large, and a few extra-larges.

The mistake I see over and over is bands having more than two designs and then printing all those designs onto every possible permutation of T-shirt color and size, such as a regular T in skinny, small, medium, large, and extra-large in black, red, and white, as well as a V-neck skinny, small, medium, large, and extra-large in black, red, and white, and a polo type in skinny, small, medium, large, and extra-large in maroon, black, and blue…the list goes on. Printing this many types of shirts is just a waste of your money. You will have to place minimum print runs (at least 50 of each design and size type to be cost effective), so you would be ordering a massive amount of stock.

By having this many designs, you are giving your fans too many choices. Choice at the mall is good, but choice at the concert merch stall is bad. A display of every conceivable design, color, and size permutation will not result in more sales. Instead, it will lead to your merch stall becoming a changing room with every prospective customer trying on every permutation of shirt design and size. This is great in the high street, but disastrous for you. You do not have acres of space for your shop—at most, you will have a table with a (hopefully) huge crowd around it. You need to make lots of sales quickly. A couple trying on your shirts will block the way for other customers and waste your time. Limit the choice of shirts you sell at the show, but make sure you have merch available to buy by mail order. When you are starting out, I would advise the following for your T-shirt range: a medium shirt and a girls/skinny fit shirt in one design only.

The black rock shirt does not work for all music genres. Hip-hop fans are used to having their musical heroes running clothing brands anyway (FUBU, G-Unit) and will not be impressed by your simple black T-shirt. Techno and turntablist acts should think very carefully about T-shirt design. Bright solid designs on pastel and earth-color shirts seem to do well. "One of the big changes is we sell a lot more women's shirts, a lot more different styles," says Dell Furano of Signatures, a major entertainment merchandising company. "The shirts are starting to reflect the boutique trends in L.A. and in New York, a soft feel and an artsy design."

Always print your shirts on good accepted brands, such as Fruit of the Loom, Hanes, Russell, and Jerzees. It will cost more initially, but put yourself in your fans' place: How would you feel when the shirt you bought off your brand-new heroes fades and fall to pieces after two washes?

One or two colors for the actual print are much cheaper than a full-color design, regardless of the size of the actual print. Design your shirts accordingly. Design your logo so it will look good when seen as white on a black shirt, as well as the other way around. And, obviously, a big problem with a T-shirt design is actually coming up with a design! You have poured sweat and blood into your music, the album cover, and the logo—can you really be bothered to do it all again for a bunch of T-shirts? I would advise you to spend the maximum effort you can—this is you, your life, and your brand you are trying to sell, so you should take it very seriously.

When designing your shirts, you should ask yourself the same kinds of questions that any designer asks. What are you trying to achieve? Are you going for a portrayal of you and your band with the logo and CD artwork as a prominent feature, or are you aiming for a more esoteric, cool design that can be worn as a lifestyle shirt? I cannot give you the answers, but you should think about your target audience. It may be better in the early days to get your band's name and the logo exposed as much as possible. On the other hand, a more esoteric design may get people talking and could become a must-have design.

After finalizing your design and shirt types, you are ready to print up your shirts. I doubt you have the equipment to do this yourself—at least to the standard expected by modern consumers—so you will need to approach a clothing printing company. Concert-associated apparel is a huge business, so many companies now operate to cater for this demand. You should obviously shop around for deals when printing up your shirts. Ask other bands, look in newspaper ads, and search the Internet. Avoid the gimmick and corporate apparel printers— they simply cannot offer good enough deals to cash-strapped young bands. You may find a cheaper deal on the Internet from an out-of-town company, but make sure you check the delivery charges. Fifty T-shirts is one big, heavy box! Perhaps wait until you have a good run of shows or a tour lined up; that way, you can order shirts on the initial run, paying less per shirt, but then be able to sell for a better price.

> "Start slowly and then gradually expand the range [of your merchandise]. Don't invest too much unless you're certain there's a demand for it."
>
> —Andy Allen, Backstreet International. Supplies tour merchandise for Metallica, the Rolling Stones, and the White Stripes, among others.

Other Apparel

I am always slightly wary of other types of clothing, such as jackets, sleeveless shirts, panties, and so on in concert merch stalls for emerging artists. It is true that you may shift a few hoodies and beanie hats if you are a rock band touring in the winter, but if you do not sell all that stock, you will be stuck with it until the next winter tour. The same goes for big-ticket items, such as leather jackets, dresses, and so on. I know the Rolling Stones did a tie-in with Agent Provocateur (UK lingerie manufacturers) to produce a fantastic range of clothes, but is that your audience? I do recognize the importance of the "band as brand" and the fact that you can lend your name to most things. I also know that a concert is a high-pressure environment—time and viewing availability are limited. Your fans will have already bought the concert tickets and paid for transportation, gas, parking, food, drinks, and coat check just to see your show. Yes, you want them to buy stuff—just don't dilute the offerings.

If you do want to sell other clothing items, I recommend you stick to hats (baseball or beanie caps) and perhaps hoodies, depending on your musical genre.

Note: If you are playing any of the major European outdoor festivals, then you should definitely print your logo and webpage onto a load of cheap disposable raincoats or ponchos and just give them away! It is bound to start raining at some point during that weekend, and when it does, the people who received your free gift will start wearing it. Those people will mentally thank you (you have made a new fan) and will be advertising your name to the rest of the festival!

CDs

Three simple rules: If you press up, print, and control the distribution of your own CDs, then get them on that merch stall and sell them. If you press and print your own CDs and have a separate distributor, then buy a load of CDs back from the distributor and sell them on your merch stall. If you are signed to a label with a distributor, then don't sell your CDs at your show. Why not? Because it will adversely affect any chart placing your CD may have and will cost you more in the long run.

I have worked with quite a few bands that were signed to labels—major or indie, it does not really matter. The bands or their management decided they would buy a few hundred CDs off the label (at cost price) in order to sell them at the shows on the tour. Usually the label would say no, and for good reason. This kind of sale has no bearing on the chart placing, and although you and I might think the sales charts are completely irrelevant these days, record companies still rely on them to prove their worth to the radio stations that will hopefully play the records released by that company. It is a vicious cycle, and one that neither the record companies nor the radio stations really wish to break.

The bad news for bands would be if the label actually said yes and sold them a couple of boxes of CDs. First, you should never buy off the label. The deal will be atrocious and will not count toward total sales—the label will probably sell them to you out of its stock of promotional copies, for which you will not receive a penny. The second problem is that every CD you sell at your show then will not be sold in a record store the next day. This means you receive neither the royalty on the sale nor the notification of the amount of sales. Yes, you have made a sale, but have you made any money? How much did the label charge you for each CD?

Selling label CDs at your shows also means a lot of angry record-store owners—why are you selling your CD at the show and depriving them of business?

If you really must buy your own products from your label to sell on tour, then at least buy them from the distributor. CDs bought this way will count toward total sales, and you may receive your royalty on them.

Other Products

Are you familiar with the term "up-sell?" It is a marketing term, referring to the practice of suggesting higher-priced products or services to a customer who is considering a purchase. In rock band merch speak, this would be like saying, "You can buy this T-shirt for $9.99. If, however, you buy two T-shirts, I will throw in this set of button pins for free." Up-selling works in band merch because you have access to low-cost, high-visibility items such as label and button pins, patches, stickers, and lanyards, all with your logo printed on them. These same items can be sold in their own right for massive profit. The cost per item for stickers and buttons is pennies, but I always try to sell them for a dollar (or a pound) each—a huge markup! Because the initial cost per item is so small, you can offer the same items as an incentive for buying multiples of your more expensive items and not lose money. Let's face it, you would have to sell an amp-head case full of button pins to make the money to pay for a tank of gas. However, if you gave five button badges away to people who bought one extra T-shirt or CD, then you probably have your tank of gas right there.

The up-sell products you choose will vary from genre to genre. Think about what inexpensive item you or your fans would perhaps need at a show—earplugs, for instance—and go about getting your logo printed on a few and selling them. In my experience, the following items always work well:

- Button badges
- Label pins
- Cloth patches
- Stickers—high-quality vinyl
- Lanyards
- Disposable lighters
- Postcard sets
- Earplugs or packets for earplugs
- Bottle openers
- Disposable raincoats/ponchos
- Plastic bags in which your fans can carry home all their new merch

Your Shop

I stressed earlier in this section the importance of making the most of your available selling space—the merch table. Retail store owners spend thousands of dollars and hundreds of hours researching and designing the shopping environments we inhabit. Their motivation for this expense is getting shoppers and customers to feel comfortable enough to make purchases. Your aim is the same. Unfortunately, your retail environment is the entrance hall of a rock club or bar, which is often noisy and crowded. Not the ideal environment to persuade a potential customer to part with cash! Lucky for you, your audience is predisposed to make a purchase—buying a T-shirt, cap, or CD is part of the concert-going ritual.

Your shop will never be an ideal selling environment, but you can take maximum advantage of the opportunity by thinking about the points in the following sections.

Location

Music fans will browse on the way in and buy on the way out. Therefore, position your stall or table so that it is visible to greatest number of people on the way out of the venue. Try not to position your stall very close to other areas of high activity, such as the cloakroom/coat check or bars. The crowd activity will mask your little stall.

It is always tempting to set up your stall in the main room so you can watch the other bands. In my experience, this does not work. Music venues are often dark and obviously noisy. Audiences will tend to leave a concert room for fresh air, for toilet breaks, to get to the bar, and at the end of the show. Make sure you are there to catch them on the way out. After all, you are there to sell merch, not to watch the show!

Display

Always have a couple of small clip lights, a long mains power extension cable, colored lighting filters (gels), gaffer tape, and a microphone stand. People can only buy what they can see, so make sure people can see your merch! Position the lights to illuminate the shirts on the wall and to create a focal point. (The microphone stand is there to clip the lights onto—placing lights on your desk will make the beams shine straight into your eyes!)

Make your display as neat and tidy as possible. Hang shirts on hangers or on cardboard "torso" shapes to stretch the shirts—this will help to display the shirt design better. If you have to use gaffer/duct tape, then tape behind the shirt, using small rolls of tape. (See Figures 9.7 and 9.8.)

Figure 9.7   Wrong! Do not just tape your shirts to a wall—it will make your merch look tatty.

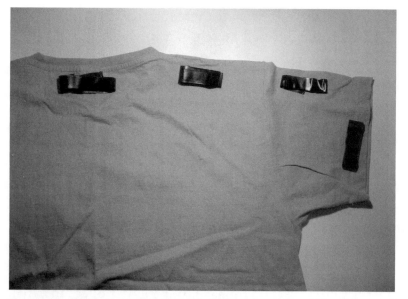

Figure 9.8   Display your shirts neatly by hanging them with rolls of gaffer on the back of the shirt.

Use signs to educate as well as inform. Do not just list prices—list up-sell offers as well, such as "Buy two CDs and get a free Millions of Americans bottle opener!"

Take CDs out of the jewel cases and gaffer-tape the cases to the table.

Selling

Many people are uncomfortable with the ideas of selling and being a salesperson. These words—"selling" and "salesperson"—instantly conjure up clichéd images of heartless, "a sale at any cost" types who pester innocent people until those same people sign on the dotted line for products and services they cannot afford. You may indeed feel the same way.

In reality, your situation is completely different. As an artist (or crew person), you are engaged in selling 24 hours day, whether you like it or not. The commodity you are selling? Why, yourself of course! You, your music, your sound engineering skills—if you do not go out and sell your skills and talents, you will not get that next gig or that recording contract, and you will not make any money.

So do not approach selling your merch as selling—just treat it as a part of spreading the love about you and your music. Enjoy the experience, make friends, and be honest!

If you are still a bit unsure about selling on a merch stall, then follow these hints and tips:

- Be at your merch stall after you perform. You are the biggest advertisement for your merch. Never, ever consider yourself too cool to get to your own merch stand. I work with all types of acts; the ones that sell a lot of merch (and therefore make lot of money) are the ones who get to their merch stall after their set and generate that interest. These bands have people who actually take the money and hand over the shirts, but it is the immediate contact with the band members that excites fans.

- Be confident. Never apologize for the quality of your merch or recordings. If you don't believe in them, who else will?

- Have plenty of change.

- Generate excitement. As well as being at your merch stall yourself, try giving away lollipops, candies, balloons, or buttons. Better still, go into the crowd and give away lollipops, balloons, or buttons.

- Have plenty of change.

- Have a way of collecting e-mail addresses. A simple paper form will suffice. Print it in landscape format, have lots of copies, and have plenty of cheap pens next to the forms. Landscape format will give people more room to write. (Someone has to enter all these addresses into a database—the more room people have to write, the more intelligible the handwriting will be.) Encourage everyone to sign up for the mailing list, regardless of whether they bought your merch. Give away a lollipop or candy as a way of saying thank you. Your mailing list is a potential goldmine, as I will explain in Chapter 10, "Marketing."

- Have plenty of change.

- Never put items on hold until after the show for a potential customer. They have to buy now! Explain to the fan that all the merch is going to sell out very quickly and that they should buy their shirt now.

- Likewise, never offer to store purchased goods until after the show. You will have limited space anyway, but most importantly, you do not want to be looking around for this item during the post-show sales rush; you should be selling more shirts and CDs instead of acting as a cloakroom!

- Have plenty of change.

- Think about the up-sell. Work out your profits per item and your potential two-for-one prices. Memorize these deals or have them on your display. Suppose a couple comes to your stall looking for a shirt. You should say, "One shirt? There are two of you! Is only one of you two fine people going home with a Millions of Americans T-shirt tonight? I can do you a deal on two shirts; it will be cheaper than you think."

- Have plenty of change.

- Sign stuff. Do not wait to be asked. When someone makes a purchase, ask, "Would you like me to sign that for you? What is your name?"

- Make it fun. Talk to people!

- Oh, and have plenty of change.

After Sales

Always make sure all your merch is available by mail order for when you are not actually playing out. Many fans may be potential paying customers for your merch, but they may be unable to actually purchase at the time for numerous reasons. They may have spent all their money, or perhaps they cannot decide what to buy, they have to get the last train home, or they just were too shy to come to the stall. Whatever the reason, you need to have some way to sell to them after the event. You do not need a major e-commerce website, just some way for fans to write to you, order stuff, send you money, and get their goods in return. PayPal, for instance, has very simple tools that enable you to get orders from your website, and MySpace will now help you sell your music online. For more information on marketing your music on MySpace, check out *MySpace for Musicians* (Thomson Course Technology PTR, 2007).

Prices

If I were to ask what your considerations were when setting a selling price for your merch, you would probably say that you need to sell your merch at a profit, but not at a price that will deter potential customers. You would be right, and yet I constantly work with acts who sell their T-shirts and CDs at a ridiculously cheap price. There seems to be a "we are doing it for the kids" attitude that, although altruistic, is wrong. If you want to be altruistic, then just give everything away. If you are going to sell stuff, add a sensible markup so that you are making some decent profit for all your hard work. You are not going to make much money from performance fees in the early stages, so you have to make it on the merchandise.

Note: Give It Away, Give It Away, Give It Away Now UK-based act The Crimea recently gave away their second album for free. By doing this, they obviously are hoping to widen their fan base and ultimately make more money from touring, merchandising, and licensing deals than they would from sales of the album. Despite selling a respectable 35,000 copies of their debut album, last year the band was dropped by their record label, Warner Music.

"We've always strived to get the music out to as many people as possible," said The Crimea's drummer, Owen Hopkin. "We want to harness the power of the Internet. If it's on there for free, we'll reach more people than the orthodox route of selling the record."

Customers will respond to sensible pricing; it helps them to make a positive decision about a purchase. Your T-shirts may be $6, but your customer will be thinking, "Six bucks for a shirt? There must be something wrong with it."

Price to sell. Look at your competitors, especially the successful ones, and study their prices and their up-sell offers.

Licensing Deals

As I already discussed, music concert merchandising is big business. In 2004, Ozzy Osbourne grossed $35 million in concert sales and another $15 million directly from merchandise sales, while Mötley Crüe's 2005 Red, White & Crüe tour averaged $10 in merchandise sales per concert-goer per show. Not surprisingly, specialized companies have emerged that work to grab a slice of this business.

Specialized merchandising companies offer you a deal to take care of all your merchandising, design, manufacturing, distribution, and sales for you, on tour or in retail stores. You basically license the right to use your name and logo to them, and they offer you a royalty rate for the merchandise they produce and sell. You then receive an advance on this arrangement, which obviously can be a pretty hefty chunk of change. The deal offered will vary, but you are usually looking at receiving around 20 to 35 percent of the gross retail price.

Nigel McCune of the Musician's Union advises, "The problem is, unlike every other deal that you're doing in the record business, advances in merchandising are recoverable as well as recoupable. So if someone says, 'We'll give you $50,000 for the right to produce your T-shirt,' they might come to you two years later and say, 'We got $30,000 back, so can we have our $20,000 please?'"

At the top end of the scale, companies such as Musictoday create huge revenues for their artists. The company (recently bought by Live Nation) has 700 clients, including newcomers such as Legend, legacy bands such as the Doors, and everyone in between—Kenny Chesney, Justin Timberlake, Taylor Hicks, Janet Jackson, and Britney Spears, to name a few. By the end of 2006, Musictoday sold more than $200 million worth of concert tickets, CDs, merchandise, and fan-club memberships.

The attraction of licensing deals is obvious—professional expertise, a distribution network, and a big load of money upfront. For many bands, this cash injection provides the necessary startup money to tour in the first place. However, you really need to think long and hard about signing your rights away. Have the deal studied properly. In particular, look at the territories covered—does the deal cover individual countries or world rights—and the timing of advance payments. Ideally, your agreement will be set up on a short-term, tour-by-tour basis.

Performance Royalties

Performing rights societies, such as ASCAP, BMI, SESAC, and PRS, work to collect any royalties due to you from the public performance and broadcast of your works. If you own the copyright to your songs, and they are performed or broadcast in a public place, you will get paid. This collection of royalties is primarily concerned with radio, TV, and nightclub play, but also extends to live shows, hence the inclusion here.

You should join a performing rights society anyway, because you will receive royalties for radio play and plays in public places. When you have joined, you will be eligible for payment of royalties from your shows. In the UK, for instance, the PRS will pay you for live performances at the majority of venues in the country, regardless of whether the show is part of a tour. In the US, you will only receive royalties on live performance if you perform on one of the top 200 grossing tours (as decided in *Pollstar* magazine).

Sponsorship

Sponsorship is one other income stream you could consider, although in my experience it only really works for higher-level acts. To understand this, you need to examine the relationship in a sponsorship deal. You want money or services that the sponsor can supply. The sponsor, in turn, wants to use your mass appeal to further spread its name. It is another form of advertising, and one that can work well, but only if the relationship is equal on both sides. Obviously, a sponsor will not achieve much exposure if you have no fan base or audience draw.

Major companies are seeing music as a good way to extend their brand reach. European mobile phone giant Vodafone, for instance, now concentrates on live music sponsorship, spending at least 20 percent of its $117 million (£60 million) annual advertising budget in this area. Obviously, here is a greater chance for you to attract a sponsor. The problem for you is finding companies who see live music as being a good fit with their advertising plans. Those companies receive hundreds of applications for sponsorship—how are you going to stand out?

The first step in securing sponsorship dollars is to create a professional proposal presentation. The potential sponsor needs to see the benefit of entering into a deal with you. They need hard facts and statistics, the same kind of statistics you used when approaching concert promoters (refer to Chapter 8). The emotional aspect of you and your music ("We are the best band since the Beatles") is irrelevant. Your potential sponsor wants to know that if they give you $2,000 and paint their logo onto your van, you will be seen by a certain number of people—people who will have an interest in purchasing the products or services of your sponsor.

You will need to provide a demographic analysis of your fans and your potential audience. You will need to identify their sex, age group, purchasing power, influences, and influence. This data is readily available if you know where to search for it. For instance, you could call up the radio stations that play your kind of music and ask them for their demographic reports. The radio station targets a certain demographic of the population by playing the same kind of records that you make; they will have custom reports detailing information about their listeners that they use to attract sponsorship and advertising of their own. If you can get a copy of these reports (or the distilled information), you can supply accurate demographic data to a potential sponsor.

At this point I would agree with you if you are starting to think it is all a little daunting. My advice is to forget about sponsorship until you are in a position where you are actually approached by a potential sponsor. Concentrate on increasing your audience and your concert draw. It does not matter how many professional sponsorship proposals you send out, no sponsor will be interested if no one is buying your records or attending your gigs.

> "[Playing live] is the medium through which an act's art can flourish the best and where they can explain or extend the material they've recorded. It also enables an artiste to build a following and then learn how to handle an audience."
>
> —Joel Harrison, A&R manager, Island Records Group.

10 Marketing

The Oxford English Dictionary defines marketing as "the activity of presenting, advertising and selling a company's products in the best possible way." In terms of getting your show on the road, you are the company. I hope it is fairly obvious to you what the products are—your music, your image, and your merchandise.

You may have the same attitudes toward marketing that you do toward selling—that it is not something you are comfortable with and that you have no interest or skill in it. But the reality is that unless you do not want anybody in the world to ever hear you or your music, you are involved in marketing. Marketing is not simply selling a product for money; look again at the definition. If you are still having problems with the idea of the word "marketing," then swap it for "promotion." Whatever the term, all you are interested in is presenting your band's music "in the best possible way."

In the real world, beyond dictionary definitions, marketing involves spreading the news about your band's shows and tours to the widest audience. This audience is not only comprised of concertgoers, but it also includes artist managers, booking agents, promoters, and record label A&R people. Different marketing methods will work for different audience types—the following sections describe some of those methods (see Figure 10.1).

Posters and Flyers

You have to let potential gig-goers know that you are playing a show. Putting up posters and handing out flyers is simple and cheap way of doing this. In fact, I would imagine this to be the primary marketing activity that most bands will engage in when starting out. Make it effective by following this simple advice.

Figure 10.1 Marketing—you may have to be a bit more subtle than this.

I often sit on tour buses, headed into town on the morning of a show, maybe with band members looking out the windows. Sooner or later, one of the band members will turn round and say, "Dude. I don't see any of our posters up." To which I always reply, "Well, I bloody well hope not! If your posters are visible, it means they have only just gone up, which means no one knows about tonight's show, which means we might as well keep going to the next town 'cause there is not going to be a crowd tonight!"

Timing is important when putting up posters and flyers because there are limited places to stick posters in most cities, and as soon as you put them up, new ones will be posted over them. Make sure you put posters up in good time to promote the show, but not so soon that other posters are plastered over them before the show. Your audience might not have had a chance to absorb the information before new posters are put over yours. I would recommend putting posters up no sooner than one month before a small club or bar show. However, stick the posters up too late, and your fans will not know about your show until the last minute. They may have already made plans and they may not be able to get to the show.

Even so, posters are effective, especially if they can be seen during commute times and over weekends or public holidays. The promoter of your show or tour will usually take care of all the traditional marketing methods—posters and flyers—but they can only do this if they have the necessary artwork and information. Make sure you or your team supply logos, website details, and current/forthcoming release details as soon as the show or tour is confirmed.

Obey the law. You may be putting up your own posters for a show. Do not be arrogant and plaster your posters or flyers over every public space you can. Every major city with a healthy music scene will have strict laws governing posters and flyers on private and public property. Boston, for instance, will prosecute and fine people who post illegally a minimum $300. In the UK, you can be prosecuted under the following acts: Town and Country Planning Act, Highways Act, Anti-Social Behaviour Act, Local Government Act, and Clean Neighbourhoods and Environment Act 2005—all of which lead to a significant fine and a possible prison sentence. Whatever your views on civil liberties or the freedom of speech, you have to know that the authorities will catch you. Your name is all over the poster! Those same authorities will visit the club or venue you are advertising, elicit your details from the promoter, and track you down.

Posters are a useful part of your marketing efforts, but you have to work very hard, spend a lot of money, and potentially break the law in order to make your work stand out. Obviously, the situation will change with a label or a national promoter behind you; high-impact poster campaigns on official billboards and other paid-for space are extremely effective in raising awareness of a new album release or tour.

Flyers, on the other hand, can be just as effective without the high cost or legal ramifications. A flyer is usually a small piece of paper (A6 or one fourth of a letter page) that can be printed in either color or black and white and can be single-sided or printed on both sides. Flyers are designed to be studied. You hand the flyer to someone, and the person can read it, rather than glimpsing the information from a speeding automobile or train (as with posters). You can present more information in your flyer than you would be able to with a poster.

Flyers are also cheaper and easier to produce. You can simply create a design, add the relevant text (venue, show date, admission pricing, and so on), copy four lots of that design onto a single piece of letter-size paper (or A4 paper if you are outside the US), and print up as many as you like. You can do this with any home computer and a black-and-white printer. If you copy 100 sheets, you will have 400 flyers—after you have cut them up, of course!

Postcards are similar to flyers in that they are small and can present a lot of information. But they are not cheap to produce, being printed on cardstock, and you will have to use a specialized printer to actually print them.

I prefer flyers and postcards to spread the word about a band and a tour. Flyers are cheap, can contain more information, and can involve the personal touch—you can actually hand a flyer to someone. This brings me to personal invitations....

Make It Personal

Handing out flyers and postcards at other shows and clubs is effective, but handing out *invitations* is even more effective. What do I mean by invitations? I am talking about making your flyers personal or including a special offer (see Figure 10.2).

You can put up posters that advertise the dates and venues, but that will not necessarily entice a potential gig-goer; posters merely inform the public of an event. Instead, print up flyers and postcards with a personal message or offer, along with the conventional day, date, venue, and CD details. Even if you have carefully targeted your audience, you need to give them a reason to attend your show.

A special offer could include:

■ **Cut-price entry offer.** Can you make a deal with the venues you are playing to provide free or half-price entry for anyone turning up with one of your flyers?

Figure 10.2 An interesting use of a flyer or give away. In this case the band has printed up plastic flyers the size of a credit card and given them away at every venue in which they perform. The card asks you to do just one thing—send your e-mail address to the band!

- **Mail-in offer.** "Mail this flyer back to us with your street and e-mail address filled in, and we will send you a free Millions of Americans CD!" Yes, you might give away a lot of CDs, but they are cheap to produce and, more importantly, you are getting the e-mail and mailing addresses of potential fans—fans who you then can tell about forthcoming shows or special offers on merchandise.

- **Members-only password.** Include a password on the flyer for a "members only" section of your website that includes live clips, free downloads, or special offers.

- **A competition.** You could set up a lottery in which fans enter their e-mail address or mobile phone number, and you pick a couple of lucky winners on a designated date. Prizes could be free entry to the show, T-shirts, or an opportunity to meet the band backstage.

The idea of these invitations is to entice a potential concertgoer to one (or all) of your shows. And concert-going is not a solo activity—people attend shows as couples or in groups. If you give free entry to one person, that person is bound to bring some friends along, and you will have then sold more tickets.

Postcards and flyers will also attract the attention of industry figures—put some in the mail to your target list of booking agents and promoters as an invitation.

I think you will agree that the combination of a personal offer and direct contact (handing out the flyer or postcard in person) is extremely effective. But what if you cannot make that personal contact? You will be or are playing out-of-town shows—it is not possible to visit each town ahead of the show and hand out flyers, is it? No, it is not. However, you can send the various promoters these personalized flyers. The promoter can use them as part of his or her advertising for your show.

Getting promotional materials to out-of-town promoters is a vital part of your marketing efforts. As well as helping them publicize the show, it shows the promoters that you care about their success. You are helping them to sell the show.

Upon confirming a show with an out-of-town promoter, you should arrange to send as many flyers or posters as necessary to the club or bar. Also inquire about the local papers and radio stations in that town. Chances are the promoter will automatically place listings and ads in those local outlets. Can you approach the papers or stations with an interesting story that might generate some further interest? If so, you will need to do a press release, so read on....

Press Releases

Newspapers, magazines, radio, and TV stations need content—they need stories and information to print or to fill their programs. You supply the news, and they will print or broadcast it.

The process of supplying news to the media is done by issuing a press release. Figure 10.3 shows a typical band press release.

As well as the factual information (tour dates, venues, and ticket information), the press release gives editors story-based information. This can be printed verbatim ("Jay Leno's favorite band is back") or

**PLEASE CONTACT ANDY REYNOLDS T: +44 (20)771 886
E: andy.reynolds@tourconcepts.com FOR MORE INFORMATION**

-start-

Jay Leno's favourite band tours the States this Spring in support of their debut album, 'Male Caucasian'.

MILLIONS OF AMERICANS (Sheffield, England based rock band) gained notoriety in the US following an appearance on the 'Jay Leno Show' (NBC) in September 2006 on which the band members sprayed the host, Jay Leno, with beer. Leno and his production team subsequently banned the group from the studios of NBC.

MILLIONS OF AMERICANS have just finished a tour with YOUR MATERIAL STORY in the UK and have their debut album, 'Caucasian Male' out now on Mega Global Records.

MILLIONS OF AMERICANS will play the following venues:

Sat 03/31/07	Worcester, MA	The Palladium	7.30pm
Mon 04/02/07	Cincinnati, OH	Bogart's	7.00pm
Tue 04/03/07	Cleveland, OH	House Of Blues	7.00pm
Thu 04/05/07	Pittsburgh, PA	Rex Theatre	7.00pm
Fri 04/06/07	Columbus, OH	Newport Music Hall	7.30pm
Sat 04/07/07	Detroit, MI	Harpo's Concert Theatre	7.30 pm
Mon 04/09/07	Chicago, IL	Metro / Smart Bar	7.00 pm

All tickets are $16.

NOTES FOR EDITORS:

MILLIONS OF AMERICANS are a Sheffield, UK based rock band.

ALBUM DETAILS
ARTIST: MILLIONS OF AMERICANS
ALBUM: 'Caucasian Male'
Release date: 23 May 2005
Number of Discs: 1
Catalogue Number: MG045
Label: Mega Global
Distributor: PHD

Album cover image and band photos are available for downloading at:
www.presssite/050264.html

-end-

Figure 10.3 A press release. The main story (what we want the readers to know) can simply be printed as it is, saving the editor time.

incorporated into a larger piece. The factual information will go into the listings section of the publication. The idea is to save editors and writers time—be creative, write your own story (as long as it is true and relevant), and you will get it printed.

All newspapers, magazines, websites, and radio and TV stations will have an editorial fax or e-mail address to which you can submit your press releases. Obviously, you need to target your releases—local papers and radio stations initially and perhaps some national music press magazines and websites. Build up a database of contacts, but be careful and don't bombard them with information. Try to save up news about a couple of events and submit that as one press release.

Timing is vital with press releases—magazines are prepared two months in advance, for instance—so get your press releases out in plenty of time for inclusion.

Street Teams

A "street team" is way for bands (and now companies and organizations) to use their fans, the kids on the street, to spread the word. Street team members are unpaid enthusiasts who work in exchange for free merchandise and concert tickets. To market the band(s) they are representing, street team members bring friends to the shows, convince friends to buy band merchandise, put up posters and hand out flyers, request airplay on radio stations, and spend time on community and forum websites. All this activity is "viral" marketing—not actually advertising the band, but spreading the presence of the band from one person to the next, just like a virus spreads.

Street teams are certainly not as effective as they were six years ago, when the bands I was working with first started using them. I think the "viral" aspect has started to bother a lot of people; the majority of music fans can tell when they are being "street teamed" and have grown to resent it.

Don't get me wrong—there is nothing wrong with a true fan deciding to act for her favorite band and getting all her friends excited as well. If she gets a couple of free shirts from the deal, who cares? My problem is with the professional street team companies that have sprung up who act for the entire label. There is no way you can tell whether a street team member is committed and is going to work hard, especially if you are not paying that person anything. My experience has been that team members do not actually do that much work, but they still expect to be on the guest list for shows and get backstage afterward. The work they actually do has also become more like straightforward advertising ("this band is great; buy their new CD") than actually spreading the word via subtle marketing, and somehow the whole thing smacks of exploitation.

My advice would be to go ahead and motivate your existing fans to get you more fans, and then reward them for that activity. Call them a street team if you want. However, don't go with a large street team organization until you have fully examined that company's methods and the caliber of their team members.

Online Marketing

I try not to presume (because presumption is the mother of all screw-ups), but I am presuming in this case that you have heard of MySpace (see Figure 10.4). MySpace is one of a new breed of social networking sites—along with Bebo, Faceparty, and YouTube—all of which allow users to create their own connections and content. The main difference with MySpace—apart from being the biggest social networking site, with 45 percent of market share in the US—is that is was designed primarily for musicians to communicate directly with their fans. MySpace is the brainchild of Tom Anderson, a musician, who got together with Chris DeWolfe, a marketing expert. Anderson wanted to create a website where musicians could post their music and fans could chat about it.

We now know, of course, that MySpace is a vital part of any band's marketing strategy. In fact, it is part of *every* band's marketing strategy. MySpace is now seen as "traditional" media, along with radio, TV, and magazines.

> "For us it's not just MySpace. It's a combination of it all—the Internet and print. It's all about developing a community. Stuff like MySpace helps for sure, but it's not the whole story."
>
> —Eron Bucciarelli, Hawthorne Heights

Figure 10.4 MySpace. In case you didn't know....

How do you effectively use MySpace (or your website) to market your music and get shows? As with any marketing, you have to know what you are doing and work at it. Just bunging up a MySpace account and expecting to land a major concert tour is not realistic. Use your page as a point of contact and as part of an online community, so fans and industry people can instantly check out your music.

Websites work well when they have currently changing content that persuades visitors to keep coming back. You need to do the same. Work on getting your fans to your site, and then make sure they keep coming back and keep recommending your site to others.

Getting Visitors

Visitors (or "traffic") are the lifeblood of any site—there is no point in having a site if no one knows it is there! You can get people to your site in numerous ways:

- Put your website/MySpace address on everything you send out or sell. CDs, demos, letters, flyers, and T-shirts should all have the URL (such as www.mysite.com) clearly visible.

- Put your URL in the signature line of all e-mails you send or forum posts you make.

- Encourage industry people to check you out by going to your site. Many record label people prefer to do this now as opposed to receiving CDs in the mail.

- Ask other bands to place a link to your site on their site.

- Go to the MySpace sites of other bands and invite their "friends" to be your friends too.

Database of Visitors

So now you have swarms of people coming to your site. They have a look around, listen to some music, and then leave. Good, right? Actually, it is not. You have no idea who came to your site and, therefore, you have no idea how to contact those people to see whether they liked what they heard. If they did like it, you want to be able to tell them about your new CD and the shows you will be playing. You need your visitors' details so you can market to them!

MySpace makes this easy. Fans can register their interest by adding you as a "friend." You can then send mass messages to all your MySpace friends, telling them about future shows, new tracks, and important announcements (such as, "Hey, we just got signed!"). This messaging can only be done through MySpace. You do not have the actual e-mail addresses of your visitors, but you do have something very important—a database of likeminded people who have expressed an interest in your music.

If you run a non-MySpace site, then you should have some way of collecting visitors' e-mail addresses. Unfortunately, there is no way to instantly discern a person's e-mail address from his or her visit to your site. (If there was, then spammers would have access to billions of e-mail addresses.) Instead, you have to ask people for their address.

A simple way to do this is to offer something free in exchange for your visitors' details. This could be a free song download, access to a special section of the site, or a promotion code for money off at your next show. Install a simple form script on your site that will ask the visitor to enter his or her name and e-mail address. (Ask the people who built your site to do this, or do a quick Internet search for more information on this topic.) Once visitors have "subscribed," they receive the gift. More importantly, you have another name to add to your database!

Keeping Your Visitors

MySpace works for bands because it allows you to communicate directly with your fans. If you do not communicate with them, though, they will forget about you and move on to the next thing. Make your friends/subscribers feel like part of your community. Keep your subscribers informed with regular postings, newsletters, and messages.

In direct contrast to my advice about press releases, I would advise you to update your website/MySpace page regularly, even if you have no news. Remember, you may have worked really hard to attract all your subscribers, but this does not mean these people are your fans. According to Andy Davies, a BBC radio producer, "When you receive promotional material saying a band has 15,000 friends, you have to remember that none of it directly correlates to musical appreciation. It's just 15,000 clicks of the mouse."

> "As an artist and musician, you should know where your strengths lie. Don't go to somebody empty-handed just because you can sing and be like, "Make me into a star." You have to drive yourself, and if you don't, you're gonna end up heartbroken."
>
> —Derek Safo, a.k.a MOBO award-winner Sway.

11 Getting Onstage: Advanced Information

Your musical career is going well. You are playing shows, organizing tours, setting up street teams, and talking to professional artist managers, booking agents, and label A&R people. You are set to get to the next level—those big shows and headline tours. It is all fantastic, and you know you deserve the success.

But being successful does not mean playing enormodomes and staying in fancy hotels. True success involves knowing when *not* to stay in fancy hotels. Large-scale touring means lots of expense and logistical headaches. Organizing a tour is not the same as playing a hometown bar show.

This chapter deals with the advanced logistics and costs of a modern tour. I strongly advise that you read this chapter and understand how touring works, even if you then decide to hire professional tour managers. (If you are a budding tour manager, this chapter will be especially interesting to you!)

You saw in Chapter 7 the common mistakes that bands and crew can make when starting out. Just because you are selling out huge venues does not mean the mistakes stop happening. In fact, due to the huge amounts of money involved, any mistake will have extreme financial implications.

Budgets and Costs

In Chapter 9, I explained how promoters cost out their shows and how that affects how much you get paid. None of that took into account how much it costs you every time you perform at a show. Even playing to 100 people in a bar will cost you. You need to put gas in the van, perhaps rent a van, buy guitar strings, pay for rehearsals, and the list goes on.

Imagine paying those costs every day you are on tour. We have seen what kind of income you can expect from each performance, but will that be enough to cover the cost of your sleeper coach, road crew, equipment hire, and hotels? You won't know until you list all those possible expenses and work out your profit or loss, as I explained in Chapter 2.

Figure 11.1 shows the tour budget sheet that I use when working out costs for a tour. (You can download your own copy from www.the-tour-book.com).

I use this sheet as a memory aid as well as a financial tool. Working through the sheet reminds me to organize different aspects of the tour. It does not really matter what level of show you are doing; most of the expenses you are likely to encounter in a modern tour are included in the budget sheet. I will explain them in order to give you a more complete understanding of the way a tour works.

Millions of Americans   US Tour Spring 2007

REVISION:		MILLIONS OF AMERICANS US TOUR - SPRING 2007		Days= 11 Shows= 7		
		EXPENSES SUMMARY		TOTAL COST		
TOTAL EXPENSES		WAGES		$13,860.00		
		PER DIEMS		$1,035.00		
		ACCOMMODATION		$2,055.00		
		TRANSPORT		$18,797.56		
		SOUND		$0.00		
		LIGHTS		$3,520.00		
		VIDEO		$0.00		
		BACKLINE		$2,730.00		
		SET & STAGE		$0.00		
		PRODUCTION		$4,160.00		
		REHEARSALS		$1,720.00		
		OTHER EXPENSE		$2,240.00		
			TOTAL	$50,117.56		
INCOME		7 shows at $3200	$3,200.00 7 1	$22,400.00		
			INCOME TOTAL	$22,400.00		
PROFIT / LOSS						
		EXPENSES		$50,117.56		
		5% CONTINGENCY		$2,505.88		
		PROFIT/LOSS		-$30,223.43		

Millions of Americans   US Tour Spring 2007

REVISION:	MILLIONS OF AMERICANS					Days= 11		
	US TOUR - SPRING 2007					Shows= 7		
ITEM	SUPPLIER/ SPECIFIC	NOTES	UNIT COST	MULTIPLY	MULTIPLY	TOTAL COST		
WAGES								
Tour Manager	Andy Reynolds	Plus FOH sound	$330.00	11	1	$3,630.00		
Production Manager						$0.00		
FOH sound						$0.00		
Monitor sound						$0.00		
System sound #1						$0.00		
System sound #2						$0.00		
Lighting Designer	Lisa Ampy		$290.00	11	1	$3,190.00		
System lights #1						$0.00		
Spot light ops						$0.00		
Backline technician	Charlie Himp		$270.00	11	1	$2,970.00		
Backline technician	Dan Rivers		$270.00	11	1	$2,970.00		
Backline technician						$0.00		
Merchandise	Steve Wag	Plus 10% of gross sales	$100.00	11	1	$1,100.00		
Driver						$0.00		
PER DIEMS								
Band Show			$10.00	7	4	$280.00		
Band day off			$15.00	3	4	$180.00		
Crew Show			$10.00	7	5	$350.00		
Crew day off			$15.00	3	5	$225.00		
Driver(s)						$0.00		
ACCOMMODATION								
Band		2 x twins for 3 days off	$80.00	3	2	$480.00		
Crew		2 x twins & 1 single for 3 days off	$80.00	3	3	$720.00		
Driver		Single	$80.00	10	1	$800.00		
Day rooms						$0.00		
Breakfast						$0.00		
Tel & fax			$5.00	11	1	$55.00		
TRANSPORT								
Flights	British Airways	LHR-NY-LHR	$320.00	9	1	$2,880.00		
Band bus	Nite Train		$440.00	11	1	$4,840.00		
Over drives		One?	$100.00	1	1	$100.00		
Dead head days		Travle to and from base	$440.00	2	1	$880.00		
Mini Bus						$0.00		
Equipment Van						$0.00		
Fuel		45 c a mile		3400	1	$7,555.56		
Ferries						$0.00		
Trucks						$0.00		
Trailer	Nite Train	$45 a day	$45.00	10	1	$450.00		
Freight & shipping	EFM	Backline essentials	$1,232.00	1	1	$1,232.00		
Crew - public transport						$0.00		
Parking						$0.00		
Road Tolls						$0.00		
Taxi's		Radio stations etc	$20.00	7		$0.00		
Pick up & transfers	Adison Lee	To and from heathrow (£60)	$120.00	3	1	$360.00		
Excess baggage			$500.00	1	1	$500.00		
Delivery						$0.00		
SOUND								
PA hire						$0.00		
Equipment purchase						$0.00		
PA hire						$0.00		
Equipment consumables		IEM cells etc	$100.00			$0.00		
Radio Licences						$0.00		
Sound misc.						$0.00		
LIGHTING								
LX hire	Upstaging	Mac 500, truss etc - see spec	$320.00	11	1	$3,520.00		
Equipment purchase						$0.00		
LX hire						$0.00		
Equipment consumables						$0.00		
LX misc.						$0.00		

Millions of Americans   US Tour Spring 2007

	Supplier	Description	Unit cost	Qty		Total	
VIDEO							
Rental						$0.00	
Equipment purchase						$0.00	
Equipment consumables						$0.00	
Misc.						$0.00	
BACKLINE							
Rental	SST	Cabs, shells & cases	$230.00	11	1	$2,530.00	
Equipment purchase						$0.00	
Equipment consumables	SST	Strings, sticks, gaffa	$200.00	1	1	$200.00	
Misc.						$0.00	
SET & STAGE							
Rental						$0.00	
Equipment purchase						$0.00	
Equipment consumables						$0.00	
Misc.						$0.00	
PRODUCTION							
Pre - production TM			$500.00	1	1	$500.00	
Pre - production PM						$0.00	
Mobile phone TM			$30.00	11	1	$330.00	
Mobile phone PM						$0.00	
Tour Books			$70.00	1	1	$70.00	
Insurance	Robertson Taylor	Musical equipment, cancellation	$1,700.00	1	1	$1,700.00	
Legal & accounting						$0.00	
Visas & work papers	Traffic Control	Embassy service - £40 per visa	$80.00	9	1	$720.00	
Visas & work papers	US Embassy	Visa Charges	$80.00	9	1	$720.00	
Catering - supplies						$0.00	
Catering - wages						$0.00	
Laundry		$100 a week	$100.00	1	1	$100.00	
Gratuities		$20 a day	$20.00	1	1	$20.00	
Medical						$0.00	
Copying						$0.00	
Misc.						$0.00	
REHEARSALS							
Wages		3 x£100	$600.00	1	1	$600.00	
Rehearsal studio	Terminal	£270 a day	$560.00	2	1	$1,120.00	
Equipment hire						$0.00	
Venue Hire						$0.00	
						$0.00	
Transport						$0.00	
OTHER EXPENSE							
Agent's commission			$10.00			$2,240.00	
Management commission			$0.00			$0.00	
Foreign Artist Tax						$0.00	
				TOTAL		$50,117.56	

Figure 11.1 The Tour Concepts tour budget sheet.

Wages

As explained in Chapter 2, the crew members who work directly for the band—such as FOH engineers, tour managers, and so on—are freelance and charge a daily or weekly rate for their services for the duration of the tour. When preparing a budget, some of these wages will appear directly. Others will be included in supplier's costs—for example, the lighting company's quote will include crew but will expect the touring production to feed, house, and transport their crew. Wages are usually paid on completion of the tour unless the tour is more than one month long, in which case wages are paid monthly.

Looking at the budget in Figure 11.1, you will see that wages account for nearly $14,000. Can you really afford to pay all those crew members that money? You may try to negotiate lower prices with the crew. Be warned, though: Pay level in modern touring is a hotbed of controversy. Wages have not increased significantly in the 20 years I have been involved in the industry, yet the workload and responsibility have increased. Is it fair to ask your crew to work 14-hour days for less than minimum wage?

Per Diems

From the Latin meaning "per day," this is a small stipend paid to the touring artist and crew, supposedly for sustenance. Per diems range from $10 to $25 a day and are paid in cash while the crew is on tour. I do not pay per diems for show days if we are carrying catering on tour; the band and crew are being fed a proper meal every show day and therefore do not need money for sustenance.

Accommodations

Being on tour means being away from home, and being away from home means finding somewhere to sleep every night. In the early days of your band, this might mean crashing on friends' floors, but hopefully as your career takes off you should be able to afford decent accommodations in guesthouses or hotels.

Touring acts and crews are not expected to find or pay for their own hotels. The tour pays for the accommodations for all its touring personnel. However, all room occupants on tour are expected to pay their own incidental costs, such as phone calls, room service, movies, and so on.

The use of sleeper buses means the tour members will usually sleep while traveling to the next city. (There is a detailed explanation of sleeper buses later on in this chapter, in the "Sleeper Coaches" section.) In this case, hotels will be used as day rooms only. Day rooms can be booked for a cheaper price because they are only in use from 9:00 A.M. until 4:00 P.M. Day rooms are primarily used for people to take showers and have breakfast.

On average, a decent hotel will cost between $80 to $130 per night per single or twin room, plus tax. Budget hotels can be had for $40 to $70 per room per night. In Figure 11.1, you will see that I have tried to save money by only having hotels on the days off, and I have not booked day rooms. Even so, I am predicting that I will spend more than $2,000 for seven shows.

Booking rooms for each night of a tour is a time-consuming business, but thankfully there are specialized travel agents who can deal with this for you. These travel agents can negotiate better deals for you with the hotels and will hopefully know what hotels are near the various venues. However, some hotels are known to be more band-friendly than others, and the travel agent will usually book you there, regardless of the hotel's proximity to the gig!

One of my favorite hotels is the Columbia Hotel in London (see Figure 11.2). Famous for its '70s-style decor and late bar, the Columbia has become an institution in its own right. On any given night there are at least three bands and crews staying there, inevitably meeting up in the bar to swap tour stories.

Travel

Touring means travel, and travel is expensive. It would be unreasonable and a logistical nightmare for the crew to make their own travel arrangements, so I determine the best modes of transport. The tour then provides and pays for all travel for its touring personnel and equipment. As well as planes, buses, and limousines, this includes reimbursing band and crew for travel to and from the tour. Once on tour, we use the following transportation methods:

- Air travel
- Sleeper coach
- Splitter van
- Passenger van

The next few sections will discuss these transportation methods in more detail.

Figure 11.2   The Columbia Hotel, London. The author has spent thousands of pounds here and still cannot get a free drink at the bar.

Air Travel

Flying is the best way to crunch those tour miles, whether by commercial scheduled airlines or by private rented jet. If you have to spend money on airfare, it is often worth booking business class. It may cost a bit more, but the increased leg room and baggage allowance, coupled with the shorter check-in and deplaning times, can pay off. A specialized, music industry travel agent will be able to get you good deals on business-class airfares.

Commercial scheduled flights will often get you there in time and with less expense, but in these days of increased security checks and excess baggage charges, you might be better off renting a jet. "Chartering a jet is not as expensive as people might think," says Paul Mansfield, marketing manager at Bookajet. "If you wanted to send six or eight people to mainland Europe (from the UK) business class, it would typically be around $1,500/£800 per seat, which adds up to $12,500/£6,400. For that sort of price, it's worth chartering a private jet." This is especially true if you take into account the excess baggage charges.

There has been an explosion in no-frills, low-cost airlines in Europe and the States. Airlines such as Southwest, Virgin Blue, Ryanair, BMI-baby, and easyJet provide ridiculously cheap fares and frequent flights. The budget carriers' service is often top-notch despite the low price to the consumer. The success of the no-frills carriers means more music groups can fly to shows outside their usual territories and fly to and from tour legs. This can save a band a lot of time and money.

However, in my experience, they are not always the bargain solution you have been looking for! I recently flew an ultra-budget airline to Italy. Our return flight was cancelled at the very last minute due to fog. All 150 passengers then stormed the ticket desk for refunds (yeah right!) and alternative flights. After waiting in line for 90 minutes (!), we were eventually reassigned onto a flight that evening from an airport 150 kilometers away. Luckily, we still had our hired car available to us and we were able to make the flight. We did arrive at our destination, but 12 hours late! The show was obviously cancelled, and the band and promoter lost money. Therefore, I have some tips for you regarding budgeting and organizing travel using budget airlines.

Most budget airlines are point-to-point and offer no guaranteed connections with other flights, even with the same airline. It is a bad idea to try to plan travel with connecting flights using budget airlines. If the budget airline does not fly from your departure to your destination directly, then you should use an airline that either can offer guaranteed connections or has direct flights. (Budget airlines often don't offer alternative transportation or accommodations in case of problems!)

Also, check the actual destination of the plane. Most of the budget carriers have deals with older and smaller airports, which can be many, many miles from the advertised destination city. Extra transportation costs and time to get into your destination city may outweigh the savings of the budget airfares.

Music groups travel with a lot of luggage. Even a couple of guitars, a snare drum, a cymbal case, and personal luggage can amount to a substantial load. Always check the baggage allowance of any airline, especially the budget airlines. Most airlines have an allowance based on weight (although some operate based on the number of pieces of luggage). That allowance is usually (per passenger):

- First class: 40 kg (88 lbs)
- Business class: 30 kg (66 lbs)
- Economy class: 20 kg (44 lbs)

Obviously, there is no first or business class on the no-frills airlines!

If you exceed the allowance, you are charged per kilo of excess luggage. Prices vary, but usually fall around £4.50/ $7/€7 per excess kilo. Some airlines (notably Ryanair in Europe) have introduced a fixed fee for all bags placed in the hold in an effort to reduce operating costs and to improve turnaround of their aircraft.

The cost savings from flying budget could be negated quickly by these excess baggage costs. In the past, I have paid out more than $300 in excess baggage costs on a budget airline. Every single band and crew member was over the limit with his personal luggage, and we were carrying guitars, basses, and pedal boards.

With any airline, show up as early as you can to the check-in counter and flirt like crazy with the check-in staff. I am serious! Don't be creepy, but give the staff lots of smiles and eye contact. Why? Well, the earlier you turn up, the greater the chances of your luggage and musical instruments actually making it on board the aircraft. (Large and heavy boxes are the first to get bumped off a full flight.) You will also reduce your chances of having to pay any excess baggage costs. You might even get an upgrade! Therefore, depending on how much luggage the group is carrying, you should give yourself at least three hours for long-haul flights and two hours for everything else (even domestic flights).

Finally, you may save money on excess baggage fees, but the touring party is going to have a *lot* of time hanging around in the airport (see Figure 11.3). I try to build in an extra £10 per diem for that day. If the artist or crew starts to grumble, you can hand off the per diems for them to "lose" in the airport.

Figure 11.3 An empty airport. How much time do you want to spend here in order to save money?

Sleeper Coach

Sleeper coaches are the standard travel method for modern tours (see Figures 11.4 and 11.5). Sleeper coaches are standard coaches converted to include 8 to 16 bunk beds on board. The bus travels overnight between shows. This allows the band and crew to sleep and travel at the same time. The benefits are obviously enormous: No hotel rooms are needed; there is less traffic at night so journey times are quicker; and the backline equipment can often travel in the bays of the bus, saving other transport expense.

However, bus life can be hard. Most people find it very difficult to sleep in a moving bus. Hard economics often dictate that the bus will carry both band and crew, and that can total 10 to 14 people, all living in a confined space for weeks on end.

The bands you see on tour do not own their buses; they are rented from specialized music touring companies for the duration of the

Figure 11.4   A sleeper bus. You can see the lounge extension wings (above the front wheel). These wings are extended when the bus is parked in order to make the lounge area wider. (Photo courtesy of Nitetrain Coach.)

Figure 11.5   Inside a sleeper bus. This view is looking down from the front lounge into the bunk area. (Photo courtesy of Nitetrain Coach.)

tour. Sleeper buses cost between $450 and $500 a day, depending on the mileage traveled and the quality of the bus. You have to pay extra charges for road tolls, taxes, the driver's wages, and so on. In the US, the driver expects to be provided with a hotel room during the day, and you need to factor in those costs as well. In the UK and Europe, drivers sleep on the bus and are paid a small amount of money to compensate for this hardship.

Note: Get a breakdown of all the extras when renting from a sleeper bus company. Many companies will charge you extra for bus oil changes, A/C fluid, satellite TV access, and even bed changes on the bus. These charges are all quite legitimate, but they can come as an unpleasant surprise if you have not budgeted for them!

A lot of planning is involved with a sleeper bus tour; most of this is concerned with the driver's working hours. You cannot just leap onto the bus after the show and expect to be in the next city the next morning. Drivers have to obey mandatory rest break and working hour regulations for your safety as well as theirs. The regulations vary in the US and Europe, but the consequences of not anticipating these breaks are the same—plan journeys with your driver in advance, or you could find yourself taking an unexpected day off somewhere.

If your driver exceeds his permitted driving hours, he *has* to pull over and rest. The rest period can be up to nine hours, depending on the driving he has done so far that week. I once spent a day in a German truck stop 20 kilometers (12.5 miles) outside of Berlin after our driver "ran out of hours." He pulled over and that was that—we were there for nine hours, stuck on a bus. And only 12 miles from the city!

Note: Always Book Your Tour Transportation Early If you do not book your tour transportation early, you may not have any transportation, and you will not be able to tour. Really busy periods in the touring calendar are March and April, the summer festival season

(June through August), and October/November. Reserve transportation even if you only have a rough tour period with no specific dates booked. You or your tour manager should have good contacts with ground transportation suppliers, and you can explain the situation to them. Most entertainment suppliers are used to this approach, and although it is not perfect, it is honest.

Keep in regular contact with your suppliers until you confirm your order. Explain to your transportation supplier that budgets and plans have not been finalized, but you are keen to give them your order, and please can they make sure they don't let this bus/truck/van/skateboard go out on another job without at least letting you know. This is vital! You really do not want any last-minute surprises.

Likewise, let your suppliers know as soon as the tour is scrapped, moved, or postponed. Finally, you should arrange for transportation bills to be paid in advance if possible, to "double confirm" your order.

Splitter Van

A UK/Europe phenomenon, splitter vans are basically large converted vans with a bulkhead providing equipment storage in the back and seating, tables, TV, and video in the front for six to eight people, plus a driver. Splitter vans are good for short travel distances and very low-budget touring. Self-drive splitter vans cost about £120 to £160 ($235 to $300) per day; this price excludes fuel and oil.

Passenger Van

Touring the US usually means hiring a passenger van. All your gear goes in a trailer or in a separate cargo van. Passenger vans cost $40 to $80 per day, and again, this price excludes fuel and oil.

Which method should you choose? It's a matter of looking at the travel distances involved, the routing of the tour, and other logistics to determine the most cost-effective transportation method. My rule of thumb is that if you have a touring party of eight or more people, then you should consider a sleeper bus. In the case of the budget in Figure 11.1, I looked at the distances involved and decided that a sleeper coach would be the best option.

Parking and Road Tolls

Do not forget to include parking and road tolls in your budget. These random, inexpensive costs can mount to hundreds of dollars!

> "The most common mistake bands make in the live environment is trying to take the emphasis off themselves as players and personalities by introducing expensive film and set. The audience (if there is one) came to see the band, not the film or set. All the toys on stage can make bands slack.
>
> The other most common problem is bands' lack of understanding of the financial workings of record, publishing, and performance contracts, particularly in relation to recoupable investment. Actually, there is one other big issue which seems to rear its head very often—royalties. Make sure everyone knows who is getting what as early as possible, as lots of bands split up when it becomes clear that one or two members are going to become rich and one or two are not.
>
> One final mistake—tequila slammers. Avoid those, and you will have a long and productive career. If only I had known that when I was starting out...."
>
> —Chris Taplin, tour/production manager for clients including The Darkness, Super Furry Animals, Bjork, and Morcheeba

Sound

Larger-capacity venues (holding 700 or more people) do not generally have an in-house sound system—at least not one that would be up to concert sound standards. In these cases, the promoter will find a PA system hire company and rent a PA for the performance. In practice, an act touring venues of this capacity would probably hire a PA itself for the duration of the whole tour to ensure continuity of sound. The band would then be responsible for transporting the equipment plus any additional personnel. The promoter would refund the artist a previously agreed-upon amount for the PA based on the promoter's show costs. (See Chapter 9 for a more detailed explanation of promoters' costs.) Even though the act is in theory getting the touring PA paid for by the promoter, there are additional transportation, personnel, and logistical costs that will add to the bottom line for the act, basically costing them more money than they get paid by the promoter.

In this case, Millions of Americans are playing venues that have in-house systems, and we therefore do not need to carry a PA.

Lights

As with sound, professional acts may elect to carry their own lighting production, for which the promoter will reimburse them. The same transportation and logistical costs apply.

Production

Production costs are directly related to getting the tour on the road and keeping it on the road. Although most of these costs are self-explanatory, you may be unfamiliar with the ones discussed in the following sections.

Pre-Production

A tour takes a ridiculous amount of work to organize. As a tour manager, I can be working on various aspects of the planning of the tour for a couple of months, on and off. I am freelance and charge for the days I am on tour; I then also charge a fee for the amount of pre-tour work I do. This is the pre-production fee.

Tour Books

No, not free copies of this book! Tour books are the printed itineraries that detail times, addresses, and travel arrangements for the band and crew on the tour. Figure 11.6 shows an example of tour book pages. I compile all the information I receive from the promoters about times, addresses, and technical information as I go, entering it into a special template I have created. You can download a template of these pages from www.the-tour-book.com.

Tour books were an absolute necessity in the days before the Black-Berry and the mobile phone. The only effective communication method between the touring party and associated offices was by fax. I vividly remember checking into hotels, only to find 20 or so faxes pushed under my door.

THE ALL-AMERICAN REJECTS

TUESDAY 24 AUGUST 2004
SHOW DAY - LONDON, UK   GMT

VENUE: Empire, The	**FORMAT:** Indoor
Shepherds Bush Green	**CAPACITY:** 2000
Shepherds Bush	
London	
W12 8TT	
England	
TEL: +44 (0)20 8354 300	
FAX: +44 (0)20 873 3218	**ROMOTERS REP:** Graham Lambert
PROD TEL: +44 (0)20 8742 926	**MOBILE:** 07966 25817█
PROD FAX: +44 (0)20 8742 B18133	**EMAIL:** ▓▓▓▓▓▓▓@▓▓▓▓▓▓
PROMOTER: SJM	**PRODUCTION:** Emma Edgar
TEL: +44 (0)161 907 3443	**TEL:** +44 (0)161 907 3443
FAX: +44 (0)161 907 3449	**MOBILE:**
	EMAIL: ▓▓▓▓@▓▓▓▓▓▓

TRAVEL:

BAND DEPART:	14.00. Do not check out!
BAND ARRIVE:	15.00
CREW DEPART:	11.00
CREW ARRIVE:	12.30

SCHEDULE:		**PROMO:**
ACCESS TO VENUE:	13.00	
PA & LX LOAD IN:	n/a	
BACKLINE LOAD IN:	13.00	
SOUND CHECK:	15.00	
DINNER:	Buyout	
DOORS:	19.00	
LARUSO:	19.30 - 20.00	
TERRA DIABLO:	20.30 - 21.00	
AAR:	**21.30 - 23.00**	
FINISH:	23.00	
CURFEW:	23.00 STRICT? You bet!	
AFTER SHOW CLUB:	After party in bar	

HOTEL - BAND: Columbia Hotel	**HOTEL - CREW:** Columbia Hotel
95-99 Lancaster Gate	95-99 Lancaster Gate
Bayswater	Bayswater
London	London
W2 3NS	W2 3NS
England	England
TEL: +44 (0)20 7402 0021	**TEL:** +44 (0)20 7402 0021
FAX: +44 (0)20 7706 4692	**FAX:** +44 (0)20 7706 4692
CONTACT: Pauline Barbour	**CONTACT:** Pauline Barbour
RES. NUMBER:	**RES. NUMBER:**
DETAILS: 4 twins, 3 singles	**DETAILS:** 4 twins, 3 singles

AFTER SHOW:

BAND:	To hotel
CREW:	As band

TOMORROW: Depart UK back to USA

NOTES:	**LOCAL MONEY:**	
	£1=	£1
	$1=	0.57p
	e1=	0.69p
	LONDON:	Same
	LA:	-8 hours
	NYC:	-5 hours

Tour Concepts - Concert Tour Management
T: +44 (0)7762 551886
E: andy.reynolds@tourconcepts.com
W: www.tourconcepts.com

THE ALL-AMERICAN REJECTS

TUESDAY 24 AUGUST 2004
SHOW DAY - LONDON, UK   **GMT**

PRODUCTION INFORMATION

VENUE:	Empire, The
	Shepherds Bush Green
	Shepherds Bush
	London
	0
	W12 8TT
	England
TEL:	+44 (0)20 8354 300
FAX:	+44 (0)20 873 3218
PROD TEL:	+44 (0)20 8742 926
PROD FAX:	+44 (0)20 8742 B18133

TRANSPORT:	
PARKING:	Very difficult. Truck parking in Ariel Way off Wood Lane
PERMITS:	required
LOAD IN TYPE:	Flat roll to stage via ramp at left of building
LANDLINE:	No

FACILITIES:	
DRESSING ROOMS:	Five
SHOWERS:	3 in DR 1, 3 &4
CATERING:	Kitchen top floor
PRODUCTION OFFICE:	Yes

PRODUCTION:	
STAGE SIZE:	15.5mW x 9.85m D(8.5m to pros arch
CLEARANCE:	9m
PROSCENIUM:	Arch height 9m x 9m W
PA WINGS:	No
FLYING POINTS:	Vision Truss in house. 10mx6mx52cmx52cm box grid

POWER:	3P 300A(camlocks). 3P 63a CEE-form

SOUND:	
HOUSE PA:	EAW KF850 X14, SB850 X8, CREST AMPS
DESK:	Heritahe H300
MON. DESK:	Midas XL3 40 ch.
MIXES:	12 wedge on 8 mixes + cue
FOH MIXER AREA:	Platform on dance floor
S/C CURFEW:	None
RESTRICTIONS:	None

LIGHTING:	
HOUSE LX:	Par 64, Source 4, Goldenscan x 8
DESK:	Avo Sapphire & Pearl 2000
DIMMERS ETC:	Avo FD 72 way. 24 spare channels
HOUSE SPOTS:	Pani 1202 x2
SMOKE ALARM:	Yes

GENERAL:	
BARRIER:	In house - permanent
MERCH AREA:	Three, concessions
MERCH FEE:	25%
PERSONNEL:	All techs Techs@Shepherds-Bush-Empire.co.uk.

NOTES:	

Tour Concepts - Concert Tour Management
T: +44 (0)7762 551886
E: andy.reynolds@tourconcepts.com
W: www.tourconcepts.com

Figure 11.6 Pages from a tour book. Copies of the book are given to the associated offices of booking agents and managers, as well as the touring band and crew.

Tour books are not as vital now, and in fact usually end up unread, in a huge pile in the back lounge of the bus. It's funny, though—everyone moans if the tour manager does not make the tour books, which is why I always budget for them.

Legal and Accounting

There is a lot of money involved in modern touring, as I keep mentioning. Look at the amount of money being paid out in Figure 11.1!

All this money needs to be accounted for, just as with any business or household. To account for tour expenses, I keep accurate records of all cash payments and fees received on the tour. I get a receipt for every single purchase, even gratuities, and then enter the amounts into my cash accounting spreadsheet. (I used to use Quicken, but the record company accounts could not open the files I sent them, so I'm back to using Excel.) At the same time, there are other, larger payments being made to suppliers. These are usually administered by the band's or manager's accountants, and it makes sense to have someone qualified to deal with this.

Every penny of expenditure and income must be accounted for, especially if you are relying on record company tour support. The label will want a complete reconciliation of all the money they have "lent" you for tour support. I am good with figures, but I am not an accountant—it's best to pay someone to help with this part of the process! I therefore include something in the budget for this.

Visas and Work Papers

You are considered to be working when traveling to different countries to perform. It follows that you may need a work permit or visa to enter that country, or you risk being fined and thrown in jail. Depending on the country you are visiting, applying for visas is an extremely complicated and long process. It is also extremely expensive.

For instance, P-1 visas for entertainers and their "essential personnel" are needed to enter the US. These visas for UK bands and crew currently cost $1,600 for the US application procedure per group, plus £114 per person for the UK admin. You now also have to go to the US Embassy in person.

Likewise, the UK government wants to change its rules for non–European Union bands acts performing there. The new rules mean that each band member and crew person will have to apply individually for his or her visa, which could cost each person up to $580/£300. Ten thousand foreign artists tour the UK every year and are currently paying a total of nearly $3 million in work permit fees.

Ideally, the promoter in the destination country will help you arrange the necessary visas and permits. Luckily for you, the countries that have a large number of acts arriving from overseas—such as for summer festivals—often instigate a temporary visa waiver period.

A word of warning: Having done all this work, paid all that money, and been given your visa, there is still no guarantee you will be let in when you arrive at your destination. Entry is subject to the judgment of the immigration officer on the day—arrive drunk and belligerent, and you may be on the first plane back home!

Insurance

A touring artist should ideally insure himself to cover cancellation and public liability claims. (Public liability covers you if someone is injured or killed while attending your concert.) Many bands remain uninsured on tour because, typically, the live music industry has been seen as very risky by insurers. This has caused the insurance premiums to be very high.

As the industry has become more professional and health and safety legislation has become more pertinent, specialized brokers have emerged who understand the risks better and are able to provide cheaper premiums and better coverage.

At the very least, make sure your equipment is insured. Two bands I have worked for have had their equipment stolen while on tour. The first band was not insured. The truck was stolen from outside the hotel, and their manager had to do some fast talking to convince the record label to cut loose some extra tour support money. We needed new equipment so we could play an extremely important show in New York the next day.

"We've found out that for a small up-and-coming band, cancellation cover is not viable," says Rick Inglessis of Swinglehurst specialized brokers. "Those tours run at a loss, so we stress bands should at least take out musical equipment cover in case anything is stolen or broken."

Laundry

There is a laundry run once a week on tour. Band members and crew leave their dirty clothes in a clearly labeled bag in the production office. Then someone, usually the venue runner, takes the clothes to local laundry service. I consider this a favor to my crew, so I do not expect them to pay for washing their clothes, which is why I budget something toward the cost.

Gratuities

Airports, hotels, taxis—everyone wants a tip for helping you out. As a tour manager or leader, you really do not want to pay all these out of your own pocket. Include a reasonable amount per day for gratuity in your predicted expenses.

Rehearsals

I like to separate costs associated with rehearsals, because some record companies will not allocate tour support funds for rehearsing. Also, rehearsal pay rates for musicians and crew are often different from touring rates.

Other Expenses

Wages, per diems, accommodations, travel, technical equipment, and legal affairs are the main areas of expense when touring today. You should definitely have proper lists of predicted expenses for these items in place well in advance of heading off for the first show on the tour.

There are also other expenses you should consider.

Contingency

A budget should always have a contingency fund. This is your emergency money. Although modern tours are planned to the finest detail, things do go wrong, and often money is the only way out of a situation. I personally work out a contingency based on a percentage of the total expenses (say, 3 percent).

Agent's Commission

The booking agent will take a cut of the gross income of the tour. This is often overlooked when preparing tour expenses, but if you look at Figure 11.1, you will see that the agent's commission amounts to $2,240. It is a legitimate tour expense, so make sure you budget for it.

Foreign Artist Tax

As I mentioned in Chapter 3, all countries have some sort of "foreign artist tax" to claim a percentage of your revenue while performing in that particular country. This taxation is administered by the relevant government department in each country. Some countries charge higher levels of taxation than others. For instance, Germany, which is a big market for US acts, currently levies a whopping 24.9 percent on fees of €1,001 ($1,000) or more! (However, this situation may be changing soon thanks to the work of the major German promoters. These promoters have successfully lobbied the German government to get the amount of taxation reduced for visiting artists.)

Because the promoter will deduct these taxes at source (in other words, when you get paid), it is vitally important that you budget properly for these expenses. When touring internationally, it is extremely important that you and your band tour manager scrutinize show offers to make sure the fee offered is "net and free of all local taxes." If a gross figure is offered, then do the math quickly to determine whether you will make any money off the show at all! You should always specify in your contract that you have to be paid in your domestic currency. Getting paid in Swiss francs for a show, for instance, means you'll lose money when you have to change those Swiss francs back into US dollars.

Advancing

Having worked your way through the budget sheet in Figure 11.1, you will have organized the various aspects of the tour—ordering the equipment you need, negotiating wages with crew, and booking your travel and accommodations. You also know how much you stand to make or lose and whether you are actually going to do the tour!

Assuming you are going to do the tour, the next step is to advance the tour. Advancing is the process of contacting all the promoters and venue production managers on the tour and ensuring that they are ready for your visit. You have issued a contract and contract rider the terms of which, in theory, the promoter will honor. You should never assume that this is the case, though—contact them and ask them about the points covered in these last few sections.

Contract and Rider

Has the promoter received the contract rider? More importantly, has the rider been passed on to the technical crew at the venue? Does the promoter have concerns or issues with the catering and hospitality rider?

Arrival and Parking

If rock and roll is supposed to be about fantastic lifestyles, frenzied fans, and glamorous showbiz parties, why on earth am I talking about parking? Believe it or not, I spend a considerable amount of my advancing and on-the-road time worrying about parking.

Is Parking Arranged for When You Arrive?

The parking arrangements are always important if you are traveling on a sleeper coach. There is little point to traveling overnight if you cannot park near the venue when you arrive the next morning. On arrival at the venue, you really want to get your trucks and buses parked in the loading bay or at least on the street outside the venue as soon as possible. The driver may be running short on his allotted driving hours and may need to get parked as soon as he arrives. He will not be able to drive around the block several times while waiting for a parking place to open. If he does go and park away from the venue, he may not legally be able to drive back to a suitable place near the load-in.

This parking space advancing applies equally to touring in a van. Think about the last time you tried to park in a busy section of your hometown. You can easily waste 30 to 45 minutes driving around looking for a parking space. The problem becomes worse if you actually need to park next to a specific shop or business. The same is true of trying to park a van and a trailer at a venue. If you do not have a pre-allocated space next to the load-in, you will be faced with carrying your gear from the van along the street to the venue.

When advancing the show, ask the promoter to block off street parking outside the venue or apply to the local authorities for the appropriate parking permits. (That is the reason why I put the vehicle plate number and model/make on the rider.) Specify the approximate time you will arrive at the venue. This will give the promoter adequate time to block parking spaces if necessary.

Landline/Shore Power

Modern sleeper buses require power for the lighting, A/C, DVD players, and PlayStations they carry onboard. Buses can run their engines or internal generators to provide this power. However, running big diesel engines is noisy and consumes a lot of fuel, and it is forbidden in many cities worldwide. A more common practice is for the bus to run off mains electricity.

Venues involved in modern concert touring are aware of the power needs of modern sleeper buses. This power is called *landline* or *shore power,* and it consists of nothing more glamorous then a heavy-duty 32-amp cable running from inside the venue to the bus. Upon arrival at the venue, the bus driver simply locates the cable and plugs it into the power distribution board inside his bus.

Of course, the landline will not be there if you have not told the venue you need a landline or you have not given an approximate time of arrival for your bus.

Good advancing practice is to notify the venue or the promoter of your landline needs and an approximate time of your arrival. That way, the cable will be left out for you!

Venue Access

What time can you get into the venue for showers and coffee? Usually this will be the same time as equipment load in, but negotiate with the promoter to have earlier access to the toilet facilities at least—the golden rule of tour buses is "no solids."

Equipment Load In

Your rider should stipulate how long you need for equipment load in and sound check. Does the promoter have any problems with this? An unusually early load in may mean crew overtime pay. If the promoter has signed your rider, then he has agreed to this and will have to pay those costs himself.

Noise Curfews

Does the venue have any noise restrictions or curfews? Always ask about this when advancing your show. You may not be able to make noise (in other words, start your sound check) until after business hours. In this case, you may elect to load in later. There is no point loading in early and then hanging around until 6:00 to start the sound check.

Support/Opening Acts

You may be traveling with a tour support act. If you are not, then get the details of any opening act the promoter has booked. It is good to know what your crew will be dealing with on the night of the performance. I often joke about having a 32-piece Brazilian thrash-jazz band as the support act on particularly tiny stages—I am sure one day someone will arrange one just to teach me a lesson!

If you are traveling with your own chosen support act, then by all means mention them to the promoter when advancing the show. Be careful, though—you may end up sharing your rider and dressing room with that act. Some promoters assume that because you are touring with another band, you are all traveling as one big happy family. That may not be the case at all. Make sure any opening act you tour with has its own production and hospitality riders and that these have been passed along to the promoter. Whoever you are advancing the show with should understand that the support acts are to be treated as separate entities.

After-Show Club

An after-show club (when the music venue you just performed in turns into a nightclub or disco) is a pain for any touring band to deal with. Pack down and load out suddenly become a frenzied rush, often accompanied by flashing lights, stage smoke, and drunken audience members getting in the way.

Your advancing should always inquire about any after-club disco. You need to find out how much time you've got to tear down and load out if the venue turns into a club night after your show. Is the load out exit the same as the load in entrance? Often the load-in will be the front door and across the dance floor—a dance floor that will now be full of dancing people. It is dangerous and time-consuming to try to push your gear through a dance crowd. If this is the case, you need to find out how far the crew will have to push the gear to get it back on the van/truck/bus.

Merchandise Fee

A venue or promoter may charge you to sell your own merchandise (T-shirts and CDs) at your own show. This charge will be a flat fee, percentage of the total gross sales, or a percentage based on audience attendance—for example, $50 per 100 ticket holders. You may not agree with this charge (and many, many industry people do not), so you should try to make a different financial arrangement with the venue during the show advance process. Ask the promoter what the percentage is and whether sales tax is also deducted. Then see whether they will lower or waive the percentage.

If, during the advancing, you cannot come to an amicable arrangement with the venue, then at least you will know not to bother lugging your shirts into that particular venue on the tour.

Ticket Sales

Finally, always ask the promoter how well the show is selling. As well as giving you information about possible sellouts and percentage deals, it is only polite to show some interest in the promoter's business. You want the night to be a success for the both of you!

Working in the Live Music Industry

12 Working behind the Scenes

"Most TMs and engineers I have met have been friendly and very open with advice and help. Talking to people who do the job is invaluable and will teach you a lot. I try to be the same; you never know when you need some help, and they may be the only people that can help you out at that point."

—Timm Cleasby; tour manager, the Artic Monkeys

In my work as a band tour manager, I receive many inquiries from people who want to work in the live music industry, usually along the lines of, "I wanna be a roadie; take me on tour." This worries me slightly because obviously the image of "roadies" (I loathe that word!) in most people's minds is of a group of people so unskilled that anyone can suddenly become one!

If you have read Chapters 2 and 7 already, you will have some appreciation of the technical skills and personality traits that a successful road crew person must possess. Being on the road is not a case of simply hanging around with pop bands; to be effective and to keep your job, you need to be skilled, professional, selfless, and compassionate. You are going to be dealing with insecure and worried artists, artists who are sometimes completely out of their league in the concert environment. You cannot panic when things go wrong. You are paid to make sure things go right every time the band sets foot on a stage. You will have very little opportunity for hanging around with the band!

It is true that years ago bands would employ a general "roadie" who would shift cases, set up gear, and generally take care of everything to do with the stage. Today, that role is still applicable to some bands, especially in the early days of a band's career. That kind of road crew person does have a lot of contact with the band he works for; this kind of crew gets seen with the band at social events and can become almost like one of the family.

I suppose the image of this kind of person excites potential road crew people. They see the roadies having direct contact with the band, living on the same tour bus and staying in the same hotels—even in the same hotel rooms—as band members. The life looks glamorous and makes potential road crew people excited. This excitement is slightly misguided, though. Let me give you some warnings.

The Cons of Life on Tour

To try to give a more rounded exploration of the role of the road crew, here is a list of several of the downsides to life on tour.

Money

Ninety-nine percent of the tour crew I know work freelance. (The *Oxford English Dictionary* describes freelance as "earning money by selling your work or services to several different organizations rather than being employed by one organization.") Being freelance means we are free to choose when we work and for whom. We have to search for the work, but usually there is enough to sustain us throughout the year. All the crews I know go through periods of incredible abundance with plenty of work, hot leads, and money rolling in. And then, for whatever reason, there is no work.

A tour can get cancelled, for instance. Or perhaps it is a quiet time of the year, and there simply isn't any work. Even worse than no work is late payment (or nonpayment) from your client. No current tour work and no income can leave you facing financial ruin.

Before you accept any freelance work, you should always check out the financial position of a new client. You may be offered a road crew job by a booking agent, artist manager, or business manager. However, these people do not actually pay your invoice. In nearly all cases, your salary as road crew is paid by the band, either from their own vast cash reserves (if they are U2 or the Dave Matthews Band) or, more likely, from record company tour support. I mention this because it is very easy for an artist manager to call a freelance touring crew person, order that person's services, and then not pay the crew person.

Get written invoicing details for your work before you actually go out to work: "*Xxx* artist care of *Xxx* business manager" or "*Xxx* record label." Many bands set up a small company to administer the finances of their touring (such as Millions of Americans Touring, LLC), in which case your invoice should be sent there. In other cases, all invoicing is handled by the artist's record company.

When you have found out the invoicing details, you should find a live person in the relevant record company accounting/accounts payable office. Drop that person a line to let him or her know who you are and what your role is, and tell that person to expect your invoice!

Ask whether you need a purchase order number or other reference. Large organizations do not accept invoices for purchases that have not been authorized. Many record companies I work for also require you to be on their supplier list before they will accept an invoice from you. You will therefore have to fill out some forms and return them, a process that can take two to four weeks. Only then can you submit an invoice!

Draw up a contract. Insist on at least one third of your salary for the road crew work on the tour in advance. Getting a portion of the money up front will help your cash flow and shows commitment from the artist's business team. Likewise, if the tour is going to last for three months or more, then insist on being paid monthly for the duration of the tour Can you really afford to work for three months without any income from the tour, and then have to wait another 30 days once the tour has finished to get paid? Again, it's all about cash flow. You may be on tour, but your rent/mortgage/bills still need to be paid!

Any terms you have for payment should be clearly stated in your contract for road crew work.

The Production Services Association has produced a very useful contract for freelance crew. Although the PSA is based in the UK, the style of the contract is applicable to any freelance technician. You can download a copy of the contract from their website, www.psa.org.uk.

> "I learnt as I went along, watching other people, and used a bit of common sense...."
>
> —Scott McKenzie; backline technician, Muse, Sigur Rós, The Dammed, and Super Furry Animals

Health and Conditions

If you like comfort, regular food, lots of sleep, a modicum of privacy, and job security, then touring life is definitely not for you. Especially sleeper bus tours. I always liken touring on a sleeper bus to being in a traveling frat house—mess, noise, unsociable behavior, and more people than there should be packed into a small space. There is *no* privacy on a tour bus, a fact that seriously irritates and upsets many people.

I am serious—this is not a glamorous life.

Your health will also suffer. A combination of lack of proper sleep; moving from hot, sweaty rooms to the cold outside; lack of decent food; heavy lifting; and too much drinking and partying will soon take its toll. At the very least, you will get a bad cold—a cold that will spread around the bus in no time.

Learn to live and function without sleep. It may seem harsh, but your body will adjust. You cannot allow yourself to get cranky because you have not slept—no one sleeps properly on tour.

This is how I survive touring:

- Make sure you learn how to nap—sleep anytime you possibly can.
- Buy earplugs and eyeshades to enable you to sleep anywhere.
- Make sure your cell phone has the loudest alarm known to man.
- Get a backup alarm as well.
- Never rely on hotel wakeup calls.
- Drink plenty of water all day.

- Make the tour manager strike meats and cheeses from the rider deli tray. Meats and cheeses go bad pretty quickly in a warm dressing room. This can cause food poisoning.

- Don't store any food in the bus fridge. Food left in a tour bus fridge tends to stay in there for a long time because no one is responsible enough to tidy up the fridge. Eventually, this old food will get moldy. Mold can contaminate other food, again causing food poisoning.

Finally, this job is murder on relationships. Friends, family, and significant others get resentful of the amount of time that you are away. The worst part is when you promise to call, and some disaster takes place on the tour, and you end up being super busy when you should be calling home. This does *not* go over well.

Work hard at keeping your communications current—an e-mail or text message twice a day will keep you in people's heart and minds.

> "The worst thing about being on tour? Being away from family and loved ones. Having to live with the same people 24/7 for months on end. Never being able to hold a regular place in your Sunday football or cricket team."
>
> —Andy Dimmack;. backline technician, Franz Ferdinand, Super Furry Animals, Pavement, ... And You Will Know Us by the Trail of Dead

Pay Rates

I mentioned in Chapter 11 that the wages paid to touring crew are a huge bone of contention. The economics of the touring market have not really supported an increase in pay amounts in the last 10 years or so.

The other problem is that, as a freelancer, you need to work. If you have just finished a two-month arena tour with an international superstar, then you may have been paid pretty well and you may be doing okay financially. You are going to have to go back to work at some point, though, and what if your next job is with four kids in a van playing bars? You cannot charge them arena-tour rates, despite the years of skill and experience you have built up. My point is that it does not matter who you have worked for and how long you have been touring; you cannot simply set a fee and expect to get it.

There is no international standard pay scale for touring road crew. You charge what you think you are worth. I think I am worth my weight in gold, but I cannot realistically charge that for a tour. (At the time of writing, gold is $20,600/£10,500 per kilo. I weigh 71 kilos—you do the math.) If you are challenged by a prospective employer about your proposed fees, then you need some formula that you can use to explain how you arrived at the daily rate. A good starting point is to take the minimum wage for your state or country, multiply it by 10 (for the average 10 hours a day you work), and then add what you feel is appropriate, depending on your skills and experience.

Suppose you live in California and you have been hired by a band that you have previously worked with, but who has just been signed. They used to pay you $50 a day with no per diems and no wage for days off. You want to take things to a more professional level with them, so you ask for $105 and a $15 per diem for days off. They balk at your request until you explain your reasoning.

Minimum wage in the state of California is $7.50 at the time of this writing. You work an average of 10 hours a day, so $7.50 × 10 = $75. Add another $30 for the skills and experience you can bring to them, and this gets you $105 per day. You then explain that you do not really need a per diem on show days because there will be food and drink provided by the promoters. However, you would like $15 per diem on the days off because there will be no supplied catering and you will have to fend for yourself.

The band can either accept your offer or not; the point is that they can see the reasoning and that you are not simply doubling your fees because they have been signed!

In case you are wondering about wages of the top dogs, the backline crew for U2's Elevation tour was paid $2,500 a week.

> "From the band's point of view, playing live is good because you
> get to present your songs the way, and in the order, that you

choose. It is especially useful if you can play new songs live a few times before actually recording them. It is fun being on tour!"

—Mark Parson, tour manager, "!!!," Squarepusher, Autechre

When Things Go Wrong

You may be attracted to the glamour and power of working with a touring act—the parties, expensive hotels, and international travel. I have tried to point out that it is not all glamour and it is in fact really hard work. In case you still think you want to work for bands on tour, I have one final sobering thought.

On February 20, 2003, the tour manager for the band Great White detonated stage pyrotechnics as part of the band's show at the Station nightclub in West Warwick, Rhode Island. The pyros (called *gerbs*) ignited the soundproofing behind the stage and started a fire that killed 100 people and injured 200 more. The tour manager, Daniel Michael Biechele, was prosecuted and eventually sentenced to 12 years in prison.

I am sure that during all the fantastic shows, thousands of miles traveled, and good times with friends and fans on the road, Mr. Biechele considered himself to be a lucky man, leading a fantasy lifestyle. Then 100 people lost their lives at a rock show, and Mr. Biechele ended up in prison.

The fire was a tragedy and a terrible reminder that accidents happen. The fact that you work for a rock band on tour does not mean you are exempt from the responsibilities of life. Look out for yourself and everyone around you.

13 How to Gain Work and Keep It

"I have been touring for around six and a half years now. I started working in a club mixing sound for a tiny, and I mean tiny, amount of money. My touring career started when a band came through who needed a sound guy. I dropped everything and went on the road with them."

—"Supa" Dave Rupsch, production manager and FOH engineer, My Chemical Romance

I have tried to put you off working on tours, but it seems you still want to find out more. I don't blame you. Working for a top rock, pop, or country band can be both financially rewarding and an amazing experience. There is the opportunity for foreign travel, a unique lifestyle, and a sense of community that brings immense satisfaction to people in the touring industry.

However, like most niche industries, it is difficult to break into this kind of work and to establish yourself. Then, once you have made the entry into the industry, you face even more hard work. I have witnessed so many musicians (and crew) who really mess it up for themselves by being unprepared, unprofessional, or ignorant. It always strikes me as being a shame when artists and crew act that way. Surely this is the dream they have been working toward—why throw away the chance of a lifetime by being unprepared?

Be Prepared: Get the Answers!

Most of the questions I answer involve information about training courses and career paths, such as, "Where can I train to be a tour manager/roadie/crew person?" The short answer is that you cannot.

377

The live music production industry is largely unregulated and made up of freelancers who bring specialized skills to the industry. These skills have been gained by specific training in a certain area—such as sound or lighting—or (more likely) have been learned through years of actually working on the road. As yet there is no organized career progression for live show production and no one-stop, internationally accredited training organization.

Most of the people I work with in the touring industry fell into working on tours. A combination of desire and an aptitude for the work meant my colleagues and I quickly established ourselves and gained more work, eventually leading to careers.

> "I didn't do any formal training to become a tour manager. It was all on-the-job training—you learn how to do it, or it doesn't get done. No one taught me or gave me any lessons, and the same goes for engineering. The best knowledge I gained was, and still is, always from other TMs' and engineers' experience and experiences. When you hear that someone has messed up royally, you feel bad for them but you also make a mental note not to do the same thing. Talking to people who do the job is invaluable and will teach you a lot."
>
> —Timm Cleasby, tour manager, the Artic Monkeys

Get to Know Local Talent

When I am asked, "How do I become a tour manager/roadie/crew person?" I simply always say, "Find yourself a band!" Think about it. The biggest and most successful bands and artists need the best crew—crew who have skills, expertise, and years of experience. You may not have that experience right now. Don't worry, though—the top bands of today started out very small. Find yourself a band and grow with them.

> "I used to work in a club so I knew lots of the local bands, including one who had just gotten a [record] deal. They started doing lots of gigs, and I used to tag along in the van, sitting on the gear in the back (no tour buses in those days). After a while they got fed up with me drinking all their beer, so they decided to give me something to do—carrying their gear and tuning their guitars."
>
> —Anthony Oates, backline technician for Nick Cave and the Bad Seeds, Goldfrapp, Tindersticks, Roni Size and Reprazent, and Apollo 440, among others

Find the best emerging talent in your town, area, or venue and make yourself indispensable to them. The musicians you know or work with may not be technically oriented. If you have live concert experience and training, you may be able to help these people.

Ask yourself:

- How many times do I hear bands complaining of house sound engineers, weird feedback, bad stage sound, or inattentive bar managers?

- How many times are musicians late for shows and sound checks? How many times do people forget instruments, get lost, or assume they are able to borrow other bands' equipment?

Can you see the potential here?

With a little forethought and technical ability, you can make yourself indispensable to all the "little" bands in your town. This is especially true if the band in question is playing out of town or out of state. Any organizational or technical skill will be invaluable to a group of musicians who are tired and far from home. Hone those skills and make yourself known. Build up your network.

Yes, I know what you are saying: "I don't have a network. I'm just starting out!" Or maybe, "I live in the middle of nowhere!" Or even, "I'm still in school!" To all of these issues, I would reply: "You would be surprised at the number of people you already know." Think about it:

- Do you go to shows?
- Do you know DJs or people in bands?
- Do you know people who work in clubs, bars, or record stores?

If you can answer yes (or maybe) to any of these questions, then you have a network that is applicable to what you want to achieve!

Then you need to use your network and spread your wings a bit further. You can do that by:

- Advertising your services in local musical instrument shops, rehearsal studios, record stores, and venues.

- Ensuring that venue managers, rehearsal rooms, and musical instrument stores know about you.

- Keeping track of touring acts coming into town and who is opening up for them. When one of the local acts starts to do well, make sure you are part of their team. The success of this small local act may also be a stepping stone for your own career.

Obviously you will not get paid much (if anything) in the early days, especially working with an up-and-coming band. Do not be discouraged, though. You *have* to think long term. This investment of your time and expertise now will be worth more in the bank in the long run. A positive, can-do attitude when dealing new bands, venue managers, or local agents will get you noticed. And getting noticed is your main priority.

As "Captain" John Jackson (stage manager and drum technician for the All-American Rejects, shown in Figure 13.1) told me, "There are a lot of techs out there who started out as a friend to the band, and will always be a friend to the band, but have gone on to do real well

Figure 13.1 "Captain" John Jackson.

because they sought advice from other techs and bands and were willing to work hard and learn."

So, if you are working in a venue as sound, lighting, or stage crew, make sure you are always nice, polite, and attentive to the visiting artists—especially local support/opening acts. The fledgling bands of today are the superstars of tomorrow and, as you know, people value loyalty. That local band could be on their way to a large record company deal with lots of tour support money—they could be looking to hire *you* as a crew member!

I know many engineers in small, provincial clubs, such as "Supa" Dave Rupsch (My Chemical Romance, All-American Rejects), who have been offered touring jobs with touring national bands, all due to:

- Doing a really good job on the night of the show

- Being polite, attentive, and professional toward the visiting artists, which is what you should be doing in your job anyway

> "I got started in the job by getting on to the crew in the student union when I was at university. When I graduated, I got in with a small PA company and did three years with them, followed by a bigger PA company, then direct work for bands."
>
> —Craig Donaldson, monitor engineer for Tricky, Morcheeba, Blur, the Rapture, and Super Furry Animals, among others

Training

As I mentioned earlier, you cannot really train to be a tour manager or a crew person. Until recently, there was no real one-shot school or college that would teach you everything you need to know about working on a rock tour. That situation is changing, though. As live music continues to grow as an entertainment phenomenon and a viable source of employment, the importance of structured career training and guidance has been recognized.

Modern concert production is evolving constantly, and the roles of touring personnel are becoming increasingly specialized, as we shall see. LED screen engineers, camera people, hydraulics engineers, FOH and monitor audio engineers, instrument technicians, audio systems engineers, riggers, production managers—the list of modern touring jobs goes on. It therefore pays to get training in at least one skill. Although it is true that there is still a demand for the jack of all trades when working with emerging acts, it is also true that you should have one skill, preferably acquired through training, in order to gain a competitive edge in this industry.

> "I have never trained specifically for this job, but I did study music at college. This exposed me to a lot of emerging technology of the time (MIDI and digital audio), which helped a lot when I came to tech for bands. I also play a lot of instruments, which makes understanding how the stage setup works a little easier than it would be for a non-player. Training is more important now that the job is becoming more technical."
>
> —Chris Taplin, tour/production manager for the Darkness, Super Furry Animals, Bjork, and Morcheeba, among others

Courses

Colleges and courses do exist to teach technical stagecraft for theatre environments; a quick search on Google will turn up courses and colleges in your area. (Search for show production courses, stage management courses, and theatre technical training.) I have also found degree courses in event management, which will teach you some of the skills necessary to become an effective band tour manager.

Courses also exist that teach audio engineering. Understanding audio is pretty important if you want to work touring with bands. Learning the basics of signal paths, microphone technique, and the different types of connectors and cables will prove invaluable while on the road. Audio engineering courses at your local college may be more studio-based—in other words, based on the making and mixing of records—and, in my experience, there is a huge difference in mixing audio for stage and mixing for records.

The fact remains that any qualifications you gain show that you have commitment and dedication. I would thoroughly recommend you investigate studying a related skill. You could still work part-time for bands or in a club running sound while studying. The experience you gain from your actual show work will make your studies more relevant.

Always keep an open mind when while training or learning. For instance, you may love lighting and be totally absorbed by the new lighting technology, but please do not dismiss the audio, video, and staging aspects of modern concert touring. Try to obtain a rudimentary knowledge of other disciplines and make sure you subscribe or have access to industry trade magazines, such as *Total Production, Live!,* and *Audience.*

Readers in the UK will also be interested in the proposed National Skills Academy for Live Performing Arts. A proposal and more information about this exciting training opportunity can be downloaded from www.ccskills.org.uk.

Broaden Your Skills

So you have gone out and found the bands and musicians most likely to succeed in your area and you have offered your services. You have applied for a theatre or production skills training course. That's great; you should not skip these steps.

What else can you do to gain and keep work in the live music industry? If you called or e-mailed me right now, I would ask you:

- Are you musical? Can you play an instrument?

- Can you string a guitar or set up an amp or a drum set?

- Do you own or can you drive a van or truck?

If you can say yes to any of the questions above and you are serious about gaining and keeping a career in the live music industry, then you are in an excellent starting place already.

I mentioned being trained is a fabulous way into concert touring. Specializing as a sound engineer or a lighting person will eventually get you work in this industry. The work may be low level and the pay may be very basic. However, you will get better-paid work if you have other relevant skills.

For instance, I work primarily as a tour manager. I can also mix FOH sound and monitor sound. I tour as a tour manager. Sometimes I tour as an audio engineer only. I have an advantage, though—I can suggest to the client that for only x a day over my usual daily rate, I can combine the two jobs, saving the client money and gaining me more work.

I have told you that crew wages, as well as the amount of money available to tour suppliers, has remained the same for the last 10 years or so. And while you do not want to be doing two jobs for one wage, it does make sense to be able to offer other skills in order to get that contract. Many of my colleagues can double up as TM/FOH engineer or as driver/backline technician. You can do the same.

Think about the following:

- Make sure you learn basic backline skills. By this I mean stringing and tuning guitars and basses. Learn how drum kits are assembled (and disassembled).

- Talk to musicians and find out timesaving hints and tips for setting up gear. Learn how to operate the most common MIDI and computer-based samplers, sequencers, and modules.

- Study massage and reflexology. I am serious! Understanding and practicing good massage techniques shows you are a caring and thoughtful person—someone who understands the needs of others. It's very useful for life on the road.

Again, the trick is to make yourself indispensable to any client—whether the client is a local act struggling to get noticed or a top international touring band.

Get That Experience
The problem with any training or when starting out in a job is that you do not have the experience that makes you invaluable to your employer. It's the same old problem—you can't get the work until you have the experience, and you cannot get the experience until you have worked in the industry. So how do you get around this problem?

Figure 13.2 Local crew at load-in.

You should try to work on shows and events doing jobs that do not require much (if any) experience. Two jobs spring to mind immediately: stagehand/local crew person and band merchandise seller.

Stagehand/Local Crew Person

Inquire at local venues and find out who they use for stagehands or local crew. (For an explanation about the role of the local crew, refer to Chapter 2.) On larger shows the stagehands will be employed to load in all the set, staging, lights, PA, wardrobe, catering, and production equipment (see Figure 13.2). A typical large theatre/arena–type show will involve about 20 to 40 local crew each for the load in and load out. The work of a stagehand is really, really hard and not that well paid, but it offers two benefits—an insider's view of the various methods and equipment used in modern touring *and* direct contact with touring personnel.

Stagehands who possess any technical skills or training, who work hard, and who are sensible and have a good attitude will soon find themselves moving away from the straightforward unpacking and packing of trucks. They will often be assigned more interesting tasks throughout the put-up process of the show.

When I load into a venue, I always ask the stagehand crew boss to assign the more capable and intelligent of his crew to me directly. I can then work with those stagehands, directing them to assist my sound and lighting department heads, knowing the stagehands have the relevant knowledge to really help my crew.

All major concert cities will have at least one crewing agency or organization that will supply stagehands/local crew to promoters and venues. Make the necessary inquiries and sign yourself up for this kind of work. Get employed at as many shows as possible, observe what is going on, and ask lots of relevant questions.

Tour Merchandise Seller

As you saw in Chapter 9, any band playing live should have merchandise to sell at shows—T-shirts, hoodies, CDs, and badges/pins. I also told you that my number-one tip for gaining and keeping work in the live music industry is to find those younger emerging acts and approach them with your technical and organizational skills. If you have no technical or organizational skills, then they may have no use for you and they will definitely not pay you if you do work for them! However, what if you can combine your enthusiasm and positive attitude with a useful service?

Offer to sell merchandise for the band, as well as carrying amps or driving the van. Prove yourself as reliable and trustworthy. As I said, the merchandising operation for most bands is their financial lifeblood. Every band I have ever worked for has told me how important it is to them to have someone capable and trustworthy to look after the merchandising operation.

For you, the selling of the merchandise means you get to work on shows and perhaps go on tour with little or no experience. As soon as this happens, you need to capitalize on the opportunity.

Offer to help out wherever you can, not just with the merchandise selling. During show days you are only really busy as a merchandise seller after the audience is let into the venue. During the load-in and sound check you are free to help out the band you are with, the other bands, the promoter, whomever! The touring scene is a small family affair. Once your face and reputation are known, you can tout your desire to do touring work to other bands.

Another approach is to find the companies who supply T-shirts, posters, and so on that the bands sell on the road and perhaps get a job with them as a touring merchandise seller. You will not work directly for the band and you may not be able to get to know them very well. Again, though, merchandise selling leaves you lots of time in the day when you can make yourself useful to the tour manager and crew!

How Do You Keep Working in the Industry?

Having gained a foothold in the industry, you will need to work extremely hard to then find further employment. In my experience, as a band becomes successful, they become less responsible for actually finding and hiring their own crew. Hiring is usually done by the artist's management or the band's tour manager. Booking agents may also be asked to hire crew for their acts, although this is not as common.

> "Basically, over the years I've gotten to build up a list of people in that [tour crew] position who I like and trust and would have no problems recommending to my clients when they ask."

> —Geoff Meall, the Agency Group

How do the managers and bands find their crew?

From experience, I know that artist managers, booking agents, and bands choose their touring crew through previous contact with crew or from direct recommendation. I recently polled some of my clients on this subject, and 90 percent indicated the same process in hiring touring crew. Not one of my clients mentioned looking at CVs/resumes or advertisements. No one mentioned responding to cold phone calls or e-mails as a way of hiring crew.

It's simple: To get the work you need to be recommended. Forget about cold calls, bulk e-mailings and web-based "crew sites"—the top businesspeople in the modern live music industry work from direct contact or recommendation. In fact, the live music business uses its "suppliers" just like anyone else uses an electrician or plumber.

For example, I for one do not go around all day thinking about a list of potential plumbers I can call upon if I need to. Rather, when I find myself suddenly needing a plumber, I will either look in Yellow Pages or, better still, call someone I know who has used a plumber recently and ask for a recommendation.

My experience with live music industry professionals is that they think in the same way about tour crew. Although booking agents and managers plan tours and concerts for a living, the actual provision and selection of crew, especially tour managers, comes as almost an afterthought. The priority of the manager and booking agent is to get the band on tour, to get advertisements in the press, to get sponsorship deals in place, and to get the tour funds sorted out.

Record companies and booking agents are *not* employment agencies for touring crew. Working with my clients over the years has led me to the conclusion that you, as a potential/experienced touring professional, should view yourself as one of the plumbers of the tour-planning world and recognize that your potential clients do not sit around all day planning how to utilize the numerous crew (including you) who have sent in CVs and e-mails.

Ms. Agent instead will probably say to herself, "Well, that's the tour planned; the band leaves in two weeks. Oh, better get a tour manager and a front-of-house engineer, I suppose. Does anyone know a good TM?" It does not matter how keen you are or how much experience you have, you need to have a previous or current client singing your praises and passing along the word about your skills.

> "We don't choose at all really, we just recommend either having worked with them or having them recommended to us by someone we work with. Kind of like six degrees of separation, which can be quite hard for tour managers and crew to break into."
>
> —Eileen Mulligan, Primary Talent

Getting Those Recommendations

You need referrals and recommendations to get employed on a tour or an event. To get those referrals you should adopt these strategies:

- *Do not* send out e-mails or letters to managers, agents, record companies, or bands if you have had no previous relationship with them. If you are going to contact someone cold (that is, you have had no previous dealings with them), at least call them on the phone.

  The advent of e-mail means it is easy for anyone to send off 20 or so e-mails and then sit back, waiting for the recipients to take action. While this is not actually spam, this kind of work-seeking e-mail is just as annoying for any music industry professional as spam is.

  Making a cold phone call is an uncomfortable and nerve-wracking process for many of us. However, it shows more commitment and a desire to actually make a situation happen. Many music professionals, me included, appreciate the effort of a phone call. Yes, we may be busy, we may not be able to take your call, or we may be unable to help you. Still, the fact that you actually made a phone call instead of sending an impersonal e-mail is always more impressive.

  When making an employment-related call, you should always be brief and polite and ensure some follow-up action. Introduce yourself to the potential employer, ask whether you may send a CV/resume by post or e-mail, check all the necessary spellings, and hang up, thanking the person for his or her time.

  The CV/resume you send should always reference when you first made contact, such as, "I called you today (01/02) regarding possible jobs on the *xxxx* tour. I am pleased to enclose some information about myself." Offer to follow up the call again in two to three weeks to see whether the situation has changed or whether there are other opportunities.

- *Do* make friends with other crew members and keep in regular contact. All successful tour crew get offered employment that clashes with existing work. This happens to me all the time and I simply say, "Thanks for the offer of the work. I'm sorry I am not available for that period. However, I know this really good person who may be able to help." That person could be you!

> "Never be rude to people that are trying help you. Screaming and shouting is not the fastest way to get things done. People are much more inclined to help calm, friendly people."
>
> —Sarah Newton, SJM Concerts

- *Do* your research. Find out who is touring, as well as when and where. Look on promoter and venue websites. Subscribe, or have access to, industry trade magazines, such as *Audience* and *Billboard,* and to websites, such as CelebrityAccess.com.

  Remember that most tours are booked between four and eight months in advance, with tickets going on sale only two to three months before the tour goes out. The booking of crew can be done at the very last minute (as discussed previously), but it does no harm to know well in advance that a tour is happening and to make yourself known to the relevant artist manager or tour manager.

- *Do* keep in touch with previous clients. It sounds obvious but, as I explained previously, artist managers and booking agents do not really have your employment welfare at the top of their list of priorities. They will not be thinking constantly about giving you work. Keep in touch, make sure you are on their radar, and at least appear to be genuinely interested in the career of the band they represent. A reminder e-mail or call every two to three months should do the trick. At the very least you will get a copy of the band's new album before it is released in the stores!

- *Do* get testimonials and recommendations from satisfied clients. You have already seen that these recommendations and referrals are what will get you future work; make sure you publicize the work you have done. By all means have a website, brochures, and a CV. These are tools that will help you get work, but if they do not contain testimonials and referrals from previous clients, then the effectiveness of these sales materials will be lost.

As soon as you have finished a tour or an event, write to the person who directly employed you and ask him or her to jot down something for you to use in your resume or on your website. Be polite and, if necessary, write out a rough version of what you would like that person to say about you. Always make sure you seek the person's permission to publicize any comment he or she may have written without solicitation, such as a thank-you e-mail.

I seek testimonials and comments from my clients immediately after I have finished a contract. I then post these testimonials on my website. You can see them at www.tourconcepts.com/clients.htm. You can do the same—set up a MySpace page or a website, list the people you have worked for, and get those testimonials on there! In the same way that promoters and A&R prefer to check out a band online, a prospective employer can check to see that you are capable and that you have experience by simply going to a webpage and seeing what people have said about you.

> "Never act like you know everything [when working for a band]. Always act like you have no idea what is going on. Don't have an ego."
>
> —"Captain" John Jackson, stage manager and drum tech, the All-American Rejects.

The Future

14 The Future of the Live Music Industry

There can be no doubt that live music today is in an extremely healthy state. But what does the future hold?

Cycles

Changing music tastes in the UK during the late 1980s and early 1990s had a profound effect on the UK live music industry. The so-called "Second Summer of Love" (which actually lasted two years!) saw the prevalence of the drug Ecstasy fuel an explosion in youth culture. Music fans jammed into illegal warehouse parties and outdoor raves, all but abandoning the live music of the day.

Live concerts continued, but the post-rave era of the early 1990s saw massive growth in legal clubbing as "DJ culture" grew. Live music promoters, especially those dealing with student venues, definitely felt the pinch and had no choice but to move into this area of promotion as well.

There are no specific figures to illustrate the financial impact the DJ-culture years had on live music in the UK, but I remember vividly speaking to promoters at that time who were predicting the death of live music. In their view, paying a couple of hundred dollars to a guy with a box of records was a lot easier than dealing bands, trucks, sound checks, and lighting rigs.

The late 1980s and early 1990s was obviously the bottom of a cycle for live music in the UK. Could that happen again? I'm not sure. Live music seems to be so powerful these days. Powerful enough to tempt people out of retirement....

Reforming

The lure of concert ticket cash, merchandise, and associated sponsorship deals is enough to tempt the most unlikely bands out of retirement. Motley Crüe, Take That, Genesis, and now the Police have all reformed and have toured or are planning to tour. It is interesting that none of these acts has released any new material, nor are they planning to. The immense earning potential of a quick world tour involves nothing more than rehearsing all your old material.

These reunion tours are a huge boost for the live industry as well. The Police tour is predicted to gross around $175 million; on top of that, you still have bands such as the Rolling Stones bringing in $138.5 million for 39 shows.

Concert-Going Experience

One major change for the live music industry appears to be the role of the promoter in creating a concert-going experience for the audience. Michael Rapino, CEO of Live Nation, says, "For 20 or 30 years, every promoter was a business-to-business brand. It was about servicing the artist and the artist community, not the consumer." To change this approach, Live Nation bought Musictoday, a global entertainment merchandise supplier and branding company (see Chapter 9). "Our mission is no longer limited to the two-hour concert," says Rapino. "It's about taking that two-hour experience and turning it into a 12-month relationship. There's so much around the show itself that we realized we should be selling: a photo at the show, song downloads, the concert poster." Fans can already buy CDs of the concert they have just seen; this same CD can also be sold to fans who did not go to the show.

Live Nation has also started collecting contact details for the audience (e-mail address), something they had not thought important before because the audience was not buying tickets to see Live Nation the promoter, but to see the band. That situation has not changed; audiences pay to see the act on stage, not the guy promoting the show. Still, if the audience has a lousy time at a show because of bad parking, poor facilities, or high ticket prices, then the promoter will lose customers. Promoters are learning to listen to their audience and can get direct feedback about the venues the promoter owns and the shows it promotes. Rapino explains, "If you went to a show at Jones Beach, we'll send you an e-mail and say, 'Thank you for going. Would you like to participate in our survey? We have some ways of rewarding you if you do.' Was the parking good? Did the food suck? The sight lines? How can we make it better?"

As the superstar agents demand higher fees and the promoters increase ticket prices to pay those fees, making the concert-going experience better for the fans can only be a good thing.

Globalization

With its increased health and wealth, the live music industry is behaving like any other trillion-dollar industry and moving more toward globalization. The larger promoters, such as AEG and Live Nation, have had a busy couple of years acquiring smaller promoters, both domestically and in other countries. These takeovers are creating global super-brands out of the promoters.

On a smaller scale, two large US-based booking agents have recently opened offices in London, tempting the cream of the UK booking agents, along with their artist rosters, to head up their new offices. William Morris Agency and Creative Artists Agency (CAA) now operate in London, New York, and Los Angeles, with CAA also in Nashville.

Is the reason for these new offices to expand globally or just to acquire a whole new roster of clients overnight? Gaining a new client roster is certainly a possibility. If you can tempt a superstar agent to your company, you will undoubtedly also gain the high-profile acts on that agent's roster. Because bands have a relationship with their agent, regardless of what company the agent works for, you would find it very difficult to tempt a top act to your new agency without bringing the agent along with them.

Ticketing

One big change in the future of the live music industry will be ticketing. Until quite recently, a promoter printed and sold the tickets for the show using a distribution system that involved the venue box office, a few record shops, and sending tickets in the mail. The promoter would collect the money from sales as they were made and hold onto it until the settlement.

Now a whole raft of ticketing purchasing and distribution systems are available. You can purchase your ticket online or via your mobile phone, and then print it out at home or have a code sent back to your mobile phone. You take your phone to the show where it is scanned, allowing you entry. No more waiting for the mail to arrive or standing in line at a box office to buy tickets.

This technology is great for ticket-buying fans, and its use is only set to increase. Some estimates put the sale of print-at-home tickets or mobile-phone-code tickets at 80 percent of all tickets sold in five years' time. There is a problem, though. The promoter is no longer receiving the cash directly—it is going to the ticketing companies. Could this mean that the larger ticketing companies—such as Ticket-master, which sells 15 million tickets a month—could just cut out the promoter and deal with the bands directly?

There is also the increasingly thorny issue of "secondary ticketing," or scalping. As if the promoters did not have enough to worry about with the primary ticket sellers perhaps taking their business, they now have to contend with companies such as StubHub, who are making massive profits from the promoters' hard work (see Figure 14.1).

StubHub (which was acquired by eBay) is a secondary ticketing company, giving people with unwanted concert tickets the chance to sell them online. This is reported to be a $10 billion industry, and StubHub (and others) sell tickets for an average of $145 each. (The average price for a concert ticket in North America in 2006 was $50.35.) This is not the original price for the ticket—if you were unfortunate enough to want to buy a Rolling Stones ticket after they sold out, you would end up paying $263 for a $137 ticket through StubHub. Indeed, the average markup paid to StubHub is $67.50 per ticket. Of course, the artist and promoter don't get any of that extra money; the deal has been done on the original ticket price, and StubHub walks away with a nearly 100-percent profit.

No one is accusing secondary ticketers of ripping people off—these companies are simply being entrepreneurial. What annoys bands,

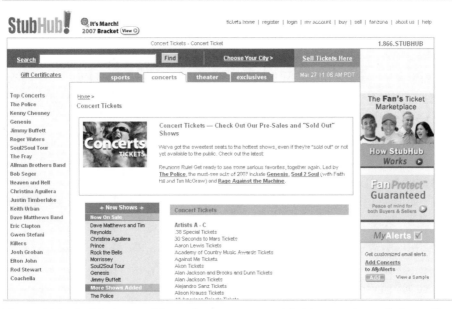

Figure 14.1 StubHub.com. They take your unwanted tickets and re-sell them. They're great if you are a fan looking for a ticket to a sold-out show. They're not so good if you are the band, booking agent, or promoter, because StubHub keeps all the money.

their management, and the promoters is that the secondary ticketers are letting the promoters do all the hard work and then sitting back and making huge profits.

Your Future

What is your future in this new world of after-show DVDs and global booking agents? How will you and your music fare?

DIY

A consensus sweeping the industry is that bands do not need record labels anymore and that DIY (do it yourself) is the way to go. As CD sales decline, labels are increasingly demanding a share of their artists' entire income—live performance, merchandise, and sponsorship. EMI Records, for instance, signed singer Robbie Williams for a reported $90 million in 2002. The deal included EMI receiving income on all Robbie's touring and merchandise income, as well as CD sales. Other artists, outraged by this apparent greed by the labels and encouraged by the opportunities of the Internet, are increasingly staying away from the major labels. The focus is on building multiple revenue streams and not relying on album sales. "We are in a different business now," says Michael Hausmann, who manages Aimee Mann. Mann has released three albums on her own label, SuperEgo. "We can license a song onto TV or a film and make twice as much money (as we would on a major label), or we can book a tour or whatever."

Other artists agree that DIY is the way to go. "People will make a lot less money, but more people will make money. I could give away all my music for free and still make a living from live shows and T-shirt sales," says Akira the Don, an independent artist who was signed to Interscope Records.

Wait a minute, though. I have spent most of this book telling you that touring is expensive and that you are very unlikely to make much in the way of performance fees when you are starting out. How are you going to be able to tour without support from a record label? Enter the sponsors....

Bands as Brands

Bands as brands. Remember those words—you will hear them all over the place. Artists who are perhaps shunning the labels still need investment in order to go out and make thousands of dollars playing live. Bands are now leveraging their brand appeal—that is, working with companies who want to use their image to advertise their products. This goes beyond mere sponsorship. Bands are becoming brands and receiving cash from non-music-related products. Young British singer/songwriter Lily Allen now has a deal with a High Street fashion chain. Despite being only 21, Lily Allen has already had a number-one single in the UK and has toured extensively. The deal with the clothing brand will see her advertising the chain, as well as designing a collection for the shops. Obviously, she will earn money from both activities.

You may not have the brand value of a Lily Allen yet. If you are thinking about going down the DIY route, you should start to look at how you can turn yourself into a brand. Don't be put off by possible accusations of selling out. In a recent survey by Entertainment Media Research of 900 males and females aged 15 to 50, 51 percent said they thought brand involvement in music was appropriate.

Figure 14.2 Apple iPod and U2. Neither really needs the other to carry on selling, but both are now powerful brands. Each gives the other the impression of quality, technological innovation, and lasting appeal.

Being appropriate does not mean your musical audience (or the consumers of the products with which you are involved) will actually agree with the promotion tie-in. The survey also found that 46 percent of those asked thought that the tie-in between Apple and U2 (see Figure 14.2) was a "good fit"—in other words, it was appropriate. In contrast, only 13 percent thought the sponsorship deal between McDonalds and Justin Timberlake was a good fit—in fact, 28 percent of the people asked thought it was a bad fit.

Investment

Another recent innovation in the wake of the labels losing their hold on artists is the advent of music venture capital trusts. Venture capitalists (VCs) work by persuading people to give them money, which they then invest in startup companies or use to aid growth for established companies. Traditionally, VCs operated in the millions-of-dollars territory, and attracting investment into the music industry was not even in the same state, let alone the ballpark.

Now the situation has changed. Patrick McKenna, chairman of Ingenious, a media investment and advisory business, says, "The demand for live entertainment, in all forms, has increased significantly in recent years as consumers look for new and unique entertainment. This consumer-led growth in live revenues has been fueled by brands wishing to sponsor and advertise around major events of both an entertainment and a sporting nature." See—it's that bands as brands thing again!

Ingenious has two music venture capital trusts, which are set to raise $98 million (£50 million) for investment in companies producing and promoting new and established live events. This is an amazing amount of money and a new development that has fantastic implications for an already booming industry.

Make sure you are part of it!

Epilogue: That Story!

Throughout *The Tour Book* I have shown you the benefit of understanding the industry you are in. Playing shows and going on tour is a vital part of any artist's career. It also is really good fun!

However, things can (and do) go wrong at shows and on tour, even for the most experienced musicians and crew. Hopefully, sharing my knowledge and experience with you will help you avoid making mistakes that can cost you time, money, and cancelled shows and can seriously affect—and even end—your career.

To prove this point, I want to share with you a true story. It is tale of rock 'n roll touring at its most absurd, so be warned!

A Tale of Two Drummers

In December of 1997, I was approached by the management of a recently re-formed English alternative rock band. The band had been lured out of retirement by a lucrative record deal with Universal Records, and the management wanted me to work as tour manager for a March 1998 tour of North America and Canada. I met the band and its management in London and agreed to manage the tour.

Now when I say "band," what I actually mean is a duo that used the latest cutting-edge technology to reproduce their albums on stage. This onstage technology was augmented by a live guitarist and drummer, both of whom the band hired on for the tour. The duo had done this previously and, although it was expensive, they felt it worked well.

In January of 1998, the duo and the hired musicians started work on transforming the songs from the new album into a live set. Initially, they did this in the duo's home studio in the suburbs of London with the

403

intention of moving into a suitable band rehearsal space a week before the start of the tour. At the same time, I was busily sorting out the pre-production; booking transportation (international and domestic flights, tour buses, and internal transportation); securing work permits and visas, hotels, and equipment (including a full lighting rig); finding crew for the tour; and creating a budget list of possible expenses.

As part of these pre-production responsibilities, I was tasked with arranging the production and purchase of a set of IEM monitors for the session drummer. As it does now, the process involved the musician in question having molded impressions made of his ears. The manufacturer used these molds to create the earpieces. IEMs were becoming very popular at that time, and a combination of demand and new technology meant they were not cheap! I arranged for the drummer to nip up to a specialized audiologist just off the world-famous (and very expensive) Harley Street in London.

Have you noticed how many times I have mentioned how expensive things were? It's going to get worse!

March 20, 1998: London

In March of 1998, the band moved into a major London rehearsal room for a day of production rehearsal in order to create the show. The previous week the band had rehearsed in one of the smaller rooms at the same studio, and I had popped in every now and then on business. During these visits, I noticed that there was a mattress and a sleeping bag on the floor behind the drum kit. I was told that the drummer was in fact sleeping there overnight. "Wow, that's dedication," I thought.

By the time we moved into the large room at the complex, I had hired the necessary crew for the tour: a backline tech (Mr. A), a keyboard tech (Mr. L), a monitor engineer (Mr. K), and a lighting designer/operator (Mr. D). As well as tour manager, I would also mix the FOH sound. The crew was told to be there on March 20th for the production rehearsal—to meet the band and to start to get a handle on the forthcoming technical requirements. I also arranged for the lighting equipment and extra sound to be delivered to the rehearsal studio so we could have a full production rehearsal.

One major problem all international touring bands face concerns their personal instruments and backline: How do you get that equipment to another country? You cannot take it with you on the plane as checked luggage; band equipment is deemed too big and too heavy to be considered luggage. It is therefore classed as freight, which the airlines will happily transport for you—at a considerable cost!

To reduce the costs of this tour, I arranged for the really vital and personal equipment—guitars, amplifier heads, cymbals, snare drums, samplers, synth modules, and so on—to be freighted across the ocean from London. (Specialized rock 'n roll freighting equipment companies deal with this kind of thing—you tell them where and when you need the gear, and they somehow make it happen.) All the generic equipment the band needed—guitar cabinets, bass amp, drum shells, cases, and lights—were being rented in the US for the duration of the tour. This was cheaper than freighting everything; there is little point in sending an Ampeg SVT amplifier and an 810 cabinet halfway across the world when you can rent one locally!

I have done this kind of thing many times, and experience has taught me to always have a prep day in the destination country before the first day of the tour. This prep day gives the band and crew a chance to make sure all the rental gear works and that the gear is compatible with the equipment we have freighted to the destination. I booked a rehearsal studio in Manhattan for this prep day, the idea being that the day after we arrived in New York, we could have a good day in this other studio. We would check all the incoming and rental gear, wrap at 8:00 p.m., load up the bus, and then head up to Toronto for the first show. That was my idea, but the reality proved to be very different.

Back at the London studio, things were not going well. The backline tech, Mr. A, introduced himself to the guitarist and started familiarizing himself with the guitarist's equipment. (This is what backline techs do— you cannot fix a musician's system in the middle of a gig if you are not familiar with the way it has been put together.) While poking around in the back of the guitarist's effects rack, Mr. A received a rather severe electrical shock from the equipment. Mr. A obviously was not very happy about this, and he complained—using four-letter words—to the guitarist. The guitarist, obviously not used to having his parentage or his equipment criticized, also got upset, and an argument broke out. It blew over fairly quickly, but tension remained in the air for the rest of the day.

There were other technical problems throughout the day, and tempers were fraying by the time we finished.

That evening, I was told by the band and the management that Mr. A would have to go—he was not welcome on the tour. Great; now I had three days to find a backline tech before we flew to the States. I spent the next couple of days on the phone, calling all the techs I knew. However, the hunt was pretty futile because even if I found someone who was not already working, there was no way I would've been able to arrange the necessary US work permits in time. On the last day before we left, I decided that we would have to try to find someone in the States, so I sent a few faxes and e-mails out to people I knew in the US and left it at that.

March 24, 1998: Flight UA907

On March 24, 1998, the band and crew assembled at Heathrow Airport. I personally was looking forward to sleeping for the whole United Airlines flight—the last week had been extremely hectic, and this was a good chance to get some rest.

The first signs of trouble came when three of the band members were caught smoking in the bathrooms. No-smoking flights had recently been introduced, and my charges were finding the six-hour fight a bit difficult. They were given a stern warning by the cabin attendants, but they were allowed to return to their seats. Sensing all was calm again, I settled down in my seat and started to doze.

I was awoken by the guitarist shaking my shoulder. "Andy, you need to sort things out. The drummer's acting really strangely." I looked around to see the drummer, previously sitting in a crowded row of five seats with children and grandmothers around him, now all on his own in the deserted row. And he did not look happy.

"They won't give me another drink," he snarled when I approached him. "You're the tour manager. Get me another drink!"

I replied that if the cabin crew would not serve him, there was very little I could do.

"Great tour manager you are. You're as bad as those other [*various sexist and racist expletives deleted*]. Get me a drink!"

I looked at my watch and realized we were only one and a half hours into the flight and that this guy, as well as being drunk, was also a pretty nasty person. Deep joy.

"Calm down, mate," I said. "If you don't act like a drunk, then maybe they'll serve you in a bit. Why don't you drink some water and have a nap?"

By this time the drummer was on his feet in the aisle, clearly getting very agitated. I managed to get him to move back to rear of the cabin and into the galley area, where there was more room. One of the cabin crew asked us both to take our seats because we were upsetting the other passengers. I explained that I, the tour manager, was somewhat responsible for the situation and would therefore try to deal with it. We were joined by Mr. L, the keyboard tech, who was also trying to calm the drummer. He had no effect, though, and the drummer rapidly got more and more agitated. At some point, I looked around the cabin and saw that where there once had been a plane full of families and couples, there were now empty seats and frightened-looking people cowering in the front of the cabin.

As we continued to try to reason with the drummer, word reached the captain that there was a disturbance aboard. Knowing that some of our party had already been cautioned for smoking in the bathrooms, he obviously figured we were a rowdy bunch and he therefore was taking no chances. The captain sent back his first officer, who carried a pair of "Tuff Cuffs"—the plastic temporary restraints that cops use.

"The captain requested that we restrain your friend," the first officer told me.

"He's not my friend. I just happen to be the tour manager for this group. I don't think restraining him is a good idea; he is clearly agitated. I will calm him down and get him back to his seat," I replied.

"Okay, I will inform the captain that you are taking responsibility."

At this point, the drummer finally lost it. Shouting, "I want to get off! Let me off!" he lunged for the aircraft door at the rear of the plane and tried to open it. Mr. L, the first officer, and I managed to grab him before he could reach the handle, and we wrestled him away from the door. We got him down and somehow we got the Tuff Cuffs on him. We got him to a seat and wrapped a couple of seatbelts around him, and I sat down next to him. The remaining passengers were moved out of harm's way.

The captain definitely was not taking any chances now. Apparently, the drummer had been using extremely sexist and racist language toward the cabin attendants before he became violent, and this—coupled with the attempt on the aircraft's door—prompted the captain to call the FBI. (Interfering with a flight crew is a federal offense and in 1998 carried a maximum penalty of 20 years of imprisonment and a $10,000 fine.) Because we previously came to the attention of the captain (thanks to the smoking warning), he assumed that all nine people making up our party posed a threat, and therefore he also asked for the police to be on standby. I was informed of all this by the first officer.

"Your friend is causing a lot of trouble for a lot of people," the first officer said.

"He is not my friend. I just happen to be in a position of responsibility," I replied wearily.

I could see this tour evaporating before we even landed, and all of us spending a night in jail. I did some fast talking and managed to persuade the first officer that the rest of the party was innocent, that I would take full charge of the drummer, and that there was no need for anyone else to be detained when we landed at Newark. Luckily, he agreed. I then went over to the remaining band and crew and told them to keep their heads down, be quiet, and act like saints for the remaining flight time. Upon deplaning, they should go straight to the hotel and wait for me there. The tour was off.

I spent the next two hours of the flight in a nearly empty rear cabin with nothing to do except listen to the ravings of a psychotic. Oh, the glamour!

We landed at Newark, and the plane was stormed immediately by New Jersey's finest. The other passengers were told to remain in their seats as the drummer and I were escorted off the plane.

"Your friend here is in a lot of trouble, Mr. Reynolds," the cops informed me.

"He is *not* my friend," I replied through gritted teeth.

We were met by federal agents and taken to the New Jersey Port Authority building. The drummer was placed in a holding cell while I was questioned by the FBI, the police, and the INS. It was explained to me that the drummer's visa had been revoked and that the US authorities would be holding his passport; he was *persona non grata* (unwelcome and unacceptable in this country). It was up to me to arrange legal representation for the drummer, and we would be held here until such time as he was arraigned or released (which was very unlikely). I dealt with all this, a ton of paperwork, more references to my "friend," and TV news reporters. I finally managed to leave the New Jersey Port Authority building at about 8:00 P.M., three and a half hours after we landed.

I hailed a cab and arrived in Manhattan at about 9:00. I was tired, pissed off, and expecting a full night of work ahead of me. The tour was obviously off; I would have to cancel everything and deal with the insurance, the promoters, and the travel arrangements to get us all home again. I also had to contact the band's lawyer to handle the drummer's affairs. I was upset by the whole stupid affair. I expected the band to be devastated.

In fact, the band was having drinks and a huge meal in the hotel restaurant. They seemed to be upbeat—almost happy.

"What are you doing?" I almost screamed at them. "The tour's off, we have a guy in jail, and you lot are sitting here, ordering expensive food, and getting drunk!" (I was tired.)

"It's okay," said the lead singer. "We've got our old drummer flying in as we speak. Everything's cool. Have a drink. Relax."

It turns out that while I was dealing with half the law enforcement agencies of eastern America, the band had very thoughtfully rung up their old drummer and asked him if was free to come out to the US to help continue the tour. Never mind that he had not been in the band for five years, he had not heard the new material, and he had no airline tickets or US visa. Remember, it was almost 2:00 A.M. in London, and Drummer #2 had just gotten in from a nightclub. He obviously was not thinking straight when he said yes, and the band immediately phoned an airline and spent a ridiculous amount of money to get him a ticket on the first flight out of Heathrow that morning.

March 25, 1998: New York—Preparation Day

The next day was the most intense day I have ever been a part of. It was supposed to be a nice, easy prep day with everything in place and just a few technical adjustments to make. Instead, and in no particular order, I had to:

- Liaise with the band's lawyer regarding the future of Drummer #1, still languishing in the NJPA cells.

- Find a US backline tech. (This still had not been sorted out.)

- Rewrite the tour expenses budget, file it, and arrange for extra funds to be wired to the tour account.

- Change travel arrangements for Drummer #1 and make new ones for Drummer #2.

- Change all the rental drum equipment. Drummer #1 was left-handed and played a completely different type of kit than the one Drummer #2 preferred.

- Check all the freighted equipment and make sure it was compatible with the rented gear.

- Make sure Drummer #2 knew all the songs.

- Oh, and get all this done, using only a payphone in the studio, before we left at 8:00 P.M. to go to Toronto.

Drummer #2 arrived at the studio in Manhattan at midday on March 25th. He was not a happy bunny. What had seemed like a "wizard jape" (a jolly good idea) at 2:00 A.M. had turned into sordid reality upon touchdown at JFK, and he was hung over and tired. He had basically walked out of his normal life at a moment's notice, with no planning, and he was full of regret about this. On top of that, he faced a whole day of rehearsals to learn the new songs that made up the majority of the band's set.

All I can say is that we walked into that studio on Avenue A in Manhattan with nothing and came out with a rock show. The band really pulled together and hammered the set into some kind of order. Drummer #2 learned all the new songs, furiously scribbling notes while listening to the tracks over and over on his Walkman. The crew soldered leads, made cables, marked settings, and made the production able to tour. I was either on the phone all day or programming settings into the digital Yamaha desk we were using.

The bus arrived to pick us up, and we loaded out—a lot later than I had planned. Stopping briefly at the hotel to shower and check out of the rooms, we headed off for the nine-hour overnight drive to Toronto. Drummer #2 stayed in Manhattan for the evening and flew up to Toronto; I didn't have time to organize his entry visas for Canada, and therefore he could not travel on the bus with us. (It is not uncommon for a bus full of entertainers with work permits to have a non-permit-holder aboard. The manager of the band, for instance, is not deemed to be employed by the promoters and therefore is basically there on business. Drummer #2 did not want to risk pretending to be the manager, so he elected to travel independently, posing as a tourist.)

March 26, 1998: Toronto—Lee's Palace

Despite the somewhat shaky start to the tour, the show at Lee's Palace in Toronto was a total success. This was a band that had not played together before, and with a drummer who had learned nine new songs in eight hours. Yes, the set was a bit hesitant in parts, but we had 11 more shows to play on this tour, and the band, crew, and I were confident that we could pull this off. A small celebration took place after the show, and then we made ready to set off back across the border for the next show in Cleveland, Ohio.

Because Drummer #2 had no US work permit, he again could not travel on the bus with us. He did not want to pretend to be a manager or a hanger-on, so I booked him a flight from Toronto to Cleveland, leaving in the morning. He could just say he was a tourist. Before we left, he asked us to take his suitcase on the bus with us to save him having to carry it around on his journeys to and from airports. I gave him his flight details, more cash for taxis, and the venue details for the next day. With that, we set off for Cleveland.

At about 3:00 A.M., 10 minutes after we crossed back over the US border, my pager started to go berserk. (Yes, pager. US cell phones were too expensive to rent back then.) Message after message kept coming, all from the same number. I quickly identified the number as being that of the hotel in Toronto where Drummer #2 was spending the night. With a sickening feeling in my stomach, I ordered the bus to pull over at a payphone, and I called the number on the pager.

"My passport is in the suitcase I gave you!" Drummer #2 wailed. "How am I going to get out of the country?" Hmmm. Good point, well presented. I told him to calm down and not to worry. I could not do anything now (it was the middle of the night), and the rest of us would be in Cleveland nice and early, at which point I would make some calls and organize things. I told him to get up early and be at the airport for his scheduled flight.

March 27, 1998: Cleveland—Odeon

The bus pulled into Cleveland and parked at the venue at about 6:00 A.M. Thankfully, I had managed to fall asleep, despite the calamity raging around me, so I was still asleep when the driver switched off the engines and went off to the day rooms to sleep. I woke at about 9:00 A.M. We could not get into the venue until midday, so I found a breakfast place with a payphone and started to make calls.

I had to think fast. I was told by US immigration that Drummer #2 would not be able to travel to the US from Canada without his passport. Canadian immigration said the same thing and also wanted to know how, if he had no passport, Drummer #2 had gotten into the country in the first place? I could not say he had lost his passport because that would've meant trips to embassies and even more embarrassing questions. Besides, Drummer #2 had entered both the US and Canada on short notice and without the necessary work permit—not a fact I wanted to share with either immigration service I invented some story to keep them happy and asked what a possible solution could be. For instance, if I could get Drummer #2's passport to him, he would be allowed to fly, right? Canadian and US immigration both said yes. Okay, that was a start.

These calls took a couple of hours; it was then time for load in. Remember, I have seven other people to look after, and I am supposed to be mixing FOH sound. This looked like it was going to be another long day!

While taking care of the logistics of the day, I started to hatch a plan to rescue my drummer. Toronto was six hours by car. I could hire someone to drive up there, with the passport, collect Drummer #2, and then head back. That would bring Drummer #2 into Cleveland at about midnight, which would be two and a half hours late. The only alternative was to fly the passport up there and hope Drummer #2 could make a connecting flight back into Cleveland. He had already missed his original flight from Toronto; I checked with Air Canada, and they had an evening flight from Toronto to Cleveland that would arrive just in time for him to play the show. He would miss sound check, but at least the fans would get to see the band perform, which is all that is important on tour. The show must go on!

Now the question remained, could I get Drummer #2's passport to him in time? Air Canada informed me that there was a flight leaving Cleveland in an hour. The staff was very helpful and told me that Air Canada would be more than happy to fly the passport up to Toronto (for a full adult last-minute fare!) and hand it off to Drummer #2. I had no time to take a trip out to the Cleveland airport and back, so I called a cab company and explained the situation. A car quickly arrived and, after I tipped the driver a ridiculous amount of money, the passport was on its way to the Cleveland airport and eventually Toronto.

Meanwhile, in Toronto, Drummer #2 was having a nervous breakdown. He had stationed himself at the Air Canada ticket desk at the airport and was now receiving call after call from me as I kept him updated with the news. I had changed his flight to the evening one (at more considerable expense). The poor bloke was in a right state at this point, but I assured him that his passport was on its way and that he would be back with us soon.

The cab company in Cleveland got the passport to the Air Canada staff at the airport, and they placed it aboard the Toronto flight. At last, a break! I still had not let on to the promoter about our little situation. The news about Drummer #1's escapades had been in the papers and on the TV news, and I did not want to give the promoter any other cause for concern. I told the band to remain quiet and keep out of the way. We continued sound check with the new backline tech on drums and acted as if nothing had happened.

The Air Canada flight landed on time in Toronto, and the staff found Drummer #2 and handed him his passport. This gave Drummer #2 about 20 minutes to check in, get through security, and get onto the flight. He paged me just before boarding; I called him back, wished him a pleasant flight, and told him we would see him at the show.

At this point, dear reader, do you get a sense of dread reading those last words? It's all going too well, isn't it? I have overcome disaster, planned an alternative, and now it's merely a matter of time before everything's back to normal. Isn't it?

I had been advised by the Air Canada staff in Toronto that there was a storm building over Toronto, and that the Cleveland-bound flight might be delayed slightly. This was supposed to be good news for me because this potential delay actually gave me more time to get the passport up to Toronto. What the Air Canada staff did *not* tell me was that the storm was potentially capable of worsening to the point where air traffic would be grounded in Toronto.

Guess what? The storm worsened, and the flight with Drummer #2 and his passport was aborted after takeoff and returned to Toronto! We were *that* close, only to be defeated by Mother Nature!

You can imagine my total despair when I found out. To make things worse, I had to tell the band and, even worse, the promoter. He was, of course, furious and threatened legal action. I managed to calm him down (been doing a lot of calming in this story, haven't I?), and we agreed to cancel the show for the evening and rearrange for the next day. The venue was available, but I am sure a lot of fans went home that night unable to make the show the next day. We did play that show, and then continued the tour, the only further mishaps being the occasional hangover.

And what of Drummer #1? The band's lawyer (who I had dragged out of a black-tie dinner on the evening of the original flight) applied for bail for Drummer #1, and it was granted. Drummer #1 was released from the NJPA jail on the same day as we were in the rehearsal studio, and I had to make arrangements for him. Manhattan's hotels were full, and Drummer #1 ended up staying in the penthouse suite of the hotel we had previously occupied—the only place I could find for him. He was arraigned the next day, when a very lenient judge decided he had mental health issues, slapped a hefty fine on him, and banned him from working in the US again.

The story is not over, though. I still had to get the idiot back to the UK. United Airlines would not take him, and neither would most of the other carriers. In the end, American Airlines agreed to take him on the condition that he flew in the first-class cabin, where he could be "adequately observed." So he stayed five nights in a penthouse suite and then flew home first-class. I also had to send him cash for living expenses while he stayed in New York!

So there you go: A tale of two drummers, stupidity, and the resulting calamity.

Appendix

SOURCES

This appendix contains a list of the quotes and figures and the appropriate sources or copyright owners.

CHAPTER 1
Quote by Olly Parker: ©2007 *Audience* magazine

CHAPTER 2
Quote by Andy Ross: ©2007 *Audience* magazine
Quote by Ben Kirby: ©2007 *Audience* magazine
Quote by Andy Farrow: ©2007 *Audience* magazine
Quote by Andy Taylor: ©2007 *Audience* magazine
Quote by Bob Gold: ©2007 *Audience* magazine
Quote by Kevin Doran: ©2007 *Audience* magazine
Figure 2.3 photo by Krittiya Sriyabhanda

CHAPTER 3
Quote by Matt Willis: ©2007 *Audience* magazine
Quote by Gerrard Phillips: ©2007 *Audience* magazine
Quote by Alex Gilbert: ©2007 *Audience* magazine

CHAPTER 4
Quote by Phil Catchpole: ©2007 *Audience* magazine
Quote by Jonny Simon: ©2007 *Audience* magazine
Figure 4.3: ©2007 Fotolia

CHAPTER 5
Quote by Jamie Graham: ©2007 *Audience* magazine
Quote by Colin Schaverien: ©2007 *Audience* magazine
Figure 5.1: ©2007 Music Bank Ltd
Figures 5.4, 5.8, and 5.10: ©2007 Fotolia

CHAPTER 6
Figure 6.11: ©Midas Consoles
Figure 6.14 photo by Krittiya Sriyabhanda
Figures 6.12, 6.15, 6.24, 6.25, 6.27, 6.29, 6.30, and 6.31:
    ©2007 Fotolia

CHAPTER 7
Quote by Gareth Dobson: ©2007 *Audience* magazine
Figure 7.2: ©2007 Matt Snowball Music
Figures 7.6, 7.8, 7.10, 7.16, 7.17, 7.18, and 7.23 photos by Krittiya
    Sriyabhanda
Figure 7.13: ©2007 Meyer, Inc.
Figures 7.11 and 7.19: ©2007 Fotolia

CHAPTER 8
Quote by Doc McGee: ©2007 *Audience* magazine
Review by Paul Travers: ©2005 *Kerrang*! magazine
Quote by Vuz Kapur: ©2007 *Audience* magazine
Figures 8.2, 8.4, 8.8, 8.9, and 8.10: ©2007 Fotolia
Figure 8.3 photo by James Sharrock

CHAPTER 9
Quote by Marek Leiberberg: ©2007 Der Speigel
Quote by Mick Jagger: ©2002 Fortune.com
Quote by Del Furano: ©2007 *Fast Company*
Quote by Andy Allen: ©2007 *Audience* magazine
Quote by Owen Hopkin: ©2007 *The Guardian*
Quote by Nigel McCune: ©2007 Musicians Union
Quote by Joel Harrison: ©2007 *Audience* magazine
Figure 9.1: ©2007 Fotolia

CHAPTER 10
Quote by Eron Bucciarelli: ©2007 *Music Week* magazine
Quote by Andy Davis: ©2007 *The Times*
Quote by Derek Safo: ©2007 *Music Week* magazine
Figure 10.1: ©2007 Fotolia

CHAPTER 11
Figures 11.5 and 11.6: ©Nitetrain Coach

CHAPTER 14
Quotes by Michael Rapino: ©2007 *Fast Company*
Quote by Michael Hausmann: ©2007 *Music Week* magazine
Figure 14.2: ©2007 Apple Computer

Index

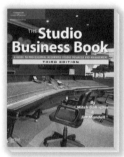

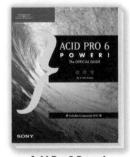